Democracy and Money

T0362171

The authors of this book argue that postwar fiscal and monetary policies in the United States are prone to more frequent and more destabilizing domestic and international financial crises. So, in the aftermath of the one that erupted in 2008, they propose that now we are sleepwalking into another, which under the prevailing institutional circumstances could develop into a worldwide financial Armageddon.

Thinking ahead of such a calamity, this book presents for the first time a model of democratic governance with privately produced money based on the case of Athens in classical times, and explains why, if it is conceived as a benchmark for reference and adaptation, it may provide an effective way out from the grim predicaments that state managed fiat money holds for the stability of Western-type democracies and the international financial system.

As the United States today, Athens at that time reached the apex of its military, economic, political, cultural and scientific influence in the world. But Athens triumphed through different approaches to democracy and fundamentally different fiscal and monetary policies than the United States. Thus, the readers will have the opportunity to learn about these differences and appreciate the potential they offer for confronting the challenges contemporary democracies face under the leadership of the United States.

The book will find audiences among academics, university students and researchers across a wide range of fields and subfields, as well as legislators, fiscal and monetary policy makers, and economic and financial consultants.

George C. Bitros is Professor of Political Economy, Emeritus, Athens University of Economics and Business.

Emmanouil M.L. Economou is Adjunct Lecturer at the Department of Economics, University of Thessaly.

Nicholas C. Kyriazis is Professor at the Department of Economics, University of Thessaly.

Routledge International Studies in Money and Banking

For more information about this series, please visit: www.routledge.com/
series/SE0403

Democracy and Money

Lessons for Today from Athens
in Classical Times

George C. Bitros,
Emmanouil M. L. Economou and
Nicholas C. Kyriazis

Routledge
Taylor & Francis Group

LONDON AND NEW YORK

First published 2021
by Routledge
2 Park Square, Milton Park, Abingdon, Oxon OX14 4RN

and by Routledge
52 Vanderbilt Avenue, New York, NY 10017

Routledge is an imprint of the Taylor & Francis Group, an informa business

British Library Cataloguing-in-Publication Data
A catalogue record for this book is available from the British Library

Library of Congress Cataloging-in-Publication Data
A catalog record has been requested for this book

ISBN: 978-0-367-50917-0 (hbk)
ISBN: 978-1-003-05180-0 (ebk)

Typeset in Times New Roman
by codeMantra

To the many scholars of the ancient Athenian society and economy on whose contributions particularly in recent decades this book has been based.

Contents

Exhibits

Figures

Tables

Preface

Over ten years have passed since the 2008 financial crisis erupted in the United States and spread quickly around the globe, and all indications are that we have entered into a period in which responsible leaderships in the United States behave as if nothing happened. They have an excuse. The U.S. economy has returned to growing near its potential. Unemployment has declined to historical lows. Monetary authorities have even trouble pushing the inflation rate up to their 2% target rate. After a brief retreat more recently, asset valuations have resumed their upward trend, etc. Yet experts in international organizations, universities and independent think tanks have not stopped submitting credible analyses and evidence to the contrary.[1] Not everything is alright, they insist, because the underlying trends that led to the 2008 crisis have remained intact, if not worsened.

For an example, consider the global financial imbalances. According to Mohan (2009, 1), then deputy governor of the Reserve Bank of India (RBI):

> The proximate cause of the current financial turbulence is attributed to the sub-prime mortgage sector in the USA.[2] At a fundamental level,

[1] See, for example, the most recent assessments by Blinder (2019).

[2] U.S. banks from within and outside the Federal Reserve System have been consistently encouraged, and bank managers operating for their own self-interest, but also under the threat of social stigmatization, if they do not go along, have been persuaded to offer mortgage loans to low-income households priced at commensurate interest rates. For many years, the demand for such loans was brisk, their stock accumulated to several trillion U.S. dollars, and banks faced no debt-servicing problems. With the exception of two bank failures in early 2007, the significance of which was missed by the responsible authorities, ominous signals earlier might have been easily construed as regular data blips. However, under the semblance of normality, some very bad trends were evolving. These amounted to increasing rates of unemployment, accompanied by declining labor force participation, increasing poverty, accompanied by declining labor share, and increasing inequality, accompanied by an extraordinary accumulation of income and wealth in the top 1% of U.S. households. Therefore, one might reasonably assert that it was not the sub-prime interest rate loans or the lax policies that led to the crisis but the declining labor share and the rising poverty which rendered large masses of working people unemployed and unable to service their housing loans. Moreover, as argued by Bitros (2018), the timing and the severity of the crisis might have been instigated by other forces emanating from the real side of

however, the crisis could be ascribed to the persistence of large global imbalances, which, in turn, were the outcome of long periods of excessively loose monetary policy in the major advanced economies during the early part of this decade.

Several years later, Bitros (2015, 70–77) assessed the evidence for the United States from where the crisis started and concluded that to some significant extent culpable for what happened were lax monetary, housing and other primarily bank related policies. Have they been confronted in the meantime? Not really beyond certain superficial macro- and microprudential interventions because, in order to forestall the crisis from getting out of hand, the U.S. Federal Open Market Committee (henceforth Fed) loosened monetary policy through three waves of easing in the quantity of money, and indeed to such an extent that now it stands prisoner of the dilemma expressed very precisely in the *Global Financial Stability Report* issued last year by the International Monetary Fund (2018). On page vii, we read that:

> A more significant tightening in global financial conditions will expose financial vulnerabilities that have built over the years and will test the resilience of the global financial system.

That is, in view of the world dominance of the U.S. dollar and notwithstanding the recent stern opposition by the current U.S. administration, if the Fed attempts to return to normalcy by confronting the overly loose monetary policies since 2008, the Fed risks a new global financial crisis. It is a terrible impasse with the stability of the international financial system hanging on the balance.

Unfortunately, looking forward, the terrain of policy choices in this regard is extremely foggy. Errors by fiscal and monetary authorities in the United States can be committed quite unintentionally and the consequences can be catastrophic for advanced and emerging countries alike. It goes without saying therefore that if there was ever need for some fresh inspiration, the time is now. On this motivation, we decided to go back and search for insights in the fiscal and monetary arrangements Athens had put in place in classical times, when it reached the apex of its military, economic and cultural influence in the Eastern Mediterranean and beyond. Since the Attic drachma became in those centuries as dominant as the U.S. dollar in the postwar period and money served the best interests of Athens as it has done for the United States, we thought that perhaps a comparative assessment of the main differences in the two cases might be revealing and helpful. We hasten to add that we have been encouraged to embark on this venture by the literature from over 100 years of research into every possible aspect that enabled Athens during those

---

the economy, partly independently and partly because of the effects of prior initiatives or lack thereof by monetary and fiscal authorities.

two centuries to achieve accomplishments well beyond the exceptional. In particular, we have drawn heavily on the contributions by Andreades (1928), Rhodes (2013) and Pritchard (2015), regarding public finance; Cohen (1992, 2008), Figueira (1998) and von Reden (2010), regarding currency and money matters and policies; Engen (2010) and Woolmer (2016), regarding trade policy; Harris (2016), regarding property rights; Morris (2004) and Ober (2010, 2015), regarding economic growth; Bresson (2016a), regarding the structure of institutions and markets; and several tens of other distinguished researchers, who have added many precious details in the explanation of the emergence and staying power of Athens in classical times. As to our research approach, we draw on Cohen (1990). We follow his lead by applying mainly forensic types of analysis and resorting to cliometric methods only when appropriate. Thus, in recognition of our intellectual debt, we are very pleased with the opportunity to devote this book to all of them.

Athens did not have a central bank. It maintained control over the standards and the organizational safeguards of its currency, it pushed for the currency's adoption among its allies, and it operated a mint where the state as well as anybody who had silver bullion might convert it into drachmae at a small fabrication and seigniorage cost. The mint was supervised closely by the *Council of 500* or *Boule*,[3] which served as the executive branch of government, whereas the *Ecclesia of Demos* or *Assembly* was the top decision-making body with all legislative and select ultimate-degree judicial and auditing powers. Members of the *Assembly* were all male Athenian citizens over 20 years of age, the quorum for the meetings was 6,000 in a male population that ranged from 30,000 to 60,000 depending on the period, and the number of meetings was at least four times a month (or a *prytany*, a tenth of the year). We mention these well-established details early on in order to stress a key difference. Athens was governed by *direct democracy*. In this system, the interests of those who govern coincide with the interests of those who are governed, and thus, it was to the benefit of all to manage the finances of the state and the currency as prudently as their own. On the contrary, the system of governance in the United States and in the other contemporary democracies is *representative democracy* and as a rule the interests of *politicians-agents–representatives* align only rarely with those of the *principals-citizens*. As a result, U.S. governments have managed public finances and the dollar in line with the short-term and expedient interests of those elected in positions of power at any one time, as well as unelected wider classes of bureaucracy, lobbyists, organized interest groups, quasi-government banks like Fannie Mae and Freddie Mac, and even quasi-government institutions like several well-known think tanks. Keeping in mind this inherent weakness in the structure of representative democracy should go a long way toward

---

3 For further information regarding the meaning of the Greek words, see the Glossary of Greek terms at the back of the book.

explaining the precarious shortcomings of fiscal and monetary policies in the United States and the other advanced democracies.

Can anything be done to reduce the likelihood of a worldwide disaster? In view of the inertia in the *status quo*, and since history suggests that proposals like the one made recently by the Governor of the Bank of England (BOE) in favor of the introduction of an international Libra-like reserve currency to end the dominance of the U.S. dollar are unlikely to materialize any time soon, if at all,[4] the least ambitious aim would be to strengthen the independence of the Fed in the expectation that it might forestall the excesses of U.S. governments. A possible reform in this regard would be its constitutionalization as a fourth branch of state powers, along with the legislative, the judicial and the executive. If the Fed retains control over its policy instrument, that is, the Federal Funds Rate (FFR), this reform might prove durable and effective. But if further research continues to ascertain the lack of such control, which we consider most likely, the next best reform would be to scrap the Fed and opt for a system of free banking based on a commodity state-sponsored currency unit and private issuing of notes and credit. If and when developments lead to that course, assuming of course that a worldwide upheaval does not precipitate regime changing reforms in the meantime, the best free banking alternative is the Athenian because it offers the potential to combine one *eponymous* Uniform Official Currency (UOC) with the anonymity of digital ones, the potential of which draws increasing interest from central as well as commercial banks and other independent issuers.[5]

Friedman, Schwartz (1986, 8, 11) set two prerequisites for establishing the possibility of viable money without a central bank. The first is the existence of a successful historical precedent in which money was linked to a commodity and the government remained aloof to its functioning in the economy, and the second is that money was produced by private enterprises operating in competitive markets. The information on which we draw from the above-mentioned sources about Athens in classical times is so credible that it permits us to claim that the Athenian model of free banking meets both these conditions. But due to the relative scarcity of hard data in the modern sense of the term and the inherent blurring of telescopic faculties looking backward into the distant past, it is reasonable to expect various reservations. For

---

4 See Karni (2019). Libra is a digital currency that the giant U.S. company Facebook, Inc. plans to introduce and manage as part of its worldwide social media network. However, as of August 2019, its launching continued to remain under consideration.

5 Scrapping the Fed and the central banks in general and replacing them with monetary systems based on commodity currencies and competitive banks all possessing equal rights to trade is not recommended only by the successful historical precedents of the Athenian, Scottish, and numerous other country episodes of free banking over the millennia. In addition, it has long been recommended by the panoply of arguments found in the voluminous literature in the tradition of Smith (1936/1990). For a review and assessment of this literature, see Sechrest (1993/2008).

example, some readers may be tempted to argue that what we know about Athens in classical times derives from "opinions expressed by authors like Aristotle, Thucydides, Xenophon, Demosthenes, etc." or, at most, contestable "expert testimony." Some others may find our approach to the Athenian system of public governance biased because of missing emphasis on the follies of direct democracy. And still some others may question the idea that insights drawn from a precedent 25 centuries ago may be useful in tackling thorny present-day problems. To all of them, we suggest that even if they were right and the case of classical Athens that we present is more imaginary than well grounded in facts and experiences, it has helped us highlight a model of free banking with potent properties for confronting the current precarious financial situation in the United States and the international economy.

The organization of the book is straightforward. In the introductory chapter, we trace the path of the ideas and policies that are responsible for the prevailing ominous trends in the United States and in the international financial system, because of the world dominance of the U.S. dollar. We find that the core problems are the *intoxication of representative democracy* with unsustainable public and private debts, and the complacency of the Fed in accommodating this intoxication through persistent quantitative easing in the supply of fiat money and the lowering of policy interest rate to the zero bound. Having arrived at this diagnosis, we turn to classical Athens in search for any helpful insights. In Chapters 2–5, we explain in good detail how Athens: (a) managed to conduct frequent wars and at the same time construct the monuments we so admire today without deficit spending and accumulation of debts; (b) through far-reaching institutional arrangements, it established the Attic drachma as the dominant currency in the then known world; (c) provided superb quality of governance which enabled the private economy to function through home and market-oriented activities in agriculture, manufacturing, services, and export-import; and (d) left it to the banking industry to provide the required credit to finance the private economy.

Drawing on these fundamentals, in Chapter 6, we present the analytical framework through which we envision that financial markets determined equilibrium values for such crucial variables as the amounts of currency, bullion and bank credit, the interest rate and the bank reserve ratio, and the general level of prices for goods and services. Central to our book are Chapters 7 and 8. In the former, we assess the performance in the United States relative to that in ancient Athens by reference to the rates of unemployment, inflation, long-term interest rate and economic growth. *Mutatis mutandis* we find that with the possible exception of significant economic growth in the recent century of Western-type democracy standards, the economy in Athens performed well. Encouraged by these findings, in Chapter 8, we investigate the prospects of four alternatives to central banking and arrive at the recommendation that we spelled out above. Finally, in Chapter 9, we explain why it is imperative in present-day representative democracies to reestablish the sovereignty of citizens over political parties and politicians, and how the advances in electronic communications in recent decades have rendered the transition to substantive, if not direct democracy, technologically feasible.

Aside from the available rich literature, which enabled us to search in the glorious past of the Athenian democracy for possible enlightenment on how to confront the treacherous problems that beset the status of money in present-day democracies, we have benefited from many trusted friends and colleagues who read advanced versions of our book and offered us constructive criticisms and advice.[6] Without implicating any of them in the views we express and in the possible errors of fact and interpretation that may still remain in the text, we should like to acknowledge with much affection and gratitude: Christos Baloglou, Kyriakos Revelas and Efthymios (Mike) Tsionas, for drawing our attention to several ambivalent statements and issues of historical and analytical significance, with the coverage of which we were able to sharpen our arguments; George Georganas, who must have spent considerable time thinking about the analysis particularly in Chapter 6 and took us to the task of reworking it until we gained confidence in its present form; Constantine Christidis, for helping us clarify a good number of expositional gaps and linguistic obscurities; Geoffrey Hodgson, Joseph Huber, Theodore Lianos, Anastasios Malliaris and Athanasios Skouras, for their encouragement and support; and Thomas Figueira, a world-renowned researcher of the Athenian society and economy in classical times, but not only.

Referring to the latter eminent scholar, we would like to add that we have been enormously privileged and remain truly grateful that he gave our manuscript the hard reading for which he is known, particularly in those aspects of ancient Athens on which this book is based. We have spared no time and effort to take advantage of his comments, suggestions and insights, while keeping some with which we could not deal presently in the treasure vaults of our future research. So, to conclude, if there is a wish to make, it is this: may the impact of this book be such that in retrospect all those mentioned above and those who are too many and who we could not thank by name will be pleased for having shared with us the effort of building a centuries-long knowledge bridge toward the problems that current and future democracy-loving people throughout the world will have to confront.

George C. Bitros
Emmanouil M. L. Economou
Nicholas C. Kyriazis
Athens, Greece, Winter 2019

6 For reasons of easy accessibility to our sources by international readers, early on we decided to abstain from all references to the rich contemporary research published in Modern Greek. However, on the other hand, we did not wish this decision to be interpreted in any way as a judgment on our part about the value of the insights that this literature offers regarding the subtleties of ancient Greek society and economy. To bridge this gap, in addition to our assurance and advice that this literature is of the highest quality and that it is worth reading, in a section at the back of the book, we provide a representative sample of authors and study titles dubbed into English.

1 Introduction

Unlike the Athenian democracy, which functioned by direct participation of its adult male citizens in the state's decision-making process, all democracies established in more recent centuries have been erected upon the *principle of representation*. Drawing on it, the citizens as *principals* assign to elected officials as *representatives* or *agents* the authority to legislate and govern. If the elected officials could be held *strictly* responsible for honoring the terms of an *explicit* contract with the citizens, the relationship of representation would not be problematic. But this is not the case. Because in theory and in practice, the authorization to legislate and govern has been construed to mean that after the officials are elected, they are *free* to decide on the various issues of the state. To see the problem that arises, let them be free until the following elections.

Since the latter are held normally several years later, the citizens may be safely presumed to have little or no memory of what they were promised in the previous elections, and hence the elected officials become *de facto* able to pursue with relative impunity their own self-serving interests instead of those of the citizens. That this proposition is the rule rather than the exception is corroborated by numerous old and new sources. For an early one, consider the following testimony from the autobiography of the great politician and philosopher Franklin (2005, 87).

> Few in public affairs act from a meer view of the good of their country, whatever they may pretend; and, tho' their actings bring real good to their country, yet men primarily considered that their own and their country's interest was united, and did not act from a principle of benevolence.

As for another more recent, it suffices to mention that a wholly new field in economics, that is, Public Choice Theory, has been developed for the expressed purpose of explaining the behavior of elected officials and devising mechanisms to maintain democratic control over the ways they use the power entrusted to them by citizens.

Bitros, Karayiannis (2013) assessed the two models of democracy and found that because of the above inherent weakness, representative democracies are prone to developing serious distortions, some of which are accompanied by high risks of becoming degenerative. Such a grievous one on the political side is, for example, the advancing erosion in the representativeness of governments. The constitution and the related laws and ordinances set out when and how elections are announced, how they are conducted, who participate as candidates and who make up the constituency, and how the winners are nominated. Yet in many democracies where two political parties often alternate in government, either through implicit or explicit agreements, they introduce changes for the purpose of perpetuating their hold on power. As a result, the case is rather common that governments hold majorities in the parliaments, despite receiving less than half of the votes of the electorates, thus enabling them to vote for laws opposed by most of the population. Moreover, governments that are elected by nonproportional electoral systems justify doubts about their representativeness, thereby leading citizens to perceive their decisions as illegitimate, and to resort to behaviors that aim to annul the results intended by the laws.

The list of distortions in public governance is long. However, here we are interested in the domain of the economy, and upon turning to it, two very worrisome trends stand out. These are first, the persistence of deficit spending along with the accumulation of huge public debts, and, second, the loss of control of the money supply by monetary authorities, particularly in large reserve currency countries. Our plan is to explain briefly in this introductory chapter why these trends are unsustainable and why it is absolutely urgent to confront them ahead of the next big crisis; then, to make a digression to find out what we can learn about these issues from Athens in classical times; and finally, drawing guidance from our findings, to return in the concluding chapter to highlight the question of how it would be advisable for contemporary democracies to go about the tasks for reversing these trends.

1.1 Deficits and debts in contemporary democracies

Up to the 1929 economic crisis, democratically elected governments applied fiscal policies under Adam Smith's dictum that "what is prudence in the conduct of every private family can scarce be folly in that of a great kingdom." To alleviate short spells of unemployment, they resorted to deficit spending mainly to finance infrastructures and found it imperative to balance them out later in the upturn of the business cycle. So, no public debts accumulated. But, when the crisis erupted, the recession that followed was so deep and protracted that it shook the confidence of people in the free market economy and rendered the millions of ordinary people who lost their livelihood receptive to government measures that offered even the faintest ray of hope. Thus, although now we know that this calamity was instigated and exacerbated in the United States by failures of the Fed, the change in the economic and social climate enabled politicians to depart from the prevailing fiscal orthodoxy and to implement policies that allowed the state to intervene deeply into the private economy.

In the following three decades, for reasons that trace back to the *principal-agent problem* outlined above, governments widened gradually the range of deficit spending to include an ever-expanding list of consumption expenditures, and hence public debts started to pile up at increasing rates. Perhaps to absolve himself from all responsibility in case the proposals he put forward in 1936 were abused, shortly thereafter Keynes (1942, 277–278) came back to state that:

> I should aim at having a surplus on the ordinary budget, which would be transferred to the capital budget, thus gradually replacing dead-weight debt by productive or semi-productive debt …. But I should not aim at attempting to compensate cyclical fluctuations by means of the ordinary budget. I should leave this duty to the capital budget.

However, his precaution proved needless. Because the genie that Keynes (1936) thought he had closed firmly in the bottle of his general theory escaped as the interpreters of his propositions, collectively called Keynesians,[1] set the course of developments in the direction so accurately noted in the following excerpt from Hayek (1960, 304–305):

> …democracy will have to learn that it must pay for its own follies and that it cannot draw unlimited checks on the future to solve its present problems. It has been well said that, while we used to suffer from social evils, we now suffer from the remedies for them. The difference is that, while in former times the social evils were gradually disappearing with the growth of wealth, the remedies we have introduced are beginning to threaten the continuance of that growth of wealth on which all future improvement depends.

Thus, by the time Buchanan, Wagner (1977) were writing, democracy in deficit had been established already as the new normal. Entitlements kept increasing at unsustainable real rates of growth; servicing of the unproductive public debts absorbed ever-increasing chunks of Gross Domestic Product (GDP), along with aggravating income inequality; the United States turned from creditor to debtor country, thereby eroding the value of the U.S. dollar as the preeminent currency of the world; with few

---

1 Despite Keynes's admonitions to the contrary, under the influence of Keynesians, democracies got addicted to deficit spending as if future generations would be wealthy enough to weather the deadweight from the accumulated debt. Even worse, democracies are called now to get accustomed to a new fad by the name of *New Monetary Economics*, which is no more than a new toxic form of statism bound to erode further democracy and individual freedoms through heavy taxation of fiat money by means of negative interest rates. Instead, in this study, we stand by the wisdom of the so-called balanced budget doctrine by drawing on the fiscal policies that Athens applied in classical times and centuries later democracies adopted as the preferred normal until 1929.

exceptions, public sectors expanded everywhere by crowding out the more productive private sector and limiting its share to around 50% of GDP; and last, but not least, regulatory arrangements designed to keep the markets open to actual and potential competition have become themselves part of the problem rather than the solution by failing repeatedly to perform effectively according to expectations.

Where are we now and what are the risks looming ahead? Owing to the almost miraculous combination of inventiveness with entrepreneurship, the fears that this wealth producing engine may stall under the burdensome profligacy of democratic governments have not materialized, at least not yet.[2] Fortunately, wealth continues to grow and as a matter of fact to benefit countries which had remained behind in the past. But the underlying trends are very worrisome because public debts continue for several decades now to increase faster than wealth. To highlight this point, for reasons that will become apparent shortly, a key example to draw attention to is the United States. Figure 1.1 depicts the time series of Gross Federal Debt (GFD), Gross Domestic Product (GDP) and their ratio (GFD/GDP) since 1939. Observe that from 1939 to 1980, GFD increased slower than GDP and that the indebtedness of the federal government declined even below the prewar years. This outcome emanated from the exemplary performance of the engine of growth to which we hinted above. But, as one can glimpse by

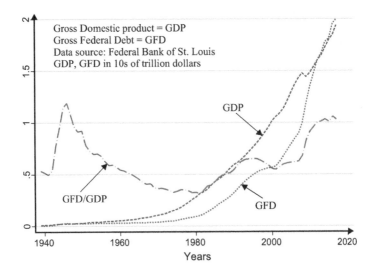

Figure 1.1 Federal government indebtedness in the United States 1939–2017.

2 Already from the Obama years, the rise in public expenditures, which was accompanied by (a) excessive and to a large extent arbitrary regulation of the economy, (b) expanding rent seeking activities by organized minorities and (c) rampant manifestations of crony capitalism, gave a foretaste of imminent stalling in the engine of economic growth. Interested readers in the literature on secular stagnation in the United States may wish to look at Bitros (2020).

looking closer at the slopes of the curves GDP and GFD, from 1980 on the rates of economic growth decelerated, while those of the federal debt accelerated, thus pushing the index GFD/GDP relentlessly upward. As a result, last year this index stood at 103% and all indications are that by 2025, if not much earlier, it will climb to 125%.[3] This is more than double the level of 60% that was considered safe by the European countries when in 1992 they entered into the Maastricht Treaty.[4] Therefore, the risk of a worldwide financial Armageddon cannot be discounted.

Contributing mightily to this outlook are several considerations. One is the extent to which the U.S. dollar is used outside the United States as a means of payments and store of value. By all metrics analyzed by Martin, Mukhopadhyay, Homebeek (2017) of the Bank of England, it is the currency of choice by central banks in which to keep their reserves; it dominates in cross-border lending among banks, debt issuance particularly by emerging countries and invoicing in the export–import trade of goods and services[5]; and not the least, as Figure 1.2 amply demonstrates, it holds by far the top rank in the execution and clearing of daily foreign exchange transactions. Despite the gains recorded by the Euro and a few other currencies in recent

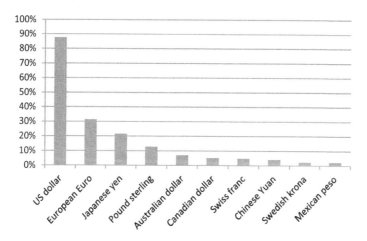

Figure 1.2 Share of daily transactions by currency.
Note: Trading volume adds up to 200%, because each currency trade has a pairing; Data as of April 2019.
Source: https://www.bis.org/statistics/rpfx19_fx.pdf

---

3 According to Gordon (2016, 428), focusing on the federal debt ignores the unfunded pension liabilities of many states and localities. If these were included, the index of public indebtedness would be considerably higher than this figure.

4 In 2017, the indices of Debt-to-GDP for the Euro Area and the European Union were 81.6% and 86.7%, respectively. For these and other related data, see https://tradingeconomics.com/country-list/government-debt-to-gdp.

5 According to Bank of England calculations, 64% of central bank reserves are in U.S. dollars and 39% of new issues of world debt involve transactions denominated in U.S. dollars.

decades, the position of the U.S. dollar in international transactions remains little changed.[6] But because of this role, in case of trouble, the Fed will not be able to print dollars at will to bail out the federal government without undermining its international value and risking an upheaval, if central banks in their efforts to avoid big losses decide to unload their dollar-denominated reserves.

While this risk may be viewed as an outlier in normal times, it is urgent that U.S. leaders hear the admonition expressed in a recent interview by Brown (2018), former prime minister of the United Kingdom:

> The cooperation that was seen in 2008 would not be possible in a post-2018 crisis both in terms of central banks and governments working together. We would have a blame-sharing exercise rather than solving the problem. In the light of the trade war launched against Beijing by the US, China would not be as cooperative a second time.

In short, the United States must stop behaving as if there were no other countries strong enough to oppose the nationalistic policy choices of their leaders. For, insisting on the present course, it is the perfect recipe for provoking the next major financial crisis.

A second consideration is that the U.S. federal government, even ignoring the politics of raising the statutory limit on the federal debt, cannot borrow at will without pushing the interest rates up and driving many emerging and poor countries into extreme hardships and bankruptcies. This is what is happening currently, and it will not take long before the interest rates on the ten-year *treasury* bills hit the 4% mark. Then, to recycle their debts, these higher risk countries will be obliged to pay considerably higher interest rates, investment and growth will decelerate, and the Aeolus sac of social and financial problems may open worldwide. How likely is such a dreadful scenario? The experts who wrote last year's report of the International Monetary Fund (2018, 22) think that it is likely, because otherwise they would not bother to state the following:

> In the United States, the tax overhaul and higher spending will widen the fiscal deficit, which was already set to deteriorate over the long term because of aging-related spending. Against the backdrop of record low unemployment rates, the deficit expansion is providing a short-term boost to activity in the United States and many of its trading partners, but at the cost of elevated risks to the US and global economies. The larger deficit not only will leave fewer budget resources to invest in supply-side reforms, but will add to an already-unsustainable public debt and contribute to a rise in global imbalances. With the US economy already

---

6   The hold of the U.S. dollar over world financial markets is such that Coy (2018) did not shy away from referring to the situation as "tyranny." If not tyranny, we hasten to add, it is certainly a powerful nuclear device imminent to explode even by accident.

operating above potential, expansionary fiscal policy could lead to an inflation surprise, which may trigger a faster-than-currently anticipated rise in US interest rates, a tightening of global financial conditions, and further US dollar appreciation, with potentially negative spillovers for the global economy.

Obviously, speaking courageously, the IMF experts do not shy away from warning that the U.S. public debt is unsustainable and that as long as its upward trend is not harnessed, the world is in a course for highly unpleasant surprises.

Next source of anxious concern is the level of the private debt in connection with the lack of pertinent reforms in the banking sector. After some moderate deceleration in the aftermath of the 2008 financial crisis, the private debt as a percentage of GDP stood last year at 202.8%. Hence, as real interest rates will be trending upward in the coming years, interest payments may be expected to act as a powerful drag on disposable incomes and returns on capital, thus dampening growth rates and worsening the deadweight of the overall debt on the economy. That is why we think that barring an unexpected event which might force an abrupt turnaround, the prevailing structural imbalances in the United States will remain highly precarious for the financial stability of the international monetary system. The 2008 crisis presented the authorities in the United States with an excellent opportunity to prepare for the worst by facing up to the problem of the extreme concentration of economic power by the so-called "too-big-to-fail" banks. It is true that now the few gargantuan banks in question are better capitalized and stronger to weather a crisis of comparable proportions. Presumably, now they operate also under some more stringent microprudential arrangements. However, given that crises are getting ever more disruptive because of the increased interconnectedness in the world, the force of the next one cannot be second-guessed, so the prevailing oligopolistic structure in the banking sector stands as a profound challenge to U.S. democratic institutions. Because, if for some hard to predict reasons one of these banks fails, the crisis that will ensue may get easily out of control in view of the animosities that the present U.S. trade policies arouse among former amicably trading countries.

Lastly, we should like to take exception of the extremely elevated risks emanating from the outstanding worldwide indebtedness. In the first quarter of 2018, the level of world debt amounted in absolute terms to 247 trillion U.S. dollars and in relative terms to the corresponding GDP to 318%.[7] Part of this debt was in the home currencies of the various countries and part in assets in foreign currency. Of the latter in 2015, over 55% of foreign debt assets held by countries were denominated in U.S. dollars.[8] Thus, on ac-

---

7 For further details regarding other aspects of the global debt, see www.cnbc.com/2018/07/11/global-debt-hits-a-new-record-at-247-trillion.html.
8 In the same year, external debt denominated in Euro amounted to about 20% and the rest in other currencies. For further details, see Bank of England (2017, 3).

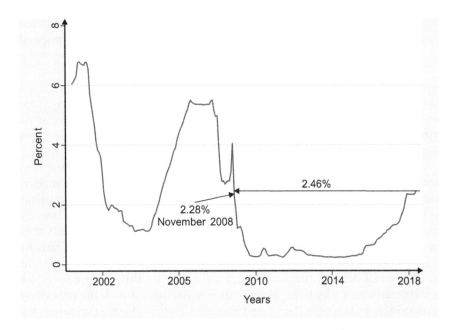

Figure 1.3 Three-month U.S. dollar LIBOR (London interbank offered rate).
Source: Federal Reserve Bank of St Louis, series USD3MTD156N.

count of these figures and the evidence presented above on the role of the U.S. dollar, there remains no doubt that looking forward the stability of the international financial system is intimately tied to what happens to the value of the U.S. currency and the interest rates associated with it. On this critical issue, Figure 1.3 signals developments that are very alarming. For what the sharp rise of the three-month Libor in the last two years indicates is that the excess demand for U.S. dollars, taking place in a period when the Fed is on a course of tightening the money supply, will continue to push the interest rates upward and lead to an appreciation of the value of the U.S. dollar. But from the Bank of England (2017, 1) simulations, it follows that for every 10% increase in the exchange rate of the dollar, real GDP growth in emerging countries declines by 2%. Thus, even if no surprises take effect regarding the risks involved, the huge global debt in conjunction with the prevailing trends in the U.S. dollar denominated interest rates should mobilize demo-cratic governments across the world to take immediate steps to unwind not just public debt but debt across corporations and households as well.

Will they? We are afraid that deficit spending is so ingrained in the nature of representative democracy that adopting policies yielding benefits over the long haul is sheer wishful thinking. However, the risks we analyzed above will not go away, and if some of them flare into another crisis, events may get out of hand quite easily. That is why thinking ahead of such events requires reforming representative democracy. So, going back to classical Athens, where democracy was based on self-government and there was neither deficit spending nor public debt,[9] may give us some useful guidance on how to tackle them.

1.2 Complacency and acquiescence of the central banks

Continuing with our benchmark case, we focus on the United States and the U.S. dollar. The *Federal Reserve Reform Act of 1977* states:

> The Board of Governors of the Federal Reserve System and the Federal Open Market Committee shall maintain long run growth of the monetary and credit aggregates commensurate with the economy's long run potential to increase production, so as to promote effectively the goals of maximum employment, stable prices, and moderate long-term interest rates....[10] Nothing in this Act shall be interpreted to require that such ranges of growth or diminution be achieved if the Board of Governors and the Federal Open Market Committee determine that they cannot or should not be achieved because of changing conditions.

From the sentence we have underlined, it follows that the Fed enjoys full independence from the other branches of government. Literally speaking, they are so free to pursue the objectives set for them that the Act avoids even to make any reference to the imperative that they ought to coordinate with the fiscal authorities since in the relevant economics literature, it has been well established that in order to achieve the stated objectives, monetary and fiscal instruments must be finely adjusted to each other. Anyway, operating in this institutional framework, one would have thought that the Fed would have prevented the ominous trends discussed above. So, the question that arises is: Did the Fed use their independence for the benefit of the United States at

---

9 During times of war, Athens borrowed massively from cults and the *treasury* of goddess Athena on the Acropolis. After the wars, these loans plus interest were repaid through budget surpluses. However, as Pericles predicted by drawing on the limited capabilities of Athens to conduct protracted wars, owing to the low levels of productivity, savings and investment, the huge loans accumulated during the 30 years of the Peloponnesian War could not be repaid and Athens in 404/403 BC went bankrupt.

10 With this provision, the U.S. Congress set four objectives for the Fed, that is, money growth commensurate with the economy's long-run productive potential, maximum employment, stable prices and moderate long-term interest rates. Over the years, both the wording and the number of these objectives changed. For example, in the "Statement on Longer-Run Goals and Monetary Policy Strategy," adopted in January 24, 2012, and amended in January 29, 2019 (see www.federalreserve.gov/monetarypolicy/files/FOMC_LongerRunGoals. pdf), the Board of Governors of the Federal Reserve System refers to the three last ones. Until specifically indicated otherwise, we shall continue to construe that the Fed has remained always mindful of its responsibility to keep real GDP growing close to the growth of potential GDP, no matter how in the meantime various U.S. Congress Acts expressed the policy objectives that it ought to pursue.

large? The evidence suggests that the monetary authorities became part of the problem because (a) while they are formally independent, in essence they have acted as if they are influenced decisively by politics, and (b) the policy instruments at their disposal are ineffective. So, let us look into these issues.

The United States canceled in 1971 the direct international convertibility of the dollar to gold. Although initially the cancelation was provisional in the sense that it might be reestablished after the revision of the Bretton Woods agreement, negotiations failed, and the regime of fiat money has continued ever since. This date is important because it marks a shift in the substantive independence of the Fed. For, as long as the fixed exchange rate regime under the Bretton Woods agreement and the convertibility of the dollar were in force, monetary authorities could withstand political pressures and even their own temptations from following lax currency and credit policies, since they had to abide by the constraints involved in these arrangements. But once they were withdrawn, the Fed's independence ebbed. To corroborate this view, a convenient criterion is to look at what happened to prices, the stability of which has always been in the mainstay of Fed's policy objectives.[11] Table 1.1 displays the changes in prices for various subperiods over the years from 1960 to 2016. During the period 1971–1982, consumer prices rose abnormally because of the two sizable increases in the international price of oil, whereas in the period 2008–2016, the rise in consumer prices was abnormally subdued because of the economic crisis. So, excluding these periods, inflation from 3.35% in the pre-1971 period increased to 5.72% in the period after 1971. This finding confirms that the Fed failed to keep prices stable and that it resorted consistently to deliberate erosion in the value of the dollar. A possible explanation is that they stepped up the rates of inflation because it was recommended by the U.S. Phillips curve for attaining high levels of employment. But a more credible explanation is the following.

In the previous section, Figure 1.1 shows that the indebtedness of the federal government started to rise already from the 1960s. A similar figure for

Table 1.1 Changes of consumer prices in the period 1960–2016

Subperiods	Cumulative (%)	Average per annum (%)
1960–1971	41.4	3.35
1971–1982	138.3	12.57
1982–2008	148.7	5.72
2008–2016	11.5	1.43

Notes: The data for the Consumer Price Index (CPI) comes from the database of the Federal Reserve Bank of St. Louis and correspond to the series CPALTT01USA661S.

11 Later, we shall conduct a wider and more detailed assessment of the Fed's failure to achieve the objectives set for it in the *1977 Federal Reserve Reform Act*.

the private sector would show an equally sharp upward trend. Why did the Fed accommodate the accumulation of so much debt? It doesn't take much economics to contemplate that they did so because, at the rate of inflation they built into their calculations: (a) the real burden of the overall U.S. debt was eroding at the rate of 2.5%–3.5% per annum, and (b) the international savers everywhere in the world who held their savings in U.S. dollars subsidized the United States at the same rate. Apparently, there was no problem until the 2007–2008 crisis erupted, deflation set in and now prices cannot rise at the previous pace (see inflation figures for the period 2008–2016 in Table 1.1) because the Fed has to go into a currency and credit tightening mode. Thus, in the present juncture, something must give before the United States goes again into a tail spin and drags with it weak emerging and poor countries. In principle, what must give is a quick and decisive rolling back of the debt, public and private. Yet as we stressed earlier representative democracy has shown itself to be profligate, virtually despising fiscal policies that impose burdens on the current generations of voters, whereas the impact of monetary policy on the private sector is uncertain because Fed's control over the conventional instruments of monetary policy is highly problematic.

The difficulty that the U.S. monetary authorities face stems right out of their mandate as spelled out in the excerpt we quoted above from the *1977 Federal Reserve Reform Act*. In the pursuit of the four objectives set out for them,[12] it is only the short-term interest rate that they have any chance to control, since once this is set, the rates of inflation, unemployment, economic growth and long-run interest rate are all determined in the markets. But controlling the short-term interest rate is an exercise in futility, and the same is true regarding Fed's control over the "money supply."[13] Figure 1.4 highlights the basis for this assessment. Diagrams (a) and (b) depict, respectively, the domestic and the foreign markets for dollars. Assume that at some initial point in time, indicated by the upper index 0, the central bank has complete

---

12 Notice that in addition to the objectives of price stability, maximum employment (minimum unemployment), and economic growth in line with the economy's productive potential, the *1977 Federal Reserve Reform Act* sets for the Fed a fourth objective, that is, the achievement of "moderate long-term interest rates." This provision has not attracted attention in the relevant literature. But to us it seems rather amazing that the Act sets objectives in terms of the instruments of monetary policy; For it legitimizes the government to object to particular interest rate policies, and hence to vitiate the independence of the Fed.

13 In the past, central banks adopted fractional reserve systems of banking to conserve on the scarce precious metal, which constituted the basis of their currency. As a result, money supply included the amount of currency in circulation plus the amount of credit that banks created on the basis of their obligatory reserve ratio multiplier. Even though paper money is costless, for reasons that are hard to understand, contemporary central banks have continued to apply fractional reserve systems. In this context, to distinguish between the money created by the central bank and the money created by the monetary system-related banks, it is customary to refer, respectively, to the *base money* or *outside money* and *inside money* or *money supply*.

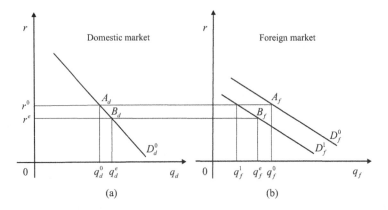

Figure 1.4 Central bank control of money supply.

knowledge of the level and slopes of the corresponding demand curves, which are denoted by the symbols D_d^0 and D_f^0. Drawing on this knowledge, let the central bank reckon that the total amount of dollars to print is $Q^0 = q_d^0 + q_f^0$, which upon entering into the markets determines the interest rate r^0, and the domestic and foreign markets settle at points A_d and A_f.[14] Now, suppose that for reasons that need not occupy us here, the demand for dollars abroad suddenly declines and the demand curve in diagram (b) shifts downward to the position D_f^1. At the prevailing interest rate, we observe that the amount of dollars demanded declines from q_f^0 to q_f^1. The excess supply of dollars in the foreign markets will express itself as a relative decline in the prices of U.S. goods and services, and hence by increasing their demand, it will push gradually the supply of dollars in the domestic market to q_d^e and the interest rate to r^e. What this simple analysis confirms is that the equilibrium interest rate for dollars r^e depends on the preferences of the domestic and foreign economic agents to hold dollars, that is, on the preferences that determine the distribution of Q^0 between q_d^0 and q_f^0, which are beyond the ability of the central bank to even predict, because they change continuously under political, economic and natural events.

That the Fed has lost control of the money supply, if it ever had any, can be confirmed also by at least two pieces of factual evidence. The first is the abandonment by the Fed of all efforts to target monetary aggregates like the M1 or M2.[15] Beginning in 1970, the Fed declared every week the path of M1

---

14 It should be clear from theory that since the central bank has the monopoly of printing dollars, it may set either their amount or the interest rate, but not both at the same time.
15 Money supply measured by M1 includes cash, demand deposits, and traveler's checks. M2 includes M1 plus savings and time deposits, certificates of deposits, and money market funds.

and indicated their preferred behavior for M2. This approach to controlling money supply changed in 1975, and the Fed begun to announce publicly targets for money supply growth. However, even though in the following years they experimented with various operating targets, experience was disappointing and particularly during the period 1979–1982. As a result, the Fed started to deemphasize the use of monetary aggregates, and in 1987, they declared that they would not even set targets for M1. Finally, upon testifying in Congress in 1993, Alan Greenspan, then chairman of the Fed, submitted that they would no longer use any monetary targets, including M2, as a guide for the conduct of monetary policy. This was equivalent to witnessing that any measure of money supply is too volatile to be used as a policy instrument.

The second piece of evidence leads to the same conclusion by drawing on more recent events. Let us assume that the base money is 100 dollars and that the reserve requirement is 10%, so that the official upper limit of "money supply" that commercial banks can provide to the economy is 1,000 dollars. Under the prevailing economic circumstances, commercial banks may decide to lend less or more than this limit. Is this possible? Certainly it is and we observed the former case right after the outbreak of the crisis in 2007–2008, when the commercial banks stopped lending altogether and the financial markets imploded. As for lending in excess of the official limit, what happened in the period preceding the crisis is quite revealing. Because of a multitude of errors of omission and commission by the federal government and the Fed, which are summarized in Bitros (2015, 73–77), commercial banks used fractional reserve controlled deposits to finance voluminous loans against risky asset-backed securities from outside the commercial banking system, and they did so without adequate capitalization to self-insure for the high risks they assumed. Again, but the hard way this time, it took a systemic breakdown to understand that the Fed cannot possibly control the money supply.

Next, we turn to interest rate targeting. In the 1980s, as it was becoming apparent that money supply could not serve as a viable policy instrument, central bank and academic thinking turned gradually to devising rules based on the interest rate. Classic among the latter has been the one proposed by Taylor (1993, 202), which suggests that the central bank's policy must strive to equate the interest rate on short-term loanable funds with the sum obtained by adding the rate of recent inflation, plus half the percentage difference of real GDP from its trend, plus half the difference between the rate of recent inflation from its target rate, plus two. Even though it is unknown whether the Fed followed it, over the so called *Period of Great Moderation* (1993–2001) the data show that the central bank behaved as if it did follow this rule and much of its success was attributed to having done so. But in the following years, the situation started to unravel until the housing bubble burst in 2007–2008 and the crisis broke open. In the light of this event and its aftermath, experts started to raise doubts regarding the ability of the central bank to control the interest rate. For example, one year into the crisis, Garrison (2009, 198) writes:

> Once the current recession… is behind us, there can be no simple return to normalcy. Money-supply targeting is operationally nonviable, and interest-rate targeting will be seen (by the market and, it is hoped, by the Fed) as nonviable.

And two years into the crisis, Phelps (2010, 137) visits this crucial issue and states at no uncertain terms the following:

> One of the towering lessons of the present crisis is that it has made vivid to us what has long been obvious to all but the most doctrinaire academicians. Radical uncertainty, known as "Knightian uncertainty," is always present in some respects and is always a significant consideration—at least, in a modern economy or even a traditional economy operating in a modern global economy. …<u>An important consequence of this flare-up of uncertainty is that the central bank does not know the level to which to set the "policy rate of interest" and thus the direction in which to start moving the policy rate</u>.

Moreover, for those who remain unconvinced, Fama (2013, 198) came along with the following data-based assessment regarding the viability of the interest rate as a monetary policy instrument:

> In sum, the evidence says that Fed actions with respect to its target rate have little effect on long-term interest rates, and there is substantial uncertainty about the extent of Fed control of short-term rates. I think this conclusion is also implied by earlier work, but the problem typically goes unstated in the relevant studies, which generally interpret the evidence with a strong bias toward a powerful Fed. Finally, for the period that starts with the lingering recession of 2008, a less ambiguous conclusion is possible. The decline in short-term rates after 2008, despite massive injections of interest-bearing short-term debt (reserves) by the Fed and other central banks, is a cautionary tale about how market forces can limit the power of central banks even with respect to the short-term rates that are commonly taken to be their special preserve.

Drawing on the above, we feel confident in concluding that interest rate targeting is an exercise in futility, exactly as the targeting of monetary aggregates was back in the 1970s and 1980s.[16]

---

16 Moreover, it should not escape attention that by trying to control the interest rate, the Fed applies direct control on the price of paper money and hence it distorts its allocation in

In this conclusion, we are not alone. Convinced that neither the money supply nor the interest rate can serve as viable instruments of monetary policy, several economists have suggested that central banks would be more tenable to target variables like the exchange rate and asset prices.[17] We sympathize with their efforts, but we do not believe that thinking ahead of the next world financial crisis affords the luxury of further experimentations of the Fed in these directions. Instead, we feel that in the United States and in other reserve-currency representative democracies, it is high time for fundamental reforms to reverse the prevailing ominous trends.

1.3 Conclusion

Present-day democracies are based on *the principle of representation*. They differ from the direct democracy in ancient Athens in that the elected officials and those whom they appoint in the various branches of government as a rule pursue interests that differ from those of the people. Because of this mismatch, large segments of citizens have become alienated and abstain from voting, the degree of contestability in the political market has vanished, the political parties which alternate in power behave as if they have been captured by minorities of organized special interests, and quite frequently those who are elected to govern represent less than one-third of the electoral body.[18] Hence, as could be expected, representative democracy by its very nature is inherently weak and prone to serious distortions. Many of them, like the ones just mentioned, emanate from the setup of the political institutions, whereas many others have to do with the institutions and the functioning of the free market economy.

In this book, we are interested in finding out what enlightenment we can obtain from the case of Athens in classical times that could be useful in confronting the two money-related problems that threaten the stability of Western-type democracies. These are, first, the excessive indebtedness in the United States and the world at large, and second, the complacency and acquiescence of monetary authorities in accommodating this alarming trend.

---

exactly the same manners in which direct price controls distort the allocative mechanism in the commodity and services markets.

17 Just to mention a few, De Grauwe (2008) presents arguments in favor of the view that central banks may be able to improve macroeconomic stability (i.e., lowering the variability of output and inflation) by targeting stock prices; Teo (2009) compares the welfare implications of exchange rate and interest rate targeting and finds that under certain conditions the former gives results which are superior to the latter; and Shiratsuka (2011) recommends that central banks incorporate into their models information from macroprudential analyses regarding changes in investors' attitudes toward risk taking.

18 That the rate of abstention of registered voters from the electoral process is appallingly large can be glimpsed easily from the U.S. elections in 2016 and the EU elections in 2019. Relevant results and analyses may be found in www.telegraph.co.uk/news/2016/11/14/us-election-2016-voter-turnout-fell-to-58-per-cent-this-year-est/ and www.euronews.com/2019/05/10/low-turnout-at-the-european-elections-what-s-wrong-with-eu, respectively.

To identify the forces that catered to the profligacy of representative democracy, we looked into how the ideas of Keynes played into the hands of so-called Keynesians, who in turn offered populist politicians the pretext to expand the accumulation of public debt through unrelenting deficit spending. To be sure, raising public debt to unsustainable levels, and mainly for social consumption purposes, is appalling for any country. But it becomes unfathomable if it is adopted by a country like the United States, which stands as the dominant banker in the world. For, aside from exposing the United States itself to the risk of default, it has encouraged the U.S. private sector to amass levels of debt that are too precarious, should a crisis like the one in 2007–2008 erupt again anytime soon. This prospect should not be discounted, particularly not in the present juncture, when interest rates are climbing, and the President of the United States supported by his political party has declared openly his opposition to the Fed's preferred course of action to unwind the exceedingly easy money policies they applied throughout the post-2008 period.

Can we trust that the situation is manageable? Not really, for three reasons. First, because the U.S. government will find it hard to slow down deficit spending, since politicians in general are nearsighted, meaning that they detest the political cost which would be involved in any attempt at returning to balanced budgets, let alone to realizing public surpluses. Second, because under the present institutional setup, the Fed is typically independent but substantively subservient to politics. It is true that since 2016, they have adjusted several times the rate of the Federal funds upward in line with the rising interest rates in the market. But, given the pressure from the present U.S. administration and the recent developments in the share prices, it is doubtful whether they will continue their efforts toward tightening monetary policy, even though the instruments at their disposal are ineffective. Third, because, should a new crisis break out, the Fed cannot expect the kind of cooperation that countries with major reserve currencies like China and the European Union (EU) offered in 2008, since current U.S. policies have undermined significantly their solidarity.

That is why, we maintain that the social cost of central banking exceeds by far its social benefits and that it is high time to reform it drastically either by insulating institutionally central banks from politics, so as to enable them to safeguard the integrity of money, if they still control the interest rate as their sole policy instrument,[19] or otherwise to replace central banks by a market-based monetary system. In the latter event, we shall argue that the monetary system in classical Athens, to the presentation of which we shall devote the next several chapters, stands as a highly meritorious model case to emulate.

---

19 Central bank independence is a necessary condition for preserving the value of paper currency. But it is not sufficient, because at the same time a central bank must have control over its policy instruments, that is, the "quantity of money" and the "interest rate" on its loanable funds. For, in the absence of such control, central banks lose the *raison d'etre* for their existence.

2 Money-related institutions in classical Athens[1]

From Amemiya (2007), Engen (2010) and numerous previous scholars of the society and economy of ancient Greece, there remains no doubt anymore[2] that the state of Athens could be conceived to consist of four activity sectors. These were: (a) the public sector, which included the military; (b) the private sector, comprising the subsectors of household production and consumption, market-oriented production and distribution, and money and banking; (c) the import–export sector with its supporting capabilities of shipping, insurance and warehousing; and (d) the system of *agoge* for the upbringing of young Athenians and maintaining their ethos through life.[3] In this section, we focus on the setup of public and private institutions, which are known to have maintained direct and/or indirect affiliations with the processes of currency and credit.

2.1 Public governance and Archai in charge of the currency

The Athenian democracy was ruled by three entities: The *Ecclesia of Demos* (congregation of citizens for decision-making purposes) or *Assembly*, the *Council of 500* or *Boule* and the *Dikastiria* or *Courts*.[4] The *Assembly*, in

---

1 The generic term in Greek of a public agency or authority or institution is *Arche* and in the plural *Archai*. Below, when referring to public entities, we shall use these terms interchangeably.

2 Later on, we shall refer in passing to the modernist-primitive controversy that dates back to the late 19th century (The Bucher–Meyer Controversy) as well as to how it evolved after Finley (1973, 1981). Now, the general consensus is that the economy of Athens in classical times was developed to a considerable extent in terms of market-oriented productive activities and financial institutions. That this was the case will be ascertained also amply by the presentation in the following chapters.

3 The system of *agoge* defined a domain in which the public and the private sectors interacted. As such, it was more of a Public–Private-Partnership, that is, the so-called 3P, rather than a distinct sector of productive activities. However, because of the paramount importance Athenians attributed to character education, we shall treat it here as a separate sector.

4 To maintain uniformity in the use of terms, unless specifically mentioned otherwise, henceforth we shall refer to these three entities as the *Assembly*, the *Boule*, and the *Courts*.

which participated all adult male Athenian citizens, exercised the top legislative and governing responsibilities. It convened four times during each *prytany* (tenth of the conciliar year), which lasted from 36 to 39 days, and at least 40 times per year in total (Thorley 1996, 30).[5] It could be in session only when more than 6,000 citizens were present. One of the four meetings of each *prytaneia* was devoted to discussion and decision-making on issues of governance, defense, foreign policy, provisioning of food and other supplies, including welfare, while the other three dealt with various issues. The *Boule* consisted of ten groups with 50 members each from the ten tribes of Athens. The 50 members of each tribe served in the *Boule* for one-tenth of each year and were replaced by another group at the end of each *prytany*.[6] In practical terms, each tribe that held this post actually ruled the city with full executive rights (Lyttkens 2013, 59, 76). Among its main duties were: (a) to prepare the so-called *probouleumata* (preliminary decrees) and submit those which were approved for final discussion and voting in the *Assembly* (Demosthenes, *Against Neaera*, 59.4); (b) to prepare the agenda for each meeting of the *Assembly*; (c) to care for the arming and manning of warships as well as the cavalry; (d) to supervise the execution of the budget, the management of the *treasuries of the gods*, and the operation of the mint; and (e) to be in constant contact with the public officers who were appointed to manage the affairs of the state on a daily basis (Aristotle, *Athenian Constitution*, 46.1, 49.1–2).

In particular, administration on a day-to-day basis was exercised by the *prytaneis*, the nine *archons*, the public administration, the ten *strategoi* (generals) and several categories of magistrates distinguished by their dedicated functions. The nine *archons*, all of whom were equal among themselves, although one had the title of *eponymous* (the most important of the nine *archons*), carried out specific projects and responsibilities. For example, the *archon* in charge of defense was responsible for collecting all public revenues earmarked for the financing of the army, and paying all related expenses (Tridimas 2012, 4).[7] The public administration consisted of various departments, providing services to enable compliance with building codes, enforcement of regulations regarding food and other supplies, orderly conduct in the markets, and the design, construction and maintenance of public infrastructure, among others. The ten *strategoi,* each coming from one of the ten Athenian

---

5 However, the precise number of *Assembly* meetings is still open to debate (Rhodes, Lewis 1997, 13, 14).
6 The 500 men who served in the *Boule* were chosen by lot at the *deme* level, each of them having been allotted a certain number of slots proportional to its population. At this time, membership was restricted to the top three of the original four property classes, that is, the *pentacosiomedimnoi*, *hippeis* and *zeugitai*. The class of *thetes* acquired the right to elect members in the *Boule* later. By contrast, a considerable number of the 700 officials assigned to administrative tasks were elected by vote from lists of knowledgeable and experienced Athenians. For more details on this very significant issue, see Aeschines (*Against Ctesiphon*, 29) and Aristotle (*Politics*, 1317b15–1318a3).
7 We will discuss more about the place and the tasks of *Archons* in Section 9.3.4.

tribes, oversaw the armed forces, and were appointed by and reported to the *Assembly*. Their service was annual, and depending on the evaluation of their performance, they could be reappointed (Lyttkens 2013, 52). At the end of each *prytaneia*, a vote was taken as to whether they had performed their duties adequately, and those who were found inadequate lost their office.[8] As for the *tamiai*, we shall explain shortly that they performed key tasks in the system of public finance as treasurers and managers of various *funds*.

Finally, the judicial powers rested with the *Courts*, which heard cases in the civil, maritime and penal domains. Competent to adjudicate civil disputes were the *Dikasteric Courts* (*Popular Courts* or *People's Courts*). These dealt with most cases, albeit scarcely in a law-based fashion. On the contrary, as argued by Cohen (1973) and Lanni (2008), the *Maritime Courts* and the *Areios Pagos,* which handled maritime disputes and most homicides, respectively, functioned in a precedent setting manner from a legal standpoint. The Supreme Court called *Heliaia* comprised 6,000 judges and served as a *Court of Appeals.*[9]

The institutions in charge of the state's budget and the currency were embedded in the above organizational structure with enough autonomy from the central authorities to pursue effectively their tasks, but at the same time their administrators remained under closed supervision and brevity of tenure, so they were discouraged from resorting to abusive discretionary practices. The presentation below aims at identifying the institutions that were in charge; characterizing the range and the nature of the mandates under which they operated; and lastly, highlighting the arrangements through which they were controlled by citizens.

2.1.1 Making the best of the Laurion mines

Ancient Athens started cutting silver coins from 545 BCE. As per Exhibits 2.1–2.3, they showed on the obverse the guardian goddess of the city, Athena, and on the reverse an *owl*, the sacred bird of Athena, symbol of wisdom. These coins, with main denominations at various periods in *obols-drachms-didrachm-tetradrachm-dekadrachm-minae-talent,*[10] were commonly called

---

8 Pritchard (2012, 48–49, 2014, 8) argues that the *strategoi* were often required to finance by themselves the means to perform their *strategia*, that is, to fulfill their annual responsibilities.

9 *Heliaia* convened very rarely in its full membership. The bulk of cases were brought in front of the *Popular* or *People's Courts,* which constituted particular chambers of *Heliaia* specialized according to the nature of the law they applied and the importance of the cases they heard. For example, the *Maritime Courts* was a chamber of *Heliaia* dealing with maritime cases. The higher the social importance of the cases a chamber dealt with, the larger its membership was in terms of participating judges. Worth noting is also that before the reforms of Ephialtes and Pericles in the 460s and 450s BCE, respectively, the judicial functions of *Heliaia* were performed by the *Assembly*, which stood as court.

10 One didrachm was equal to two drachmae; one tetradrachm was equal to four drachmae; and one decadrachm *was* equal to ten drachmae. Each obol contained 0.72 grams of silver.

Exhibit 2.1 Illustration of the Athenian *obol*.
Note: Athens. After 449 BC. AR Obol. Helmeted head of Athena right. Owl standing right.
Source: With the permission of wildwinds.com:
http://www.wildwinds.com/coins/greece/attica/athens/SNGCop_053ff.jpg

Exhibit 2.2 Illustration of the Athenian *tetradrachm* (four drachmae).
Note: Athens AR tetradrachm. ca 449-430 BC. Head of Athena right in crested Attic helmet.
Owl standing three-quarters right, head facing, olive spray and crescent moon behind, all in square incuse.
Source: With the permission of wildwinds.com: http://www.wildwinds.com/coins/greece/attica/athens/starr_xxiii-11.jpg

Thus, since there were 6 obols to a drachm, 100 drachmae to a mina (or mna) and 6,000 drachmae to a talent, these two denominations contained 4.3 grams and 26.17 kilograms of silver, respectively. Smaller coin denominations made from copper and called *chalkos* and *kollyboi* were introduced and used for small value retail transactions. The principal places of copper production were Chalkis and Cyprus, both of which derived their names from copper, Anatolia in Asia Minor, Etruria, Brutium and Elba in Italy, as well as Spain (von Reden 2010, 30, 32). Two such coins are shown in Exhibits 2.1 and 2.2.

Exhibit 2.3 Illustration of the Athenian *dekadrachm* (ten drachmae).

Note: Illustration of the Athenian decadrachm (ten drachmae) having the goddess Athena on the front side and the owl with the inscription ATHE (of Athens) on the back side of the coin.

Source: With the permission of wildwinds.com: http://www.wildwinds.com/coins/greece/attica/athens/sg2516.jpg

glauke (the Greek name for *owl*).[11] They were of excellent craftsmanship, and of high and stable silver content for about three centuries. Thus, they became the main currency of the Eastern Mediterranean world (Thompson, Mørkholm, Kraay 1973; Kraay 1976; Kroll 2011). As discovered hoards show, they circulated from the Black Sea to the Persian Empire, Egypt and Italy and as far as today's France and Spain. They were used as a means of payments in trade with very wide acceptance, like today's U.S. dollar (Kleiner 1975; Van Alfen 2011) and the other international reserve currencies.

To mint the coins for their currency in the 6th century BCE, Athenians obtained silver mainly from the mines of Macedonia and Thrace.[12] But these mines were occupied by Persians in 512 BCE and the Athenians were forced to look for silver more intensively within the bounds of their borders. These efforts were met with great success when in 483 BCE they discovered a new rich vein of silver in the Laurion location of the Southern Attica known as

11 *Glauke* was the sacred bird of the goddess Athena, a symbol of wisdom, prudence, and farsightedness. Thus, perhaps the Athenians chose to use this symbolism in their coins, because they understood that issues related to money required wisdom and prudence.

12 For example, during the period of tyranny in Athens (560–510 BCE), Peisistratos and his son Hippias were paying wages to a mercenary body of 300 men, called *Doriphoroi*, which was used as a means of enforcement of the regime, and this amount of money originated from those silver and gold mines in Macedonia and Western Thrace (Lavelle 1993, 7). However, various authors include also among the sources of silver in this period places like Siphnos, Lydia, and even Laurion.

Maroneia.[13] Mining there started much earlier, most likely as far back as the Bronze Age. But it became particularly intensive and very productive during the 5th and 4th centuries BCE, because it was exceptionally lucrative. For example, revenue from silver mining in the 4th century has been estimated at about 70 drachmae per ton of ore, whereas expenses for enriching the ore were about 38 drachmae per ton. This left a gross profit of 32 drachmae, which amounted to a margin of 45.7% (Conophagos 1980, 213–273, 341–359; Christesen 2003).

In turn, this discovery instigated the need for the enactment of state institutions to undertake large-scale extraction and processing of the mineral. To this effect, they activated the *board of poletai* in association with certain related tasks assigned to *Boule*. It should be noted that the silver resources of Laurion were owned by the city-state of Athens (henceforth the state)[14] even when found on private property, meaning that different property rights applied for resources above and below ground, as is the case today in many countries.

2.1.1.1 The board of poletai (sellers)

Provisions for the establishment of this *board* had been included already in the constitution that Cleisthenes introduced in 508 BCE.[15] Quite likely its invention reflected the pressure Athenian leaders felt at the time to mobilize in order to search for alternative sources of silver, including more intensive exploitation of their own mines. But we know neither whether it played any role in the discovery of the new vein of silver in Laurion, nor when exactly it took over the administration of the mines. Presumably, given that the program for building the 200 warships that Themistocles had proposed started very shortly after 483 BCE, a reasonable guess is that by that time the *board* must have given out significant numbers of leases and that mining activities under its supervision must have accelerated significantly.

---

13 That the vein was rich indeed is verified, among others, by Aeschylus (*Persians*, 236–238) when Atossa, the Achaemenid Persian empress and daughter of Cyrus the Great asks about the Greeks: "And what else have they besides? Do they have sufficient wealth in their homes?" and the Chorus responds: "Of silver they possess a veritable fountain, a treasure chest in their soil." Obviously, Chorus refers to the Athenian Laurion mines.

14 In 483/482 BCE, Athenians allocated 200 talents from the newfound Laurion riches to build 200 warships. This suggests that the state owned the mines. But aside from this direct evidence, we have several indirect indications to the same effect. For example, whereas Aristophanes' (*Wasps*, 655) implies that the mines were owned by the state, Aristotle (*Athenian Constitution*, 22.7) is more reassuring. On the contrary, Thomas Figueira has suggested to us that the regime of ownership of the Laurion mines was probably more complex.

15 However, references to *poletai* as sellers of public contracts, confiscated properties, and sacred lands date back to the times of Solon.

It auctioned leases for silver mining[16]; monitored the application of contracts by mining contractors; applied various deterrents to discourage defrauding of the state; collected the fees from the leases as well as the state's taxes in the form of silver; and in general it strived to administer the mines effectively.[17] Additionally, based on the extant evidence discussed by (Walbank 1983), it conferred land leases in compliance with the practice followed in sales of confiscated property; collected the taxes from the concessions; and even though the evidence to this effect is scanty, according to Hansen (1999, 260) and Papazarkadas (2011, 53), it was tasked with the leasing of the so-called sacred properties.

In classical times, it was managed by ten governors or financial magistrates, one each from the ten Athenian tribes. They were elected by lot annually, they reported directly to the *Assembly* and their decisions were subject to various controls (Aristotle, *Athenian Constitution*, 7.3). For example, the contracts for selling confiscated and sacred properties had to be ratified by the nine *archons*.

2.1.1.2 Mining-related tasks of Boule

The prospects of newfound riches to strengthen Athens militarily and economically rendered the Laurion mines too important for politicians and citizens to entrust their management completely to the *board of poletai*. The stakes were very high and the same was true regarding the temptations of the public officials involved to enrich themselves fraudulently, if left unattended. Thus, aside from all other safeguards, the *Boule* was assigned to exercise supervisory authority over the *board* in certain key areas like the allocation of leases and the final certification of contractors.

---

16 Hallof (1990) has suggested that the auctions conducted by the *board* may not have been as open as usually assumed and that in effect, the successful bidders were preselected individuals. However, Papazarkadas (2011, 55), based on epigraphic evidence (*SEG* XXVIII 103 ll. 23–24; *IG* II² 1241 ll. 52–53, *IG* II² 2492 ll. 34–36) argues that Hallof's view is questionable because, given that: (a) land leasing throughout Athens followed identical practices; (b) auctions constituted a normal practice, and (c) decentralized institutions tended to operate in unison with those in the level of the polis, it is legitimate to surmise that in organizing auctions the *board* followed specific procedures originally employed at the polis level.

17 According to Aperghis (1998, 6–8, 13), mining leases were differentiated along the following lines: A *kainotomia* (new-cutting) was leased for one to three years, at which time, if silver was discovered, the mine was reclassified as an *ergasimon* (a workable mine) and leased for three years; after this period, the mine was reclassified again into an *anasaximon* (a mine that could be re-equipped) with a ten-year lease period and perhaps with a renewal option for another ten years; if the mine was abandoned or left idle for more than a year and then brought back into operation, it was classified as *palaion anasaximon* (a mine that once had been *anasaximon* with a ten ten-year lease period).

Mining operations were run almost exclusively by private contractors, individuals, or consortia, who won the rights to mining specific tracks of the mines by participating from time to time in an auctioning process conducted by the *board of poletai* under the supervision of *Boule*. In particular, the 50 *bouleutai* (*councilmen*), who served in the *Boule* every *prytaneia*, had to be present in all phases of the auctioning process, that is, from the publicizing of the calls for bids in mining specific tracts in the mines, to appraising the submitted bids and to announcing the winners; their presence at this stage assured citizens about the integrity of the competition and dissuaded possible acts of favoritism on the part of the governors of the *board of poletai*; and essentially this supervision took the form of democratic control.

Additionally, the *Boule* exercised a key prerogative over the winners of the competition, which consisted of an examination regarding their technical capabilities to perform in accordance with the expected terms in their contracts. Depending on the tract of the mine for which a contractor had won in the bidding, the *bouleutai* examined to their satisfaction whether the contractor(s) had the manpower, the resources and the previous good record to do the job, and only then could they proceed to sign off the contract.[18] Thus, transparency in this process went hand in hand with best practice and the results in all historical accounts corroborate that it served the state and its citizens very well.[19]

Various fixed and recurring expenses appear to have been associated with the leases and the extracted quantities of silver. For example, contractors were expected to pay an initial license fee of 20 drachmae, which could go up to 150 drachmae,[20] to agree to a tax of 4.125% on the revenue from the extracted silver, and to cover the expenses for renting the slaves and the excavating lands from their owners (Van Alfen 2011, 16, ftn 47). State taxes and rents amounted to about 10% of the market value of the extracted silver. The rest belonged to the consortia or individual entrepreneurs, who received their share in the

18 After passing these capabilities tests, the winners at the auctioning process received a contract which lasted from three to seven years, depending on the prospects that emerged regarding the amount of silver that might be extracted (Van Alfen 2011). The consortia were the forerunners of later joint stock companies like the medieval Venetian *colleganza*, the Genoese *Mahona* of Chios and Phocaea, and the early modern Dutch and English joint stock companies such as The Dutch East India Company (**VOC**) and the East India Company (EIC).

19 Documentation about this assessment can be found in Papazarkadas (2011, 56) and Ober (1985, 28).

20 It appears that the fee of 20 drachmae was paid to the state in order to secure the right to search for silver in a given tract. Once silver was found, another auction took place, this time with an entry fee of 150 drachmae. At this stage, any third party could outbid the initial contractor. We do not have details about the auctioning process. But it seems that the initial fee was very low because there was no guarantee of finding any silver, whereas if silver was found later on the fee of 150, drachmae was variable depending on the risk that interested entrepreneurs were willing to take. The amount of 150 drachmae was not negligible. According to Loomis (1998, 241), an unskilled worker during the 4th century received a daily wage of 1.5 drachmae.

form of silver ingots (bullion). They were free to dispose their take in any way they chose, including selling it to the state at a large scale price discount of about 10%. This discount covered an estimated cost of minting of about 2%, the remaining 8% being profit for the state and/or seigniorage. Alternatively, the entrepreneurs were free to sell it as commodity to the highest bidder in a free market (Van Alfen 2011, 19). This again is an indication of the existence and functioning of one of the earliest commodity markets.

2.1.2 Minting of coins and maintaining their integrity

Van Alfen (2011) reports that between 460 and 404 BCE, Athens produced a colossal amount of coins, mainly *tetradrachms* from two streams of silver, that is, the Laurion mines and the tributes contributed from its allies. From the sheer size of this coinage, it follows that Athenians had managed to put in place institutional arrangements for large-scale minting of exceptionally high quality coins, and maintaining their integrity in domestic and international transactions. Fundamental among them were the mint and the *dokimastai* (testers).

2.1.2.1 The Athenian mint

The ancient Greek word for a mint was *nomismatocopeion* and since in Athens the dominant quantity of coins was made of silver, the mint was also called *argyrocopeion*, literally meaning silver-mint.[21] In Exhibit 2.4, the large rectangular building, situated next to the Southeast Fountain house and behind today's Church of Agioi Apostoloi, has been identified as a mint.

It was built probably sometime between 430 and 420 BCE. Only its foundations have been preserved, showing a building that measures 27 × 29 m, with its northern half open to the sky. Its southwest room contained furnaces and water basins. Clear signs of metalworking activities were also found in the form of metal slag and several tens of unfinished coins (so-called flans or coin blanks). The latter were used to produce small bronze coins from at least the 3rd century BCE. Before that time, this mint probably served as the place of manufacturing the official lead and bronze weights that were used to check the weight of goods sold by merchants.

Coinage was the prerogative of the state. The operations of the *Athenian mint* (henceforth the mint) were directed by a *board of epistatai* (supervisors) who served for fixed terms and, as in the case of the *board of poletai*, they

---

21 Drawing on the archeological information, we believe that in Athens there were three sources supplying coins. A state mint located in the *agora*, but yet of unknown location, which fabricated the fine Athenian silver coins. Another one, very likely owned also by the state, which produced bronze coins of small value; and many private metal working shops which cut bronze coins taking advantage of the mismatches that developed between supply and demand for such coins. The mint to which we refer in the text is the *argyrocopeion*.

Exhibit 2.4 Location of the foundations of an Athenian mint.
Source: American School of Classical Studies at Athens, Agora excavations: http://agora.
ascsa.net/id/agora/image/2012.59.0041

were answerable to the *Boule* and ultimately to the *Assembly*. There were
ten *epistatai* plus a secretary.[22] In the presence of the 50 *bouleutai* serving
in each *prytaneia*, the *epistatai* weighted the silver coming in for minting
from the mines and from the market; they logged the old coins that were
delivered to be demonetized or reminted; and they managed the production
and delivery of the minted coins to the appropriate *tamiai*, etc. Judging by
the volume of the coins that it turned out every year as well as their superb
technical craftsmanship, it is rather certain that the mint was a relatively
large productive unit with very knowledgeable and skillful workers (slaves).

2.1.2.2 Dokimastai (testers)

Currency-related Athenian authorities were very keen on protecting it from
fake and adulterated coins. For this purpose, Engen (2005, 369), Ober (2008,
222, 237) and Harris (2013, 29) among others report that sometime in the
first quarter of the 4th century, they appointed public slaves as officials to
examine the integrity of the coins brought to them by people involved in
market transactions. If these officials, called *dokimastai* and located one in
the *agora* and another in the port of Piraeus, determined that the coins had
been struck by the mint, the law required that they be accepted as means of

---

22 From a number of inscriptions that have been found, such as *SEG* 21.667, dated before
356/355, as well as *PA* 6681 and *APF* 220, we know even the names of some individuals who
served as *epistatai*. For example, mention is made of Anaphlystos, Doros, and Aimon, son
of Theogeiton of Aphidnai, a municipality that belonged to the tribe of Aiantis (Develin
2003, 13, 292–293).

payment in Athens. In case they found that the coins were good but unofficially struck imitations of the Athenian coins, they returned them to their owners; lastly, if the coins were found to contain cores from bronze or lead, or be debased in any other way, they were categorized as "counterfeits" and by being confiscated they became the property of the state.

Of the later, those deemed as fakes were slashed and dedicated to the sanctuary of the *Mother of the gods*, which acted as a *public fund*, that is, an institution about which we shall say more shortly below. Such fake *owls* have indeed been found near *metroon*, where this sanctuary was located. The rest were brought to the mint where they were melted, and the silver thus gained was either deposited as bullion in the above sanctuary or used to fabricate Athenian coins. If during testing arose conflicts, the interested parties could take their case for resolution in the so-called *People's Court*. But, if a seller refused to accept coins approved by the testers, all his goods on display that day were confiscated by state officials.

How the testing process created strong incentives for those involved to behave with transparency, it is not difficult to glimpse through. The *dokimastai* chose at random one coin out of those brought to them and, except for inspection, palpation and touchstone indications, they used special precision scales, sealed by state authorities, in order to examine whether it had the proper amount of silver.[23] If the coin passed the test, the seller had a guarantee as to the coins he was receiving in payment. But if the coin was found undervalued or adulterated, that is, a case of attempted fraud, the whole lot was confiscated. Hence, the merchants had strong incentives not to attempt fraud, because if they did and got caught, they would lose all the coins in the lot.

On the other hand, as we mentioned, the *dokimastai* were public slaves. If they did not fulfill their obligations as expected by the trust that the state bestowed on them, the law provided for severe punishments, such as whipping. Hence, they had strong incentives to do their job as truthfully and effectively as they could. We suggest that the state purposely entrusted this task to public slaves as against citizens, because the latter could not be subjected to such severe punishments under the Athenian law. Therefore, by assigning the task of testing to noncitizens with "diluted" rights and by monitoring closely the testing process, the state established conditions that enhanced the reputation of the Athenian currency and facilitated the smooth functioning of local and international markets.

However, aside from the coins struck by the mint and their imitations that were struck unofficially, foreign coins were occasionally, yet apparently

---

23 For detailed descriptions of the legal provisions that applied in the testing of the coins, of the consequences that applied to those that took part in the circulation of fake and adulterated coins, and how differences were resolved, see, for example, Engen (2005, 369), Ober (2008, 222, 237), Harris (2013, 29), Woolmer (2016, 84) and Rhodes, Osborne (2003, 115). According to the latter, anybody refusing to accept a coin that had been declared good by the *dokimastai* was punished by having his merchandise for that day confiscated.

legally, used in private exchanges of goods and services. About the latter we know neither how extensive was their use nor whether the *dokimastai* or other currency-related state authorities were involved in any way. Our knowledge in this regard is limited to the evidence cited by Figueira (1998, 57), who argues that the main foreign coins that circulated in Athens were those of Aegina, Chios and Kyzikos, and the indications highlighted by Kleiner (1975, 14), who suggests that coins struck by foreign mints could be accepted in transactions taking place in Athens by drawing on Aristophanes (*Frogs*, 717–738).

Based on the above, we surmise that the introduction of the post of *dokimastai* was a key institutional arrangement because it contributed significantly to the establishment of the Athenian currency as the dollar of the times on at least three grounds. First and foremost, with their presence, they provided a constant assurance to market participants about the commitment of state authorities to stand by the integrity of the Athenian coinage. Second, they acted as a filter mechanism that cleansed the market from adulterated coins and increased the trust in and hence the demand of the Athenian currency; and third, by offering a low cost process for checking on demand the integrity of the means of payment, the function of *dokimastai* reduced the cost of transactions and stimulated the incentives of doing business in Athens.

2.2 Financial intermediation in the private sector

Literary and epigraphic evidence brought into the forefront of scholarly attention, particularly in recent decades, ascertains that 5th and 4th century Athens had an extensive market and monetary system. Citizens and *metics* pursued mining, handicraft, manufacturing, export–import and other services, and became quite wealthy. Especially active were entrepreneurs and craftsmen from the class of *metics*. Thus, gradually over the span of these 2 centuries, Athens became the center of expanding nonfarm activities, which aimed at covering local needs as well as generating exports.

Along with the deepening commercialization of the Athenian economy during this period, there emerged a vibrant sector of financial intermediation, which could function much like the ones we observe in present-day market economies, although of course the disparity in the sophistication of banking services between then and now is great. To substantiate this claim, we shall return later on to explain the services they offered and the influence they exercised in the operation of the economy. Here, we shall limit the presentation to a bare introduction.

2.2.1 *Trapezai (banks)*

Banking grew important mainly in the 4th century. The reasons coincide with those we know today from development theory. After the intensification of the exploitation of the Laurion mines in the 480s BCE and the enactment of the big naval program of 483/482 to which the unexpected increase in public revenues gave impetus, the Athenian economy started to evolve away from agriculture and into other forms of value-adding activities.[24] Concomitant with these changes was the gradual shift in the holding of wealth by individuals. Rich persons moved away from a focus on holding land and instead they stored increasingly their wealth in silver coins, bullion, bullion substitutes such as domestic silver utensils and ornaments, and interest-bearing bank deposits. If there is any doubt that it was this transformation that generated the incentives and the opportunities for the expansion of banking, it ought to be dissipated in the light of the evidence cited on the one hand by Cohen (1992, 191), which indicates that the rich shifted their focus from visible property (land) to invisible (*aphane*) property to conceal their wealth, and on the other by Aristophanes (*Ecclesiazousai*, 600), who put his protagonist Blepyros to say[25]:

> ...And how about the man who has no land, but only gold and silver coins, that cannot be seen?

Most likely, the expansion of banking was stimulated also because the state of Athens did not license the undertaking of financial activities. Entry into banking was completely free. Anybody, Athenian or foreigner and citizen, *metic*, or even slave could become a banker and act in lieu of a bank by undertaking transactions yielding in the words of Demosthenes (*For Phormio*, 11): "hazardous revenue from money which belongs to others." Who survived in this industry and became wealthy and who failed and got in trouble with his depositors and debtors was decided in the banking market and the state did not mingle up taking the side of the one or the other. It was a case where the chief arbitrator of success and failure was the forces of the market and whenever suspicions about fraud and malpractice arose, it was left to the responsibility of those who transacted to resolve their differences through arbitration or by going to courts.

It is also of interest to note that since the law did not recognize the existence of business entities with rights and obligations separate and autonomous from the individuals who acted on their behalf, a bank and a banker were indistinguishable. In everyday life, people would say either "I have a deposit at Pasion's bank" or "I have a deposit with Pasion." But as Cohen (1992, Ch. 4) has firmly documented, the identification of a bank by its owner was not one man's show. Even though banking was a strictly personal

---

24 For further details about this transformation process, see Halkos, Kyriazis (2010).
25 The distinction between visible and invisible property to explain the lack of transparency in fulfilling one's tax obligations was used in the public discourse much earlier than the close of the 5th century BCE when Aristophanes wrote this comedy. For more details on this important behavioral shift, see Azoulay (2018, 153).

business, banks employed several employees and projected the necessary continuity of operation in the trust of their customers through certain social norms foreign to the Athenian society at the time. In particular, although it did not hold as a general rule, when the banker died, it was customary for the ownership of his bank to pass to one of his trusted employees, most likely a slave, who then joined his wife in marriage.[26]

At its peak, the banking industry numbered not less than 30 *eponymous* bankers and presumably numerous more anonymous ones, owing to the secrecy under which they conducted their operations (Cohen 1992, 31). Pasion, whose name was mentioned above, was the wealthiest banker and manufacturer of his time. He began his career as a slave owned by the bankers Antisthenes and Archestratus, who had a bank in the port of Piraeus. During his slavery, he quickly rose to chief clerk, called *argyramoibos* (see Section 2.2.2), in charge of a money-changing table at the port. He proved so successful that by 394 BCE through his services to the state, he managed to become a freed man and thereafter an Athenian citizen. Eventually, he got ownership of the bank in which he was working and established also a shield factory.

As an Athenian citizen, he donated large amounts of money to the state and extended loans without interest to many people in high places (Davies 1971, 428). When he died, his banking business, valued at around 80 talents, passed to his slave Phormio, who also later became an Athenian citizen. We transfer this example from Bitros, Karayiannis (2006, 17) just to highlight the kind of open-mindedness that prevailed, despite the conservative teachings of Athenian philosophers regarding class relationships and offering of labor for hire by citizens. Pasion's example proves that in Athens, social mobility was feasible even among *metics* and *slaves*.[27]

2.2.2 *Argyramoiboi or Kollybistai (moneychangers)*

The occupation of moneychanger was older than the emergence of banks and its beginning probably dates to the end of the 6th or the beginning of the 5th century, that is, during the period when many city-states first issued their own coins and commerce was expanding all over the Mediterranean.

---

26 For a more detailed account of the practices in this regard, see Cohen (1992, 61–80) Op. cit. 24.

27 Winters (2011, 82) gives a sort of "Forbes list" of the richest people in classical Athens, albeit from various time periods. The list shown below includes several individuals and their estimated wealth in drachmae. For some of them, the literature provides two estimates, the higher of which is reported within brackets:

1. Epicrates 1,800,000 [3,600,000]; 2. Nicias 600,000; 3. Oionias 489,000; 4. Euthycrates 360,000; 5. Conon 240,000; 6. Ischomachus 120,000 [420,000]; 7. Demosthenes 90,000; 8. Lysias 84,000 [600,000]; 9. Hipponicus 1,200,000 discounted to 600,000; 10. Diphilus 960,000 discounted to 480,000; 11. Pasion 480,000 (not counted).

The banker Passion, listed 11th in this list, was formerly a slave, whereas other entrepreneurs of relatively lesser wealth came from the class of *metics*.

In order to facilitate exchanges between merchants from different cities, using different coins, the moneychangers undertook the tasks of assessing the value of coins according to their content in precious metal, usually silver, and determining their exchange rate. As Cohen (1992, 18–19) writes:

> Money changer (*argyramoibos*) was a name applied to anyone engaged commercially in the testing or conversion of coins and precious metals.

Usually, they charged a fee of 5%–6% of the value of the exchange, which was called *kollybos*. But gradually the functions that moneychangers performed were taken over by other institutions and their importance in the economy declined. In particular, as we explained above, some city-states, notably Athens, introduced the function of *dokimastai*, who undertook on behalf of city-states to guarantee the integrity of their official coinage. This change naturally should have compelled some moneychangers to turn into bankers, some others to differentiate their services in order to survive, and still some others to move into other professions. Thus, during the centuries under consideration, in addition to banks active in the changing of coins, receiving deposits and extending loans, there were also professional moneychangers called *argyramoiboi* and/or *kollybistai*. In Athens, they were located in marketplaces and in the port of Piraeus and they combined the functions of *dokimastai* and assessors of the worth of the coins brought to them for conversion. Understandably since old, imitated and counterfeit coins circulated in parallel with newly minted ones, their job must have been knowledge intensive and their trade competitive.

2.2.3 Enechirodaneistai (pawnbrokers)

In parallel to moneychangers, there existed also pawnbrokers, called *enechirodaneistai*, who took property as security deposit, as modern pawnbrokers do. They differed from banks in at least three respects. Namely in that: (a) they did not take coin deposits; (b) they offered loans in coins but no more "sophisticated" types of credit (like maritime loans, etc.); and (c) unlike the safekeeping service that banks offered, if the loan was not repaid by the due date, they took hold of the property the borrower had deposited with them.

Pawnbrokers existed also after the emergence of the banking system, as they continue to exist today. They took as guarantee (pawns) probably objects of value such as rings and jewelry, but not mortgages of land, houses and other hard to liquidate valuables.

2.3 Summary

All authority for deciding on matters of currency rested with the *Assembly*. In this body, citizens decided by voting on minting new series of coins, reminting or demonetizing old ones, expanding the supply whenever necessary by issuing gold, silver-plated and bronze coins, introducing laws to regulate the parallel circulation of local and foreign currencies, etc. Certain executive and supervisory tasks had been assigned also to *Boule*. Lastly, integral to the system of public finance were the *tamiai*, the mint and the *dokimastai*.

Given that the costs and benefits from state decisions concerned the same citizens who took them, it was in everybody's interest to act responsibly and to be open to discussion and persuasion.[28] Any citizen could come forward and make a proposal on issues that were included by the *Council* in the agenda of the meeting, thus "enriching" the stock of existing options. The *Assembly* listened, discussed, voted and adopted or rejected the proposals. But at the same time, it was very strict in the monitoring and control of the institutions that were involved in the management of the state's financial affairs. The various currency-related "officials" (*poletai*, *epistatai*, *dokimastai*, etc.) underwent reporting and voting procedures at the beginning and the end of their short tenures in order to enhance the spirit of transparency, accountability and fiscal responsibility, and to discourage embezzlement and fraud.

In the private sector, excluding production and consumption in the household (*oikos*), transactions took the form of money exchanges in a marketplace called *agora*. Thus, owing to the mediation of money and the efficiency benefits that derived from its use, parallel with the goods markets, there developed a robust money market in which economic agents could secure a wide range of financial services for the planning and management of their economic affairs. Central in this market was a significant number of private *banks* which, among other services, accepted deposits and extended loans by trying to earn a profit margin between the interest rates they paid on deposits and the interest rates they received from loans. On the contrary, the banking activities of so-called *argyramoiboi*, who dominated in much earlier times, during the 5th and 4th centuries were subdued.

Now, having identified which institutions were involved in which money-related activities, it is safe to conclude that the protagonists were the *Assembly* and the *banks*.[29] The *Assembly* influenced the economy and the money market through its decisions regarding the state's budget and the currency part of the money supply, whereas the *banks* did the same through their banking and credit creating services. Hence, the natural approach to get a glimpse into the way in which the money market helped clear the goods and services markets in the economy is to look first into the implications of the coincidence of fiscal and currency functions in one and the same authority, that is, the *Assembly*. To this, we turn in the next chapter.

28 The principle of acting in this way was called *parrhesia*. It meant that any citizen had the right and the obligation to speak freely about all matters that concerned the welfare of the totality of the people (common good), and at times even at a personal risk. Consequently, it set high moral standards and required conscious and active citizens.

29 Later on, we shall emphasize that among the protagonists were also the silver bullion holders who influenced the economy and the money supply in their own independent ways. But our focus in this chapter has been on the institutions that were active in the money market.

3 The system and the tenets of public finance

The *Assembly* had jurisdiction over a wide range of subjects. It voted on taxes, loans, expenditures, and in general on all issues that related to the financial policies of the state. Responsible for the preparation of the budget, its execution and any auditing and reporting was the *Boule*. The latter was also in charge of the oversight of the agencies and the procedures for the collection of public revenues and the settlement of budgeted public expenditures.

It is needless to say that over the decades, the nature of fiscal policies and the web of budget related agencies changed. A trend became particularly apparent after 403 BCE when Athens started overhauling democracy. Two key reforms should suffice to highlight its direction. The first concerns the reshuffling of the powers of the *Assembly* in financial matters. In particular, this reform shifted the decision-making authority of the *Assembly* first, to "laws," which of course apply automatically and are quite difficult to change, and second, to specialized institutions presumably run by "experts." In the relevant literature, some authors have interpreted this reform as a deliberate "reduction in democracy in favor of greater efficiency,"[1] whereas others think that the *Assembly* continued to have ultimate control on fiscal and currency matters and that there was no discontinuity involved.[2]

From our point of view, what should be stressed is that this is the first known instance in the controversy of "rules vs. discretion," which has attracted so much interest from economists and political scientists working in the areas of fiscal and monetary policies in contemporary democracies. The second seemingly decentralizing reform introduced sometimes in the mid-380s BCE, split the functions of the *public fund*[3] into two separate

---

1 On this issue, see among others Lyttkens, Tridimas, Lindgren (2018) and Harris (2013, 244).
2 For a detailed discussion of the views, which have been expressed on this issue and a handy summary of the relevant literature, see Welser (2011, 105).
3 The *public fund*, also known as *demosion*, collected revenues from fines, rents, and public property leases and covered public expenses such as paying the wages of civil servants and judges, as well as the cost of *trierarchy*. The personnel of the *fund* responsible for carrying out these tasks before the Peloponnesian War were called *kolakretai* (Samons 2000, 55–69).

activities. Revenues were collected by the *apodektai*. But payments started to be made at the level of the public authorities, to which money was allocated through the process of the so-called *merismos* (allocation). More specifically, the *Assembly*, the *Boule,* and the other state entities received the allocated funds in their own separate accounts, and they made payments out of them against budgeted expenditures under their own responsibility and reporting requirements. In the course of the year, as surpluses and shortfalls developed in the execution of the budget at that level, the *apodektai* would consider whether monies were transferred from surplus to deficit authorities, and in case of overall surplus or deficit, the accounts were balanced through the reserves that were held for safekeeping purposes by the *treasuries of Athena and the other gods*,[4] and remained available to the state on demand or passed as donations to their ownership.

Our objective in this chapter is to present the rudiments of a model to explain how Athenians set up a system of public finance, controllable by democratic means, which rendered it possible for them to balance the budget through war and peace, despite the well-known excesses of the Periclean era.

3.1 A brief overview of the fiscal administration

Demosthenes (*Against Timocrates*, 96) informs us that Athens maintained two public budgets: one civil and another sacred. Moreover, from various sections of Aristotle's *Athenian Constitution*, it follows that they distinguished between the "property of the polis" and the "property of the gods." From these pieces of information, we can infer that, while the civil budget comprised revenues that were earmarked for covering current and capital account expenses like paying civil servants and financing the cost of public works, respectively, the sacred budget was an aggregate statement of the audited reports that the responsible officers of sacred operational units submitted and entailed the results of sacred current and capital accounts, together with the balance of funds and valuables that were left under their guardianship either for safekeeping purposes or as donations. This section

---

4 At the beginning, the *treasury of Athena* and the *treasury of other gods* were separate *funds.* The former managed the treasures of the Parthenon, which had been established before democracy, whereas the latter, established in 434 BCE, handled the treasures of all other temples in the city. The *treasuries* were merged into one in 406/405, separated in 384, and finally merged again in 346 BCE. As we shall explain shortly, they functioned as bankers to the state during peacetimes and as lenders of last resort in periods of war. The *treasury* was administered by a series of magistrates, called *tamiai*. Their appointment was annual (Marcaccini 2015, 517) and during their term of office, they were under the supervision of the *Boule* (Aristotle, *Athenian Constitution*, 47.1). In addition to the funds it raised from the temples, the *treasury* collected funds from the payment of fines, from renting out public property allocated by the state and even from private donations. According to Samons (2000, 35–38), this *treasury* collected also the *aparchai*, meaning the tributes paid by the allies to the city of Athens.

highlights the web of agencies that were involved in the execution of the two budgets and the particular tasks they performed; maps the sources of revenues and the types of expenditures that were financed; and explains how the *Boule* made sure that the policy decisions taken by citizens in the *Assembly* would be applied in a framework of transparency and accountability on the part of the responsible officers.

3.1.1   Setup of the state's financial services

From the studies of Welser (2011) and Prichard (2015), it follows that by the first half of the 4th century BCE, Athens had managed through trial and error to put in place a sophisticated system for collecting revenues and allocating public expenditures with diligent cross controls to minimize corruption. Figure 3.1 brings together the administrative entities that are known to have played active roles at one period or another in this system, but without any pretensions that such a model existed at any particular period. For, first, some of its constituent features like, for example, the process of *merismos*, shown in Circle M, did not exist in the 5th century, whereas the *Delos* or *allied fund*[5] had eclipsed by the time that *merismos* was first introduced, quite likely in the early years of the 4th century BCE; and, second, in the span of the 2 centuries under consideration various administrations rearranged these entities by merging or splitting them, as well as creating new ones. In essence, the analysis in Figure 3.1 helps us make sense of the general process of public finance in classical Athens, irrespective of whether it is validated or not by historical details.

Having clarified this point with reference to Figure 3.1, observe that at the top of the hierarchy in Circle T was an officer called *tamias*[6] *ton koinon*

---

5 The *Delos* or *allied fund* was established in 478 BCE and its main purpose was to collect the tributes from the allied city-states that were necessary in order to apply the grand strategy of deterrence against the Persian threat, with Athens being the leader. In 454 BCE, perhaps for reasons of safety, it was transferred from Delos to Athens and placed under the guardianship of the *treasury of Athena*. Upon its arrival, there the fund started paying to the *treasury of Athena* religious offerings, perhaps as substitute payments, for safekeeping and administrative services, called *aparche,* at the rate of 1.6% on the balance of the deposits. This arrangement lasted until 404, that is, the end of the Peloponnesian War, since after the defeat of Athens by Sparta and its allies, the *First Athenian Alliance* was dissolved (Samons 2000, 70–83). Its main managers consisted of ten *hellenotamiai* whose duties included safeguarding of the treasures, drawing up of tax directories, allocating the alliance money in the event of war, and accompanying the *strategoi* in war campaigns perhaps for the purpose of covering the associated expenditures. In order to ensure the prestige and the integrity of the *fund*, it was decided that in the event of corruption and spoilage of money by the *hellenotamiai*, those usurpers found guilty after trial, would have suffered the ultimate punishments: death by drinking the hemlock.

6 The translation in English of this term is "treasurer." However, the tasks a *tamias* performed were wider than those of a treasurer who receives and pays out money and then reports to a higher authority for reasons of accountability and transparency. For example,

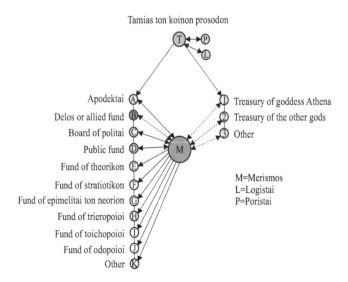

Figure 3.1 Probable setup of the Athenian system of public finance.

prosodon or *tamias epi tes dioikiseos*, all terms meaning that he was respon-sible for the overall supervision of the system for collecting and dispensing public revenues and reporting to the *Assembly*. To carry out his coordina-tive duties, he was assisted by a body of civil servants, depicted by Circle P. Aristophanes (*Frogs*, 1505) refers to them as *poristai*, implying that they were involved in the handling of financial means. Considering that in this admin-istrative structure he stood as *epistates* or chief among all *tamiai*, we may view his role as being equivalent to the present-day "Minister of Finance." But this does not imply that those in charge of the various *funds* were of lesser social prestige and influence. An indication of how important these posts were can be derived from the example of Euboulos and Lycourgos.[7] Both introduced such radical fiscal measures in the second half of the 4th century that Athens not only escaped the economic recession from the Social War (357–355 BCE) but also, as argued by Economou, Kyriazis (2016b), in

according to Bubalis (2010), the two *triremes* used in festivals, which had been built and maintained by *treasuries of the gods,* were administered by *tamiai*. Also, the *tamiai* in charge of the two speedy *triremes*, called *Paralos* and *Salaminia*, were obliged to keep them always in operational readiness.

7 Euboulos served as *tamias* of the *theoric fund* from about 354/353 to 343/342 BCE, whereas Lykourgos was appointed *tamias ton koinon prosodon* three successive times, and held this post each time for four years, beginning in 338/337 BCE. Their posts were among a limited number in which appointments were made by vote, instead of lot, and for periods that exceeded one year. The justification for these exceptions from the norm is that those ap-pointed ought to have expert knowledge and skills.

the period 355–322 BCE, it achieved impressive economic growth, accompanied by a super impressive increase (tenfold) of public revenues from 130 to 1,200 talent*s*.[8]

The two budgets mentioned by Demosthenes are associated with the two axes in Figure 3.1. The civil budget pertained to the left axis and the sacred to the right. Looking downward, we see which civil and sacred administrative agencies were involved. Their heads acted as *tamiai* in the wider sense, and in some of them, they were referred to by specific titles. For example, in Circles A and B, the *tamiai* carried the titles of *apodektai*[9] and *hellenotamiai* because, as we shall explain in the next section, they collected revenues from specific sources. Some agencies, like the *allied fund* and the *public fund,* collected revenues from specific sources and dispensed those allocated to them for specific uses by *merismos*.[10] Some others, like those of *apodektai* and the *board of poletai*,[11] collected funds from specific sources and transferred the surpluses to *merismos* for reallocation; and the rest, like the *funds* of *theorikon*[12] and *stratiotikon*,[13] just dispensed the funds allocated to them by *merismos* to cover budgeted outlays for cultural and welfare activities, building roads, fortifications, etc.[14]

Notice that we have drawn the double-headed arrow between *merismos* and the *Delos* or *allied fund* in dots and those between *merismos* and the

---

8 From the available evidence, we know with considerable certainty that the system of public finance was much less coordinated in the 5th than in the 4th century BCE. Therefore, a good deal of the spectacular increase in public revenues under Euboulos and Lykourgos must have resulted from improvements in the administration of revenue collections. But from the literature assessed by Burke (2010), we find it difficult to believe that a significant part of this increase did not come from the expansion of the economy that was propelled by the large building programs both of them implemented. An account on the parallels of this building program to that by Pericles in the 5th century BCE can be found in Andreades (1928, 262–263).

9 There were ten *apodektai*, one from each of the ten Athenian tribes. They maintained lists of debtors to the state, writing off those who settled their obligations. Debtors who were not insolvent and did not pay their obligation were punished by doubling their debt or even by imprisonment (Aristotle, *Athenian Constitution*, 48.1–2; Papazarkadas 2011, 83–86). By decision of the *Boule*, they contributed to the process of *merismos*. As for the tasks performed by the *board of poletai*, see Section 2.1.1.

10 This mechanism was introduced in the 4th century BCE.

11 In Section 2.1.1, we explained briefly the role of this agency with regard to its tasks in the Laurion mining activities. However, as we shall see in the next section, its tasks extended well beyond this area.

12 The *tamiai* of this *fund* were expected to provide each citizen with two obols covering the fee of attendance in the theatrical plays that were sponsored by the state.

13 According to Aristotle (*Athenian Constitution*, 47.2), this *fund* managed the defense budget. In cases that its revenues fell short of the budgeted expenses because of unforeseen developments, the *Assembly* saw to it that the necessary funds were reallocated from other uses.

14 The *fund of trieropoioi* financed the building of *triremes*; the *fund of toichopoioi* covered the expenses for the construction and maintenance of the city's walls; the *fund of odopoioi* was responsible for the city's roads network; and the *fund of epimelitai ton neorion* looked after the operation of the naval bases mooring the warships and possibly merchant ships.

treasuries of Athena and the other gods in dashes. We have done so to emphasize the following two aspects. According to Rhodes (1980, 410–411), the *treasury* of the *Delian League*, that is the *allied fund*, remained independent until 411 BCE and finally it was abolished in 404 BCE. Its independence, indicated by the dots, was qualified because, after its transfer from Delos to Acropolis in 456 BCE, most likely some amounts from its funds were used by Pericles to finance the erection of the golden age monuments and beautifications of Athens. By implication, even in the absence of a formal kind of *merismos* at the time, an alternative allocative mechanism did exist. The second aspect, indicated by the dashed arrows, has to do with the role that the *treasuries of the gods* played in the balancing of the civil budget to which we turn next.

The principle on which the process of *merismos* operated was to balance the budget by adjusting the budgeted expenditures to the flow of revenues at predetermined intervals within every year. If at the end of the accounting period the budget experienced a deficit, it was balanced by borrowing from the *treasuries of the gods*. But in case of a surplus, the funds were transferred to the *treasuries of the gods* partly for safekeeping purposes and partly as donations. Thus, the latter played a key role in the budgetary process. Apart from serving as safekeeping depositories, in regular times their own cash and near cash treasures were kept at arm's length from the fiscal authorities by being considered as devoted to gods and hence untouchable in all but really compelling circumstances. Davies (2001) conveys this view by arguing that these sacred *funds* functioned as monetary reserves. Besides, whenever funds were borrowed, the state had to pay interest, and this deterred all but transitory borrowing. It is believed that the *treasuries of the gods* shown in Figure 3.1 raised significant amounts of funds from public and private donations, interest remittances from loans to the state, and other sources; and that when Athens was in urgent need for funds during times of war or other emergencies, the sacred treasuries would come forward and contribute, even though Athens would return the loans whenever it could (Samons 2000, 30–50).

The sacred budget had to do with the management of valuables that were deposited in the *treasuries of the gods*.[15] As treasurers, their *tamiai* counted

---

15 According to von Reden (2010, 162–163), the monetary property of the *treasuries of the gods* derived from spoils and harvests, voluntary dedications of cash and other precious metal items, proceeds from the sale of confiscated property, penalty payments for breach of secular or sacred law, fees for cult services, public taxes, revenue from interest-bearing loans, rents of land and houses, sales of sacred property, etc. The temple inventories in Athens, Delphi, and Delos attest to the vast monetary resources some *treasuries of the gods* amassed. Furthermore, private and public benefactors provided resources for temple construction in order to enhance their standing and prestige in the cities. At the same time though, it should be noted that the temples had expenses for construction, maintenance and repair of buildings, wages, and the feeding of personnel and animals. The accounts from the *Temple of Apollo* on Delos reveal that the *hieropoioi* (the priests) bought products such as olive oil, wine, wheat, barley, firewood and charcoal. There were also regular and irregular workers employed, such as builders and flute players.

and weighted the coins they received; they prepared a comprehensive report with the property of each *treasury*, listing separately the coins from silver, gold, and other valuables; and they published on a single "stele," that is, a publicly displayed engraved stone, which served as an audited record of the report, showing the revenues they had received and the outlays they had incurred during their term in office (Blamire 2001). In most cases, temples were autonomous economic units even though they were accountable to the public authorities. In cases where the temple *treasury* was under the control of the state, public officials were placed in charge of it (von Reden 2010, 163–164).

Lastly, shown in Circle L is the body of so-called *logistai*, whose tasks according to Aristotle (*Athenian Constitution*, 54.2) entailed checking on whether public expenditures were effected in line with the provisions and the guidelines laid down by the responsible authorities. In other words, they acted as the modern-day state controllers and auditors and, if they found discrepancies, they filed a lawsuit against those who were in charge.[16]

3.1.2 Sources and uses of public funds

A fairly complete picture of the sources of funds that flowed at one period or another into the civil budget and the uses to which they were put is given in Table 3.1. Our objective here is to explain briefly the types of revenues raised; how Athens went about collecting them with the mediation of the widely decentralized administrative units we mentioned in the previous section; and what general classes of public services it financed. Regarding the latter issue, we shall limit the presentation to a mere introduction, since in Chapter 5, we look into the structure of the public sector in greater detail.

3.1.2.1 Public revenues

• *Rents from state-owned property*: Properties were let at auction to the highest bidder, usually on ten-year leases. The auction was held in the *Boule* under the direction of the *board of poletai* and in the presence of the *king archon* (one of the state's high magistrates but not the same as the *eponymous*). Rents were paid annually to the *apodektai*.[17] This

---

16 According to a lemma in the Oxford Classical Dictionary, there were three distinct bodies with the title of *logistai*. The first one, consisting of 30 experts, supervised payments to and from the various *funds* and sacred treasuries. This is the body mentioned in Figure 3.1. The second body, comprising ten *logistai*, checked magistrates' accounts each *prytany*. These were chosen by lot from the members of the *Boule*. Lastly, the third body included ten *logistai* selected by lot from all citizens. Their task was to examine the accounts of magistrates at the end of their term of office and bring before a jury those who were found to have committed punishable irregularities.

17 By using the system of auctioning in the allocation of concessions (land, mines, etc.), Athens was using a very modern procedure. Because, as we know now, auctions are mechanisms that help optimize the use of a resource since presumably the highest bidder makes the best use of it, thus promoting growth and welfare. Auctions help establish correct

Table 3.1 Flows of funds in the Athenian public budget[a]

	Sources	Uses
Above budget[a]	Rents from state-owned property	Armed forces
	Minerals and underground resources	Infrastructures
	Custom duties on import–export trade	Monuments and beautifications
	Court fees, fines, and confiscations	Remuneration of officials
		Civil servants and judges Market monitors
	Eisphora	Working of the polity through democracy *Ecclesiastika*[b]
	Metoikion	Welfare
		Theorika Pensions to disabled Care of war orphans
	Pornikon telos Miscellaneous	Miscellaneous
Below budget[c]	*Liturgies*	
		Soldier financed armaments

a From the sources of public revenue, it follows that the state's income derived mainly from taxes on trade of goods and services. With the exception of the *eisphora* tax on rich people, which became permanent in the 4th century, there was no general income taxation and whatever occasional taxes were imposed on people or their property they took the form of a flat rate on the assessed overall values of one's property. For a detailed inquiry into the tax system of Athens in classical times, see Lyttkens (2013).

b *Ecclesiastica* were introduced in 403/402 BCE after the proposals of two influential citizens (politicians) with the names, *Agyrrhios* and *Heraclides*. Under it, a reimbursement of tree obols (half a drachma) when attending the *Assembly* meetings was offered to each Athenian citizen (Tridimas 2017, 215). The idea behind this was to increase the number of citizens participating in the *Assembly*.

c While the entries in the Above-budget section relate to public revenues and expenditures, the ones in the Below-budget section have to do with the financing by citizens of certain public services.

method anticipated modern state procedures when dealing with similar matters.

• *Minerals and underground resources*: For Athens, the most important minerals were the silver mines of Laurion. As we said earlier, the mines were let out in separate concessions to the highest bidders for either three or even ten years at a time. Early on present in the auction was the treasurer of the *fund of stratiotikon* and later on the treasurer of the *fund of theorikon*. The rents were payable each year to the *apodektai*.

- *Custom duties on import–export trade*: Most important was the charge of *pentekoste,* a 2% duty on the value of all imports and exports. Its collection was assigned for a year to the highest bidders. What is interesting to note is that the highest bidders were usually a consortium of private individuals, which is an indication of the advanced level in which legal practices and property rights protection had reached in Athens.[18]

- *Court fees, fines and confiscations*: In private suits, both parties paid fees, and in disputes of private citizens against the state a citizen deposited a *parakatabole*, that is, a percentage of the value in dispute, which was returned if the plaintiff won but fell to the state if he lost. Fines in public prosecutions went also to the state. They were frequent and could amount to several talent*s*. Confiscated goods were sold at public auctions (Aristotle, *Athenian Constitution*, 52.1).

- *Eisphora*: This was a property tax. At the beginning, Athenians introduced it as an extraordinary measure to be applied only in times of extreme necessity, such as war. However, during the 4th century, when the revenues from the allied tribute did not exist anymore and the revenues from other sources were insufficient, Athenians by vote rendered the *eisphora* permanent and imposed it on the wealthier citizens and *metics,* that is, non-Athenian citizens living and working in Athens. The *eisphora* was a proportional form of property tax. Its collection was assigned to the highest bidder in an auction. The tax collectors were called *telonai* and each one was assisted by a staff of specialized employees, possibly, not only citizens, but also *slaves. Telonai* and their staff were paid by withholding a certain amount of fees for the provision of this service to the state (Fawcett 2016, 174, 188, 193).

- *Metoikion*: This was a personal tax on *metics.* According to Gabrielsen (2013, 337, 341), men paid 12 drachmae a year and women 6 drachmae. Its collection was farmed out on a yearly basis to the *board of poletai.*

- *Apeleutheroi*: Meaning those slaves who managed to gain their freedom, such as the case of the wealthy banker and industrialist Passion. They were obliged to pay a special tax amounting to one *triobolon*, that is, half a drachma per annum (Lyttkens 1994, 70).

- *Pornikon telos*: It was a license fee paid by all prostitutes to carry out their profession legally (Lyttkens 1994, 70–71, 73).

- *Miscellaneous*: Earnings from seigniorage and other irregular sources.

- *Liturgies*: Under this arrangement, early on one wealthy citizen, and later a group of them, undertook to finance the provision of a public

---

18 For a detailed analysis on this, see Hansen (2006, 92).

service. For example, one frequently mentioned is the covering of the running costs for a *trireme* warship for one year.[19] Gabrielsen (1994, 45, 124, 139–140) reports that this cost was high, averaging between 3,000 and 6,000 drachmae, and kept increasing over time. For this reason, whereas initially *Liturgies* functioned as an institution based on willful giving, eventually it was abandoned and replaced by coercion.[20]

3.1.2.2 Public expenditures

- *Armed forces*: In the 5th century Athens fought its wars by drawing partly on public revenues, partly on indirect taxation of the well-to-do citizens via the institution of *trierarchy*, and partly on the obligation of *hoplites* to finance their armaments.[21] Gradually though, the need to maintain a standing army and a naval force shifted the burden for financing most of these services onto the budget. By implication, defense services absorbed an increasing percentage of public revenues and by putting pressure on all other services, it must have turned social sentiment increasingly in favor of peace. Based on the evidence cited by Kyriazis (2009, 120), we believe that it was this trend that precipitated eventually the coming of the second Athenian renaissance under Euboulos and Lycourgos in the second half of the 4th century.[22]
- *Infrastructure*: Figure 3.1 in the previous section ascertains that in Athens, there functioned a wide assortment of funds, which oversaw and financed the construction of fortifications, ports, roads, etc. Work in each project was performed by private contractors who had won either in a competitive bidding process or in the framework of a Public-Private-Partnership. In either case, the execution was monitored by the *tamiai* of the fund concerned and corruption was deterred by the possibility that the accounts might be audited by *logistai* on behalf of the *tamias ton koinon prosodon*.

---

19 *Trireme* was the main type of ship used in sea fighting by Athenians during those centuries. It comprised a 200-member crew. For more details, see Morrison, Coates (1986).

20 For more information and analysis regarding the importance and the range of the services that well-to-do citizens provided in the context of *liturgies*, see Section 5.2.2.8 entitled "Other public services."

21 *Hoplites* were a social group of citizens that grew larger during the *Archaic Period* (750–510 BCE). They were medium-income and they could finance their personal military equipment by themselves. By participating in the so called *phalanx* formation, they provided a potent fighting force whenever they were called upon to defend their homeland, or even to expand its power and influence. For more details about this military formation, see Kagan, Viggiano (2013).

22 In our view, the evidence is such that it would be utterly farfetched to argue that the period under Euboulos and Lykourgos was not for Athens a second golden age achieved through a combination of public works, a wide program of institutional reforms, and robust expansion of domestic and international trade.

- *Monuments and beautifications*: Those who opposed Pericles' plans for the construction of the monuments and other structures of art that we so admire today[23] accused him of abusing the tribute of the allies, of spending money that was earmarked for defense purposes, and of numerous other frivolities. He responded by invoking various arguments all of which suggested that he viewed his building program as a continuation of public investments propagating the power and grandeur of Athens that he had repeatedly emphasized, as for example in the following excerpt from his *Funeral Oration* (Thucydides, *The Peloponnesian War*, 2.41):

  > ...And we shall assuredly not be without witnesses; there are mighty monuments of our power which will make us the wonder of this and of succeeding ages; we shall not need the praises of Homer or of any other panegyrist whose poetry may please for the moment, although his representation of the facts will not bear the light of day. For we have compelled every land and every sea to open a path for our valor, and have everywhere planted eternal memorials of our friendship and of our enmity.

  In retrospect, there is no doubt that he proved right, because all superpowers that have emerged ever since have adopted more or less his viewpoint regarding the employment of public investments for projecting a country's wealth and power abroad.
- *Remuneration of officials*: In the first half of the 5th century, many citizens in official positions offered their services for free. They did so motivated by the urge to represent the interests of the tribe, which had opted to place them in the state's selection process. But beginning with Pericles paying officials for their services started to expand beyond those employed in the public administration. For example, the judges called *heliastai,* who served in the court of *Heliaia* started to be paid three obols for each meeting (Hansen 1999, 184). As a result, more and more Athenians begun to exchange self-reliance and duty to serve the common good for paid employment in state offices, and besides its fiscal and other economic implications, this trend must have changed rather for the worse the nature of the bonds Athenians maintained in the past with their state.
- *Working of democracy*: As it has already been mentioned (see Table 3.1) with the introduction of the policy of *ecclesiastica*, the Athenian state provided remuneration to the first 6,000 participants in the *Assembly*.
- *Welfare*: The state aided the poor and those facing unexpected calamities. This assistance was distributed by the municipal authorities where the recipients resided for better monitoring of their needs and more

---

23 For a brief introduction into his building program, see the *Athenian Acropolis: The building Program of Pericles* at http://people.duke.edu/~wj25/slides/18%20Acropolis.pdf.

efficient delivery of the service. The aberrant behaviors, which are well-known from modern day experiences to be associated with welfare programs, were mitigated by strong incentives for Athenians to abide by the laws and regulations. These incentives emanated from the *paideia* they received in the school and in the family, the competition in daily life for social approval and recognition (fame-honor), for themselves and their descendants, and their trust in the meritocratic procedures of the state, which encouraged them to meet their communal obligations. But at same time, given that Athens was governed on the principle that "absolutely no one was to be trusted" in the management of public money, abuses were discouraged by institutions and administrative safeguards that Athenians had put in place, which provided for constant monitoring and severe penalties in cases of fraud.[24] To these institutions and safeguards we shall return shortly below.

- *Miscellaneous*: Expenditures for unforeseen events.
- *Soldier financed armaments*: Depending on the productive capacity of the farmland they owned, Athenians from the time of Solon were categorized into four classes. Two of them were those of *hippeis* and *hoplites*. When drafted into the armed forces the ones from the former class were expected to procure a horse with full implements for the cavalry, whereas those from the latter class were expected, with some exceptions like war orphans, to procure their personal weaponry.

Reflecting on the above, two remarks are worth noting. The first has to do with the *eisphora*. Athenians had strong views about the range of the individual rights that emanated from their citizenship. They believed that free citizens should normally be compelled to pay neither property nor income taxes, because doing so, it would be equivalent to accepting a regime of tyranny or servitude.[25] This explains why in times prior to Peisistratos such taxes did not exist and when they were convinced to vote in favor of the *eisphora* tax they accepted it on the conditions that it would apply only in exceptional circumstances.[26] Consequently, its imposition on a permanent

---

24 For several such cases, see Christ (2006).

25 From the research of de Jasay (2007), it follows that the issues regarding the voluntary or coercive nature of progressive taxation are nowadays as contested as ever. One such issue springs from the realization that progressive taxation is based on a right of the majority to impose higher tax obligations on the minority (wealthy). But this right is inconsistent with the principle of equality of citizens. Athenians were aware of this inconsistency and to ameliorate it, they introduced mechanisms of social pressures and rewards. The analysis by Kelen (2001, 7–58), which highlights the numerous positive effects that would result from a more voluntary and less coercive taxation, ascertains how superior the approach of the Athenians to this problem was, relative to the dominant practices in the democracies of today.

26 It may be worth noting that the *eisphora* tax had a threshold below, which it was not levied and that it crept downward in real terms with inflation and probably because of impoverishment.

basis may be the first known case whereby a democratic body of citizens decides to impose a progressive property tax and use the proceeds to finance "programs" benefiting in part the poorer citizens. The second remark relates to the inclusion in the regular uses of public funds of outlays for welfare. To our knowledge, this is the first instance in history where a collective body of citizens authorized the state to extend various forms of governmental assistance to select groups of coinhabitants in need. As a result, Athens became the first example of a "Welfare State," with all its pros and cons, including corruption.[27]

3.1.3 Democratic control of financial magistrates

Before being confirmed as *magistrates* or *bouleutai,* elected officials were subjected to a procedure called *dokimasia* (testing), which was administered by the *Boule* in cooperation with a special board appointed by *Heliaia.* This board assessed how the nominees had conducted their previous lives and decided by placing emphasis not only (or even so much) on their qualifications but also on their community reputation and moral standing.[28] Upon completion of their duties, but before being absolved of any responsibility, all appointed officials passed through a procedure called *euthune,* which was implemented by a ten-member board called *euthunoi* (Schwartzberg 2004, 312). No appointed official, not even the *strategoi,* was spared from undergoing an evaluation on how they had performed their duties (Hansen 1999, 222–224; Lanni 2016, 72). Moreover, inspections could take place at any time during their term in office (Osiander 2007, 71), and in cases of wrongdoing, sanctions could be imposed upon the officials and/or their entire collegial board (Ober 2008, 157). The inspections were carried out by the ten *logistai* in the second body of public auditors mentioned in footnote 16 (Hansen 1999, 220–221; Lanni 2016, 72).

The preceding arrangements applied to elected officials in general. For those who had been entrusted with the management of public funds in one way or another, the examination was much more rigorous. On completion of their service, the magistrates and the *bouleutai* in this particular category

---

27 We return to the welfare services provided by the Athenian state in Section 5.1.3.
28 In particular, referring to the *dokimasia* of a magistrate Fröhlich (2013, 185) writes:

> This was not a test of his competence or his ability with regards to a specific task, but rather a judgment of his status and character as a citizen in the presence of either the court or the boule, depending on his office. Any candidate for office was required to testify to his status as a citizen over several preceding generations, his civic good conduct through military service and paying taxes, and his general moral conduct (Aristotle, *Athenian Constitution,* 55.2–5). After giving his answers to all of these questions and furnishing witnesses in support of his testimony, the magistrate's case was then put to a vote of the *Assembly.* Provided the *Assembly* approved, the magistrate was then sworn in and formally entered office (Aristotle, *Athenian Constitution,* 55.5).

passed through a procedure called *logodosia*. This was initiated with the submission by each of them, within a month from leaving office, of a report detailing their activities and accounts. In their reports, the audited officials had to show that they performed their duties in accord with the standing laws and regulations and that at no time they had engaged in unlawful activities or misuses of funds. The reports were examined by a *board of* ten *logistai* with the assistance of ten *synegoroi* (public prosecutors).[29] Their verdicts were then forwarded to the *People's Court*, which decided on the guilt or innocence of the investigated officials. This part had to do only with the financial aspects in the reports. For all other aspects, any citizen could bring a suit in the *board of euthunoi* within 30 days following the examination of the accounts (Fröhlich 2013, 261). But the complainants ought to have solid evidence to back their accusations, because otherwise they were exposed to the risk of being countersued and be convicted as sycophants, which in Athens carried very severe penalties.

If during this first stage of the auditing process, the ten *logistai* or the ten *euthinoi* discovered evidence of corrupt practices, depending on their severity, they had various options. For example, they might refer the case to Boule, the *Boule* which could fine the responsible official up to 500 drachmae; or they might appoint prosecutors and instruct them to seek through the *Popular Courts* the imposition of a higher penalty; or they might send the case to a second board of ten *logistai* for a judgment in the second degree. At this level, the auditing process involved two stages. In the first stage, the *logistai* in this board inspected anew the official's financial accounts for evidence of embezzlement, bribery or financial mismanagement; and then in the second stage, they convened a popular court to present their findings and pass judgment as to whether the audited official was guilty or innocent. In these hearings, the *synegoroi* presented any charges that arose out of the audit and members of the public were invited to bring forward accusations for the jury's consideration. Through this setup, the state not only encouraged informers to report wrongdoings but also used state officials to actively seek out and prosecute financial misconduct (Lanni 2016, 72).

Officials condemned for embezzlement, bribery or other corrupt offenses faced punishments such as deprivation of civil rights (*atimia*),[30] big fines,

---

29 Costouros (1978, 41) ascertains that indeed there were three *boards of logistai*. He calls them Administration Accountants, Council Accountants, and Examiner Accountants. We believe that they correspond to the three bodies of *logistai* mentioned in footnote 16 above.

30 The bonds among people in classical Athens were based on close face-to-face relations. In such a social environment, the loss of civil rights was considered very severe punishment because it changed one's social status from "citizen" to a disconnected and denigrated "individual." Expressed differently, if a person was condemned as *atimos*, meaning dishonest, he faced general outcry that rendered him a social outcast. This explains why in Athens and in other Greek face-to-face city-states, dishonesty against the law and corruption had much more severe social consequences than in today's, mostly impersonal, societies.

confiscation and sale of their property as compensation for the damages they caused to the state, and in cases where one's malicious actions were considered too harmful to the state, one faced even the possibility of the death penalty. In view of the severity of these penalties, it is likely that some might attempt to delay or even avoid submitting to *euthune* and *logodosia*. Such behaviors were deterred by a series of other provisions. For example, an official, who failed to submit his report within a month from leaving office, was not allowed to depart from Athens, dedicate property, make a votive offering, have himself adopted or dispose of his property by will. Moreover, after the audit procedures had started, officials were prohibited from leaving Athens before *euthine* and *logodosia* were completed.

Aside from the preceding mechanisms for controlling the individualistic impulses of public funds managers, there was also one based on the experiences of citizens who came into contact with the elected officials in the course of carrying out their duties. This mechanism was called *eisangelia*[31] and worked as follows: In every major meeting of the *Assembly*, called *Ecclesia Kyria*, any citizen had the opportunity to accuse an office holder for not fulfilling correctly his duties, or abusing his position, or acting against the public interest, or being corrupt. The accused could defend himself either right then there in front of the *Assembly* or, depending on the type of accusation, in front of the courts. Again, even though this mechanism was open to abuses from politically motivated complainants, citizens had to be very careful when coming forward because they risked the trouble and the consequences of litigation.

Considering the burden of the responsibilities and the severity of potential penalties that were associated with the various posts, one wonders whether there were enough Athenians willing to get elected and serve for the public interest. We do not know how scarce or abundant the supply was. But from the results, we can surmise that on the whole those who were elected and served performed well. By implication, the state must have offered very strong incentives to attract efficient and honest officials.[32] Harris (2013, 27–28) informs us that this was exactly the case in Athens.

31 For details regarding the institutions of *euthine* and *eisangelia*, see Carawan (1987).
32 The status of being a *Bouleutes* (*Councilman*) conferred high personal prestige and re-
    spect. To distinguish themselves from ordinary citizens, *bouleutai* wore a crown of myrtle
    on their head in their public appearances. On the other hand, the magistrates had some
    important privileges in relation to ordinary citizens. While in office, magistrates often had
    a different legal status than their fellow citizens (Aristotle, *Athenian Constitution*, 45.2;
    Demosthenes, *Against Midias*, 32). If a magistrate was included among the *prytaneis*, who
    formed the executive committee of the *Boule*, then he would enjoy the added privilege of
    dining for free in the *tholos* along with his colleagues (Aristotle, *Athenian Constitution*,
    43.3; Demosthenes, *On the Crown*, 169). With this appointment, the magistrate would not
    only gain his sustenance at public expense, but also he gained access to the prestigious
    clubhouse on the western side of the *agora* in which he could socialize with his fellow offi-
    cials. Moreover, several office-holders like the jurors, the judges and the *archons* received

3.2 Balancing the budget through war and peace

Before the threat of Persians appeared on the horizon in the closing decades of the 6th century, public expenditures in Athens were extremely limited. Officials offered their services for free on an honorary basis; in domestic wars, the army of *hoplites* armed and fed themselves by their own means; and the budget for fortifications and defensive public works in general was insignificant, if it existed at all. However, the situation started to change dramatically during the turn of the 5th century, because as the threat of Persians became imminent, Athenians understood that they would not be able to repel them by staying with their traditional approaches to conducting local warfare. Thus, they adopted a "turn to the sea strategy," meaning, investing in the creation of a fleet and warships, which later led to the significant rise of their maritime economy (Economou, Kyriazis 2019b); and as they started strengthening the state's army and defenses, public expenditures began to climb and to put increasing pressure on the citizen's *Assembly* to procure the necessary resources.[33]

Eventually, the Persians did come and the Athenians with their Platean allies were able to defeat them in Marathon (490 BCE). But while that battle gave them the time to prepare for the next round of the war, the problem of securing adequate funds to cover the costs became as difficult as ever. By way of deliberate search or sheer luck, we know that in 483 BCE, they found a new rich vein of silver in the Laurion mines and that on the proposition of Themistocles, the *Assembly* approved using 100 talents per annum for two consecutive years from the newfound wealth to build and operate 200 *triremes*. According to the prevalent interpretation, in order to win over their votes, Themistocles used as pretext the war that was going on with Aegina. But his ulterior motive was the preparedness of Athens to deter a recurrence of the Persian threat and to lay down the foundations for a farsighted strategy, which under certain circumstances might offer Athens the opportunity to evolve into an incontestable state based on sea power and international trade, thus securing among others the safety of grain imports that were necessary to feed its population (Kyriazis, Zouboulakis 2004; Tridimas 2013; Economou, Kyriazis 2019b).

True to Themistocles' expectations, the Persians returned three years later and the Greeks led by the Spartans and Athenians defeated them in Salamis (480 BCE) and again one year later in Plataea (479 BCE) led by the Spartan Pausanias. These decisive victories, aside from having confirmed

---

a *misthos* ("wage" or "pay") for their services, which varied according to the precise role they fulfilled (McAuley 2013, 183).

33 Athens had already developed a maritime structure for commercial and military purposes even before Cleisthenes's reforms in 508 BCE and the large shipbuilding program that was introduced by the Themistocles in 483/482. These structures were based on the institutions of *naukraroi* and *naukrariai*, which date to the Archaic times. For details about these institutions, see Figueira (2011, 183–210) and Van Wees (2013).

the value of maintaining a strong naval fleet, gained for Athens the respect and perhaps the fear among its allies. As a result, they consented to forming with Athens the *Greek League* (also known as the *First Athenian Alliance*) with the main objective being to continue an offensive war against the Persians through sharing of the costs. For the budget of Athens, this development had two highly positive implications. First, at least until the "Peace of Kallias' in 449 BCE,[34] in addition to the flow of revenues from the Laurion mines and other public property concessions, Athens secured a second stream of significant contributions from its allies in silver currency and war ready ships[35]; and, second, after 449 BCE and until the start of the Peloponnesian War in 431 BCE, Athens continued to extract tributes from them through coercive rather than persuasive practices. With these money flows into the budget, Athens implemented a multiyear program of social subsidies and there was plenty more left for carrying out a large series of public works.[36] On this account, as we mentioned in the previous section, it is not surprising to find frequent arguments in the literature alluding to the effect that the highhanded practices by Athens alienated its allies and contributed to the war with Sparta.[37]

Coming out of this long war defeated, Athens in 404 was broke. According to some estimates, the cost of the war to the public coffers had climbed to the astounding figure of 35,000 to 47,500 talents (Gabrielsen 1994, 139–142; Morris 2009, 145). So grim was the situation that in 403/402 BCE, the *Assembly* decided to write off the outstanding debt of the state to the

34 This treaty was named after the Athenian representative who negotiated and signed this peace agreement with the Persians in 449 BCE. However, some scholars doubt that there was general peace, some others that it cannot be documented as a historical event, and still some others attribute it to a 4th century BCE exaggeration.

35 During the 20-year period of the "Peace of Kallias," the allies gradually switched to payments in currency to cover the cost of war, instead of providing ships, crews and soldiers, with a few exceptions like the islands of Chios and Samos, which continued to provide ships.

36 More specifically, under the leadership of Pericles the *Assembly*: expanded payments to many categories of officials who were not remunerated for their services before; authorized using accumulated wealth to fund an ambitious construction program of public works mainly to beautify Athens; sponsored subsidies through the *theoric fund* to low-income citizens to attend festivals and theatric plays, etc.

37 By certain historical accounts, the *First Athenian Alliance* gradually changed character and from an alliance of independent city-states, it turned into an Athenian empire consisting mainly of subordinated city-states, which at its maximum included 316 of them (Rhodes 1985; Figueira 1998, 52). According to the advocates of this view, after the expiration of the *Peace of Kallias* in 449 BCE, Athens continued to demand particularly from its weaker allies the payment of tributes. But the practices it employed were resisted, some city-states revolted, and several others switched allegiance to the other super-power of the times "Sparta." In turn, the advocates of this interpretation argue that this development tipped the balance of power in favor of the latter and gave impetus to the starting of the Peloponnesian War.

treasury of Athena.[38] Moreover, as the economy was in shambles, the prospects for raising revenues from other sources any time soon were equally bleak. The population had declined because of the casualties particularly among the younger cohorts. Production of silver at the Laurion mines had come to a standstill. The destruction of property had devastated the productive potential of the economy, thus leading to a significant reduction in the per capita income, etc. But above all, the defeat had revealed the precariousness of the fiscal policies that *demos*, that is, the citizen's *Assembly*, were capable of enacting. At the end, although the Periclean welfare programs were well conceived to maintain social cohesion, they were pushed to such an extreme that they weakened the state and laid the ground for the defeat of Athens long before it actually happened.

For the finances of the state to improve, Athens needed good many decades of peace. But the majority of the *Assembly* was under the control of citizens from social classes whose interests called for the support of rearmament and continuation of the war. In particular, experiences over previous several decades had unveiled gradually a situation of opposing interests between the populous low-income class of *thetes*,[39] on the one hand, and the much less populous middle-income class of *hoplites* plus the high-income class of citizens, on the other. The latter two classes opposed the war. *Hoplites* did so because by being absent in foreign expeditions, they could not cultivate their farms and take care of their income earning commercial activities, whereas rich Athenians were opposed because they were losing revenues from the decline of trade, banking and exports, as well as from bearing the burden of *liturgies*. On the contrary, the *thetes* benefited from rearmaments and wars because they found ample employment opportunities as rowers in the naval fleet.[40] As a result, Athens did manage to regain its sea supremacy and even defeat Sparta in Naxos in 376 BCE. But after having failed to re-institute the *First Athenian Alliance* once again, Athens ended fighting the

38 This decision was consistent with the insurance function that the *treasuries of the gods* played and to which we referred earlier in the text. From the standpoint of present-day experiences, it seems to have been the oldest instance of a PSI (Private Sector Involvement) ever recorded! But it was not because the borrowed money belonged to the Athenian state, since it was the latter that had donated this money to *Athena's treasury*. In any case, understanding the necessity to regain the high trust and the impeccable reputation they enjoyed before the war, the Athenians did not repeat such an extraordinary measure ever again.

39 The social group of *thetes* consisted of poor citizens who were exempt from taxation but also had limited rights. More specifically, they owned property producing less than 200 *medimnoi* of grain per year (1 *medimnos* = approximately 52–59 liters), they participated in the *Assembly*, but they could not be elected to the Boule. In the Periclean era, their political influence increased markedly because we surmise that their group was populous and the grains they produced were valuable for the grain shortage of Athenian state.

40 For a detailed analysis of this perspective, see Economou, Kyriazis (2016b). However, there are also indications showing that, while the decision to start the Corinthian war in 395 BCE was popular across all social classes, divisions were much more notable later on when the issue was whether or not to make peace in 387 BCE.

so-called Social War (357–355 BCE) almost as financially ruined as after the Peloponnesian War, since public revenues had declined down to 130 talents per annum whereas expenditures had soared.

The spring in the Athenian finances started to appear again only when Euboulos, an influential politician and *tamias of the theoric fund*, established in 355 BCE social peace by striking a grand compromise among the various interest groups of Athenian citizens, and possibly also *metics*, who did not vote, but exerted some influence through Athenians with whom they collaborated. That is, in exchange for stable jobs in the public sector and various welfare subsidies, Euboulos was able to win in the *Assembly* the support for his peace plan of the poorer citizen-voters, who favored the continuation of warfare, and by relieving the middle class and the rich citizens from the costs and the uncertainty of war, he managed: (a) to convince them to bear certain extra burdens in the form of *liturgies* and also, for the first time, to vote in favor of *eisphora* as a permanent wealth tax; and (b) to bring about a socially harmonious business climate in which entrepreneurs in all economic activities could pursue their plans and by so doing reinvigorate the Athenian economy, and thereby public revenues.[41] From the available evidence, we know that under the leadership of Euboulos in the period 355–340 BCE, the public budget recuperated remarkably as state revenues in 340 BCE jumped to 400 talents.[42]

Part of the peace plan was also that, in the expected expansion of the economy, the class of low-income citizens would not be left behind. For this purpose, Euboulos introduced two reinforcing policies. The first assumed the form of a law, which made it difficult to use the budget surpluses for purposes of rearmaments and warfare, whereas the second provided for an extensive program of public works aimed at rebuilding the city's infrastructures. Among others, included in this program were, a new network of roads, water supply of the city, new waterfronts and shipyards, and two newly built ports in *Zea* and *Mounichia* so that, by redeploying to them most of the warships in the naval fleet, more space would become available in the central port of Piraeus for merchant ships. Thus, as argued by Economou, Kyriazis (2016b, 2019b), employment opportunities and disposable incomes increased, public infrastructures expanded, and after a very long period, Athenians found good reasons to become optimistic about the future.

But while Euboulos pursued his expansionary policies, Demosthenes through fiery speeches tried to arouse the attention of citizens to the imminent threat of Macedonians and called in vain for war preparedness, both before and during the war. Once again though, the wisdom of the *Assembly* fell short of the challenges and the defensive power of Athens remained

---

41 He served as Head of the *theoric fund*.
42 Detailed arguments in corroboration of these assessments are found in Economou, Kyriazis (2016b).

lopsided.[43] They had the most powerful fleet on the sea but weak army on the land. So, when they confronted the Macedonians in the battle of Chaeronea (338 BCE), they were defeated and with their allies and other Greek states, they were forced in 337 BCE to sign the so-called *Common Peace* which recognized the hegemony of Macedonians over all Greeks, except Lacedaemonians. This arrangement and the respect that Alexander the Great had for Athens allowed enough leeway to Lycourgos, who was elected head of the Athenian state *treasury* in 337 BCE, to continue and even expand on the legacy left by Euboulos. In particular, he launched a vast program of public works, second only to that of Pericles, which included a new sewage system for Piraeus, monuments such as the theatre of Dionysius beneath the Acropolis and the extension of the Pnyx, the place where the *Assembly* of citizens took place, a prominent water clock, and the Lyceum.[44] Owing to these Lykourgan policies, the significant recovery, which started with Euboulos in 355 BCE, continued to 322 BCE, that is, the year when Athens was defeated both on land and at sea by the Macedonians and lost its autonomy in foreign affairs and democratic self-rule at home.[45]

Perhaps, given the large budget surpluses that the fiscal management under Lycourgos had secured, if the *Assembly* had not ignored the warnings of Demosthenes about the imminent threat posed by the Macedonians and instead they had exercised the farsightedness of Themistocles in the 5th century, this onerous outcome would not have occurred because the Macedonians would have faced an Athens ready to defend itself. But this view is speculative and hotly contested among historians.

43 That the Macedonian threat was real transpired to almost every Athenian, when: (a) in 357 BCE the Athenians suffered the definite loss of the strategic city of Amphipolis, an area rich in gold minerals, and (b) king Philip II in a surprise move seized a fleet of 240 Athenian merchant ships carrying grain.

44 To appreciate the economic robustness of Athens even under the unfortunate circumstances of its defeat by the Macedonians, we cannot help but invoke the following assessment from Van Wees (2013, 1):

> Ancient Athens most under-appreciated achievement is the sheer scale and sophistication of its system of public finance. In one peak period, the city's chief treasurer Lycurgus is said to have spent 18,650 *talents* over twelve years (336–324 BCE), an average of about 40 tonnes of silver a year, for a total population of about 250,000, or 160 grammes per head. No modern European state exceeded Athens's financial performance before Britain in the Industrial Revolution made a quantum leap to another level.

45 After the defeat of Athens in the so-called Lamian war in 323/322 BCE, a Macedonian guard was placed in the city of Athens, turning it into a satellite state. An oligarchic regime was established during 322–318 and then during 317–307, Athens was governed by a new pro-Macedonian oligarchic regime under Demetrios of Phaleron. Democracy was restored during the 306–287 and 286–262 periods and after 229 BCE till some time before the Roman conquest (Habicht 1999).

3.3 Public budget and lenders of last resort

According to Aristotle (*Oeconomica*, 2.1.15), the principle on which the Athenian state managed its finances called for keeping the annual budget balanced by holding public expenditures at most in line with public revenues. In this passage, he sides not only with a stance fervently discussed in our days, but also he stresses that this position had been adopted and practiced by the Athenians as common in their private and public affairs. Moreover, on this very crucial issue, he informs us that the *Boule* supervised the way in which the budget was applied in any given year by striving to avoid systematic deficits.

The importance of good governance is emphasized also by Xenophon (*Memorabilia*, 3.4.7–12.) in the following dialogue between Socrates and Nicomachides, where Socrates argues that there is no difference between a businessman and a general, because leadership by either is of paramount importance for the efficient management of operations in both the private and the public domains[46]:

> That is just where it will be most helpful. For the good business man, through his knowledge that nothing profits or pays like a victory in the field, and nothing is so utterly unprofitable and entails such heavy loss as a defeat, will be eager to seek and furnish all aids to victory, careful to consider and avoid what leads to defeat, prompt to engage the enemy if he sees he is strong enough to win, and, above all, will avoid an engagement when he is not ready. Don't look down on business men, Nicomachides. For the management of private concerns differs only in point of number from that of public affairs. In other respects they are much alike, and particularly in this, that neither can be carried on without men, and the men employed in private and public transactions are the same. For those who take charge of public affairs employs just the same men when they attend to their own; and those who understand how to employ them are successful directors of public and private concerns, and those who do not, fail in both.

To be sure, in reality, the state's budget was not always balanced on a yearly basis. Surplus and deficit years were balanced with the intermediation of the various *funds* and *the treasuries of the gods*. As we mentioned earlier, all cash and near cash valuables were deposited with the *treasuries of the gods* partly for safekeeping purposes and partly as donations. Presumably, for safekeeping were the deposits, which had been earmarked for covering public expenditures but had not been paid out during the year, whereas the rest

---

46 For further arguments substantiating the view that Xenophon may have been the earliest specialist or guru in the analysis and applications of management science, see Figueira (2012) and Bitros, Karayiannis (2012).

represented donations of the state to cover possible public outlays in cases of unforeseen circumstances in the future. Included in the latter amounts of accumulated wealth were also the donations by private individuals, which in all probability were of much lesser importance in comparison to the donations by the state.

As we mentioned earlier, in years during which the public budget experienced shortfalls, the deficits were covered by loans from the *treasuries of the gods*. Thus, whenever the state "borrowed" cash from them, actually it put back into circulation currency that it had entrusted to them and by doing so, the *treasuries of the gods*, aside from their religious purposes, served also for at least two subtle functions. That is, they operated first as managers of the state's currency reserves that were available on demand, and second, as schemes of insurance or lenders of last resort from which the state could borrow funds on interest to cover expenses arising from unforeseen contingencies like, for example, cost overruns in public works or a war expedition. In this latter function, the *treasuries of the gods* acted of course like contemporary central banks but with two key differences. The central banks of today are highly centralized authorities with almost unlimited decision-making powers and almost nonexistent democratic control over issues of currency and credit, whereas the *treasuries of the gods* were decentralized centers of authority with decision-making powers limited by their own resources and the strict mandates set annually for their officials by the *Assembly*.

On top of the above, it should be noted also that: (a) the *treasuries of the gods* deposited surpluses with private banks to earn interest income[47] and extended loans to the state on which they charged interest rates of 1.2% to 6%[48]; (b) these interest rates were low in comparison to the those for "landed" loans of about 12% (Demosthenes, *Against Aphobus 1*, 9) and for "maritime" loans even exceeding 100% per annum[49]; (c) the interest rates

---

47 Regarding the disposition of surpluses by the temples, for example, Andreades (1928, 189) finds that:

> ..., the shrines, as having abundant surpluses, could accumulate vast treasures and could thus become the bankers of the Greek world, loaning money to individuals and to states. For this reason most of the above-mentioned studies on loans and banks have to do with the finance of the temples; and vice versa what is written about the shrines contains much that concerns public credit and the banks.

48 According to Budin (2004, 113), the *Temple of Athena* during the period 433–427 BCE loaned money to the state at an interest rate of 6%. However, Rhodes (2005, 93) reports that for the sums of money that the state borrowed in these years, it paid interest of 6% to 427 BCE, but only 1.2% from 426 BC onward. Moreover, just anticipating our arguments later on, these interest rates were "real" in the sense that they were free of inflationary influences, because of the absence of general inflation under the currency's silver standard.

49 Maritime loans included high rates of insurance for the great risks that were involved in transport journeys over sea lanes. For further details on this issue, see Amemiya (2007, 87–103).

paid by the state were decided either by the *Boule* or the *Assembly*; and (d) the charging of interest on these loans was meant to imply tacitly that the state ought to be careful with its finances because borrowing involved citizens in extra burdens. From these arrangements, it follows that in their financial capacities, the *treasuries of the gods* in the short run functioned on the one hand as "lenders of last resort," that is, by acting as buffers against the benign imbalances that were generated by the cash management of the public budget, and on the other as conduits for returning surpluses to the economy and through the generated interest income subsidizing the interest rates that they granted to the state. In the longer run, the *treasuries of the gods* acted as insurers and wealth managers on behalf of the state, but considerably insulated from its power by the sanctity and the respect they carried in the minds of the Athenian citizens.[50]

3.4 Summary

The evidence is that after 403 BCE, and perhaps because of the criticisms that were attributed to the policies implemented in the Periclean era,[51] the decision-making authority of the *Assembly* in fiscal matters became more dispersed, horizontally over the sources and uses of funds and vertically in line with the principle of subsidiarity.[52] But as all officers continued to be elected by the *Assembly* and reported to it at the end of their short periods in office, the *Assembly*, that is, the supreme body of Athenian democracy, in essence never surrendered its authority over fiscal and currency affairs. Even though more recent scholarship casts doubts, it may very well be the case that the fiscal policies adopted by the *Assembly* were responsible for the demise of the Athenian democracy.[53] Yet on balance, there is little doubt

---

50 Perhaps, with the exception of the last attribute, the *treasuries of the gods* stood in their relation with the state as the *Sovereign Wealth Funds* of today.
51 The accusations levelled against Pericles concerned his program of public works, and particularly the building of Parthenon. Its construction lasted from 447 to 438 BCE; its decoration until 432 BCE; and its overall cost exceeded 9,000 Talents. At the time this was a colossal amount of money and, if Plutarch (*Pericles* 12.2) is to be believed, some funds might have come from the reserves of the allied tribute. As a result, although many researchers attribute the defeat of Athens to mistakes in military strategy, there are some who argue that the outcome of the Peloponnesian War might have been different (victory of Athens, defeat of Sparta), if those funds were alternatively used for boosting military defenses.
52 It stands as a guideline, which recommends that budget and nonbudget issues should be dealt with by officials in charge at the most immediate decentralized level consistent with their most effective resolution.
53 For example, Andreades (1928, 267) concludes that:

> ...More particularly the *Theorikon*, which was the culmination of the policy initiated by distributions and payments of salaries, was rightly characterized by Boeckh as the chief reason for the state's fall - as the cancer that caused its death.

that it used the power of the *demos,* that is, of the citizens, in a unique and exemplary manner.

Having assessed the evidence regarding the management of public finances in Athens over the period from Cleisthenes in 508 BCE to the Lamian War in 322 BCE, we feel confident to state the following findings:

- The public budget, made up of the current account in the form of Government spending-Government revenues plus the capital account in the form of Government investment-Government saving, for all practical purposes was always balanced.[54] This implies that in principle, the budget could not provide for deficit spending as a matter of deliberate policy. Further assurance about this finding comes from Rhodes (2005, 58), who states in no uncertain terms that:

    > ...The state could not straightforwardly run a deficit.... It could not spend money unless it had the money, and we hear, for instance, of occasions when the law *courts* were suspended because there was no money to pay the jurors' stipends....[55]

This does not imply that there were not unintended deficits in the execution of the budget. Normally, there were. If in some year, the budget experienced deficit, depending on its transitory or more permanent nature, it was covered either by funds that had been deposited with the *treasuries of the gods* from surpluses in the previous years or by loans from the same source.

- The state did not borrow from the private sector. This is a very important finding, because it enables us to surmise that the interest rates that were determined in this sector by market forces were not influenced by fiscal policies. The interest rates that were set in the public sector were determined through negotiations between government authorities and the *treasuries of the gods.* In these negotiations, the state had always the upper hand, and in conjunction with other parameters of the loans, the interest

---

54 However, during the Hellenistic period, this practice was abandoned. City-states borrowed not only from the god's treasures but also from private persons. There are some important cases that attest to this. Here, we mention only the issue of a woman called Nikareta, a citizen of the Boeotian federal state who sued the city of Orchomenos, a city-member of the Boeotian state, which failed to repay a loan to her. She had lent to Orchomenos consecutive sums of 10,085 drachmae and 2 obols, 2.500, 4000 and 1,000 drachmae. Nikareta brought her claims to a federal court seeking justice and she was vindicated. Finally, the city-state of Orchomenos and Nikareta reached a new agreement. Similar cases are those of Kleuedra and Olympichia (Schaps 1979, 13, 63–65; Mackil 2013, 103, 415–448).

55 If this shutdown is reminiscent of similar threats by the executive in the United States whenever the Congress bulks at raising the debt ceiling, the difference should be clear. In the case of Athens, the shutdown lasted until the necessary expenditures were covered by tax revenues, whereas in the United States, the politics usually end with the raising of the debt ceiling so that the government may cover deficits by borrowed funds.

rates were systematically low relative to those prevailing in the private markets.[56] In 403/402 BCE, when Athens became completely broke from the high expenses of the Peloponnesian War, it did write off unilaterally its debt to the *treasury of Athena*. But even though it amounted to the single largest destruction of assets in the entire history of the Greek *poleis*, this was a one-off decision and it was never repeated again.

- At their own discretion, the *treasuries of the gods* deposited their surpluses with private banks to earn interest income and even loaned funds to private parties and third city-states. The business environment in which they carried out these activities is nicely summarized in the following excerpt from Homer, Sylla (2005, 35):

> Temples made loans to states and to individuals. But after 450 BC, and especially after 400 BCE, investment in productive capital became common. Recorded estates of wealthy Athenians then showed little ready cash and large holdings not only of land but of rental housing, slaves let out for hire, business investments, and loans bearing interest. Even Socrates, the philosopher, had a friend to whom he entrusted his investment problems. At going rates of profit and interest the fortunes of minors often doubled or trebled in a few years. Traders and manufacturers borrowed to carry their stock, and farmers borrowed on land.

In other words, temples loaned their surpluses to banks and individuals to earn high interest rates, and in turn they extended loans to the state at low and extremely subsidized interest rates. From this arrangement, it follows that, irrespective of what god or goddess they served, the temples acted like efficient wealth maximizing capitalists in the service of the state.

- Last, but not least in order of importance, is the finding that by the time of Euboulos and Lycourgos, Athenian policy makers had become aware of the potential afforded by public works to maintain social peace through state jobs. If by building roads, aqueducts, water system, etc., they applied policies to keep in check temporary spells of unemployment and subdue the evils it is accompanied with, the results they achieved are a good indicator of the wisdom in the fiscal policies they implemented. That another golden age was almost repeated under their leadership simply confirms that, with the turn of the social sentiment

---

56 Athenian orators proclaimed the public usefulness of loans at reasonable interest rates as a means for stimulating trade (Maloney 1971, 79). The ordinary interest rate for someone who borrowed money from a bank varied between 12% and 18%. There were also cases of even lower interest rates. Loans contracted at an interest rate of 10% were considered very favorable for the borrower (*ibid*. 80). On the other hand, there were also cases of usurious loans, which were considered ethically wrong (*ibid*. 79–88).

from war to peace, fiscal policies were reoriented appropriately toward productive facilities that serve the common good.[57] However, from the experiences in the long aftermath since the Keynesian revolution in the first half of the 20th century AD, we have come to know that policies toward public capital are first best only to the extent that the private economy cannot sustain full employment. For, otherwise, widely popular public projects may elect and stabilize governments in democracies, but at the same time they drain valuable resources that can be directed to economic growth enhancing activities, and hence to the creation of cumulative wealth both for the state and its citizens.[58] So, our final assessment on this score will have to wait until later in our presentation.

57 Allowing for the significant difference in their scales, Pericles's building program in the 5th century BCE weighted heavily toward temples and city beautifications, whereas that under Euboulos-Lykourgos in the second half of the 4th century BCE was loaded with networks of public facilities. From this difference, we surmise that the building programs in the two periods aimed at tenets that reflected different social and economic circumstances. In our view, the shift from building, say, soft public capital like temples and city monuments, to building hard public capital, say, like aqueducts and water systems, signifies the fundamental shift that took place in social priorities, from a regime of regional dominance based on frequent wars, mobilizations, and expeditions in the first period, to a regime in the second that aspired to rekindle the past glory of Athens through home-grown economic prosperity.

58 Plutarch (*Pericles*, 12.4) explains the merits of the Periclean fiscal policies for achieving full employment and social peace in amazingly contemporary terms. But what escape his perception are their implications for economic growth. For, it is not unlikely that the lack of significant rates of economic growth during the 5th and the 4th centuries, and according to Van Wees (2013) even earlier going back to Solon, might have resulted from the extreme emphasis on the construction of public works, city beautifications, and the large public expenditures on cultic performances and festivals.

4 Main currency-related policies

In the opening paragraph of this book, we indicated that the currency of Athens, that is, the drachma, by the close of the 5th century had gained already the status of a world currency like the dollar and the other international reserve currencies of today. Because of its high reputation and the benefits that accrued for them and their state, Athenians throughout the 5th and the 4th centuries were adamant supporters of its integrity and the *Assembly* went to great pains to preserve it by putting in place institutional arrangements that maintained its silver content and its stability in world markets. Above, we found that they pursued and managed to apply fiscal policies of balanced budgets. Today, we know from economic theory that this is a necessary condition for keeping the external value of a state's currency stable. So, it is surprising that they practiced this fiscal policy as a matter of public choice, even though the state could borrow from the private sector.

The discovery of the new rich silver vein in Laurion in 483 BCE must have sent powerful waves of shocks locally and internationally. Suddenly, instead of importing the bulk of the necessary silver to mint the required quantity of coins,[1] Athens could procure it from local sources by leasing its mines to private contractors. *Ceteris paribus*, the decline in imports would have resulted in a significant appreciation of the drachma, unless for example simultaneously cheaper imports of other goods increased, dearer exports declined and/or government and economy wide savings increased so as to bring the balance of payments into a new equilibrium. From the evidence that the drachma dominated in a competitive international environment of multiple parallel currencies, we may surmise that it held its value very well and that,[2] with the exception of the ruinous period 412–403 BCE, it was considered in modern jargon as a safe haven currency. So, our objective in this

---

1 There are indications that Laureotic silver was used to some degree from the earliest days of Attic minting.
2 From Figueira (1998, 493) and from the extremely valuable comments he has offered us, we are aware of his view that in the period 483–413 BCE, that is, a period of sound money, there was notable price inflation. We shall discuss this issue later on in good detail. However, for the moment, we should like to note that the implied contradiction is more apparent than real, because technically speaking "general inflation" as defined presently was

section is to summarize the policies through which the Athenians achieved this high measure of success and assess the drivers for the respected public choices.

4.1 Economics of minting in classical times

The history of coinage in ancient Athens is clouded in dense uncertainty. According to a common view, the first so-called *archaic owls* were minted in 510 BCE, that is, at about the same time as the establishment of the Athenian democracy by Cleisthenes. However, we find the evidence-based arguments of Schaps (2004, 126) quite more convincing and adopt his interpretation to the effect that:

> It was probably under the rule of his sons (authors note: He means the sons of Peisistratus) (though there is a good deal of debate as to the precise date) that Athens began to mint larger coins for export, at first featuring a Gorgon device and later the famous Athenian "owls." These were minted from the native Attic silver of the Laureion mines, and Athenian coins spread throughout the Greek world.

Presumably the Archaic *owls* that Athens cut were silver coins *tetradrachms*, that is, valued at four drachmae, of excellent quality and stable silver content, because as such they gained wide acceptance in domestic and international transactions all over the Mediterranean basin. But in 478 BCE, emboldened as it was by the new-found silver mines in Laurion, Athens started minting a new generation of such coins, known in the numismatic literature as *classic owls,* which survived and shined for 2 centuries.[3] In particular, with a few exceptions, like those that emerged under the extraordinary circumstances of the period 412–404 BCE, these coins weighted on the average 17.04 grams with purity of 96%, giving net silver of 16.36 grams.

Thus, aside from its contribution to the finances of Athens, to which many scholars, mostly historians, attribute its survival from the onslaught of Persians,[4] as well as the efflorescence of the golden age that followed, the discovery in 483 BCE of the new silver deposits in Laurion acted also as a powerful shock in the currency markets. For here you had within distance of 30 kilometers from Athens plentiful ores of high silver content, whereas

---

impossible. That is, we concur with him that there was indeed "price inflation," but it was "sectoral" not "general."

3 *Classic owls*, sometimes called *old-style owls*, were introduced in 478 BCE and likely continued to 393 BCE. However, hoard evidence suggests that the minting of the *early classic owls* ceased sooner than previously thought. Consequently, more numismatists now regard the minting of the so called *mass owls* to have started earlier than 449 BCE.

4 For an assessment of Themistocles' *Naval Decree* from an economist's point of view, see Kyriazis, Zouboulakis (2004), Tridimas (2013) and Economou, Kyriazis (2019a).

most other city-states that minted their own currencies had to import the metal from abroad.[5] By itself, the distance from the source, frequently over risky sea lanes, placed the mint in Athens at a significant cost advantage relative to the mints of all other states. This advantage was further reinforced by several factors, including the following:

- In Athens, the production of coins took place under economies of large scale. To see the cost implications of this aspect, consider the fact that the number of coins cut from each series by the mint was much larger than those in the other city-state because the economy in Athens was much larger than theirs. So, the setup cost, that is, the fixed costs for preparing the molds and the dyes for each series, was distributed over a larger number of coins, thereby reducing further their average production cost.
- The high silver content in the *tetradrachm* implies that the Athenians had found new and more efficient methods for the extraction and enrichment of the ore to the highest technically and economically feasible degree of silver purity (Christesen, 2003). Consequently, in addition to the quality of workmanship and the stability in its silver content, this coin was lighter per gram of pure silver and, as we would say today, it offered more value for the money, since it was easier to carry and use in transactions.
- Based on the above, transactions became easier, faster and more secure, the velocity of circulation of coins increased, and all these developments translated into significant reductions of transactions costs, thus establishing Athens and particularly the port of Piraeus a prime hub for international trading.

The above four cost advantages quite certainly would be sufficient over time to drive the mints of all other states out of business. But on account of its efforts to render the Attic drachma a global currency that would gain for Athens the prestige and the profits associated with it, the *Assembly* sponsored three profoundly assertive policies. The first was that the "price" for converting bullion to coins on demand was kept at a markup of only 5% (Kroll 2011,

---

5 It is certain that three cities, that is, Aegina, Athens and Corinth, with significant commercial activities during the 5th century, minted their own coins since the late 6th century BCE. Athens had the silver deposits in Laurion and Thorikos. In northern Greece and in particular in Macedonia, gold and silver ore veins were found near Mount Pangaion, and Thrace and the island of Thasos. These helped finance the Macedonian imperial ambitions in the 4th century BCE and raised coin circulation to a new level. Gold and silver ores were also found in the Aegean islands of the Cyclades and in particular in the island of Siphnos, which had established mints even as early as the *Archaic Period* (von Reden, 2010, 29). It appears that Aegina, Corinth and the rest of the Greek city-states did not have deposits of precious metals on their lands. Thus, they must have imported them from other places.

236) over the commodity price of the bullion, of which about two percentage points covered minting costs. By implication, the intention was to keep the cost of seigniorage low so as to maximize the profits of the state through the widest possible diffusion of the Athenian currency.[6] The second policy took the form that the mint abstained from minting certain supplementary coins. For example, we know that during the late 5th century, small value bronze coins called *kollyboi* (see Exhibit 4.1) were issued by private persons, not by the state mint (Aristophanes, *Peace*, 1199–1201). These were introduced because there was insufficient currency in circulation in small denominations to cope with daily retail transactions of recurrent small value goods like, say, for purchasing bread. Thus, the private sector covered a need not covered by the official mint. One reason that the state did not issue bronze coins may have been that it did not have the capacity to do so (insufficient qualified personnel for the production of low value coins) and/or that the cost incurred in relation to any seigniorage was deemed to be too high to make the production of bronze coins by the state mint worthwhile.[7]

The third policy was an ingenious one in that it reflects a deep intuitive understanding of economic principles. In particular, depending on the prevailing circumstances in the currency markets, they altered the terms under which they accepted old (worn-out) coins for restriking and/or silver bullion held by private citizens for turning it into coins. If they thought that there was shortage (oversupply) of currency, they lowered (increased) the "price" of minting so as to bring the demand and the supply of the currency into equilibrium.[8] Essentially, by following this policy, the mint acted like a

---

6 Recall from Section 2.1.1 that the seigniorage on large-scale bullion purchases by the mint was about 8% out of a price discount of 10%. Athens earned seigniorage profits on each coin minted, whether the source was freshly mined silver or the silver coins of other cities. In the decades preceding 478 BCE, many states minted their own coins, which circulated freely everywhere in competition to each other. Therefore, if Athenians wished their coinage to gain grounds and even displace the other currencies, the *Assembly* ought to impose a low cost for the right of seigniorage. The traders and merchants of other cities, in turn, liked *owls* because of their easy exchangeability. *Owls* thus became the world's first great international currency, and they were followed in this role by among others Alexander the Great *tetradrachms* and *staters*, the Roman *denarii*, the Byzantine *solidus*, the Spanish American *pieces of eight* or *Spanish dollars*, the Dutch *lion dollars*, the Austrian Maria Theresa *thalers* and the American *dollars*.

7 In this case, we see a kind of specialization of each sector: silver, and in extraordinary circumstances such as during the Peloponnesean War, silver plated (and gold) coins by the state, and bronze by the private sector. This, again, is one of the earliest examples of the issuing and circulation of private coins, which are common in electronic form in the 21st century (bitcoin, ethereum and about 1200 types of electronic coins in total).

8 The historical evidence on the issue of government controls, primarily over the quality and secondarily over the quantity of the Athenian currency in classical times, but also over the silver industry more generally, was reassessed recently by Bissa (2009, 31–66). Our view that the state mints were accessible by private holders of silver and bronze bullion metals coincides with her meticulous examination, particularly on page 57, of what we know in this regard with relative certainty.

Exhibit 4.1 An Athenian *Kollybos* issued between 400–300 BCE, probably depict-
ing a horse.

Note: Attica, Athens AR Hemitartemorion, (1/8 obol), 1.08 gm. 8.5mm. 430–322 BC. Helmeted head of Athena right, archaic style / AΈE, Owl standing right, head facing, olive sprig
to left all within small incuse square. Mionnet 26cf; BMC Attica Pl. V, 22.

Source: With the permission of wildwinds.com: http://www.wildwinds.com/coins/greece/
attica/athens/Mionnet_26.jpg

modern central bank which intervenes in the currency market by injecting
or withdrawing liquidity through appropriate changes in its price, which in
the case of paper money is the discount interest rate.[9]

Finally, it is important to point out that the *Assembly* had put in place strict
legal and institutional arrangements to monitor the circulation of counterfeit and fraudulent coins, and to intervene with duly appointed officers so as
to maintain their value and enhance the trust of users in their integrity. As
we stressed in Section 2.1.2, coins that were found by the *dokimastai* to be
substandard in any respect were demonetized, either by withdrawing them
from circulation or by sending them to the mint for restriking.

4.1.1 Taxing through reminting

As has already been said, after the so-called Social War of 357–355 BCE,
and in view of the lack of tribute payments emanating from the secession
of its allies from the second *Athenian League*, Athens experienced financial
difficulties with the state revenue having plunged to as low as 140 talents

---

9 Henceforth, we shall use the term "paper money" to imply that the paper currency represents
  a promise of the issuer to convert it into an amount of specie on demand. When the paper
  currency holds no such promise, we shall refer to "fiat money." Moreover, at times we may
  refer to the respective systems of currency as "commodity standard" and "fiat standard."

per year. So, Euboulos, the leading politician and *tamias* of the *theoric fund* at the time, undertook extraordinary measures to increase revenue. One among them was that through a decree authorized by the *Assembly*, he ordered the recoinage of older coins and the issue of new ones to replace them. The new coins had a premium or seigniorage for the state of 3%–5% over the price of silver as commodity. By normal Athenian numismatic standards, this coinage was unsightly and badly minted because of the necessity to mint big quantities quickly. Still, despite the low quality of the coins in terms of appearance, the international demand for them was brisk. The Athenian coins remained the most highly sought-after in the Eastern Mediterranean until they had to compete for the preferences of the public with the highly artistic silver and mainly gold coins of Alexander the Great in the 330 BCE (Kroll 2011).

The reminting that was involved, being an extraordinary and not repeated measure, was a kind of excise tax. In essence, it taxed heavier the rich than the poor because presumably the former possessed more coins than the latter. This made the proposal attractive to the majority of citizens who participated in the *Assembly* and it illustrates the working of monetary policy under direct democracy.[10] Further, it was a "tax" paid not only by citizens but also by all residents of Attica, *metics* and slaves, sailors, ship's captains, travelers who did business or visited Athens, etc., since the new coins were legal tender. The decree was intended to raise revenue and, because of the amount of cash circulating in the highly monetized Athenian economy, it was probably successful, although we lack information regarding the amount of revenue the Athenian *treasury* collected. Still, we know that state revenues at the end of Euboulos' tenure in the 340s BCE had increased to 400 talents and that in 322 BCE under his successor Lycourgos, they had grown to as high as 1,200 talents (Economou, Kyriazis 2016b, 11), that is, a truly impressive achievement, since it is comparable to the state revenues realized during the "imperial" era of Athens (Ober 2008, 68).[11]

4.2 Regulatory framework of coinage

By contemporary standards, the advantages of a reserve currency are *tactical*, *operational* and *strategic*. The tactical advantages accrue from activities

---

10 The implication being that monetary policy served the interests of the many, not of the few. However, it is advisable not to read too much into the nature of this tax because, as we stressed, it was applied on a one-off basis, only rarely at the reminting process of older series of coins, and certainly remained flat.

11 In 355 BCE, state revenues stood at about 130 talents per annum. Hence, in the 33 years to 322 BCE, they increased 9.23 times. To the best of our knowledge, this implies the highest average rate of growth ever recorded even under confiscatory autocratic regimes, let alone under the democratic governments that prevailed in that period. Indirectly, it implies also a huge growth of trade, since customs duties of 2% on exports and imports were an important part of the public revenues.

and policies of the issuing country that change the external value of the currency or, in more technical jargon, its exchange rate with respect to the currencies of other countries. These are the easiest to understand because, in the first place, they translate into immediate results by accelerating exports, employment and gross national income. Unlike them, the operational advantages spring from policies aimed at achieving intermediate-level objectives like for example establishing a common currency in the context of an alliance among countries. As we will see in Section 4.2.4, by reference to the currency issues in the context of Greek Federations, things get more complicated because of the difficulties that arise from the parallel circulation of currencies that are issued at the country and the alliance levels.

Lastly, regarding the strategic advantages, these obtain when two or more countries pull together in pursuit of objectives like defending against external threats or enhancing their economic and political influence in the world. This level is the most complex because it brings economics, politics and national antagonisms into play. To understand how complex it is, consider for example the project for the political unification of Europe. Presumably the Economic and Monetary Union (EMU) is useful from a strategic point of view because it contributes toward the successful completion of this project. However, despite the progress achieved so far in the front of EMU, the political unification of Europe remains highly elusive.

Thinking in the context of the above analysis, classical Athens employed its currency not only for reaping tactical advantages by maintaining favorable terms of trade and making money through seigniorage but also by pursuing wider operational and strategic objectives. In the previous section, we referred to certain policies, which rendered the Athenian mint dominant in the international currency markets. These were tactical in the sense that they pressured the mints of the other states to close down and through the wider diffusion of its currency Athens enjoyed significant seigniorage and trade benefits. Besides, by issuing Attic drachmae on a large scale and providing sufficient quantities of currency for economic activity in the Eastern Mediterranean and beyond, the mint in Athens undermined the rationale for the operation of smaller regional mints.

Our focus in this section is on the currency-related policies that Athens pursued for operational and strategic purposes. Relevant in this regard are on the one hand the ones that were embedded in the *Coinage Decree* or *Decree of Coinage Standards*, the *Law of Nicophon* and the *Kallias Decree*, and on the other hand, those that can be traced in the framework of so-called *Federations*, sometimes referred to also as *Sympolitiai* or *Koina,* which were more or less loose unions of states[12] bound by an agreement or formal treaty

12 The degree of federalization of Sympolitiai remains open among historians and other scholars. Some characterize them as loose unions of states or confederacies and some others as federal states. For an introduction on this issue and the relevant literature, see Economou, Kyriazis (2016a).

to pursue not only certain common objectives, mainly defense, but also co-operation on cultural and ritual matters, economic exchanges, etc. To them, we turn below in the same order.

4.2.1 Coinage Decree (449 BCE)

The so-called *Coinage Decree* was found on two separate stone inscriptions and since then it has fueled continuous discussions among historians as to the visual restoration of the text, its date, and, more importantly, its relevance.[13] A careful assessment of the literature regarding the date of the decree was undertaken recently by Ellithorpe (2013), who concludes that:

> The continuation of the debate in more recent scholarship has produced no radical change in consensus, nor new revelations in interpretation, as no new fragments have yet come to life, and the issue of chronology can be best summed up by Figueira, who stated as recently as 1998, that "the date is controversial, but a date in the early 440s based on the Cos fragment in Attic lettering is widely preferred; it is also the better option."

Among those who accept this conclusion, most scholars date the decree at around 449 BCE and thus they link its adoption with the currency policies during the early stages of the Periclean era, which have been considered frequently as stages of increasing imperialist posture on the part of Athens. For example, some historians such as Buckley (1996, 206–207) suggest that the adoption of the decree was nothing else but sheer exercise of imperial power. To support their view, they call attention to the nature of the wording used in its composition. They find that its language is harshly authoritarian; that it makes no references to the alliance; and that by implying that there will be Athenian officials in all states, possibly as many as 314 in the 450s BCE, to attend to its implementation, the decree creates the impression of a clear attempt by Athens to compel their allies to stop minting their own coins and instead adopt the Attic drachma as their single and only currency.

Be that as it may, the question that arises is what to make of the objectives that Athenians tried to accomplish with this decree. Certain other historians, while conceding that its language smacks of an imperialist attitude, find considerable indications to argue that the decree was no more than an attempt to project "a selfish monetary policy of a regional power; and selfish

---

13 Readers interested in the origins of the *Coinage Decree* and the differences in the interpretations among historians regarding the date of its authorization and its policy objectives are advised to start from Figueira (1998, 324–325). The *Coinage Decree* builds on the idea that since many Greek *poleis* in the 5th century traded with and paid tributes to Athens in the context of the *First Athenian Alliance*, naturally Athenian "owls" became legal tender far beyond the boundaries of Attica.

monetary policy is not imperialism." Last but not least, a third group of historians side with the interpretation presented by Figueira's (1998, 310–411), according to which the tenets of the Decree were to introduce the Attic drachma as the legal tender in the alliance along with common weights, but without either prohibiting the minting of coins by other states or forbidding the parallel circulation of their coins.[14] Supportive of this view is also that non-Athenian coins were not demonetized, recalled to Athens or replaced, and that the allies who chose to mint their own coins were obliged to pay their contributions to the alliance in valid Athenian coins, while their mints continued to strike their own coins.

However, it is likely that the Athenian state did accept payments in bullion at least in the 5th century and at least in large-scale transactions. This possibility can be inferred by an event that took place during the Peloponnesian War. More specifically, in 415 BCE, the Egestaeans of Sicily arrived in Athens to plead for the support of the Athenians in their war against the city-state of Selinus, which was aided by the Syracusans. In the words of Thucydides (*History of the Peloponnesian War*, 6.8.1):

> Early in the next spring the Athenian envoys returned from Sicily. They were accompanied by Egestaeans who brought sixty *talents* of uncoined silver, being a month's pay for sixty vessels which they hoped to obtain from Athens. The Athenians called an Assembly, and when they heard both from their own and from the Egestaean envoys, amongst other inviting but untrue statements, that there was abundance of money lying ready in the temples and in the *treasury* of Egesta, they passed a vote that sixty ships should be sent to Sicily;

Notice that the Egestaeans brought with them uncoined silver worth 60 talents. If Athens accepted payments in foreign coins, the Egestaeans might have an incentive to coin this quantity of silver themselves and make the payment in their own coins. Instead, they brought in bullion, which of course would be turned into "owls" in the Athenian mint. So, if there was not a cutoff amount of payment over which inhabitants in Attica and foreigners could settle their obligations to Athens in bullion, the Egestaeans

---

14 According to von Reden (2010, 76–77), another possible reason why the Athenians wished to implement such a decree is that they may have hoped to gain silver through the fee they charged for reminting foreign coins into their own species, since the allied city-states were forbidden to produce their own silver coinages anymore. However, examining extant hoards of coins and historical evidence, Figueira (1998, 176) shows that even after the decree, there were at least 11 and possibly as many as 24 mints of allied city-states still in operation, this being a proof that the decree did not prohibit the minting of coins by non-Athenian mints. Mints that remained active after 440 BCE still exceeded the number of those that terminated their coining activities between 455 and 450 BCE. Von Reden (2010, 76) concedes this point when she writes that in the end there is no evidence that the Athenians were successful.

lacked sufficient integration in the Aegean economy and paid for foreign goods and services in bullion. We believe that large transactions with the state could be settled in bullion, but we have not been able to highlight this issue by reference to ancient and modern sources of information.

Our view is that the last interpretation stands above all others for an additional reason, not emphasized in the literature. In the preceding section, we explained that the economic dynamics in the minting markets were so profoundly in favor of the mint in Athens that those in the other states participating in the *First Athenian Alliance* would have closed down anyway. Also, drawing on the minting policies in Athens, one may even argue reasonably that the *Assembly* did seek deliberately to precipitate the closing of the other mints. But it is rather unlikely that the Athenians sought with the Decree to bring about by unilateral and authoritarian actions an outcome that would result naturally through the course of market forces. For such an interpretation would require assuming that, in order to gain some small *tactical* and *operational* economic advantages, Athenians were ready to risk the major *strategic* advantages the *Alliance* offered them.[15]

To conclude, we do not doubt that the *Coinage Decree* impinged on the autonomy of the states participating in the *First Athenian Alliance*. But it did so in a context in which Athens attempted to establish a *common economic area* within which free exchanges would take place with the help of different currencies in competition with each other but following homogeneous weight standards, with the purpose to reduce transactions costs and expedite trade-enhanced economic prosperity. On account of this interpretation, we side with Bury (1900, 226), Hammond (1959, 306) and von Reden (2010), who have long argued that the decree encouraged the flow of trade through the Aegean and especially between Athens and the allied states. In a wider sense, one may even argue that the *Coinage Decree* introduced

15 The main coins in circulation in the alliance and the Eastern Mediterranean were predominantly but not exclusively Athenian. During some periods, they were supplemented by electrum coins, which were phased out during the first half of the 5th century, gold bronze and silver-plated bronze coins. This happened during the close of the Peloponnesian War and it is an indication of the financial difficulties that forced Athens to resort to extraordinary measures. It issued silver-plated coins, that is, with a bronze core, at a value far exceeding its metallic content, thus at a high seigniorage. This coinage could only have held value in Attica and in places where governmental authority sustained its value as legal tender. It circulated in parallel with older higher value silver coins (Figueira 1998, 508). With the exception of this period, which offered Aristophanes (*Frogs*, 718) the opportunity to state for the first time the idea behind Gresham's law, there is no evidence to suggest that Attic silver coins were demonetized. As we shall explain further in Appendix 8.7, this law applied inversely in Athens because, among other possible conjectures: (a) the supply of silver-plated coins might not have been sufficient to cover demand, thus necessitating the parallel circulation of the older silver coins, and (b) prices for goods and services might have adjusted to allow for payment in plated coins at a premium (or discount in silver coins), that is, in a way similar to the practice of today of getting a discount in some instances when paying in cash instead of credit cards.

a system of parallel currencies within a *common economic area*, whereas *Nicophon's Law*, to which we shall turn after the next section, regulated the circulation of parallel currencies within Athens.[16]

4.2.2 The Decree of Kallias (434/433 BCE)

Kallias was a soldier, diplomat and statesman. He became widely known public figure in 449 BCE when he negotiated with the Persians the so-called Peace of Kallias to which we referred earlier. The decree[17] that he introduced and became law in the late Periclean era had to do with the reorganization of the Athenian system of public finance and the web of linkages it maintained with the *treasuries of the gods*. As is the case with all decrees, historians disagree on the precise date that it was authorized. But the date 434/433 BCE, that is, shortly before the outbreak of the Peloponnesian War in 431 BCE, is considered highly likely, while some others such as Marcaccini (2015, 515) propose the date 433/432.

From its content, we understand that it was partly an accountability report, partly an authorizations bill to introduce certain reforms that would render the management of public finances more efficient, partly an effort to arrest the tendencies that were observed at the time toward running budget deficits, and partly a framework for the concentration of the treasures in the various shrines in Attica to the temples in the Acropolis, perhaps in anticipation of the war with Sparta (Kallet-Marx 1989, 108–113). For example, from the decree we learn that: (a) in accordance with an earlier resolution of the people, 3,000 talents had been deposited in the *treasury of Athena*; (b) the debt owed to the *treasuries of the other gods* remained unknown; and (c) an outstanding issue was the appointment of *tamiai* to administer the latter sacred *treasury*, which was situated at the back of the temple of the Parthenon.

---

16 Introducing some common currency standards has been the rule in all past attempts to form federations, customs unions and common trading areas or zones. For example, this was the case with the Greek Achaean, Aetolian and Boeotian federations, the German Zollverein, the European Economic Community, the Eurasian Economic Community, etc. The objective of the standards is to manage the exchange rates of the currencies of the participating countries so that no one may gain unfair advantage over the others by devaluing its currency unilaterally.

17 According to Bradeen (1971):

> ...we do have two decrees, proposed by the same orator, passed on the same day, inscribed upon the same stone; anyone seriously searching for the reasons behind them must face the question of why there were two decrees, not just one. The answer seems clear; despite the fact that they were closely related because both dealt with financial reorganization, they were separate because they dealt with separate finances. Decree 1 clearly concerns the treasures and *treasurers of the other gods*. Decree 2 just as clearly concerns the treasures and *treasurers of Athena*."

In the authorizations section, the decree starts off with a reminder that all decision-making authority on borrowing in times of necessity, as during wars, and disposing of surpluses, as in times of peace, rested with the *Assembly*. This body then was asked and decided to provide by vote indemnity to the *treasury of Athena* for loans exceeding 10,000 drachmae (Stevenson 1924). Additionally, it provided a roadmap for the management of the budget over periods of war and peace. War operations were to be financed firstly out of current income, and only when this proved insufficient, with borrowing from temple funds. Imposing some order in this regard was necessary because expeditions and sieges were especially expensive and could last for years, thus rendering the state budget unbalanced on a yearly basis. This experience called for balancing the budget over a period of years. In particular, deficits in times of war were to be covered by borrowing from the *treasuries of the gods*, whereas surpluses during peacetime were to be used partly to repay previous loans and partly, to the extent possible, to beef up the reserves in the sanctuaries for unforeseen contingencies.

The most important message from the decree was this. By passing it, the Athenians who participated in the *Assembly* attested that they were well aware of the risks associated with the temptation of giving in to extravagant public expenditures. So, to control themselves from their worst impulses to spend beyond their means, following the example of Ulysses, who tied himself to the mast of his ship to resist the bewitching song of the Sirens, they tied themselves to a firm institution that they all respected, that is, the *treasuries of the gods*. At times, they did indeed run the reserves in the temples perilously low. But in contrast to what is happening in contemporary democracies, Athens did not run systematic deficits, which would require financing through accumulation of public debt. This constitutes a fundamental difference between direct and representative democracy, and we shall expand on it in our concluding chapter.[18]

4.2.3 Law of Nicophon (375/374 BCE)

In the Athenian direct democracy setup, the ultimate decision makers on all currency issues were the citizens, irrespective of whether they were educated or not. Based on due process and discussion, they took responsibility for the enacted policies, the procedures and the institutions for safeguarding the currency's reputation, and the selection and monitoring of officials who were put in charge of the various currency-related tasks. To carry out their duties in this regard, citizens received advice from "experts," who were

---

18 Just to anticipate the thrust of our arguments, we find it expedient here to note that it was not the nature of their currency that induced Athenians to detest deficit spending and the accumulation of debt. In our view, their attitudes in this regard emanated from their system of values, which was reflected in the posture and the working of their institutions.

empowered to introduce proposals in their areas of expertise. Nicophon, after whom this law[19] is named, was such an expert in currency matters.

Unlike the uncertainties that surround the date and the objectives of the *Coinage Decree* and to a lesser extent the *Decree of Kallias*, in the case of *Nicophon's Law*, the views of historians vary along a much narrower range. In their great majority, they agree that it was introduced in 375/374 BCE and that what it sought to accomplish was to increase state revenues by stimulating trade through free circulation of all good coins within Attica. That Athens was in great need to raise fresh revenues at that time we may infer from the expenditure that was required in order to maintain the 86 *triremes* with which it defeated Sparta at Naxos in 376 BCE. Simple calculations suggest that the expenses amounted to about 700 talents per annum.[20]

To raise this amount of revenue, an obvious approach was to boost trade and a policy option to attain this objective was to liberalize the currency market so as to reduce the cost of doing business in Athens by allowing foreign coins to circulate freely. What this meant was, for example, that an Athenian trader selling his wares to, say, a Massaliot buyer,[21] could accept as payment, if he wished, the massaliotic silver currency, without having to change it into Attic drachmae, thus avoiding the conversion charge that he would have to pay to moneychangers or banks. In today's terminology this effected a reduction in transaction costs, which was considered a proven means to increase the volume of trade within a region or country.

Nicophon's Law does not provide explicitly for the parallel circulation of coins. Indeed, it would be utterly farfetched if it did, because then it would undercut the efforts of Athens to promote its currency among its allies. However, in the supposedly Solonian tradition, whatever was not forbidden explicitly by the laws was considered legal behavior. Therefore, when Ober (2008, 225) writes that *Nicophon's Law* provides:

> ... for the tacit certification of certain silver foreign coins as good, and for the confiscation of bad coins,

in essence, Ober, Rhodes, Osborne (2003, 113), Engen (2005, 370) and others, who hold the same view, agree that it was market forces that determined

---

19 Note that "laws" differed from "decrees" in that the latter passed through either the *Boule* or the *Assembly*, whereas the former might be authorized through different procedures. On this distinction, see among others Schwartzberg (2004).

20 This cost may be estimated as follows: Each *trireme* had a crew of 200 persons remunerated at one drachma per day, for a period of eight months (240 days, excepting winter months). Thus, a *trireme* cost 48,000 drachmae for each period, and the 86 ships at Naxos a total of 4,128,000 drachmae, or about 700 talents. This cost excludes operational expenses for the one-year maintenance of a ship, which according to Gabrielsen (1994) was covered by the *liturgy* of *trierarchy*. For a detailed analysis of such calculations, see Economou, Kyriazis, Metaxas (2015).

21 Marseille, in today's southeastern France.

whether and to what extent coins issued and stamped as Attic by various foreign states circulated in parallel in Athens. Should there be any doubt about this interpretation, here is how Shipton (1997, 408) reinforces it:

> We thus appear to have an open system where 'good' imitation *owls* are free to circulate alongside silver currency from Attica. And since only the tester in the Piraeus is a new appointment, it is clear that at some point between the setting up of the *board of the nomothetai* and the decree itself, Athens had already taken steps *to ensure an open system*.

As a result of this reform, even though the parallel circulation of currencies within the alliance and Athens itself (certainly after *Nicophon's Law*, but quite probably even before) continued, foreigner's demand for Athenian coins became so high that in order to acquire Athenian coins, foreign merchants who came to trade in Piraeus quite likely offered their wares at a discount, if paid in Athenian currency. This again benefited both the Athenian state, which received a small margin of seigniorage, but for a vast amount of coins, so that the revenue could have been substantial in total, and the Athenian citizens, who paid in discounted prices for foreign goods. What becomes clear from *Nicophon's Law* is the sophistication and openness of the Athenian economy. It is as if Nicophon was aware of Coase's theorem 2,400 years before its formulation,[22] and also of the benefits of the parallel circulation of currencies, which promotes economic activity, and which today applies only in a few economies, like Switzerland where there is in fact a parallel circulation of the Swiss franc, the Euro and digital currencies like Bitcoin and Ethereum.

To sum up, following the interpretations by top economic historians, we accept that the decree's ultimate tenet was to reduce transaction costs by establishing a transparent and effective framework of arrangements to: (a) ensure equal and fair access to a system of quality assurance of the parallel coins used in Athens, and particularly in the port of Piraeus; (b) expedite the resolution of conflicts that arose in everyday transactions; and (c) remedy problems associated with the presence of counterfeit coins circulating alongside those that were officially struck by the mint. For its implementation, the law drew on the institution of *dokimastai* in the *agora* of Athens and

---

22 Because of human and institutional limitations, the basic assumptions of efficient markets, like anonymous, atomistic and rational actors, perfect information, homogeneous goods, absence of liquidity constraints, etc., fail to hold. As a result, transacting in markets becomes costly and whatever arrangements reduce this cost propagate economic efficiency and economic growth. Coase (1937) proved that the establishment of firms to undertake part of the production process is such a transaction cost reducing process. Hence, since *Nicophon's Law* aimed at reducing transaction costs by facilitating the parallel circulation of currencies, it is in this spirit that it served as if it anticipated Coase's theorem.

in Piraeus and provided for exceeding stiff penalties to discourage fraudulent practices.[23]

4.2.4 Currency issues in ancient Greek Federations[24]

In the period following the Peloponnesian War, there developed a very intense rivalry between the strong states on mainland Greece and the kingdoms outside Greece that were controlled by Greek political entities, such as the kingdoms of the Macedonian dynasties in Asia Minor, Egypt and Asia (Persia and India). As a result, many states on the mainland sought to increase their security and influence by building alliances with neighboring states along federal lines (Ager 1997). Two such Federations (*Sympoliteiai*) that emerged in the first half of the 4th century were the Aetolian and the Achaean. The latter, in which we shall focus here as one of the most powerful and influential, was established during the second half of the 4th century, possibly as early as 389 BCE,[25] by drawing on an older alliance of 12 states around the Corinthian Gulf, in the North-Western Peloponnese, which in turn had been founded during the 5th century BCE and quite likely served as a model. During the period 389–338 BCE, it managed to expand gradually its territorial, geopolitical and economic strength in the Peloponnese. But after the Battle of Chaeronea in 338 BCE, it became gradually a Macedonian protectorate, for a period it dissolved, then it reemerged in 280 BCE as a successful political and economic Federation, and lasted until the Battle of Leukopetra in 146 BCE, where its defeat marked the end of Greek independence, the abolition of democratic regimes and the turning of Achaea into a Roman province.

The Achaean Federation was led by three "pan-Achaean" institutions: The *Federal Assembly*, the *Federal Boule* or *Council* and the *Federal Government*. Citizens from the participating states acquired the Achaean citizenship and with it the right to participate and vote in the Achaean *Assembly*, which was held one or two times a year, provided they had completed the 30th year of their age. All matters of federal interest like, for example, foreign policy, declaration of war or peace, economic policy, and currency, were discussed and decided in this body. Responsible for their implementation were the specific executive officers of the federal Government to whom the corresponding authority and responsibility had been assigned at the

---

23 In particular, attempts to circulate debased coins fraudulently were punished by death. On this, see Demosthenes (*Against Zenothemes,* and *Against Timocrates*, pages 24 and 210–214, respectively).

24 For readers interested in ancient Greek federations, a good source of analysis and a rich compilation of the related literature is Economou, Kyriazis (2016a).

25 Some authors such as Rizakis (2015) provide evidence that the federation was already in existence even before 417 BCE.

time of their election that took place once a year.[26] As for the *Federal Boule,* by its composition, it acted as a representative body of the participating states and its duty was to prepare the agenda of subjects to be discussed in the *Assembly.* With this brief introduction into the Federation's political and administrative structure, we are ready now to turn to the issues of coinage.

Ancient "Koina" (Federations) introduced the pivotal institutions of *isopoliteia, enktesis* and *epigamia. Isopoliteia* conferred political rights at the federal level and Mackil (2013, 102) characterizes this institution as *full citizenship, available to any individual who chose to domicile himself in another region* of the Federation. *Isopoliteia* agreements were further extended to include not only member-states within a Federation but also a Federation and another state, that is, irrespective of whether the latter was a Federation or a single state. For example, the alliance between the Aetolian and the Acarnanian "Koina" enabled their citizens to own land in both of them. Regarding pure economic institutions, the main economic rights were that of ownership (of land and houses) by a citizen of one member city-state in another, called *enktesis,* and the right of intermarriage, called *epigamia. Enktesis* rights were granted by a popular resolution to foreigners and native inhabitants, enabling them to acquire land or a house (or both) everywhere in the federation. *Epigamia* conferred the right of transferring property in the form of women's dowries (Mackil 2013, 103, 2015, 491; Economou, Kyriazis 2016a, 99, 105). These rights proved highly beneficial to all member-states because, by abolishing border barriers and encouraging commercial interactions among them, the volume of trade and the mobility of resources increased all around, thus boosting efficiency and economic growth (Economou, Kyriazis 2019a). This trend was facilitated further by the introduction of federal currencies. These were issued by any member-state and circulated everywhere within the borders of the Federation. However, strong member-states retained the right to issue also local coins conforming to common weights and measures, which circulated exclusively in the specific states that issued them. In particular, according to von Reden (2010, 67–68), upon entering into a Federation, states introduced new series of coins to render their currencies compatible with those of the other member-states so as to communicate across political boundaries their readiness and interest to attract business.

Exhibit 4.2 shows a federal *hemidrachm* (half a drachma), dating back to the period 160–150 BCE and produced in the *Mint of Argos,* showing on

---

26 The head of the federation, called *strategos,* held simultaneously the highest political and military posts. But aside from him, there were several other senior government officials with dual powers in the federal civilian administration as well as in the armed forces. Some examples are the *nauarchos* (admiral), the *hipparchos* (cavalry highest commander) and *ypostrategos* (major general). Also, there was a so called *grammateus,* literally meaning the "secretary" who had responsibilities similar to those of a modern head of state archives, and further responsibilities that are not yet known. The federal government included also a series of extra high-ranking officials called *damiourgoi* or *synarchontes.*

Exhibit 4.2 Achaean *hemidrachm* produced in Aegion between 160–150 BCE.
Source: With the permission of Wildwinds.com: http://www.wildwinds.com/coins/greece/
peloponnesos/achaia/aigion/Clerk_044.jpg

the front side the portrait of Zeus Omarios and on the back the inscription
"AX" (meaning, "of the Achaeans," thus denoting that the coin was a Federal one), with the name "Aristodamos." Exhibit 4.3 shows a hemidrachm
believed to have been coined in the city-state of Messene between 191 and
183 BCE. It depicts the head of Zeus on the front and the letters "AX" on the
reverse, thus indicating that the coin was issued under the authority of the
Federation. On the reverse side and at the lower part, observe that it carries
the inscription "M." This suggests that the coin was fabricated by the *Mint
of Messene*. Also, worth noting is the date of the coin. It reveals that it was
produced as soon as Messene became a member of the Federation in 191
BCE because it is in that year that Messene acquired the right to issue coins
bearing the characteristic inscription "AX." According to Mackil (2013,
251), coins bearing the inscription "AX" and the figure of Zeus Omarios,
denoting their federal status, have been found and used since 373 BCE, that
is, at the time of the *First Achaean Federation* around 417–280 BCE.[27]

In accord with the preceding, Thompson (1939), having looked into the issue of currency circulation in the Peloponnese, reports that there were some
states such as Megalopolis, Argos, Sicyon and Corinth, which retained (at
least, for some period) the right to issue currencies with their local weights
and standards in parallel with the Achaean federal type currency. That is,
the quantity of money issued for local transactions, say, with the insignia of
Megalopolis was not accepted for exchanges with the other members of the

27 Caspari (1917, 169) claims that between the years 470 and 360 BCE, the front side of these
    coins depicted the goddess Artemis and that this image was substituted with that of Zeus
    with certainty in the period 280–146 BCE.

Exhibit 4.3 Achaean *hemidrachm* made in Messene between 191–183 BCE.
Source: With the permission of Wildwinds.com: http://www.wildwinds.com/coins/greece/peloponnessos/messene/Clerk_106v.jpg

federation. Instead, they had to use federal type of coins. More specifically, on page 143, she argues that:

> There is every evidence, in the form of coin types with the MEΓ lettering, to prove that Megalopolis, as well as Argos, Sicyon, Corinth and other cities, exercised the privilege of independent coinage even after she gave allegiance to the League. Not impossible is the conjecture that at that time she decided to keep the Pan type for her local uses, adopting the syrinx as her city symbol on the League denominations.

For an example, Exhibit 4.4 shows a *triobol* (three obols, a hemidrachm) issued in Megalopolis only for local usage. On the observe side, we see the head of Zeus while on the reverse, it bears the letters "MEΓ" and "AN" (possibly denoting the local god Pan). The federal coins issued by Megalopolis carried inscriptions such as those in Exhibits 4.2 and 4.3. But why did these states retain and used this right?[28]

One possible explanation is that they wished to adjust the ratio of the two currencies to the ratio of their local to federal exchanges so as to minimize

28 Plato (*Laws* 5.742a–b) had already explained the reasons behind the necessity for a city-state to introduce a system of coinage comprising both coins for local transactions, which he called *epitomic*, and universal coins for international transactions, which he called *Hellenic*. Referring to the latter he states:

> As regards the universal Hellenic coinage, -for the sake of expeditions and foreign visits, as well as of embassies or any other missions necessary for the State, if there be need to send someone abroad,-for such objects as these it is necessary that the State should always possess Hellenic money.

Exhibit 4.4 A *triobol* issued in Megalopolis between 151–146 BCE.
Source: With the permission of Wildwinds.com: http://wildwinds.com/coins/greece/arkadia/
megalopolis/Dengate_72a.jpg

transaction costs. Still, we do not find it convincing because producing and dealing in one federal currency on a completely voluntary basis would yield comparatively larger efficiencies for every participating state. So, the explanation of why they issued two currencies one local and one federal should be sought in political rather than economic reasons. And none seems to be more obvious than the choice on the part of the states to retain a modicum of bargaining power vis-a-vis the federal authorities by projecting their independence and flexibility to quit any time without disrupting their local economies, since transactions would be able to continue smoothly in the local currency. Assessed from the point of view of the Federation, it might appear that by granting this right to some specific states, the federal authorities risked the issuing of too much federal currency, and hence giving rise to the possibility of inflation. As long as the local and federal currencies of the states were based on more or less precious metals, which commanded their own cost of production, such a danger did not exist. But let us look into this issue anyway because at the time it might hold some sway.

Thompson (1939, 143) argues that the federal authorities allowed freedom of issuance of any quantity of federal coinage in some but not in all member-states. Assuming that Achaean authorities were afraid of the corrosive consequences of inflation, we would expect them to impose some controls on the quantity of federal coinage by granting quantitative issuance rights on a case-by-case basis. In this context, a reasonable discriminating criterion would be to grant issuance rights by reference to the level and the composition of the valued added produced in the member-states as between local and tradeable goods and services. Applying this criterion would have limited the "freedom of issuance of any quantity of federal coinage" only to those member-states that produced values of exportable goods and services exceeding a predetermined threshold. Actually, if this criterion was accompanied also with a federation wide ratio of the value of exportables to the amount of federal currency issued, it would constitute a well-conceived mechanism for controlling the overall quantity of federal currency. But although this mechanism might be workable and transparent, the historical evidence points to the direction that the control criteria that applied were at the same time practical and political. For, along with large economically and strategically important states like Megalopolis, Sicyon, Argos and Corinth, which had "freedom of issuance of any quantity of federal coinage," other small states most likely abstained from taking advantage of this right either because they did not have the resources and the technical know-how or because they were discouraged by the federal authorities through other means. We believe that exploiting the "freedom of issuance of any quantity of federal coinage" by larger member-states must have been subject to political suasions, if not actual limits. That is why our views on this issue coincide with those expounded by Mackil, van Alfen (2006) and Mackil (2013), according to which the quantity of federal currency issued by states was not determined only by their own currency needs for export–import activities but also in conjunctions with the objectives set by a wider federal currency policy.[29]

By implication of the preceding analysis, we may surmise rather safely that, since local and federal coins circulated in parallel within the Achaean Federation, the needs that arose in local and interstate exchanges for converting them back and forth were met by coin exchangers like the *argyramoiboi* or *kollybistai* in Athens. But we have evidence neither on whether there were *dokimastai* for testing the integrity of coins nor of the existence of any banking activity at least in the larger states of the Federation. Perhaps, banking, credit and the other advanced means of payment that developed in Athens mainly in the 4th century spread to the member-states of the Federation much later. However, from Mackil (2013, 387), we do know that the federal law was very strict against counterfeiting. In the particular instance mentioned, six counterfeiters in the city-state of Dyme were arrested, tried and sentenced to death. Such a severe punishment is indicative of the importance that Achaean authorities ascribed to the integrity of the federal currency as a basic means for the efficient functioning of the markets across the member-states.

---

29 Mackil, van Alfen (2006) and Mackil (2013) argue that new quantities of currency issued by federal states were determined by the currency needs for local commercial transactions as well as by the overall federal monetary policy. These authors characterize the process of money creation under federal supervision as "cooperative coinages." Such coinages were not exclusive to Achaean practice. They were also introduced in several city states of the Aegean and the Asia Minor, the Boeotian federation and in a series of city-states in Macedonia.

The literature on matters of currency in Greek Federations extends over many more issues than the ones covered above. Some key ones have to do with the politics that were involved,[30] since the ways in which they were confronted might provide useful analogs for dealing with similar problems in present-day common currency areas. But extending it further into these issues would defeat the introductory purpose of this digression.

4.3 Summary

With the exception of a few years at the end of the Peloponnesian War, the Athenian currency in the classical period gained the reputation of the reserve and safe haven currencies of today. In an environment where many currencies circulated in competition with each other, this feat was not accidental. It emanated from the superior economics that supported it in local and international exchanges, as well as from the wisdom and determination with which the Athenians in the *Assembly* adopted policies and activated preexisting and newly established institutions to safeguard its value from the inherent fallibilities of democracy.[31] The superior economics derived mainly, but not exclusively, from four sources. Namely: (a) the low cost and secure source of procuring silver from the nearby silver mines in Laurion; (b) the availability of abundant slave labor and keenly motivated entrepreneurship; (c) the economies of scale that were associated with the minting process, since by fabricating large quantities of coins in each series their average cost declined, thus rendering the coins more cost competitive in the markets; and (d) technical advances in the purification of silver ore, which made Athenian coins lighter and hence easier to use, as well as in minting coins of standard quality and excellent designs. If to these advantages we add that Athens kept the seigniorage low so as to maximize state revenues through the currency's widest possible diffusion, it is hardly surprising that the drachma had all the economic dynamics in its favor.

Fortunately, under enlightened political and military leadership, and despite the excesses experienced at times, as we saw in the previous chapter, Athens empowered a web of currency-related institutions which, operating in the framework of policies enacted by the *Assembly*, managed the currency efficiently and effectively. More specifically, in the span of 100 years from

---

30 For example consider the following: Between 225 and 215 BCE, Sicyon, a member state of the Achaean Federation, issued and circulated a Macedonian *tetradrachm*. This complicated the situation by raising questions like: By what right did Sicyon issue Macedonian coins? Had it signed a special contract with the Kingdom of Macedonia? Had the Achaean federal government approved it? Would these *tetradrachms*, and possibly any other coins bearing Macedonian symbols and fabricated by Sicyon, be accepted by the other city-states of the federation in their "international" exchanges with Sicyon? Etc.

31 According to Schaps (1996, 81), a great deal of the credit for this spectacular accomplishment must be given to the organizational ingenuity of Themistocles who assigned the responsibility for the construction of the *triremes* to the richest citizens of Athens.

460 to 360 BCE, and even though there is uncertainty about their precise dates, Athens introduced three laws to secure the dominance of its currency among its allies and generally in international exchanges. These laws were the so-called *Coinage Decree*, the *Decree of Kallias* and the *Law of Nicophon*. With each of them, the *Assembly* sought to confront particular issues that emerged at the time but in a forward-looking manner. In the case of the *Coinage Decree,* we sided with the interpretation that it represented an attempt by Athenians to streamline the coinage standards in the first *Athenian Alliance* along those applied in Athens. The *Decree of Kallias*, among other aspects, aimed at reforming the nexus of prevailing relationships between the fiscal authorities of the state and the *treasuries of the gods*. It was a most important one because it set the guidelines on how to manage the state's budget in the light of recurring deficits without accumulating public debt.

Lastly, the *Law of Nicophon* dealt with the issues that concerned the integrity of the Athenian currency and left tacitly the parallel circulation of good foreign coins to market forces. Obvious in all these legislative efforts were the concerns of the *Assembly* to preserve the reputation of the currency by adhering to the highest minting standards, motivating the supply of coinage to meet the demand, imposing stiff penalties in cases of counterfeiting and in general keeping the comparative cost of transactions the least possible. In retrospect, we know that not only they were successful in turning the drachma into the dollar of the times, but also that they bequeathed to us considerable knowledge on how to structure the management of public finances so as to mitigate the malaises of fiat money that governments in present-day representative democracies employ so abusively.

In the last section of this chapter, we covered briefly certain currency issues in the context of ancient Greek Federations. We did so in the expectation that the solutions they gave to problems similar to the ones confronted in present-day common economic and currency areas, like the European Union (EU), may be helpful. To appreciate this possibility, one does not have to look further than Greece in the period since its bankruptcy in 2009. For if, in the absence of full EU integration, Greece had the right to issue its own local currency, within certain predetermined bounds, perhaps the dilemma to stay or quit from the Eurozone would not have emerged as acutely as it did because: (a) Greece might have avoided the extreme liquidity shortfall it continues to experience, and (b) the sharp decline that transpired in its GDP might have been moderated.

5 Structure and evolution of the economy

Contemporary economic theory provides certain propositions which hold so generally that they are perceived as iron laws. One of them expressed as a simple identity takes the form:

$$(\text{Imports} - \text{Exports}) \equiv (\text{Investment} - \text{Savings}) +$$
$$(\text{Government Spending} - \text{Government Revenues}) \qquad (1)$$

What it states formally is that irrespective of the tariffs that a country imposes on its imports, and no matter whether the currency of the country is based on a precious metal like silver or it is printed on paper, its rate of exchange with other currencies will change so as to equalize the balance in its trade account (left side of the identity) to the sum of the balance in its current public budget plus the balance in the country's capital account (right side of the identity). To make better sense of it, assume that the government runs a deficit in its current budget, which is not matched by a corresponding amount of public investment. In that event, *ceteris paribus*, the exchange rate of the country's currency would decline until changes in the country's trade and capital accounts bring this identity back into equilibrium.

In the case of Athens in classical times, for the reasons that we shall consider in due course, the Athenians held an extremely high esteem for the integrity of their currency. Most convincing in this regard is that rather than succumbing to the temptation to adulterate it when things got really bad in the closing years of the Peloponnesian War, they chose to convert into coins the golden ornaments from the statue of the goddess Athena on the Acropolis, and *in extremis* they produced plated coins and supported the token *kollyboi*. Through good times and bad times, they strove to keep the international value of the drachma stable, which by reference to the above identity implies that not only did they abstain from reducing its silver content but also that they must have applied consistently fiscal policies driven by a quest for balanced budgets, if not on an annual basis, at least over the course of a few years, so as to avoid a systematic accumulation of public debt. In the preceding chapters, we identified the institutions that were involved in money-related activities. Also, we highlighted which were their particular functions, how they evolved from the 5th to the 4th century BCE, and not least the mechanisms through which they were controlled by the *Assembly*. With them, Athenian citizens aimed at enabling the state to pursue the objectives they set for it and for the achievement of which they authorized raising revenues through taxes and other sources and approved the necessary expenditures. So, before we turn our attention to the money market and the fundamental policy issues associated with it, a major task is to lay out what we know about the structure of the Athenian economy and how it evolved in classical times.

To clear the path toward accomplishing this task, it is pertinent to start with the following delimitation. Until the 1970s, the bulk of the relevant literature regarding the nature of the Athenian economy during the period under consideration vacillated around the so-called Bucher-Meyer controversy, which, according to Reibig (2001), remained inconclusive.[1] On the one side of the debate were the "primitivists," who sided with Bucher by arguing that the economy was based on households that sought self-sufficiency in production and consumption with limited exchanges and absence of markets, whereas on the other were the "modernists," who followed Meyer by maintaining that the economy was well developed, differing only from the modern economy in a matter of degree. Then, within a relatively short time span, appeared the books by Finley (1973, 1981),[2] Austin, Vidal-Naquet (1977) and De Ste. Croix (1981), which shifted forcefully the interpretations of the available evidence in favor of the primitivists. According to them, in the ancient Greek economy, the incentives that motivated economic activities and the institutions that validated their results were embedded in the social arrangements that prevailed at the time, and hence on substantive grounds, there existed no economy that functioned separately and distinctively from society. However, in the years that followed, the arguments by these so-called substantivists lost ground to such an extent that the literature came to be dominated by the views of numerous scholars called "formalists,"[3] who looked at the ancient Greek

---

1 We use this reference only to put it mildly. Because if we take as basis the time that Polanyi was writing, the literature had started to turn in favor of Meyer's arguments long before 1970. To corroborate that this is the case, here is a most relevant excerpt from Bresson (2016a, 13):

> ... among the very diverse societies on which Polanyi concentrated his efforts, there is one that interested him particularly, given his classical training: that of ancient Greece. Polanyi thus was surprised to observe a phenomenon that was unexpected in his theory: the constitution of a market system undergoing fluctuations in prices for products made for mass consumption and extending over vast geographical areas. Certainly, Polanyi was wrong to locate the "disembedding" (to adopt his vocabulary provisionally) of Greek society at the beginning of the Hellenistic period, around 330–300 BCE. In reality, great changes in the society and economy of ancient Greece had already been under way since at least the end of the Archaic period and were situated in a line of development that began with the Greek Dark Ages (from the twelfth to the ninth century).

2 This 1981 book consists of 14 essays that Finley published in the three decades leading to 1980. His key essay appeared in 1973.
3 For a recent review of this literature, see for example Ober (2017) and Economou, Kyriazis (2017).

economy through the lenses of formal economic analysis. This turnaround has been remarkable and our presentation of the Athenian economy immediately below, together with the institutions and the laws of currency and credit that we discussed in the previous chapters, attests to the solid evidential fundamentals on which it stands as an economy that functioned substantively and formally not much differently from present-day market-based economies.

5.1 The state sector

As in all contemporary democracies, the state in classical Athens *produced*, *distributed* and *financed* a great variety of public goods and services. Certainly, it performed all three functions with reference to services such as: (a) governance, including justice, defense, policing, and finance; (b) market monitoring and regulation, including enforcement of the laws that pertained to the currency, the orderly functioning of the markets, the discouragement of collusive and speculative behaviors, the control of prices in markets susceptible to unexpected shortages, particularly of foodstuffs, etc.; and (c) maintenance of citizens who could not earn a living by working owing to various mental or physical disabilities. But in addition the state provided many goods and services by outsourcing their production to the private sector.

Here, we shall present brief accounts of the goods and services that were delivered directly by the state and refer to those that were outsourced from the private sector in the next section.

5.1.1 Governance

The *Assembly* was at the same time the supreme legislative and governing body. It published its decisions in inscriptions that were carved on *stele*, that is, slabs of stone that were placed in easily accessible locations so that anyone could read them for himself or to others who couldn't read. The decisions took the form of decrees, called *psephismata*, covered all functions of the state, and remained in force until revised or replaced by another decision. Therefore, since empires stand or fall on the strength of their governance, it is reasonable to assume that Athens had a well-organized administration which made sure that the *Assembly*'s decisions were implemented effectively and produced consistently the expected results. Central in this apparatus were agencies active in the following key areas.

5.1.1.1 Civil service

At the state level, civil service was populated by officials, some of whom like judges, legislators, military officers and magistrates were "elected by lot" and served mainly for one year, whereas some others were selected by ordination, appointed after due probation, served on a more permanent basis and were relieved from all responsibility after due audit.[4] The officials in the latter group provided the necessary continuity in government and acted much like the civil servants of today. They were differentiated into "secretaries" and "vice-secretaries," and aside from Athenian citizens, their ranks included also some *metics* and trained slaves. From a functional point of view, they performed as "informed" and "experienced" assistants to the elected officials who were put in charge of the various departments of the government and updated continuously the knowledge and skill bases of the public administration. Regarding the efficiency with which they carried out their duties, it is useful to recall from Section 3.1.3 above that in contrast to contemporary democracies, elected officials were subjected to a very strict *process of logodosia* (auditing) about their activities while in office, and that any citizen having well-founded complaints about ill management or misuses of funds could bring action against them through various channels. Quite likely therefore, in view of the serious consequences they faced, elected officials acted as true hands-on managers of the public agencies and departments that they headed, despite the quick turnover in their positions.

All involved in one way or another in the public administration were paid in line with the services they offered. The *Assembly* convened 30–40 days annually; the *Boule,* which prepared the meetings of the *Assembly* and served as the coordinating center of the overall governing complex, was in session for about 250 days; and the *Courts* were open for deliberations around 200 days. In total, at least 6,000 citizens participated in the *Assembly* on a part-time basis (quorum), whereas about at least 3,200 judges, *bouleutai*, magistrates, secretaries, vice-secretaries, etc. were employed full time.[5] Hence, if we accept the rough figures of the population cited by Amemiya (2007, 36) and transferred as Table 7.2 in Section 7.2, in 431 BCE, the state employed closed to 7% of the estimated average adult male Athenian citizens, or about 3.4% of the labor force, estimated at one-third of the average overall population in the same year.

However, aside from the officials and the civil servants who served at the state level, the public administration extended vertically and horizontally. On the vertical axis, there were the ten *tribes*, called *phylai*, their alignment into the units called *trittyes* and the *demes* (municipalities). In order to handle local issues and carry out the day-to-day exchanges with the center, certainly all these decentralized entities had some administrative structure with officials and civil servants of their own. On the other hand, horizontally we know from the preceding that there were many dispersed agencies

---

4 For more details on this process, see Aeschines (*Against Ctesiphon*, 3, 29).
5 Aristotle (*Athenian Constitution*, 24.3) claims that in the 5th century, Athens employed 700 domestic officials and another 700 in foreign locations serving its international commercial interests among allied city-states and not only. The plausibility of these figures has been assessed by various renowned authors cited in Pownall (2013, 290) and the prevailing view is that they do not appear to be unreasonable.

like the mint, the *funds*, the *treasuries of the gods* and many more, which had their own mandates and staff to pursue them. So, if at the narrow state level, the civil service was already hard to coordinate, one can imagine the degree of difficulty in supervising, guiding and controlling a system of government as decentralized and fragmented as that of Athens, and indeed with a leadership that changed constantly within the limited span of a single year.[6] That is why, judging from the results, the question that arises is: how did they manage the wonders that they achieved?

We believe that the success must be credited to two unique inventions during the 5th century BCE in the management of large and geographically dispersed and highly diversified operations. The first of them is the role they assigned to the *Assembly*. They established it to perform all the functions that the *boards of directors* play today in the great multinational companies.[7] These functions entail the unequivocal enforcement of the coordinating principles that are embedded in explicit processes of conduct and communication from the top leadership to the last employee in some corner of the earth, and always with an eye toward the overarching criterion of constantly improving the operating results by the standards of the controlling shareholders. Aside from its other political functions, in classical Athens, the *Assembly* functioned in essence as a very large *board of directors*, composed of the shareholders themselves, which sat at the top of an organization that Manville, Ober (2003) have called *A Company of Citizens*. The second invention is the discovery of a technology or an administrative system to take advantage of the expanding financial and military influence of Athens by engaging all the thousands of Athenian citizens-shareholders in the management of their "company" but without causing self-defeating waste and maddening miscommunication. The fundamental principles on which this administrative system was erected are described very compactly in the following excerpt from Davies (1994, 204):

> ... (i) to maximize participation, and to minimize the concentration of power, by creating new posts or *archai* rather than give additional jobs

---

6 To warn the readers against concluding that the high dispersion of political and economic powers in classical Athens was a by-product of "direct democracy," we should like to note that exactly the opposite is true. To corroborate this claim, Bitros, Karayiannis (2012, 290–291) explain the following:

> ...ancient Athenians had gone through a lot of hardships to trust that direct democracy was sufficient to safeguard their liberties. For this reason, having found by experienced that the ultimate guarantee of their freedoms was the dispersion of political and economic power, aside from assigning the government in the hands, not of few, but of many (the majority principle) they put in place ... appropriate institutions.

7 Aside from participating in the legislative process, the *Boule* acted also as the top executive branch of the government responsible for coordinating all government agencies in the execution of the budget. To place the emphasis on this role, in this instance, we refer to *Boule* as the *Council*.

to existing *archai*, (ii) to break down the administrative load into chunks which could be performed by amateurs selected by lot, (iii) to give them explicit terms of reference and routes of responsibility, and (iv) to operate on the assumption that "absolutely nobody is to be trusted."

To conclude, the civil service and the other mechanisms of public administration to which much of credit for the golden age of Athens must be attributed had matured by the time of Pericles and remained in force throughout the 4th century, certainly with various modifications to suit contemporary circumstances.

5.1.1.2 Defense and power posture

In the 5th century BCE, the land forces that Athens mobilized in periods of war consisted mainly of the heavy infantry of *hoplites*. We mentioned earlier that the latter financed their own weapons, so the state did not bear any expenditure for their armament. But as it was the case with England in the 16th century, Athens did maintain in constant readiness about 20 *triremes* during periods of peace and about 100 in periods of war. Thus, given that the crew of each ship was 200 men, in normal times, the state employed military forces of about 4,000 men. These, along with those employed in the rest of the public administration, raised total state employment to around 7,000–8,000 men or about 7.5%–8.5% of the labor force as estimated above for 431 BCE.

The corresponding expenses were easily forecastable, so their coverage did not create unexpected difficulties. But during periods of war, war expeditions or sieges to quash rebellions like those in Thasos, Potidaia in Macedon and Mytilene on the island of Lesbos, the ranks of the army and the navy swelled to several tens of thousands men and their substantial remuneration along with the associated outlays for the war effort had to be covered by borrowing. In the absence of international money markets to raise the necessary funds and the tacit tradition not to resort to borrowing from the private sector, borrowing from the temples and the *treasuries of the gods* created always a big issue, which was discussed and resolved in the *Assembly* together with the terms of the loans and their repayment. In Section 3.3, we explained the ingenuity of this arrangement but stopped short of drawing its implications for the money market until later. We did so for the following reason.

The budget deficits before 431 BCE were relatively small, if at all, and emanated mainly from the defensive wars that Athens fought as well as the warfare that it instigated to maintain its dominance over allies and foes. As such, they were different from the budget deficits in contemporary democracies that derive mainly from the finance of various entitlements and/or combating Keynesian type economic recessions. In the 4th century BCE, the level and the nature of military expenditures changed and so did the budget deficits. In the early years of this century, Athens had emerged from the protracted Peloponnesian War ruined; in the following decades, the enemies it faced were not as formidable as those it defeated in the first half of the 5th century; and, anyway, there was no empire to protect or hold together. Therefore, shifting to a permanent army and navy did not appear to be warranted on the basis of the prevailing threats from neighboring or overseas antagonist states. Yet this is what they decided and Athens by the middle of the 4th century BCE had both a standing army, although it was a light one consisting mainly of a cavalry force, and a standing navy, the largest in Greece and the eastern Mediterranean. The question then is: why did they change their strategy and from a land power they transformed their military posture into a fearsome sea power?[8]

One explanation is that they aimed to keep sea lanes open and safe because they had come to the conclusion that the economic future of Athens depended on the export–import activities in which most Athenians had always been engaged. This sounds credible, and particularly so in the light of the following except from Xenophon (*Hellenica*, 7.1.4):

> ...You likewise possess as peculiarly your own all the arts and crafts which have to do with ships. Again, you are far superior to other men in experience of nautical affairs, for most of you get your livelihood from the sea (Underlined by the authors); hence, while attending to your private concerns, you are also at the same time gaining experience for encounters by sea. Here is another point also: there is no port from which more *triremes* can sail forth at one time than from your city. And this is a matter of no slight importance with reference to leadership, for all men love best to join forces with the power which is first to show itself strong.

But, aside from skills and locational advantages, we maintain that for this major one-time shift in strategy to be effected, there must have been many more urgent social and economic forces that pushed in the same direction.

Another explanation is the increasing cost of land warfare. To substantiate its significance, consider first the cost of land forces. From the 5th to the 4th century BCE, land wars became more and more capital and skills intensive. For example, instead of the *phalanx* formation[9] in the battles of *Thermopylae* and *Marathon* in the first half of the 5th century BCE, late in the second half during the Peloponnesian War, the troops had turned to

---

8 Before this change, Athens entrusted its defense in times of peace to its youngest citizens who served their *ephebeia* and had no combat experience. It turned them into a capable fighting force by subjecting them to unusually strict discipline and by passing them through a program of military training under specialized instructors. But in times of preparedness for war, the *demes* populated an army of soldiers and officers who stood ready to fight at any time. During the Peloponnesian War, Athens did use mercenary personnel and later on soldiers armed with javelins and a shield, the *pelta*.

9 *Phalanx* was a block-like infantry formation of *hoplites* armed with shields, spears, swords or similar weapons. For further details, see Kagan, Viggiano (2013).

using cavalry, archers, slingers and *peltastai* (lightly armed infantry with a small shield *pelta* throwing javelins). Therefore, most of their armaments had to be paid by the state. Many of them were foreign mercenaries. Also, we know that early on in the adoption of cavalry, the horses were provided by the class of wealthier citizens called *hippeis* (Horsemen). But the war cut deeply into their ranks and fortunes, horses grew scarce and the state had to come forward and cover the shortages at its own expense. The case regarding the manpower and the fortifications was similar. Regarding the former, as the population of able indigenous males declined owing to the attrition from the war and losses from the plague (430–429 BCE), the Athenian troops became inadequate and they had to be supplemented by foreign (non-Athenian) mercenaries and certainly their payment by the state imposed extra burdens. As for the fortifications, the problem must have been insurmountable because most had been destroyed and rebuilding them was practically impossible for the lack of funds.[10]

Lastly, much at work pushing for the change in strategy were the political reasons that we explained in Section 3.2. Recall that: (a) land forces (*hoplites*) were recruited from the "middle" class, whereas the navy was manned and gave employment, remuneration and political power to the large but poor class of *thetes*, and (b) the *Assembly* was dominated by the latter and hence the project of transforming Athens into a naval power catered to their interests. Thus, the answer to the question raised above is that the Athenians decided to change their armed forces from mainly land-based to mainly sea-based because it was the rational policy to adopt in view of the confluence of strong economic and social forces that were in its favor. However, while this shift offered Athens the chance to become a dominant sea power and regain a good deal of its former glory and well-being, it was not without the disadvantages that began to emerge when the land forces of Macedon started to move southward and the pacifist regime of Euboulos, despite the repeated warnings by Demosthenes and other distinguished orators, failed to recognize the imminent threat and start a program in time for rebuilding of the land forces of Athens. Not only as a result of this failure, but also because of the changes that had taken place in the character of the Athenians, who had come to enjoy a good life and despise going to war, in the battle of Chaeronea in 338 BCE, Athens succumbed to Phillip II of Macedon and the Athenians lost their sovereignty and freedoms.

---

10 The region of Attica was probably the most heavily fortified area of Greece. There were several series of outer walls with the inner ones, called *Long Walls*, connecting Athens with the port of Piraeus from the north and the south, leaving a wide corridor in between. These walls as well as the other fortifications were destroyed when Athens succumbed to Sparta. But, as we shall explain shortly below, they were rebuilt at the start of the Corinthian War in 395 BCE.

5.1.1.3 Courts and law enforcement

Heliaia, to which we referred earlier, was the main court. Its 6,000 judges were elected annually by lot among all male citizens over 30 years of age, unless they were in debt to the *treasury* or disenfranchised, that is, deprived of their civil rights through the socially humiliating punishment of *atimia.*[11] During the periods of Ephialtes and Pericles by a landmark arrangement that was introduced, most of the penal and civil cases were transferred to this court, while the other court, called *Areios Pagos,* retained its competence only for the crimes of murder and arson. Responsible for resolving disputes that related to property rights and tax issues[12] were the *Popular Courts.* These were very important because by dealing effectively and quickly with such disputes, they contributed significantly to lowering transactions cost and hence to the flourishing of the economy.

Since the protection of property rights and the enforcement of contracts are fundamental conditions for the smooth working of a market economy, we cannot think of a better approach to emphasize the certainty that prevailed in this regard than to cite a few characteristic examples. The first, and perhaps the best for highlighting the climate that existed, is the oath given by those who were appointed to the high court of *Heliaia.* According to Demosthenes (*Against Timocrates,* 149), it read as follows:

> I will give verdict in accordance with the statutes and decrees of the People of Athens and of the *Council* of Five-hundred. I will not vote for tyranny or oligarchy. If any man try to subvert the Athenian democracy or make any speech or any proposal in contravention thereof I will not comply. <u>I will not allow private debts to be cancelled, nor lands nor houses belonging to Athenian citizens to be redistributed</u> (Underlined by the authors). I will not restore exiles or persons under sentence of death. I will not expel, nor suffer another to expel, persons here resident in contravention of the statutes and decrees of the Athenian People or of the *Council.*

Moreover, regarding the crucial role of property, Aristotle (*Politics,* 1262b, 23–25) argues that:

> For there are two things that most cause men to care for and to love each other, the sense of ownership and the sense of preciousness;

From the above, and particularly from the sentence that we have underlined in the excerpt from Demosthenes, it follows that the signal from the top

---

11 Regarding the electoral process of other officials, see footnote 6, Chapter 2.
12 For a detailed analysis of the nature and evolution of property rights in Athens, see Economou, Kyriazis (2017) and the extensive literature cited there regarding this issue.

echelons of the government and the *Courts* to the simple merchants in the markets of Athens was that they ought to conduct their economic affairs by taking full ownership of the consequences, since they could not hope for any leniency on the part of the *Courts*.

If the latter conduct is to be expected by all participants in a market-based economy, certainly it should be very striking to learn from Lysias (*On the Property of Eraton*, XVII, 4–7) that if someone owed money to a person and the state *treasury*, from the seizure of his property, the person would be paid first and then the *treasury*, if there was any money left. What this implies is that in Athens, the economic interests of the weaker party, that is, the individual, took precedence over the interests of the stronger party, that is, the state *treasury*. This in turn leads to the question: why did they have this institutional arrangement about which contemporary democracies would be envious? The answer comes directly from Aristotle (*Politics*, 1263a, 1278a), who stresses that private property ensured the preservation of individual liberties and explains why Athenians felt so adamant about this that no one could repeal or ask for its repeal by the *Assembly* (Demosthenes, *Against Aristocrates*, 61–62).

However, in view of the fairness of the state with regard to the rights and freedoms of citizens, the latter in full reciprocity ought to respect the obligations they themselves had voted for in the *Assembly* on behalf of the state. This meant that citizens had a moral duty to pay their taxes and not try evading. But knowing human nature, they had established various institutions to prevent abuses. One of them was called *antidosis* and worked as follows: Assume that a wealthy Athenian was charged with a *liturgy*, which was always related to the value of his property. If he believed that another Athenian should be charged because he was wealthier than himself, he could ask the *Courts* to decide an exchange of properties as well as of the liturgical charges that were levied on them (Ober 2008, 129–130; Lyttkens 2013, 112).

In short, according to modern literature, the protection of property rights and the enforcement of contracts are pivotal requirements for the establishment and efficient functioning of a market economy. Embedded in the public administration of Athens was a full range of *Courts* including *Courts* in which commercial disputes could be resolved quickly and efficiently as well as *Specialized Courts* and jurors. For example, Cohen (1973, 158–198) reports that during the 4th century BCE, Athens set up special *Maritime Courts* in which highly knowledgeable and experienced jurors known as *nautodikai* heard commercial cases called *dikai emporikai*, and that such cases were adjudicated within a month so that justice was provided most rapidly (*ibid.* 9–40; Woolmer 2016, 82).

5.1.1.4 Financial, regulatory and other services

Among its other tasks, the *Boule* acted as the executive branch of the government. It supervised and coordinated the agencies and the elected officials in (a) the financial branch of the public administration, (b) the orderly functioning of markets, (c) the maintaining of law and order in everyday life, (d) the building and maintenance of public infrastructures, (e) the organization of cultural and religious events, etc. In Chapter 3, we examined the agencies, the functions they performed and the elected officials who served in the system through which the state financed its budgets in times of war and peace. Therefore, to round out the presentation, this section is devoted to the wide range of regulatory, policing and other services that the state provided by focusing on the job content of the officials that were in charge.

Table 5.1 presents the titles of officials in six categories of public services. From these and the corresponding number of officials appointed in each of them, we can understand the type of service they provided and the importance that the state attributed to it. But since nowadays one finds in ready internet sources extensive accounts of the tasks they performed, just for indicative purposes, below we provide brief descriptions.

Market monitoring

- *Agoranomoi* (10)[13]: They supervised the smooth functioning of the market; the fairness of prices, based on the forces of demand and supply; that the quality of the products met accepted specifications; and that

Table 5.1 Regulatory, policing and other public services[a]

Market monitoring	Policing	Public infrastructure	Cultural events	City cleanliness	Legislative consultants
(1)	*(2)*	*(3)*	*(4)*	*(5)*	*(6)*
Agoranomoi	Astynomoi Astynomia	Trieropoioi	Athlothetai	Epimelites epi ton hudaton	Syngrapheis
Metronomoi	Peripoloi	Hieropoioi	Epimelitai ton mustirion		
Sitophylakes	Agronomoi	Toichopoioi			
Epimelitai tou Emporiou	Gynaikonomoi	Odopoioi			
	Guardians of neorion	Hieron Episkeuastai Epistatai			

a All officials mentioned below, as well as the *bouleutai*, *strategoi* and *tamiai*, and the other functionaries received from the state budget a daily allowance called m*isthos* (wage). At all times, this compensation was lower than the daily wage of a skilled worker and it was given to defray the opportunity cost citizens suffered while providing their services to the state and to enable those of them who were poor to participate in the running of public services. This remuneration was in addition to the other honors and privileges state officials enjoyed.

13 The numbers within the parentheses indicate the maximum number of individuals that were appointed, because over the decades their number changed. In those categories where there are no parentheses, we do not know precisely the corresponding figure.

the currencies were pure and unadulterated (Aristotle, *Athenian Constitution*, 51.1; Fröhlich 2013, 259).

- *Metronomoi* (10): Their responsibility was to check and make sure that the weights and measures used by sellers of goods in the markets were correct. Their job was very important because they prevented profiteering (Aristotle, *Athenian Constitution*, 52.2; Johnstone 2011, 54).
- *Sitophylakes* (10 initially, 35 later on): They oversaw the formation of prices in the wholesale and retail markets of grains, grain flours and grain products. Since they supervised the bidding process by *sitopolai*, presumably they also heard appeals for abuses and imposed fines (Figueira 1986, 151).
- *Epimelitai tou emporiou* (10): They oversaw the warehouses of imported commodities in general, and of grains in particular, in the port of Piraeus; they received and examined accusations against diverters of grain; and they made sure that the *sitemporoi* (merchants of grains) brought two-thirds of the grain they imported up to the city (Figueira 1986, 151).

Policing

- *Astynomoi* (10): Policemen of the city. Five were located in Athens and five in Piraeus. Their main responsibility was to watch over the cleanliness and keep the order in the city.
- *Astynomia* (Police): A group of 300 publicly owned Scythian slaves (the so-called rod bearers) was used under the control of the *astynomoi* to guard public meetings; to keep order and control the crowds; and to assist in dealing with criminals, handling prisoners and making arrests. Other duties associated with modern policing, such as investigating crimes, were left to the citizens themselves.
- *Agronomoi*: Responsible for supervising the drainage and distribution of rain water (Isager, Hansen 2013, 137, 147).
- *Peripoloi*: Military patrols by young soldiers who were performing their initial military service.
- *Gynaikonomoi*: Their duty was the supervision of women's behavior and public appearance in order to protect the morality and the values of the society.
- *Guardians of Neorion*: Guards responsible for the security of the shipbuilding installations and the materials deposited in them.

Public infrastructures

- *Trieropoioi* (10): They oversaw the building and maintenance of trireme warships.
- *Hieropoioi*: Civil servants responsible for preparing religious ceremonies.
- *Toichopoioi* (10): In charge of building and maintaining the walls of the city.
- *Odopoioi* (5): Responsible for the maintenance of the city's road network.
- *Hieron episkeuastai*: Repairing of temples and sacred buildings.

- *Epistatai*: They supervised the construction of public works. Their number varied from two to three, depending on the scale of the project. They were nominated by the *Boule* from lists of citizens maintained in the archives of the state and municipality. When large sums had to be spent on the construction or maintenance of public buildings or works, the approval of the *Assembly* was necessary.

Cultural events

- *Athlothetai* (10): Elected on a four-year term and responsible for organizing sport events, the most important among them being the *Great Panathenaia*.
- *Epimelitai ton mustirion* (4): They were responsible for the proper functioning of the *Temple of Eleusis*.

City Cleanliness

- *Epimelites epi ton hudaton* or *epi ton krinon* (1): A state functionary responsible for supervising the proper functioning and cleanliness of public fountains.

Legislative consultants

- *Syngrapheis*: A panel of experts tasked with submitting, in collaboration with the members of the *Boule*, special proposals to be discussed at the citizen's *Assembly*.

To summarize, governance in classical Athens was much different than in the *representative* democracies of more recent centuries. It comprised a legislative and governing body composed of all adult male citizens, that is, the *Assembly*, which exercised the supreme democratic control over all policy issues; an executive branch, that is, the 50 *bouleutai* who were chosen annually to the *Boule* by each of the 10 Athenian tribes and served as *prytaneis* for a monthly period of 36 days to supervise and guide the public administration; a judicial branch, which was endowed with a full range of *Courts* that protected sternly property rights and delivered justice efficiently and quickly, particularly in cases of commercial disputes for which speedy adjudication matters because of the transactional costs involved; and ten *strategoi* and nine *archons* who were selected and appointed by the *Assembly*. The public administration produced, delivered and financed a wide range of services either directly with the help of state paid facilities and staff or by outsourcing production and distribution to the private sector. Directly, the state produced coordination, defense, financial, regulatory and many other services, whereas *paideia*, construction of infrastructures, health services, etc. were outsourced. This explains why we decided to cover them in the section that deals with the private economy.

5.1.2 *Infrastructural and cultural facilities*

In the same way as in all countries over the centuries, public works in classical Athens varied between periods of war and peace, as well as between periods of affluent and meager state revenues.[14] During periods of war, they fell to a nadir and picked up again during periods of peace when the economy expanded and the revenues of the state increased, particularly through the reinvigoration of export–import trade. Therefore, to highlight their level and composition, we shall concentrate in the periods 460–430 BCE and 355–320 BCE, which, with the exception of the major battle in Chaeronea in 338 BCE, were relatively peaceful.

Turning to the level of public works, its first and foremost determinant is state revenues. In this regard, from the assessment of the evidence by Andreades (1928, 352), we may assume conservatively that the average state income from all sources was about 1,500 Talents per annum in the period 460–430 BCE and about 600 *talents* per annum in the period 355–320 BCE. The second determinant is the running expenses of the government. Andreades (1928, 265–266) estimates that in 420 BCE, that is, while the Peloponnesian War was in full swing, overall public expenditures were of the order of 700 Talents, out of which 555 Talents were for military purposes.[15] Hence, if current government outlays in peacetime amounted to about 150 Talents in the first period, in the second period, they could be as much as 250 Talents, because in this period, Athens had a standing army and navy and the military personnel had to be remunerated. On account then of these figures, we may surmise that the average annual capital budget in the first period was about 1350 talents and only about 350 talents in the second, thus rendering public works in the former period almost four times those in the latter.[16]

---

14 According to Andreades (1928, 232), the concept of "public works" in classical Athens was completely different from that of ours today. In his view, what they meant was building temples, statues, votive offerings, etc. to beautify the city. By contrast, we have used these terms throughout to imply all types of "public investment" ranging from public works in fortifications to public works in cultural and beautification infrastructures. We do so because if "public works" included only cultural and beautification infrastructures, a great deal of public investments would be left unaccounted. For example, whereas the program of public works implemented by Euboulos in the 4th century was a full-fledged series of public works in the modern sense of the term, in the above-mentioned conceptualization, it would not count as a program of "public works."

15 In most countries from ancient times to the beginning of the 20th century, defense has been very costly, necessitating high expenditures, which usually take more than 50%, and often during wartime as much as 90%, of total state expenditures. In this particular year, war expenditures absorbed 79.3% of total state outlays.

16 The figures mentioned above from Andreades (1928) should be construed as rough approximations because they involve estimates from evidence before the lists of the allied tribute appeared. However, if the figures quoted by Morris, Scheidel (2009, 146) for the revenues that Athens received through the decades from this source are correct, we remain comfortable with the order of magnitudes in our conclusion.

Drawing on this exceedingly large difference in the levels of public works between the two periods, it is not surprising that the first coincides with the golden years of Athens. But this outcome was achieved also on account of the mix of public works that were undertaken. The bibliography in this respect is already very rich and the evidence increases daily. So, we see no reason to take a lengthy digression in this direction. Instead, based on the presumption that the range of such investments can be described by a few characteristic examples, we limit ourselves to the following.

5.1.2.1 Fortifications

Building of the "long Walls" started in 461 BCE based on proposals submitted earlier in the decade by Themistocles and brought forward by Cimon. The western wall was 6 kilometers long and connected Athens to the port of Piraeus, whereas the eastern wall was about 5.5 kilometers long and connected Athens to Phaleron. In between the walls, there was arable land which, if cultivated, together with imports received through the port of Piraeus enabled Athens to withstand any siege. The first phase of the construction finished in 457 BCE. But later, and in particular during the years 445–443 BCE, Pericles doubled the western wall. Aristophanes (*Knights*, 817–818) informs us that Cleon built a cross-wall but we do not know where it was located.

The walls were breached in 403 BCE on the demand by the victors and as Xenophon (*Hellenica*, 2.2.23) writes:

> … the Peloponnesians with great enthusiasm began to tear down the walls to the music of flute-girls, thinking that that day was the beginning of freedom for Greece.

However, a few years later, Athens recovered from its defeat and the long walls were rebuilt at the start of the Corinthian War (395–386 BCE).

5.1.2.2 Civil infrastructures

In the periods under consideration, Athens invested heavily in the construction of civil infrastructures ranging from roads, water supply systems, waste disposal systems and even public baths, to government buildings, stadiums and athletic facilities.[17] The bulk of investments in these areas were imple-

---

17 There were three public athletic facilities, that is, the Academy, the Lyceum and the Kyno-sarges, which consisted of multiple spaces with extensive sports installations. All free citizens had access to them (Fisher, 1998). Since the 6th century BCE, there existed a stadium for racecourses, which later was developed to host the famous *Panathenaic Games* (also known as the *Great Panathenaea*), a religious and athletic festival celebrated every four years in honor of the goddess Athena.

mented in the 5th century under Pericles, whereas those built under Euboulos and Lycourgos in the 4th century were mostly supplementary.[18]

The government buildings were so luxurious and expensive that we may use them as a good indicator of the high-spirited approach with which the Athenian state pursued public works in all the above-mentioned areas. This explains why, instead of presenting a long list of these buildings, which are easy to locate and study on the internet,[19] we believe it is possible to characterize them all by referencing just one building, the so-called *prytaneion*, shown by the circular building in Exhibit 5.1. This was a structure where *bouleutai* (members of the *Boule*), public magistrates and foreign

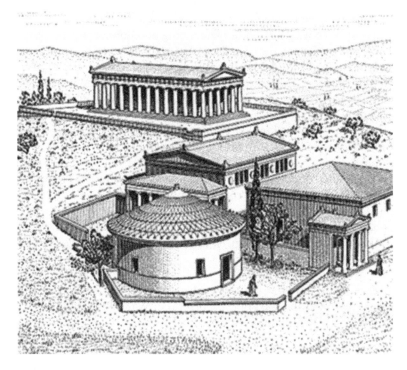

Exhibit 5.1 Prytaneion or *Tholos* and other buildings.
Source: With the permission of the Ekdotike Athinon S.A., Publishers of the History of the Hellenic Nation, Vol. A1, creator J. Travlos: https://www.ekdotikeathenon.gr/en/about-us-cp1.html

18 Among the new infrastructures that Euboulos implemented were new waterfronts, shipyards and large-scale redeployment of warships in the newly built ports in Zea and Mounichia so that more space became available in the main port of Piraeus for merchant ships.
19 For a brief but very concise presentation of government and other buildings, roads, promenades, etc. in the Athenian *agora*, see Camp (2003).

ambassadors came to take their meals during the period of their service. We do not know how many of the 500 *bouleutai*, approximately 700 magistrates, and an unknown number of ambassadors did go to lunch at the *prytaneion* every day at the state's expense. But certainly, the building must have been large enough to seat and service several hundred officials within a few hours. Even more impressive is to think of how populous and well organized the catering service must have been.

Do we have in the capitals of present-day superpowers comparable accommodations? Does Washington or Peking or Moscow have a building where several hundred congressmen, senators and other officials may lunch all at the same time day in and day out? We doubt it. That is why the *prytaneion* represents an emblematic indicator of the wealth and the power Athens projected in the world at that time, but also of the forward-looking spirit with which all state infrastructures were undertaken.

5.1.2.3 Cultural infrastructures

Construction of the temple of the *Parthenon* on the summit of the Acropolis started in 447 BCE and it was completed in 438 BCE. It was designed and built by the best architects of the time. For its construction, they employed the best materials such as the famous marble from the Mt. Pendelikon and the best craftsmen; and for its decoration, the Athenian state continued to invest resources and efforts until 432 BCE. The costs must have been enormous. This we know because throughout these years, Pericles faced sharp criticisms from his political opponents that he was spending money contributed by the allies of Athens for the common goal, that is, the defense against Persians. But Pericles stayed the course because he knew that the Parthenon as a symbol of political unity overlooking the *agora* as a symbol of decision-making based on rational discourse opened for Athens a glorious avenue to eternity, whatever might happen after he was gone.

The Parthenon was the finest and most expensive temple, but it was not the only one built in those years. Three others were the temple of *Hephaestus*, devoted to the god of fire, which is the best preserved temple in the southern slope of the Acropolis; the temple of *Athena Nike*, located close to the *Propylaea* on the Acropolis; and the temple of *Erechtheion*, dedicated to *Athena Polias* defender of the city. Moreover, aside from temples, sanctuaries and smaller shrines, the cultural infrastructures included the *Theatre of Dionysos Eleuthereus*, where the tragedies of Aeschylus, Sophocles and Euripides and the comedies of Aristophanes were played; a library, a concert hall (*odeion*), etc.

5.1.3 Social welfare

The state in Athens provided financial assistance for the orphans of those who died in wars and whoever was met by bad luck (Beaumont 2012, 135).

This assistance was distributed by the municipal authorities where the recipients resided for better monitoring of their needs (Demosthenes, *Against Leochares*, 37–38) and more efficient delivery of the services. The *Archons* in each of the *demes* were obliged by law to take care of the poor and the orphans in their region, to protect them from unfair treatment by the rich and to bury those who died in a way befitting their poor fellow citizens (Demosthenes, *Against Macaratus*, 58, 75). The orphans from wars received free meals by the state till their 18th year. They also provided to poor Athenians money to attend theatrical shows (Demosthenes, *Against Leochares*, 37–38), and all knew that those who received money were not rich. It was forbidden for someone to receive money under the *Theorikon* program from two different municipalities, and if one did so and was caught, one would be severely punished because the act was considered theft of public money (Demosthenes, *Against Leochares*, 38–39).

In Section 3.1.2, we referred to a tax called *eisphora*, which was imposed in urgent circumstances (war, natural disasters, etc.). It was linked to the citizens' income, and hence lower income citizens paid less or nothing (Christ 2006, 146). One portion of the revenues from *eisphora* was channeled to the care of war orphans.[20] During the predemocratic period, the tyrant Peisistratus introduced a law by which the people unable to go to war received health insurance from the state (Plutarch, *Solon*, 31.2), and later this was further expanded to include pregnant women.[21] Moreover, at times of food shortages, the state often distributed corn, which was either free or subsidized (Aristotle, *Athenian Constitution* 49.4; Aeschines, *Against Ctesiphon*, 3.154, 1.103–104). Disabled persons with no means of support[22] could be registered with the *Boule* and receive a subsidy of one obol and later two obols per day. Thus, we may surmise that Athens practiced the first ever recorded social welfare policies,

---

20 Diogenes Laertius (*Lives of Eminent Philosophers*, 1.2.) traces this policy back to Solon. The latter is said to have proposed that "it was in bad taste ... to ignore the exclusive claims of those who had fallen in battle," by arguing that their sons ought to be maintained and educated by the state. Although placing the origin of state-sponsored care for orphans in the time of Solon is not unlikely, it is certain that it was well established in classical Athens in the 5th century, for we have evidence from Plato (*Menexemus*, 248e–249a), Aristotle (*Politics*, 1268a 6–11; *Athenian Constitution*, 24.3) and many other most credible sources. Following the Peloponnesian War and until some point in the mid-4th century BCE, in addition to providing such support to orphans, Athens appointed an *orphanophylax* (a guardian of orphans), who was in charge of making sure that the children of killed Athenian soldiers had their needs taken care of (Xenophon, *Ways and Means*, 2.7).

21 It should be noted that any citizen had the right to denounce any official who did not follow the laws regarding the treatment of war orphans and women. Moreover, the state saw that female orphans without assets and brothers received a dowry from the next closest family member in proportion to the assets of this relative. Other cities had similar arrangements. For example, in Crete, orphans were included in the common messes known as *syssitia* and given equal portions of food with the adult men rather than the half-portions given other minors.

22 They had to own property valued at less than 300 drachmae.

since the poor citizens who were the beneficiaries paid no taxes, whereas revenues from several sources were raised to finance their implementation.[23]

At the same time though, in the management of these policies Athens
faced the same problems that beset welfare programs in contemporary democracies, that is, corruption, cheating and rent-seeking. Athenians were
fully aware that welfare allowances might give rise to negative consequences,
if they were not tied to the true ability of a person to work and to contribute toward the general well-being. For this reason, members of the *Boule*
verified the requests for assistance during certain set periods and regularly
monitored the disabilities during the period that the assistance was prof-
fered. All Athenians had the right to show up in the *Boule* and denounce
someone who received aid unjustifiably. In such instances, the members of
the *Boule* would assess the complaint, reexamining from the beginning the
prerequisites that the petitioner claimed he fulfilled. In this way, the Athenians established a welfare system that operated with compassion but with
strict rules and penalties for those who cheated. Perhaps then the welfare
states of today can improve the delivery of welfare services by looking closer
to the principles and practices Athenians applied so many centuries ago.

5.2 The private sector

Present-day advanced market economies are characterized by a sectoral
structure in which services contribute the most to employment and GDP, with
manufacturing coming next, and agriculture last. Agriculture in particular
contributes in most cases less than 10%. By contrast, in economies before the
so-called Industrial Revolution, with very few exceptions like Venice and the
Dutch Republic in the 17th century, agriculture was the dominant sector by
contributing the highest share in terms of both these metrics. Contemplated
in this context, the structure of the economy in ancient Athens was comparable to that of contemporary developed economies. Although we do not have
national accounting data to document this assessment, the case that can be
made by drawing on the available qualitative evidence in support of the claim

---

23 Athenians believed that theatrical performances had a highly valued social property in
   that they taught citizens morals, history, mythology and religion. Drawing on this view,
   they had determined that all should be able to benefit from attending. But performances
   lasted the whole day for a four-day period and this implied that poorer citizens would have
   to lose four days' wages (or remuneration from work) if they participated. Many could
   not afford this loss. For this reason, the state introduced a program called *theorica*, which
   provided a payment to poorer citizens as compensation for wages and remuneration lost,
   thus allowing them to attend the performances. Considered in this light, *theorica* was a
   program of lifelong *paideia* that the state had instituted in order to maintain the trust and
   the allegiance of a substantial part of the population. But as has happened universally
   over the centuries with similar well-conceived social programs, after a while they turn into
   black holes of public revenues and eventually become catastrophic for the state itself.

that services (retail and wholesale trade, shipping and banking) and industrial value-added activities were more important than agriculture is very strong.

To corroborate it, we submit that the economy in classical Athens could be conceived to consist of the following main sectors: (a) production of goods by households for own use and sale; (b) trade-oriented production of goods and services, including mining, handicraft and manufacturing, housing and infrastructures, money and banking, *paideia*, and other public services like policing and street cleaning; (c) distribution of goods and services, including labor; and (d) import–export activities, with supporting facilities for shipping, warehousing, and ship-building and repairing. Below, we turn to them in the same order.

5.2.1 Household production for own use and sale

The arable land of Attica was devoted predominantly to the production of wheat and barley. The productivity of land used for wheat was roughly half of that cultivated with barley, and this explains why wheat was produced only in as little as one fourth of the cultivated areas. But from Isager, Hansen (1975, 20–29), Amemiya (2007, 74–75) and many others, we surmise that Athens experienced permanently significant deficits of grains. On the other hand, husbandry flourished by raising goats, sheep, oxen, horses, swine and other animals.

Agriculture was organized mostly in small lots owned by citizens. *Metics* were not allowed to own land but they could rent farms and cultivate them for their own account. Cultivation was performed as a family activity. But there were also large farms using good numbers of slaves (Bresson 2016a, 146–148). Free married men attended farm production. There were cases of poor women who worked in the fields and sold their crops in the markets, as was the case with Euripides' mother (Aristophanes, *Acharnians*, 454). But free married women were mainly in charge of household responsibilities as, for example, spinning and knitting of wool and sewing garments with the help of one or more maids (Aristophanes, *Lysistrata*, 532; Plato, *Laws*, 805c–806a; Xenophon, *Oeconomicus*, VII, X).

Following Engen (2004), up to the first two decades of the 5th century, the economy in Athens was based predominantly on household production and consumption, with the bulk of commercial activities centered on agricultural products. The deficit in the production of cereals was covered by imports, which involved journeys over risky and uncertain sea lanes. As a result, this trade imbalance created pressures and incentives for the development primarily of sea transport services and the activities associated with them, and secondarily for increasing the range of exportable commodities and services (tradeables). However, even though making progress in this direction was favored by the prevailing institutions of democracy, private property and free exchanges, on account of other countervailing social inertias, the economy remained anchored in its archaic structure.

Assessed in this context, the discovery of the Laurion mines in 483 BCE and the decision to build the big war fleet in the short span leading to 480 BCE must have shaken the agrarian foundations of the Athenian economy very deeply. For what resulted with these developments was an unprecedented transformative process through which: (a) laborers exited agricultural and household production and entered into ship building and other associated crafts by offering their services for hire; (b) disposable incomes increased significantly and thereby stimulated the demand for all other sorts of necessities and even luxuries, thus boosting further the expansion of the nonagricultural productive activities; (c) self-interest by those who were open to new ventures precipitated the shift in the composition of production away from agriculture and toward manufacturing and services; and (d) as the newfound source of wealth was expected to last for years, the social sentiment started to change in favor of material progress through risk taking, thus encouraging investment and entrepreneurial endeavors.[24] In short, by liberating the forces of entrepreneurship in other directions away from agriculture, these developments served as catalysts in the taking-off of mining, manufacturing and services, with an emphasis on the production of tradeables that gradually gave impetus to robust export–import activities. According to Halkos, Kyriazis (2010, 256), this gradual transformation of the economy made Athens during the 4th century, the first "modern" economy, where handicraft (industry) and services contributed more to GDP than the primary sector.[25]

To appreciate the nature and the strength of the economic forces that were unleashed, below we provide brief summaries of the sectoral stylized features, which have been well documented by economic historians.

5.2.2 Trade-oriented production of goods and services

In the period between 483 BCE, when the new rich vein of silver was discovered in Laurion, and the battle in Marathon in 480 BCE, Athens built and equipped 200 *triremes*. We do not have details on how they managed this major construction feat; because, when the decision for this huge public program was taken, Athens could not possibly have the massive manpower of skilled craftsmen that was required to carry it out in the short span of two to three years. Most likely, they did it by drawing and training personnel

---

24 For a detailed analysis of the economic and to some extent political implications of the discovery of Laurion silver mines and the decision to build that big naval fleet, see Kyriazis, Zouboulakis (2004, 119–122).

25 According to Figueira (1981), the strategies toward "Turning to the sea" and "international commercial activities" were first adopted by the city-state of the island of Aegina. Hence, in the context in which we use the term "modern economy" in this book, Aegina may have preceded Athens in the historical process of transformation toward a money-based international economy.

from the other sectors of the economy, as well as by attracting immigrant craftsmen including displaced Ionians. What this implies is that the ship building industry offered the necessary wage incentives to attract workers and trainees in competition with the other sectors, thus raising disposable incomes and consumption throughout. It was a period of take-off for the Athenian economy, which was instigated initially from the discovery of the silver mines and spread gradually to the rest of the economy by boosting the demand for handicraft and manufacturing products, as well as services. That the economy flourished well beyond the end of the said public program constitutes solid evidence of the creative forces that were unleashed by these developments. Below we look at them in more detail.

5.2.2.1 Mining

Mining is characterized inherently by a lot of "luck" regarding the quantity of useful source that is found and can be extracted with cost-effective efforts. Hence, the contribution to the Gross Domestic Product (GDP) of Athens from the mining of silver ore and the associated activities of ore enrichment and silver purification must have varied considerably from one year to the next. Of what order was its value-added? According to the evidence cited by Amemiya (2007, 97), the value of silver produced per annum amounted to about 1,000 talents. Was it as huge as claimed by Xenophon (*Ways and Means*, IV) or relatively modest? We can get a feeling only indirectly. Very illuminating in this respect is the great public debate that took place with reference to the distribution of the extra income that would accrue for the state. The proposal by Themistocles, which was supported by the *Assembly*, recommended devoting 100 talents each year, for two years, to the construction of 200 warships. Thus, the estimated annual contribution of the mines to the Athenian economy was ten times the cost of 100 warships, and therefore it was a very big deal. But was it also a big deal for the public budget? Andreades (1928, 339) estimates that around 450 BCE state revenues from the Laurion mines amounted to 50–100 talents, whereas various authors having revisited the evidence more recently raise state revenues to around 160 talents. Therefore, it is not unreasonable to surmise that Athens would have been able to cover the cost of building these *triremes* with about two years' revenues from the mines. No doubt then that the discovery of the Laurion mines introduced a seminal structural break in the society and the economy of Athens.

That it did, we have further assurances from several sources. For example, Herodotus (*The Histories*, VII, 144) informs us that the revenues of Athens increased significantly and similar comments are made by Aeschylus (*Persians*, 240), and also found in the testimonies by Thucydides (*The Peloponnesian War*, 7.91), and the joke by Aristophanes (*Knights*, 362). Also, Christesen (2003) makes reference to records showing the names of 300 mining entrepreneurs, which indicate a widespread participation of persons in this activity, and Acton (2014, 119) reports that the two richest Athenians of the early 4th century, both mining entrepreneurs, were Diphylos, with a property worth 160 talents (as high as the Athenian budget in 354 BCE) and Epicrates, with 400 talents (as high as the public budget in about 340 BCE, under Euboulos).

In the light of these findings, we conclude that the mines were a regime changing source of wealth for the Athenian society and economy.

5.2.2.2 Handicraft and manufacturing[26]

In the post WWII period, households in local communities and villages all over Greece produced various homemade goods on order or freely for sale in the markets to supplement household income. So, a question that immediately comes to mind is: was the same mode of production practiced in classical times and if so how widespread was it? Spantidaki (2016) offers an example from the case of textiles by drawing on textual, iconographic and archaeological evidence. From the sophistication of the discrete and elaborate designs to the variety of material used one cannot but surmise that this was a market-driven household-based industry and that the technology of knitting and weaving had developed significantly. Very vibrant and technologically advanced was also the handicraft of pottery, which produced ceramic cups, perfume bottles, wine bottles, jewelry boxes and large storage containers for transporting wine and olive oil. The large concentration of pottery shops in the area of *Kerameikos* and the numerous vases of Attic origin found in sunken boats and in the wider Mediterranean area suggest that relative to textiles pottery was more commercialized and export oriented, yet as Arafat, Morgan (1989) have established, pottery was not less embedded in household activities, and in all indications, the same was true with the production of the plethora of farm and hand-made products that were offered for sale in the markets of Athens and Piraeus or sold directly from the shops of those who produced them and retailer merchants.

Unlike handicraft, manufacturing did not take off until the 4th century BCE. Many authors suggest that instrumental for this delay was the social hostility toward manufacturing, which was fueled by the teachings of the great Athenian philosophers opposed to wealth creating preoccupations and vulgar employments that distracted the minds and the interests of citizens away from the affairs of the state.[27] Recall though that before the

---

26 For an exhaustive and well-researched investigation of the lucrative manufacturing activities in classical Athens, see Winters (2011) and Acton (2014).

27 This is not the proper place to explain the philosophical ideas, which shaped this stance. However, on the other hand, its implications over the centuries have been too significant to leave without some hints. For this purpose, we find it convenient to draw attention to the following passage from Aristotle's (*Nicomachean Ethics*, 1140b, 1–5):

   ...doing and making are generically different, since making aims at an end distinct from the act of making, whereas in doing the end cannot be other than the act itself: doing well is in itself the end...

Peloponnesian War started in 431 BCE, everything was going very well for Athens. Pericles had managed to finance the magnificent temples and buildings that we so admire today on top of an extended assortment of social programs, and still a great treasure was left, which was stored in the *treasury of Athena*. Hence, there was no pressure for new sources of wealth. But the war and mainly the defeat at the hands of the Spartans changed all that complacency. In particular, as Garlan (1988, 65) finds, the general mentality toward manufacturing changed between the 5th and the 4th centuries BCE.

Examining this finding further, the available evidence confirms that the change in social values and attitudes must have been foundational. While in previous times people in high places who pursued wealth acquiring activities were subjected to public scorn and ridicule, after the defeat, Athenians turned to considering them more favorably. This is not to say that in the period before the war, *eponymous* public figures abstained from such activities. Xenophon (*Ways and Means*, 4.14–15) informs us that the richest Athenian in the second half of the 5th century was the General Nicias, who owned 1,000 slaves and let them to a mining contractor at one obol a day. Most likely, there were many more, perhaps of lesser social status and wealth. But after the war, we know from many sources that this trend accelerated. Just to indicate how pervasive the motivation for profit was, it suffices to mention a few socially esteemed persons who, along with their main professions, got involved in manufacturing and became wealthy.[28]

The orator Lysias (*Against Eratosthenes*, 19) was a *metic* and with his brother Polemarchos employed 120 slaves in a 5th-century factory producing shields. Famous is also the case of Demosthenes' father who maintained two factories, one producing swords and another producing beds. Demosthenes (*Against Aphobos* 1, 9–11) informs us that his father employed 32 slaves in the

---

The terms "doing" and "making" have been interpreted in the relevant literature as equivalent to "praxis" and "poiesis," respectively. It is their fundamental difference that enabled philosophers like, for example, Isocrates (*To Demonicus*, 6–7) to make the following pronouncement:

> ...wealth ministers to vice rather than to nobility of soul, affording means for indolent living and luring the young to pleasure; strength, in company with wisdom, is, indeed, an advantage, but without wisdom it harms more than it helps its possessors, and while it sets off the bodies of those who cultivate it, yet it obscures the care of the soul

Having considered this issue in Bitros, Karayiannis (2006), we concluded that gradually the emphasis on "praxis" retreated in favor of "poiesis," which in turn created the social conditions for the take-off of handicraft as well as manufacturing.

28 Lyttkens (2013, 115) conjectures that the increasing burden of taxation may have contributed significantly to this trend as well. In particular, as he states:

> the taxation pushed the population – and in particular the rich – into the market economy. Arguably both the *liturgies* and the *eisphora* entailed monetary outlays. By requiring monetary outlay, the taxation must have induced a shift towards economic activities that gave a monetary return, such as trade and production for the market, and away from a focus on land holdings, self-sufficiency and status.

sword factory and 22 slaves in the bed factory. Moreover, he tells us that his investment in the two factories was valued at about 6.5 talents the value of slaves being 4 and the value of equipment and raw materials 2.5, and that his total fortune was estimated at 15 talents, the remaining being cash, financial investments and his house and furniture. From Aeschines (*Against Timarchos*, I, 97), it turns out that Timarchos employed 12 slaves in his leather works, Kerdon 13 in his cobbler shop, and according to Demosthenes (*For Phormio*, 11), Pasion employed 60 slaves in his shield factory.

Pasion was among the richest men in Athens during the 4th century. He rose from the status of slave to *metic* and later to citizen, thus providing evidence of the existence of social mobility. Passion made his fortune in banking, whereas Demosthenes himself became wealthy by lending money and taking interests in various workshops.[29] In short, such was the range of trade activities that providers of just about everything one can think of are represented in the list of 170 occupations cited by Harris (2002, 88–99). Most active among them were professionals from the class of *metics* who acted as entrepreneurs or skilled craftsmen (Isager, Hansen 1975, 70–73).

The marketplace in Athens was located in the northwest of the Acropolis, and in particular among the hills of *Areios Pagos* and *Agoraios Kolonos*. It served as the center of the city's economic life. There were *pantopoleia* (grocery stores) selling rich varieties of goods ranging from food to *hoplite* equipment; large-scale workshops employed free citizens, women and men, and *slaves* or *metics* to produce ceramics, sculpture stores, shoes, bags, clothing and in general all goods that were necessary for everyday living. Active were also bakeries, fishmongers, florists, wine shops, workshops for musical instruments, perfume stores, shops selling women's ornaments, laundry shops and even ready-made food stores, where people prepared meals for symposiums and other social events. Particularly rich was the range of foods that could be bought or sold. Common among them were figs, grapes, pears, apples, lambs, liver and spice filling, honeycombs, chickpeas, cow's milk and other dairy products, myrtle, and various processed meat products. Just to indicate how impressive the breadth and the depth of the market was at the time, we draw on Harris (2002, 88–99) and Johnstone (2011, 22, 40) to add that one could even procure voting ballots, hourglasses, written law documents and indictments, as well as many services.

Very large was also the market in the port city Piraeus.[30] During the period 479–404 BCE, the port contributed to the Athenian economy through shipbuilding and repairing, warehousing for goods in transit,

---

29 According to the ancient sources, during the 4th century, the majority of rich Athenians no longer belonged to the old landowning aristocracy. They were "industrialists," bankers and ship owners.

30 Besides the markets in Athens and Piraeus, there were markets in all Attic *demes* such as Sounion, Eleusis, Deceleia, Kollytus and other places. Hansen (2006, 104–105) notes that "every polis had an *agora*" and that "In the Classical period the *agora* has become a marketplace, and there is next to no trace of *agora* as assembly-place."

banks, loading and unloading facilities, etc., as well to state revenues through the levy of a customs duty of 2% on the values of exports and imports. But by the middle of the 4th century, it had grown so big that it could accommodate up to 400 commercial and military ships. Adjacent to it, the famous architect Hippodamos built in 460 BCE the *agora*, which bears his name to the present day, even though nothing remains to reveal the magnificent temples and public buildings that rendered it a posh place to visit for local people and foreign sailors. Buying and selling goods took place in the *agora*, as well as through street vendors who attended various social and religious events and artisans and merchants, who visited private homes to provide goods and services.

Evidence regarding the significance of the market and the port comes from several sources. Regarding the depth and breadth of the market, Isocrates (*Panegyricus*, 4, 42) proudly proclaimed that there was no good produced anywhere in the world that somebody could not find it here:

> Since the different populations did not in any case possess a country that was self-sufficient, each lacking in some things and producing others in excess of their needs, and since they were greatly at a loss where they should dispose of their surplus and whence they should import what they lacked, in these difficulties also our city came to the rescue; for she established the Piraeus as a market in the centre of Hellas –a market of such abundance that the articles which it is difficult to get, one here, one there, from the rest of the world, all these it is easy to procure from Athens.

As for the key role of the port to the Athenian economy, perhaps no other assessment can be as illuminating and convincing as the following from Hansen (2006, 92):

> Athens must have had an enormous foreign trade, and this emerges from our sources. The most important is a passage from a forensic speech in 400 BC. The speaker, Andocides, declares that in the year 402/1 BC he took on the contract for the harbour dues of 2 per cent on all imported and exported goods; i.e. he guaranteed this sum to the state and recouped from what actually came in. The proceeds of the contract was 36 silver *talents*, and Andocides allows that he made a little profit on the transaction. So the whole of Athens' import and export trade, including transit trade, that year (which was one of the worst in the history of Athens) must have been worth more than 1,800 *talents*, which equals 11 million drachmae. A drachma was a day's wage for a daily worker, so 1,800 *talents* correspond to day-wages for 30,000 people, a whole year's wages for every single citizen of Athens.

So, undoubtedly, while in the early 5th century, the port was built mainly to bolster the state's defenses from foreign aggressors, in the middle of the 4th century large-scale public infrastructural investments had turned it into a major source of economic growth, since in addition, it stimulated private investments and boosted domestic and international trade. 1,800 talents was a huge sum of money, which denotes the economic might of the Athenian economy at that time. According to Cohen (1992, 141) in the port of Piraeus, the products imported could be sold on site and directly exported to new end-user markets. The port of Piraeus had become an international entrepôt of antiquity, as was Alexandria during the Hellenistic times, Amsterdam during the 17th century AD and among others, Hong Kong, Shanghai and Rotterdam today. Cohen (1973), Bresson (2016b), Woolmer (2016) and others write that gradually an "international trade class" was set up to handle commercial relations with other city-states. It was not only the well-preserved aristocratic class, but also *metics* and many other foreigners who stayed temporarily in the twin city of Athens-Piraeus, as traders. Many of them also served at shipyards, as *naucleroi*, meaning captains of merchant ships. Burke (2010, 397) and Engen (2010, 192–197) also provide the important information that the Athenian state, with the institution of *enktesis* rewarded any foreigner who had benefitted the city of Athens through his commercial activity, with the highest status of the "citizen of the city of Athens" and awarded him the right to legally hold landed property. And finally with this, Bresson (2016a, 414) writes:

> In the Classical period, Athens was obviously the greatest market in the Mediterranean world, the one that attracted all the merchants who wanted to sell a large cargo rapidly at a good price.

Above, we used the terms marketplace and market to indicate a wide geographical area in which all sorts of productive and commercial exchanges take place. Now, for the reason that will become apparent shortly, we should like to use the term *market* in italics to imply the meeting of supply and demand for a particular good, say, shoes. Considering that shoes were handmade, the *market* was very large and provided great incentives to the producers to devise ways by which to enhance the productivity of their workers. The situation was exactly similar to the one that pertained in the pin factory that Smith (1776/1977, I, 1.17–18) posited in order to demonstrate the *law of the division of labor*, that is, how the enlargement of the market affords the possibility to the producers to increase productivity by assigning labor to the production of the constituent parts of a product and putting it together at the end. Is there any evidence that this is exactly what the shoe and other manufacturers practiced in ancient Athens? We submit that there is, because Xenophon (*Cyropaedia*, VII, 2.5) writing at about 370 BCE could not have written the following without the benefit of some factual observations:

> Now it is impossible that a single man working at a dozen crafts can do them all well; but in the great cities, owing to the wide demand for each particular thing, a single craft will suffice for a means of livelihood, and often enough even a single department of that; there are shoe-makers who will only make sandals for men and others only for women. Or

one artisan will get his living merely by stitching shoes, another by cutting them out, a third by shaping the upper leathers, and a fourth will do nothing but fit the parts together. Necessarily the man who spends all his time and trouble on the smallest task will do that task the best (Underlined by the authors). The arts of the household must follow the same law. If one and the same servant makes the bed, spreads the table, kneads the dough, and cooks the various dishes, the master must take things as they come, there is no help for it. But when there is work enough for one man to boil the pot, and another to roast the meat, and a third to stew the fish, and a fourth to fry it, while someone else must bake the bread, and not all of it either, for the loaves must be of different kinds, and it will be quite enough if the baker can serve up one kind to perfection--it is obvious, I think, that in this way a far higher standard of excellence will be attained in every branch of the work.

From this passage, it follows clearly that this procedure was most commonly applied by manufacturers in classical Athens to boost productivity and economic growth.[31]

Lastly, it is worth noting that the markets as geographical areas in Athens and Piraeus were segmented according to the dominant activities that were pursued in them. For example, consider the area widely known today as Kerameikos. Its name indicates that it was an area where pottery shops and artisans were concentrated and where one could find everything one wished to procure made out of clay. Other areas were populated by tanners, stonemasons, wood masons, etc. This segmentation served multiple purposes of efficiency, since distances were short but transportation was very difficult. In particular, price competition among producers of similar products increased and buyers visiting the areas could compare prices and qualities easily and without spending much time to search around for bargains.

5.2.2.3 Shipping

According to some estimates (Cohen 1992), the import of grain required 600 shiploads at 3,000 *Medimni* (120 tons) per shipload. Total trade value has been estimated to average at least 13.8 million drachmae, or 2,300 talents per year (Isager, Hansen 1975).

The above numbers of shiploads give a base for calculating the size of the Athenian merchant marine and the employment it generated. Even if

---

31 Referring to the above quotation, it should be noted that Figueira (2012, 683) states in no uncertain terms the following regarding the discovery of the *law of the division of labor*:

It appears that Adam Smith reached his crucial insight that the division of labour is determined by the extent of the market from reading Xenophon *Cyropaedia* 8.2.5–6.81 one of the very passages about which it is necessary to defend Xenophon against the criticisms of Finley.

one calculates two trips per year per ship, grain imports would require 300 ships. Some of the ships must have belonged to foreign ship owners. But since Athens was the major maritime state in the Eastern Mediterranean, it is not farfetched to surmise that the great majority of ships were Athenian. To the number of grain ships, we must add a number of ships used for all other kinds of trade, although of course most ships would be used to transport export goods on the outgoing voyage and transport grain on the incoming. Still, a range of 300–500 Athenian merchant marine ships seems reasonable. Assuming an average of 20 crew per ship, this would give an employment in 431 BCE of 6,000–10,000, or 6.5%–10.5% of the labor force.

To the above estimates, we must add all the boats used for close inshore fishing; local transport as for example to the island of Salamis, which belonged to Athens, and to the western coast of southern Euboeia, which lies only a few miles east of the northeastern coast of Attica; and the multitude of land-based activities for servicing the fleet such as shipyards, loading, unloading and transporting the goods, warehousing and even banking services. If we take the upper bound of the above-mentioned range as a reasonable estimate of the overall employment, shipping was the top employment sector of the economy and ascertains once again why, as we stressed earlier, the harbor of Piraeus served as a redistribution and entrepôt center for the Eastern Mediterranean much like Amsterdam in the 17th century. Piraeus remained the leading commercial center in the region even after the political eclipse of Athens, on account of the defeat by Macedonia in 322 BCE, and until the rise of another maritime republic, Rhodes, in the beginning of the 3rd century (Cohen 1992).[32]

5.2.2.4 Money and banking

As the economy of Athens in classical times transformed from an agricultural household production and consumption basis in the 5th century into one in which manufacturing and services contributed relatively large GDP shares in the 4th century, financial intermediation expanded.[33] So, when

---

32 Recall that Piraeus served also as the main naval basis for the large fleet of Athenian warships. Referring to the contribution that the activities for its servicing made to the economy, van Wees (2013, 13) stresses that:

> the public naval dockyards in Piraeus, with their hundreds of state-owned warships in constant need of maintenance, must have been the largest industrial enterprise in the country, as was true of the naval dockyards of early modern Europe.

Hence, if we allow in addition for the contribution from the large merchant marine fleet, there is no doubt that ship-related industrial activities constituted the foremost value-added sector of the Athenian economy.

33 Referring to the Athenian financial system in classical times, the eminent economist and economic historian Goldsmith (1987, 27–28) concludes that:

> Before the Peloponnesian War financial instruments were rare as virtually all transactions were settled by payment in coins. The volume of mortgages must have still been

Cohen (1992, 2008) revisited the evidence and brought his findings to the attention of the interested scholars, the only surprise that remained was how the supporters of the "primitivist–substantivist hypothesis" could have erred so badly because banking had developed to such an extent by the 4th century that it was utterly impossible to explain the need for such versatile banking services in a household-based agrarian society.[34]

Fortunately, it is not necessary to resort to an elaborate search in the available original literature to highlight the striking range of functions that banks performed in classical times in Athens. Cohen (1992) has done all the work for us and he has done it in an exhaustive and unsurpassed manner. From this source, we learn readily and unequivocally that the Athenian banks:

- Exchanged coins and foreign currencies.
- Accepted deposits and carried out payments on behalf of their customers.
- Extended loans to various business operations, including bottomry loans in shipping and even financing of consumer credit.[35]
- Provided sureties, negotiated claims, and offered guarantees and personal advice to important customers.
- Accepted documents and valuables for safekeeping but they did not act in the capacity of pawnbrokers, and
- Facilitated export–import activities by settling payments among importers from and exporters to merchants abroad.

If the above orthodox banking activities by contemporary standards are not sufficient to raise eyebrows regarding the highly sophisticated level in which they operated, it should be certainly very surprising that the Athenian *trapezai* (banks) served their customers even in much more astonishingly modern ways. For example, they helped them hide their wealth from the tax

---

very small as land had become alienable only around the middle of the fifth century BCE, but there probably were substantial debts of tenants to landlords and some consumer debts. As the first banks apparently began to operate only in the 430s B.C., the amounts of bank deposits and loans must have been negligible. Trade credit seems to have been little used. The only financial instrument of importance was the bottomry loan...

It is clear that the period to which he refers is before 430 BCE. Yet, Ingham (2004, 101) has interpreted this conclusion to imply that the financial structure and the financial instruments remained stagnant throughout, even though the evidence discussed by Cohen (1990, 1992, 2008), Amemiya (2007) and several others erudite scholars of the Athenian economy and society ascertains beyond doubt that the extension of Goldsmith's assessment to the 4th century, if not misplaced, at least would be erroneous.

34 Drawing on the Popperian logic of scientific epistemology, the voluminous evidence regarding the development of banking in Athens in the 4th century BCE stands in direct contradiction to the "primitivist-substantivist hypothesis." So, one wonders how else this hypothesis may be falsified in order for it to escape from the charge of being utterly pseudoscientific.

35 Demosthenes (*For Phormio*, 44) recognizes that the most important prerequisite for performing successful banking activities is credit.

authorities, their creditors and in general, the eyes of their envious compatriots. To corroborate this claim, here is a quotation from Cohen (1992, 8):

> Demosthenes' father, who is known to have dealt extensively with Athenian banks, concealed much of his property throughout his lifetime, apparently completely avoiding taxes, and possibly escaping liability for his father-in-law's debts.... Even important foreigners came to Athens to use the *trapeza* to conceal funds from overseas rulers: an entire surviving court speech (Isocrates, *Trapezicus*, 17) deals with the efforts of Sopaios, a power at the Pontic court, to hide vast sums through Pasion's bank.

However, our interest in the Athenian banks is mainly for their role in the process of credit creation, to which we shall return in Chapter 6.

5.2.2.5 Construction

In Section 5.1.2, we presented a compact list of the large and small construction projects that Athens financed during the periods of peace in the 5th and 4th centuries. The institutional setup by which the state implemented these projects has been subjected to intense scholarly scrutiny and the intricacies involved can be glimpsed by looking, for example, at the inquiry and the literature cited in Schaps (1996). But for our purposes, here it suffices to note that irrespective of the scale of the projects and the mode that was employed to carry out their construction, maintenance and repairing, the only officials that the state appointed to supervise these activities are the relevant ones mentioned in Table 5.1, Column 3.

From time to time, one comes across views asserting, for example, that the road network was very poor or nonexistent. Relatively speaking, the opposite is true. Excavations in the area of *Mesogaia* have brought to light a dense and high-quality road network by the technical standards of that time, well-marked and well-signposted, where not only people but also wagons could move easily.[36] The existence of good road networks has also been confirmed by excavations in locations other than in Athens, such as the island of Crete and the state of Miletus (Asia Minor).

In contrast to the plentiful evidence regarding the large scale and the luxurious quality of building material and workmanship of public buildings, our knowledge about the houses in which Athenians lived at the time is very scanty. The following excerpt from Demosthenes (*Against Aristocrates*, 207) gives us an idea about the humbleness of the houses of the average Athenian family:

> Here is the proof: if any of you know the sort of house that Themistocles or Miltiades or any of those distinguished men of old lived in, you

---

36 The discovery more recently of a new section of this road can be seen in the picture, which is shown in the site www.tovima.gr/2008/11/25/culture/lewforos-mesogeiwn/.

may observe that it is no grander than the common run of houses. On the other hand, both the structure and the equipment of their Public buildings were on such a scale and of such quality that no opportunity of surpassing them was left to coming generations. Witness those gate-houses, docks, porticoes, the great harbor, and all the edifices with which you see our city adorned.

Because of insurmountable technical difficulties, excavations in various areas of Athens have failed to reveal what might be considered as an average house. Several decades ago, Graham (1974, 51) assessed the evidence and, with the exception of some limited indications about the size, shape, layout and quality of the more luxurious houses, he found very little that could be said with any degree of certainty about the average house. But further digging since then has enabled Bresson (2007, 77) to report that most Athenian houses had a bath with a small bathtub with a seat, while those citizens whose houses did not have this amenity, from the 4th century on could use the public baths, where for a small fee, they could take a comfortable bath with hot water.[37]

The bulk of current scholarship focuses on the financing, the construction technology and materials, and the project management that pertained to the implementation of public works. From this literature, the aspect that interests us here is the market for construction workers. In the period before the Periclean era, Athens executed its building programs by outsourcing the work to contractors under the supervision of dedicated state authorities. During the period of Pericles, this regime changed and the state hired directly the required skilled and unskilled workers and paid them either by the day or by the piece of work done. However, after Pericles, the old regime returned again gradually and public building projects were assigned mainly to private contractors. The reasons for these shifts have become the subject of considerable research. Some scholars argue that they had to do with long cycles in the structure of the labor force, whereas others like Schaps (1996, 79–80) attribute them to shifts in the balance of power at the helms of the government. From the point of view of economic analysis, their implications for the economy are much different. However, irrespective of which is nearer to the truth, common to both is the realization that the state through its public works influenced decisively the wage rate and the level of employment, and most likely not exclusively in its segments of the building trades. For then, wage rates and employment would vary in accordance with the variations in the level of the programs of public works and, depending on

---

37 Therefore, well before the famous Baths of Rome, public baths existed in Athens and in many other Greek city-states. Bresson (2007, 77) praises the system of personal hygiene of the Greeks to the point of arguing that the ordinary citizen of an ordinary Greek city would be able to give hygiene and cleaning courses to the King Louis IV of France and his courtyard (17th century AD).

their nature, they would affect positively (roads) or adversely (temples) private investment, productivity and growth in the economy.

5.2.2.6 Paideia[38]

The term *paideia* has lost its meaning even in Modern Greek. Nowadays, it is used to imply *education*, that is, a process of transferring to youth existing knowledge in various fields and through discipline of thought rendering them capable to face the challenges and take advantage of the opportunities that emerge continuously in social environments that become ever more knowledge intensive. In ancient Athens, over and above education, *paideia* comprised *agoge*, which consisted of a parallel process of building into the character of youth the required *ethos* that would enable them to become worthy of themselves and of their fellow citizens. We consider this difference very important because democracy at the time functioned as a collective of citizens, who were characterized by *individual responsibility* for their decisions and actions, that is, a quality that seems to have disappeared in modern-day representative democracies.

Young male Athenians 18–19 years of age went through the institution of *ephebeia* (Aristotle, *Athenian Constitution*, 42.1–5). This was a two-year, state-funded and organized program, instituted at least in the 4th century BCE, which focused on the military training of *epheboi* and time wise, it coincided with their two-year mandatory military service. They were trained in the usage of weapons and in military tactics, in hunting, developing self-reliance, controlling aggression, hiding, and in general becoming efficient in the arts of surviving under extreme conditions. The idea behind *ephebeia* was that if the state was ever threatened, its men would have the necessary skills and the character to defend it. And, since according to Aristotle (*Athenian Constitution*, 53.4), all eligible citizens of ages 18 to 59 might become *hoplites*, *as* listed by age group on permanent rosters displayed in the *agora* (Christ 2006, 52), an *ephebos* might be drafted into the ranks of *hoplites* at any time.

After the age of 14, boys had the option of attending secondary schooling, which included subjects such as natural sciences (biology and chemistry), rhetoric (the art of speaking or writing effectively), geometry, astronomy and meteorology. At this secondary stage, *paideia* was totally private in the sense that it depended on the choice of boys to expand their knowledge horizons and the ability of their parents to pay for the services of private tutors in the various subjects. Hence, its scale must have been limited to the well-to-do Athenian families, both in terms of wealth and culture.

The stage of primary or elementary *paideia* extended from the 7th to the 14th year of age. During these years, *grammatistai* (teachers that taught

---

38 An excellent source of information and analysis for understanding the structure and the functioning of the Athenian system of *paideia* is Pritchard (2003).

courses related to reading, writing and mathematics) introduced their students to the great poets, such as Homer and Hesiod; *kitharistai* (guitarists) taught them how to play the seven-string lyre and sing the works of lyric poets; and *paidotribai* were responsible for the physical development of the boys. They instructed them in wrestling, *pankration*, boxing, running, throwing the disc, jumping and various other exercises in the *palaistra.*[39] Some other courses such as literature, music and painting were added, but according to Aristotle (*Politics*, VIII, 8.3.1), this was not always the case.

Paideia in this stage was also voluntary. Attending was construed to imply that it was the obligation of parents to send their sons to schools. In reality, though boys from poor families either did not attend or dropped out early. Xenophon (*Constitution of the Lacedaemonians*, 3) thought that this was an unsatisfactory arrangement, because wealthy families could hire the services of *eponymous* private tutors, known as *Pedagogues*, who gave to their male children a *paideia* superior to that offered by publicly hired tutors. This critique brings us to an issue which, despite intensive research efforts, remains clouded in uncertainty. It concerns the degree of involvement of the Athenian state in the process of *paideia* at this primary stage.

Golden (2003, 19), Dobson (1963, 31) and others argue that Athenian families gave their sons the best education they could afford. Interpreted literally, this argument suggests that *paideia* in the main formative years of boys was private and that the role of the state, if any, was insignificant. However, on the other hand, some other scholars have found evidence corroborating that the state was significantly involved. For example, Beaumont (2013, 135) notes that:

> The state played no part in the provision of formal schooling with the result that all lessons were taught by teachers engaged and remunerated on a private basis and only from the mid-5th century the state intervened in the case of i) boys whose fathers died in a battle, fighting for the city ii) sons of poor unproprietied families, iii) *thetes*.

From this quotation follows that as it was the case with the provision of many other services of public interest, the state outsourced *paideia* from private tutors on behalf of the boys that came from three large low-income social classes. Hence, the state financed *paideia* in the primary stage as a "public good" of paramount importance, because presumably they believed that it was accompanied by positive externalities that exceeded significantly the public expenditures involved.

But the involvement of the state went well beyond this care. For, as explained in Bitros, Karayiannis (2011), the state showed keen interest for *paideia* by monitoring very closely the operation of private schools through

---

39 *Pankration* was a mixed martial art, developed in Sparta. *Palaistra* was the place where athletes practiced these sports.

the regulatory arrangements detailed in the following quotation from Aeschines (*Against Timarchus*, 8–11):

> Now it is my desire, in addressing you on this occasion, to follow in my speech the same order which the lawgiver followed in his laws. For you shall hear first a review of the laws that have been laid down to govern the orderly conduct of your children, then the laws concerning the lads, and next those concerning the other ages in succession, including not only private citizens, but the public men as well.
>
> In the first place, consider the case of the teachers. Although the very livelihood of these men, to whom we necessarily entrust our own children, depends on their good character, while the opposite conduct on their part would mean poverty, yet it is plain that the lawgiver distrusts them; for he expressly prescribes, first, at what time of day the free-born boy is to go to the school-room; next, how many other boys may go there with him, and when he is to go home.
>
> He forbids the teacher to open the schoolroom, or the gymnastic trainer the wrestling school, before sunrise, and he commands them to close the doors before sunset; for he is exceeding suspicious of their being alone with a boy, or in the dark with him. He prescribes what children are to be admitted as, pupils, and their age at admission. He provides for a public official who shall superintend them, and for the oversight of slave-attendants of schoolboys. He regulates the festivals of the Muses in the schoolrooms, and of Hermes in the wrestling-schools. Finally, he regulates the companionships that the boys may form at school, and their cyclic dances.

In conclusion, during classical times: (a) the state strived to ensure a minimum level of primary *paideia* for all its willing free-born male citizens and *metics* who could not afford one privately, and (b) under the influence of certain other philosophers called Sophists and Isocrates (*Areopagiticus*, 24, 44), who stressed that the labor of free citizens must be regarded an honorable activity, young Athenians were increasingly instructed to be industrious because *labor is the source of private property and accumulation of wealth.*[40]

---

40 Lest it is thought that the view about "vulgar occupations" was always the dominant tradition among Athenians, we hasten to add the following passage from Hesiod (1914, 300–315):

> ...Both gods and men are angry with a man who lives idle, for in nature he is like the stingless drones who waste the labor of the bees, eating without working; but let it be your care to order your work properly, that in the right season your barns may be full of victual. Through work men grow rich in flocks and substance, and working they are much better loved by the immortals. Work is no disgrace: it is idleness which is a disgrace. But if you work, the idle will soon envy you as you grow rich, for fame and renown attend on wealth.

Thus, over time, the majority of citizens became accustomed not to distinguish between noble and menial undertakings and the shift in *paideia* contributed a lot to the turning of Athenians from "doing" in the 5th to "making" in the 4th century that we mentioned earlier in Section 5.2.2.2. For further corroboration of these changes, we refer to the assurance by Pausanias (*Attica*, 24.3) that Athenians were the first Greeks who worshiped the goddess of "industrious Athena" (*Athena Ergane*).

5.2.2.7 Health care

In Athens and in other Greek states, health care services were provided by a parallel three-tier system. In the first tier, doctors offered their services privately and expected to be paid by their patients. The majority of doctors worked on this basis. In the second tier, doctors offered medical treatment to individual patients, but they were remunerated by the local communities per annum. The availability of medical services along this tier was considered a fundamental obligation of the state and the citizens viewed it as an acquired right.

The *demes* outsourced the services of doctors on the condition that the latter would be available on demand by potential patients. We know of this arrangement from Aristophanes' (*Acharnians*, 1027–1032) reference to Dikaiopoles, who prompts a poor and blind farmer to visit the famous surgeon Pittalos. The annual wage of public doctors in classical times was around 500 drachmae. But in the following centuries, their pay increased considerably, a famous example being the Asklepiades from Perge who in the 2nd century BCE received 1,000 drachmae from Seleucea, a city-state in Asia Minor. In order to be selected for public service, a doctor had to convince the citizens of the community of his talents and his exceptional abilities. However, this did not imply that once selected the doctor would be also the most qualified or better than the private doctors.[41]

The third tier comprised the so-called *asclepieia*. These were large medical centers surrounded by a vast assortment of facilities, like temples, baths, stadiums, gymnasiums, libraries, theaters, etc., which were thought to be

---

Given that Hesiod wrote around 750 BCE, we are nearly certain that a culture favoring work had started to form well before the 5th century and that this tradition survived and carried on to a large extent in classical times.

41 According to Plato, the candidate doctors for public service were expected to support their candidature in the best possible way. Socrates, having pointed out the pitfalls that loomed in the subjectivity of the selection process, argued that even a lawyer with suitable speech could be selected in the post of a public doctor (Plato, *Gorgias*, 456b). In addition, public doctors had to be present at public events like athletic contests so that they could immediately treat athletes in cases of accidents, and special duties during periods of military training and exercises. Doctors, both public and private, were organized in associations centered on the cult of Asklepios.

essential to the healing process. The *asclepieia* were owned and operated either by a single state or jointly by several states. Scattered throughout the ancient world operated over 300 such centers, the largest and most famous being those of Trikkala, Athens, Corinth, Epidaurus, Pergamon and the one on the island of Kos. As documented by Christopoulou-Aletra, Togia, Varlam (2009), the *asclepieia* were the first ever hospitals in the world, which offered their services in the wider Greek region.

5.2.2.8 Other public services

In addition to the cases already mentioned about the granting of mining rights by the *board of poletai* and the assignment of construction contracts in the domain of public works, the state outsourced from the private sector a wide variety of public services. Some were outsourced because the responsible state authorities perceived that they could be performed more efficiently by the private sector; some others were outsourced to reduce the uncertainty that was associated with regard to the expected outcomes; and still some others were outsourced to increase transparency and reduce the degree of corruption that accompanies as a rule noncompetitive state-managed production technologies. Thus, here we shall complete our brief inquiry into the structure and evolution of the Athenian economy, with the following three representative examples of such public services.

5.2.2.8.1 LITURGIES

Earlier, we indicated that under this institution, well-to-do citizens undertook to manage and finance from their own wealth the production of various public services. According to Lyttkens (1994, 74–76), *liturgies* were introduced at the beginning of the 5th century; the Athenians who got involved considered it a duty and an honor to perform these tasks.[42] The most common public services were the *trierarchy* and numerous *religious* and *cultural festivals.*

- *Trierarchy*: This was a military liturgy and covered the cost for the commissioning and management of a *trireme* warship for one year. Probably, it was introduced for the first time in 494 BCE in the island of Samos and some time before or shortly after the second phase of the Persian Wars (480/479 BCE), it was adopted also by Athens (Christ 2006, 156). Several authors consider that apart from altruism and *philopatry* (love for the motherland), the main motivation for a rich/aristocrat

---

42 *Liturgies* were practiced also in the rest of the Greek world, and according to Gabrielsen (2013, 343), their existence is also verified for the city-states of Mytilene, Siphnos (in the Aegean islands), Priene and Teos (in Asia Minor).

Athenian to undertake a *trierarchy* was political benefits and prestige, as well as the favor of the municipality toward him.

*   *Festivals*: Davies (1967) is the best source for a very detailed list of the various *liturgies* that were undertaken annually in this category. After counting meticulously their number, on page 40 he concludes that:

> ...the sum-total of annual liturgical appointments appears to have been over 97 at the time of Demosthenes XX (Authors' note: Speech *Against Leptines*), rising to over 118 in a Panathenaic year.

*   *Dithyrambic choruses and dramatic and comedy plays*: Most of the annual festivals were religious. But a good number of them served also cultural purposes. Among the latter, 20 were devoted to contests among Dithyrambic choruses; three for writing and staging dramatic plays; and in various periods up to as many as five for presenting comedies. The Athenians who financed these *liturgies* were called *choregoi* and the function of covering the costs involved *choregia*.

Over the decades from the 5th to the 4th century, the range of public services expanded, and the cost became too burdensome to bear even for rich citizens. In particular, to make sure that there would arise no revenue shortfalls in the difficult financial circumstances that the state confronted in 378/377 BCE, Athens classified rich citizens into *symmories* (groups) (Kyriazis 2009, 114). The few that topped each group in wealth were expected to furnish the taxes that were apportioned to their group from their own resources and then recoup the amount they paid from the other citizens in their group. But the reform was not successful because, as documented by Rhodes (1980, 411), it took tax authorities many years to collect the taxes that were due to the state by the groups.

5.2.2.8.2 COLLECTION OF CUSTOM DUTIES

This example of public service has to do with the collection of a harbor duty on the value of imports and exports, which was called *pentekoste* and equaled "the fiftieth part" of the merchandise's value or 2%. The collection was farmed out for a year to the so-called *pentekostologoi*, who had offered in the auctioning process the highest bid. What is important to note from a modern standpoint is that the highest bidders were usually a consortium of private individuals, which is an indication of the advanced nature of the legal procedures and property rights in Athens. Without the protections offered by this institutional framework, the organization of consortiums for sharing the risks involved would have been impossible. But it is also very interesting to learn from Andocides (*On the Mysteries*, 1.133–138) how those who participated in the auctioning process colluded so as to obtain the contract for collecting the duty by paying to the state the lowest possible advance. On the other hand, as argued by Lyttkens (1994, 85), the system of farming out the collection had two advantages. That is, first, it guaranteed the amount of the specific revenue for the state and, second, it minimized transaction costs, since by not knowing in advance how much revenue they would collect within the given year, those who bid undertook high risks.

5.2.2.8.3 CLEANING OF THE STREETS

According to Ault (2007, 263), Athens ensured the cleanliness of the streets by running open tenders among private contractors. An example of service in this category was the one delivered by the so-called *koprologoi,* who collected garbage and all kinds of animal feces found in the streets throughout the twin cities of Athens-Piraeus and transformed them into fertilizer for sale.[43] Aristotle (*Athenian Constitution*, 50) and the inscriptions *IG* XII 5, 107 and *IG* XII describe the provision of this service in Athens while it has been recorded also for smaller towns, such as in the islands of Paros and Thassos.

5.2.3 Distribution of goods and services

The supply and demand for goods and services met in the marketplace or *agora*. Prices cleared the market. In cases of excess demand or inadequate supply, prices increased and equilibrium was restored. But this function was only one part of the adjustment process because, in due course, the changes in prices set in motion a mechanism through which the number of firms in the market converged to equilibrium. In particular, when, say, the supply of a commodity increased while its demand remained at the same level, prices decreased and this in turn put pressure on the profits of the firms in the market. So, those of them, which experienced losses, had every reason to move to other more profitable employments. Now, any present-day economist trained on Samuelson's (1973) introduction to the principles of economic analysis would find it unbelievable that Xenophon (*Ways and Means*, IV) expressed the aforementioned dynamics of market adjustment in the following succinct manner:

> An increase in the number of coppersmiths, for example, produces a fall in the price of copper work, and the coppersmiths retire from business. The same thing happens in the iron trade. Again, when corn and wine are abundant, the crops are cheap, and the profit derived from growing them disappears, so that many give up farming and set up as merchants or shopkeepers or moneylenders.

---

43 In all probability, this was the first ever recorded recycling policy from an environmental perspective.

By reference to our current state of knowledge, the only emphasis missing is the time which might be required for shifting from the so-called market period, within which prices adjust to allocate existing quantities, to the long run, which entails a period sufficiently long to permit the reallocation of productive factors from the present to other uses as firms move in or out of the market under consideration, depending on their profit expectations.

Thinking about this text, Lianos (2014, 44) has offered two slightly different interpretations. The first is that it should not be taken literally, because farmers cannot be expected to move in and out of farming that easily, and particularly when they are in financial distress; and the second is that it may be construed to imply that markets enhanced occupational mobility by stimulating the search process for higher returns. We believe that both these interpretations are not inconsistent with our claim that Xenophon observed a truly dynamic market economy which through the price mechanism allocated labor and capital to their optimal uses in response to the preferences that the consumers revealed in the markets.[44] Hence, to have from a 4th century BCE observer, this piece of solid testimony regarding the properties of market-based allocation of resources is exceedingly reassuring about the structure of the economy that prevailed in ancient Athens at the time.[45]

Equally remarkable is also that according to Loomis (1998, 248–249, 253–254), the wage rate was determined mainly through the supply and demand mechanism, which implies that there existed a well-functioning labor market. Moreover, as we learn from Xenophon (*Cyropaedia*, IV, 5.42), in the markets buyers and sellers were coming closer and through the function of

---

44 This structure of the economy was not exclusive to Athens. Even though not as much developed, market economies in the prototype of Athens functioned in all 316 (Figueira 1998, 52) allied states, and indeed irrespective of whether they were ruled by democratic or oligarchic regimes. For example, Economou, Kyriazis (2019b) document that the Ptolemaic Kingdom of Egypt in the so-called Hellenistic period adopted many of the fundamental institutions of free market economies.

45 Referring one more time to Figueira (2012, 681–684), here is how he characterizes the model of the economy that Xenophon observed and described in the above quotation:

> This passage then becomes an important testimony on fourth-century entrepreneurial initiative, in which choices were governed by differential returns. These observations thus also reflect perceptions of autonomy and self-equilibration ... Therefore, while I am uncomfortable hypothesizing Xenophon as the *discoverer* of the 'economy' in a Polanyian spirit, we may be warranted in viewing him as the earliest extant management consultant or managerial *guru*, as the cliché would have them ... The ancient Adam Smith seems out of Xenophon's reach, but the ancient Peter Drucker might just work.

> We, instead, read this particular passage more as a paragraph out of Paul Samuelson's *Foundations of Economics Analysis* rather than Peter Drucker's *The Concept of the Corporation*.

retail merchants the cost of transactions decreased significantly and this enhanced the efficiency of markets.[46]

5.2.4 Export–import trade

Export–import activities constituted a vibrant business undertaking in Athens. Not only citizens but also *metics* established and directed wholesale enterprises in exporting Athenian products and importing grain and other commodities in which Athens was deficient in one period or another. The interest of the state in these activities was active and passive. Active trade policies were directed mostly in the importation primarily of corn, barley, wheat and charcoal, at sufficient quantities to cover the domestic demand at fair prices, but without risking shortages, and secondarily in the importation of construction materials like timber, iron and bronze. However, contrary to the presumptions maintained by certain economic historians and in the light of the evidence discussed by Bresson (2016b) and Woolmer (2016), the emphasis on grain imports should not be misconstrued to imply that the state did not adopt other policies that rendered Athens attractive to foreign traders by lowering transactions costs and expanding markets. While it is true that the focus of active trade policies was on the markets for grains and

46 Regarding the issue of state intervention in the markets and the adoption of direct price controls, we find three strands of interpretations in the literature. On the one extreme stands, Bresson (2016a, 305) who asserts that:

> ...the city did not limit itself to a passive role in matters of trade. Not only was it capable of intervening directly in the negotiation of prices in the *emporion*, but it could also act as a purchaser, thus becoming itself an actor in the market. In this way, the city had an influence on prices. Naturally, this was chiefly part of a policy of supplying the domestic market, but the city also supervised its exports, which were necessary for the life of the city as a whole. Finally, it did not hesitate to intervene directly in trade by constituting funds for this purpose, especially regarding grain.

At the other extreme, we find Amemiya (2007, 68) who states that:

> There was no price control in products other than grain and grain products.

And in between, there is the position taken by Migeotte (2009, 148–149) who, after assessing the available epigraphical and literary evidence, concludes that:

> ...It seems that, by a vote in the *Assembly* or even on the authority of the *agoranomoi*, cities had the power to cap prices, at least some of them, or even to fix maximum prices when circumstances demanded.

Drawing on the latter view, we surmise that, while the state with various officers monitored the quality and the weight of the goods sold, with the exception of grain and grain products in abnormal circumstances, direct price controls were applied rarely and for short periods, competition reigned throughout the markets of the economy, and the incentives of sellers to practice opportunism were limited, thus contributing further to the efficiency of the competitive process.

construction materials, through a wide range of passive trade-facilitating policies in the form of institutional and functional arrangements, Athens left it to the money and all other goods and services markets to bring about a balance in the trade account.

The grain policy can be analyzed from four mostly complementary perspectives. The first emphasizes the initiatives of Athens at the foreign policy level to secure the availability of adequate supplies of grains. On this, perhaps the most informative account comes to us through the following excerpts from Demosthenes (*Against Leptines*, 32–35):

> See what this amounts to. He exacts a toll of one-thirtieth from exporters of corn from his country. Now from the Bosporus there come to Athens about four hundred thousand bushels; the figures can be checked by the books of the grain commissioners. So for each three hundred thousand bushels he makes us a present of ten thousand bushels, and for the remaining hundred thousand a present of roughly three thousand. Now, so little danger is there of his depriving our state of this gift, that he has opened another depot at Theudosia, which our merchants say is not at all inferior to the Bosporus, and there, too, he has granted us the same exemption. I omit much that might be said about the other benefits conferred upon you by this prince and also by his ancestors, but the year before last, when there was a universal shortage of grain, he not only sent enough for your needs, but such a quantity in addition that Callisthenes had a surplus of fifteen talents of silver to dispose of. What, then, men of Athens, do you expect of this man, who has proved himself such a friend to you, if he learns that you have deprived him by law of his immunity, and have made it illegal to bestow it hereafter, even if you change your minds? Are you not aware that this same law, if ratified, will take away the immunity, not only from Leucon, but from those of you who import corn from his country? For surely no one dreams that he will tolerate the cancelling of your gifts to him, and let his own gifts to you stand good. So to the many disadvantages that this law will obviously entail upon you, may be added the immediate loss of part of your resources. In view of this, are you still considering whether you ought to erase it from the statute-book? Have you not made up your minds long ago? Take and read them the decrees touching Leucon.

Clearly, in order to secure the provision of the necessary quantities of grains, Athens employed all levers of its power: *Friendship*, accompanied of course with the granting of various economic and political privileges; *Intimidation*, based on the threat of blacklisting suppliers altogether and thus excluding their products from the Athenian market; *Coercion*, by blockading in this case the passage through the Bosporus straits; and not least, depending on the circumstances, *Declaration of war* as an initiative of last resort.

Employing taxes and other administrative measures to encourage, and if not to compel, importers to bring into Athens adequate supplies of grain at affordable prices for the consumers, was the second perspective. Fawcett (2016, 189) looked recently into this aspect of the Athenian grain policy in the framework of an inquiry into the applications of *eisphora* tax and offers the following summary:

> ...There was general legislation to ensure imports of grain. It was forbidden to purchase more than a certain amount of grain at a time (Lysias, *Against the corn dealers,* 6). It was a capital offense for persons resident in Athens to ship grain to harbors other than the Piraeus (Demosthenes, *Against Phormio,* 37; Demosthenes, *Against Lacritus,* 50; *Lycurgus, Against Leocrates,* I. 27). Any grain ship touching in at a harbor of the Piraeus was required to unload at least two-thirds of its cargo, and might reexport a maximum of one-third (Aristotle, *Athenian Constitution,* 51.4). It was also forbidden for persons resident in Athens to advance a maritime loan unless the ship under contract conveyed grain to Piraeus (Demosthenes, *Against Dionysodorus,* 6, 11). Although these provisions regulated import of grain, the trade itself was almost entirely in the hands of private shipowners, merchants, and retailers, who sold to individuals mainly at their own discretion. The Grain-Tax Law, however, mandated more direct intervention in the transport, storage, handling, and sale at Athens. Moreover, as we have seen, taxes were specifically used to encourage the import of grain so that it could be available to the Athenian people at an affordable price...

The third perspective is the one adopted by Figueira (1986). It follows the contemporary forensic institutional setup for resolving market disputes through the *Courts* where one or more plaintiffs, but usually the government, accuses a dominant firm of stifling competition and cornering the market for its advantage. The historical context of the case originates in a speech in front of the court by Lysias (*Against the Corn Dealers*) and it has to do with the presumed collusive practices among the domestic sellers of corn, called *sitopolai* (wheat sellers) and the intervention by the state as represented by the officers in charge, called *sitophylakes* (guardians of the wheat). Figueira finds that the collusion among *sitopolai* had been instigated by the *sitophylakes,* who instrumented the cessation of the competitive process among *sitopolai,* in an effort by the *sitophylakes* to safeguard the interests of consumers because of the particular circumstances that prevailed at the time in the market for grains. In other words, the *sitophylakes* acted as present-day competition authorities, which are empowered by law to intervene so as to guide the competitive process in the long-run interest of the consumers because certainly it would not be in the interest of the Athenian consumers if, by the intervention of *sitophylakes,* grain shortages from temporary became permanent.

Finally, the last perspective regarding the analysis of the Athenian grain policy is based on moral suasion and appeals to one's civil duties. To be sure, in a market like that of grains, in which the supply chain even today is subject to many natural uncertainties like rain, sea piracy, rough seas, etc., suppliers have wide margins to be more or less risk averse. On the average, the dominant motive under which they operate is "economic survival first." Patriotism, altruism and all other manifestations of social success and recognition are of secondary order. This was known very well to the authorities in Athens. Yet, even though policy makers operated on the dictum "don't trust anybody," they tried by all means to entice the cooperation of grain dealers by appealing to their allegiance toward Athens as well as to their quest for social fame and recognition. For this reason, as Lysias (*Against Andocides*, 49) informs us, those who were involved in these activities were considered as offering a valuable service to the city and, according to Engen (2010), the Athenians recognized that by assuming high risks grain importers deserved honors and their riches were justified.

Aside from grains, Athens imported foodstuffs such as fish, although a substantial quantity may have been fished by Athenian ships and boats, timber, luxury items like ivory, slaves etc. Timber was imported mainly for the warships, the merchant marine and the housing industries. It came from Macedon, since Attica had lost a great part of its forests, in part because of the vast shipbuilding program after Themistocles Naval Law and during the Peloponnesian War. Along with timber, imported construction material included pitch, hemp and flax, as well as iron and bronze. On the export side, the list comprised olive oil, Hymettus honey, a little wine from the agricultural sector, and primarily handicraft and "industrial" products like pottery, furniture, silver plate, artworks such as marble and bronze statues, iron and bronze domestic utensils, arms and jewelry.

Owing to the high grain imports, the trade account must have shown a deficit for Athens. On the other hand, the balance of services from banking, warehousing facilities in Piraeus, city accommodation to foreign merchants, etc. must have shown a surplus, thus narrowing but still leaving a deficit in the total balance of goods and services, which was covered by exports of bullion.[47] This conclusion is corroborated by both archaeological evidence and ancient sources, since vast quantities of Athenian silver drachma have been found in Thrace, the Bosporus, Asia Minor, Syria, Egypt and Italy (Isager, Hansen 1975) and Xenophon (*Ways and Means*, III, 2) reports that Athens attracted many merchants from abroad because they could obtain payment for their goods in sound coins.

---

47 Even though we have no evidence that cross-border barter trade took place to any extent, we believe that there may have been cases where a foreign exporter of, say, grain was paid not in coins or bullion but in goods.

5.3 Summary

Over the decades from the 5th to the 4th century, Athens made significant strides toward turning from an agrarian economy toward one based on mining, handicraft and manufacturing, and services. This trend was established under the joint effect of the discovery of the silver mines in Laurion, the need to defend against foreign aggressors, and the constant pressure for exports to finance the vast quantities of grains that were necessary to feed the Athenian population. On the way to this transformation, citizens' values and attitudes became friendly to entrepreneurship, and the accumulation of wealth through business activities came to be regarded as an exemplary sign of social success and recognition. As a result, the Athenian economy particularly in the 4th century BCE mixed robust features of a true market economy with some features more characteristic from its archaic past.

The great achievements of Athens in classical times have been associated by many authors with the invention of democracy, which permitted decision-making after due consideration of all alternatives on any one issue by a large body of citizens in a unique setting of self-government. We think that it was much more than this. For, aside of democracy, Athenians by trial and error discovered the principles of how a system of "government by the people for the people"[48] could become administratively effective without undue waste of resources and paralyzing miscommunications. That is, the equivalent of modern-day corporate governance in multinational companies that are able to manage geographically dispersed and highly diversified lines of products on a global scale. The Athenians empowered the *Boule* to act as a contemporary *Board of Directors* and in cooperation with the shareholders-citizens in the *Assembly* they laid down the rules of governance that every state agency and every official had to follow; they monitored their actions by personalizing responsibility and demanding full accountability; they insisted on short term of service of one year for most officials, and more only for few who served from *Great Panathenaia* to *Great Panathenaia*; with the exception of a few officials, who were chosen by vote for their experience and skills, all others were selected by lot; and they could be at the same time very punitive against corrupt and very graceful for meritorious civil servants and officials.[49]

---

48 As the U.S. President Abraham Lincoln declared in his famous *Gettysburg Address*, on November 19, 1863, four and a half months after the Union Armies defeated those of the Confederacy at the Battle of Gettysburg.

49 When referring to the glorious period 460–430 BCE, one comes across a view in the literature according to which Athens was under the "rule of one man," that is, Pericles. His long stay in power stands indeed in a sharp contradiction to these principles. However, Pericles, as is the case of the long serving heads of multinational giant corporations, was elected again and again by the Athenian citizens as the sole stakeholders of their state. Therefore, his case may be thought of as a judicious exception that strengthened the validity of the rule. For more on this issue, see Lyttkens, Gerding (2015).

As is the case in most democracies today, the state provided a wide range of services either directly, using its own facilities and personnel, or indirectly, by outsourcing them from the private sector. The civil service, the defense, the *Courts*, the police and an extensive body of officers with supervisory and regulatory responsibilities offered services as state servants. By contrast, services like the construction of various public works, *paideia*, health and other like the collection of custom duties and the cleaning of streets were allocated to private enterprises that participated successfully in the auctioning of the associated contracts. As such, the provision of public services could be characterized as a Public-Private-Partnership, the so-called 3P, if we wish to make use of a modern definition. However, at the same time, a word of caution is necessary, because by having abstracted from the data their historical context for reasons of brevity, the Athenian system of public services may have appeared in our presentation more robust than it was. Not all public services were provided at any one time and when offered their extent and quality cannot be ascertained with any certainty.

Of all public services instrumental for the orderly functioning of the society and the economy were the *Courts* which ensured the quick and least cost adjudication of penal, civil and commercial disputes. Being centuries ahead of their times, Athenians had concluded that personal freedoms are intimately linked to property rights, so all institutions had been endowed with a bias toward upholding individual contracts.[50] And what is more, in order to maintain a balance between the creative individualistic impulses of economic agents and the public interest, the Athenian authorities made certain that court-confirmed trespassing of the laws was enforced with the utmost consistency. For, since the contemporary terms of "collective responsibility" were unknown, every citizen, every *metic* and every slave, all were individually responsible for their actions and all knew in advance the legal and social consequences that befell to those condemned.

In our view, Democracy took roots and flourished in Athens during classical times because it allowed its citizens to shape the political framework within which they could pursue freely but orderly their economic activities. The private sector of the economy that we presented in this chapter did not emerge all at once. It morphed into a market economy gradually from the 5th to the 4th century as the needs transformed in the minds of the individuals into opportunities for profit, and those alert and risk prone among them managed successfully to take advantage. For a forceful example to this effect, recall the case of Andocides from the excerpt we cited on page.... we are informed that he paid to the state 36 talents and he received the contract

---

50 Such was the respect for individual contracts that, in profound contrast with what is happening in contemporary representative democracies, their force took precedence even before any concern might derive from them for the state. We emphasize this difference because of its far reaching implications for the market economy. For more details on this issue, see Economou, Kyriazis (2017).

to collect the 2% duty on the exports–imports in 402/401 BCE. Because of the circumstances, he made only a little profit. But he could have had a very big loss, even though he participated in the auction because on the average he may have expected to make a moderate profit. Setting up a factory to manufacture shields, advancing a maritime loan, travelling to the Black Sea to fetch loads of grains, etc. involved investment risks that some took in the expectation of profiting and not all of them were successful. However, in retrospect, the truth of the matter is that the market economy in Athens emerged owing to the efforts of all winners and losers, irrespective of the particular activity in which they ventured.

6 Money in an economy without a central bank

The readers will have noticed by now that in the preceding chapters, we never referred to "money." We referred consistently to "coins," "coinage" and "currency," but we were very careful not to identify these terms with "money" or "near money" substitutes.[1] The time has come now to clarify this distinction.

Cohen (1990, 2008) has established that the banks in classical Athens created credit by a multiple of the deposits they received.[2] However, apart from this common feature, those banks differed from the ones of the last several centuries in the following main respects: (a) the currency they dealt with was silver coins and bullion easily convertible into coins for a small striking and seigniorage charge by the state mint; (b) their resources for making loans consisted of coins and bullion they themselves owned and/ or collected through *primary deposits*; (c) the banks operated free of any state supervision as all other enterprises; and (d) since there was no central bank to generate for them *base money*[3] and require that they apply a specific

1 As "near money" is defined anything, tangible or intangible (e.g., promissory or any other form of commitment to a future money payment) that proves itself good enough in value preserving properties as well as in convenience and low transactions cost to outperform barter. However, in the sequel, we shall focus exclusively on "money" in the form of currency, bullion, bank deposits and bank loans.
2 We use the term "deposits" to signify the flow of loans from affluent individuals and shrines to bankers - cum - banks, and thus to distinguish them from bank loans for consumption and production purposes. As Thomas Figueira has pointed out to us in a private communication, deposits in the contemporary meaning of the term played a minimal role in the total economy since only a few Athenians had the resources, confidence and sophistication to use them. The only mass evidence available in this regard is archaeological/art historical, and it suggests that households held reserves in precious metal vessels. Also, evidence from hoards and temple treasures suggests that bullion was held in unusual, hard-to-exchange and worn foreign silver coins. The literary evidence is Lysias (*Against Eratosthenes*, XII.11–12, 19). Yet it is doubtful whether the three talents mentioned in these passages were in coins or not; Figueira thinks they were in coins. But that enumeration reminds us that for the affluent Athenians, there existed flows back and forth between silver and liquid gold reserves in the forms of Persian Darics and electrum Cyzicene coins. In his view, there was a hierarchy in the liquidation of sacred treasures starting from Attic coins down to metal incorporated in art work, with the statue of Athena herself the final stage.
3 In modern monetary systems, base money consists of the amount of currency that circulates among the general public, plus the currency physically held in the vaults of commercial banks, plus the commercial banks' reserves held in the central bank.

reserve ratio, the banks determined the quantity of *secondary* or *derivative* deposits they created along with all other variables in the system. The absence of a mandated reserve ratio does not imply that the Athenian banks were inclined to create excessive amounts of credit, which raised their risk of default.[4] Certainly, some banks did and, from Cohen (1992, 215–224), we know that a number of them failed. But given that depositors had all the incentives to guard against banks that overextended in the quantity and the quality of loans that they advanced, on the whole banks should have practiced restraint from the fear of having to face a run by their depositors.

The objective herein is to explain how we think that the Athenian banking system, mediating between savers and borrowers in the fully competitive environment that evolved over time, determined the quantity and the composition of money in the form of currency and bullion in circulation, primary deposits in currency and bullion held by the banks, and secondary deposits corresponding to bank credit.

6.1 Demand and supply of currency and bullion

In the Athenian economy, there functioned two markets for silver, one for silver in the form of currency and another in the form of bullion. Both markets were closely interconnected because, as we indicated earlier, for some relatively small cost bullion could be converted on demand into coins at the mint. Hence, the supply of currency in every period was equal to the quantity of bullion that was worth holding in the form of coins on the grounds of its purchasing power in terms of goods and services; or, more accurately, it was equal to the quantity of bullion worth holding in the form of coins on the grounds of its purchasing power in terms of goods and services all over the then known world, because the economy was completely open and local silver markets for currency and bullion coincided with the international ones. In this framework, let the purchasing power of drachma be denoted by a continuum of prices p^c and the quantities of the currency offered in exchange for goods and services at these prices by the symbol S^c.[5] The pairs of (S^c, p^c) define the supply side of the market for currency. Moving next to the other side of the market, assume that at the prices p^c, the providers of

---

4 Nor does it imply of course that the banks were in any discernible way any more prudent than any banks today. The critical difference is that ancient Athenian bankers had no central banker to blame if their business collapsed and they could shift the costs of their errors on to the taxpayers. On the contrary, a central bank with its monopoly power on the quantity of fiat money ends up today with significant corresponsibility with the banks and this explains why central banks frequently bail banks out upon imminent default.

5 In the past, several renowned economists have insisted that money is as subject to supply and demand as any other good or service. For example, Mill (1923, 490) writes:

> ...the value or purchasing power of money depends, in the first instance, on demand and supply. But demand and supply, in relation to money, present themselves in a somewhat different shape from the demand and supply of other things...whoever sells corn, or tallow, or cotton, buys money. Whoever buys bread, or wine or clothes, sells money.

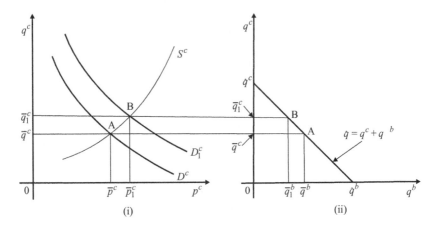

Figure 6.1 Allocation of available silver between currency and bullion.

goods and services offer to purchase D^c quantities of currency, and hence that the pairs (D^c, p^c) describe their demand for currency.[6] In the jargon of contemporary economic analysis, the aspect that would attract attention at this point would be the mechanism by which the supply and demand for currency arrived at equilibrium.[7]

We shall highlight this issue with reference to Figure 6.1. Graph (i) depicts the above-defined curves of the demand and supply of currency. The supply curve has been drawn in an upward sloping fashion because it is reasonable to assume that as the price of the currency in term of goods and services increases, for example, if a plentiful harvest or extraordinary loads of grain from the Euxine came to the market in Athens, bullion holders would be motivated to convert more and more of its quantity into currency.[8] On the contrary, regarding those who demand currency by offering goods and

6   In various periods, there circulated in Athens privately fabricated and monitored but state backed small change coins made of bronze, whose metallic value was far less than its nominal worth. These constituted in essence a form of fiat currency. However, by all historical accounts, their amount was insignificant relative to that of the silver currency in circulation and on this ground in the analysis that follows, we ignore it altogether. For further documentation on this issue, see Cohen (2008, 68–69).

7   It should be clear that at the microeconomic level, there are as many supply and demand pairs for currency as there are goods and services. But here we shall conduct the analysis as if all goods and services have been aggregated into a single commodity.

8   Notice that this constitutes a significant departure from the textbook assumption of a fixed or central bank determined supply of currency. To follow on the example, the elastic supply of currency from the stock of bullion that Athenians held provided the means to accommodate endogenously the shock of the increased supply of goods. In Athens therefore relative prices changed to cushion any shocks on the demand or the supply side of the markets, whereas nowadays shocks must be identified by central banks before they are able to prevent, if at all, the possible destabilization of the economy.

services, it is reasonable to assume that as its price rises, they will reduce the quantities that they are willing to purchase. This explains why we have drawn the curve of the demand for currency as downward sloping. But the interests of buyers and sellers of currency are opposite, because those who sell currency for goods and services wish to buy low, whereas those who sell goods and services for currency wish to sell high. Consequently, repeated exchanges among them are bound to lead to a position where everybody is satisfied with the results. Economists call this position equilibrium. In Graph (i), this situation is shown at point A, where the quantity of currency and price that prevail are marked by the symbols $\left(\overline{q}^c, \overline{p}^c\right)$. At that price of the currency, Graph (ii) shows that from the total available quantity of bullion $\hat{q}$, quantity $\overline{q}^c$ would be converted into currency and the remaining $\hat{q} - \overline{q}^c$ would be traded in the form of bullion and other wares from this precious metal.

Next, suppose that while the production of goods and services increases, the overall quantity of the available silver bullion remains fixed at $\hat{q}$. How would this change affect the allocation of bullion between currency and commodity uses? Since silver in the form of currency would become dearer in terms of goods and services, more of the silver in the form of bullion would be expected to be converted into currency and a new equilibrium would be established at point B in which the equilibrium values would be $\left(\overline{q}_1^c, \overline{p}_1^c, \overline{q}_1^b\right)$. Using the same analytical apparatus, we could examine also the opposite case in which the production of goods and services remains fixed and the overall quantity of bullion increases, as happened in the case of the discovery of the Laurion mines in 483 BCE. In that event, goods and services became dearer in terms of silver bullion and certainly some of its available quantity was converted into currency. But how much currency was necessary each time to carry out efficiently the transactions on the goods and services that were produced was determined in the two markets through the mechanism of relative prices and the competition between the opposing interests of currency buyers and sellers in terms of goods and services. So, in effect, one of the main functions of central banks in modern monetary systems, that is, the creation and management of base money, was performed by the stock of silver coins and bullion, the relative prices of which cushioned the shocks in the goods and services markets. Except that, this stock was not controlled monopolistically by one organization, but by many individual and uncoordinated economic agents who stood to make a profit or suffer a loss depending on the quantity and the composition of the amounts they held and the particular nature of the shocks.

The above analysis glosses over a very important aspect. This has to do with the presence of banks. The stocks of currency and bullion in the economy (q^c, q^b) bear no interest. By implication, those who hold purchasing power in the forms of highly liquid currency and slightly less liquid bullion forego the opportunity to make a deposit in a bank and earn interest. Economists would say that they absorb an opportunity cost. This cost motivates the holders of wealth in these forms to try and allocate it among currency, bullion, bank deposits and loans, so as to maximize their benefits. Hence, in addition to the markets in Figure 6.1, there are two more, that is, those for bank deposits and loans, which need to be integrated into the analysis. To this issue, we turn next.

6.2 Demand and supply of primary deposits

As we indicated earlier, Athenian banks provided a range of services much like contemporary banks. One of these services was that they accepted deposits and paid interest on them. By virtue of the voluminous evidence in this regard, it is reasonable to assume that there was a robust banking market where, on the demand side, we had bankers competing to attract deposits by paying the lowest possible interest rate, whereas on the supply side, we had households, enterprises and *treasuries of the gods*,[9] searching around to make deposits at the highest possible interest rates, but considering also the reputation and the riskiness of the bankers whom they would trust with their money. Figure 6.2 expands on Figure 6.1 in several ways. The first is the introduction in Graph (ii) of an additional axis, which measures the quantity of primary deposits that become available in the economy through a process by means of which economic agents strive to reallocate their current holdings of silver currency, q^c, bullion, q^b, and primary deposits, q^d, so as to reap the highest possible benefits.[10] The reallocation is achieved with the help of the relative price of the currency p^c, the implicit relative price of bullion $p^c(1-e)$, e being a percentage unit cost for converting bullion into currency, the reserve ratio k, by the inverse of which banks multiply primary deposits, and the interest rate r, which indexes the relative benefit of giving up present for future liquidity. Points marked by an A in Graphs (i)–(iii) show an initial allocation among these three components of base money q^m, for $q^d = kq^{cr}$, $0 < k < 1$, $k = k_0$ and $e = 0$.[11] So, let us trace through the changes, which would take effect in the previous example of an increase in the production of goods and services in the economy, holding the

---

9 In the financial markets the *treasuries of the gods* acted also like banks lending money at interest. For example, based on a stele from the Athenian *demos* of Rhamnous, Davies (2001, 117–128) reports that accounting records pertaining to the management of the monies of their goddess Nemesis show that the *treasury* lent about four talents at about 7% and earned about 1.7 talents of interest in seven years.

10 Bank deposits consisted of currency and bullion. Let the former be denoted by q^{cd} and the latter by q^{bd}. From the quantities of currency and bullion in the economy, quantities $(q^c - q^{cd})$ of currency and $(q^b - q^{bd})$ of bullion circulated outside the banking system, whereas the remaining quantities were held within it in the form of primary deposits and reserves owned by banks.

11 Notice that in the definition of money denoted by q^m we have included the primary deposits q^d. For the Athenian model of free banking analyzed here, this may be considered a narrow definition of money that corresponds to the base money in today monetary systems. The broader definition of money adopted in the text includes also the amount of secondary or derivative deposits q^{cr}, which corresponds to the credit that the banking system generated at the reserve ratio k_0.

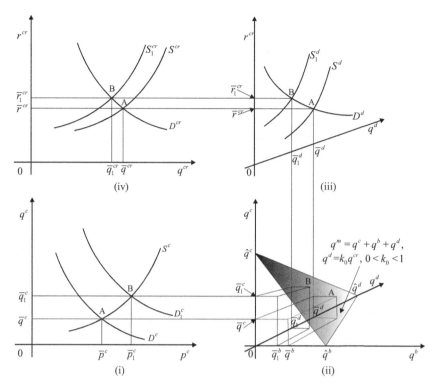

Figure 6.2 Equilibrium in the money market.

available quantity of bullion constant. The change would shift curve D^c in Graph (i) to the position D_1^c. In turn, the equilibrium price of currency in terms of goods and services would rise from $\bar{p}^c$ to $\bar{p}_1^c$, and as a result, the equilibrium quantity of currency would increase from $\bar{q}^c$ to $\bar{q}_1^c$.

Looking next at Graph (ii), we see that the rise in the use of currency would come about partly from a reduction in the form of money held in bullion, the quantity of which would decline from $\bar{q}^b$ to $\bar{q}_1^b$, and partly from a reduction in the deposits held by bankers. What would happen in the market for primary deposits is shown in Graph (iii). As these deposits would decline with the shift from S^d to S_1^d, the equilibrium interest rate and their quantity would shift from point A to B. In particular, at the latter point, the equilibrium interest rate would increase from $\bar{r}$ to $\bar{r}_1$, whereas the equilibrium quantity of primary deposits would decline from $\bar{q}^d$ to $\bar{q}_1^d$.[12] This analysis

---

12 So, a plentiful harvest in Attica or abundant supplies of grain shipped from abroad meant that the interest rate also rose. Except that the rise was moderated by the stock of bullion that served the same purpose in smoothing real economic shocks as is served today by financial market speculators.

explains the chain of changes in response to an isolated increase in the production of goods and services. But it remains mute with regard to the nature of the interest rate $\bar{r}$ and it requires some further explanation.

Keeping with the preceding analysis, in Graph (iii), we ought to have symbolized the equilibrium interest rate for primary deposits as $\bar{r}^d$, because this would represent the interest rate that the banks offer to depositors in order to secure the quantity of primary deposits $\bar{q}^d$. Instead, we use the symbol $\bar{r}$ so that we may have the opportunity to elucidate this important issue. Recall that when a certain amount of currency or bullion is deposited with the banks, they use it to extend interest bearing loans by the multiple of the inverse of their reserve ratio k. To attract the equilibrium quantity of primary deposits $\bar{q}^d$, assume that Athenians banks offered to depositors the interest rate $\bar{r}^d$. In a competitive business environment, the interest rate on loans $\bar{r}$ (see Graph (iv)), and hence on credit, has to be consistently aligned with the interest rate the banks pay to depositors, because in general, $\bar{r} > \bar{r}^d$.[13] How might this be achieved? The simplest conceptualization is to postulate that the demand curve for primary deposits D^d in Graph (iii) includes an interest rate for the attraction of deposits by affluent households and enterprises. With this issue settled, we are ready now to address the equilibrium in the credit or loans market.

6.3 Demand and supply of bank credit[14]

In Figure 6.2, relevant to the analysis of the market for credit or bank loans is Graph (iv). Let us concentrate first on the determinants of the curve labeled S^{cr}, which stands for the supply of credit. Active on this side of the market were financial and nonfinancial intermediaries, including individual Athenians not necessarily rich. For example, in Section 5.1, we noted that the *treasuries of the gods* acted like banks, whereas Harris (2002, 81) reports several cases of small loans advanced by nonprofessional lenders. Also, in order to facilitate the selling of their goods and services enterprises offered credit to buyers. From a legal point of view, selling on credit was forbidden. But *de facto* in everyday commercial relations, such transactions were quite widespread (see for example Cohen (1992, 14) and affected the overall supply of credit by expanding or contracting the outstanding stock of "trade credit." These written debt claims could be transferred to third parties

---

13 To be sure, credit money generated through bank loans is less liquid than bank deposits; So, these forms of money have an important difference, which is reflected in an interest rate differential. How larger is the average interest rate on loans in comparison to the average interest rate offered on deposits depends on factors like the operating costs of the banks, the pricing of default risks on their loans, the robustness of competition in the money market, etc.

14 Unless otherwise specified, henceforth we shall use the terms "credit" and "loans" interchangeably.

(Cohen *ibid.*, 14–18). Yet as is the case today, advances of such credit as well as loans offered by isolated individuals should have been limited in scale, so they are assumed not to have played a decisive role in the determination of the equilibrium in the credit market. For this reason, we shall concentrate on the role of financial intermediaries, that is, banks.

Since they accepted deposits and extended loans, it does not take much theorizing to establish that banks affected the supply of credit through three channels.[15] The first and very likely the most important was the well-known multiplier mechanism. In particular, drawing on the realization that only a limited proportion of the deposits they kept was withdrawn each period, banks felt confident about their liquidity to lend out the rest in the form of business and consumer loans. But some part of the latter returned to banks as new deposits. So, they continued lending up to a limit, which corresponded to so many times the initial deposit as it was warranted by the inverse of the reserve ratio k that they applied at the time. The explanation of this process and its documentation by Cohen (2008, 76–83) leaves no doubt that the Athenian banks did create credit in the same way systemic banks do in present-day democracies. More specifically, looking at Graphs (iii)–(iv) in Figure 6.2, it is unlikely to miss that the money market determined not only the equilibrium interest rate $\bar{r}$ but the equilibrium reserve ratio $\bar{k} = k_0$ as well. For, the latter can be computed readily by dividing the volume of the equilibrium credit $\bar{q}^{cr}$ (see Graph (iv)) by the equilibrium rate of primary deposits $\bar{q}^d$ (see Graph (iii)).

The second channel was the share that the banks held in the economy's base money $p^c[\hat{q}^c + (1-e)\hat{q}^b]$. As the price of the currency in terms of goods and services changed relative to the price of bullion plus the cost for its monetization or demonetization, certainly the banks would be motivated to convert bullion into currency and vice versa. Perhaps, because they found no evidence of such episodes or they construed them to be insignificant in comparison to the mass of coins in circulation, neither Cohen (1992, 2008) nor Amemiya (2007) makes any reference to such endogenously induced conversions. However, aside of this allocational effect, changes in the relative prices of the currency in terms of goods and services changed the value of the portfolios of currency and bullion held by banks (see Figure 6.2, Graph (ii)), and hence influenced the amount of credit the latter advanced.

Finally, regarding the third channel, it is helpful to recall from our earlier discussion that with the exception of state intervention in the determination of the prices of cereals, foodstuffs like oil and fish, and charcoal, markets were totally free and the same held true for the parallel circulation of

---

15 It should be noted that this is the first instance in our analysis that we refer to credit creation by banks. As it will become apparent shortly, our conceptualization is that in classical Athens, money consisted of the currency, that is, the Attic drachma, silver bullion readily convertible into currency at a small minting cost and bank credit.

domestic and foreign currencies.[16] Hence, technically speaking, the position of the S^{cr} curve in Graph (iv) would be subject to disequilibria in the trade account as well as pure arbitrage that economic agents might be motivated to undertake depending on the differences in the relative prices, including the interest rate r. For if, for example, the rise in the productivity of the economy or the discovery of new trade routes shifted curve S^{cr} to the position S_1^{cr}, thus raising the equilibrium interest rate from $\bar{r}$ to $\bar{r}_1$, and this rise was considered undue in the light of the financial conditions that prevailed abroad, other things remaining equal, importing of coins and bullion would shift the curve S_1^{cr} to the right and the amount of equilibrium credit would shift from $\bar{q}^{cr}$ to $\bar{q}_1^{cr}$.

Turning next to curve D^{cr} in Graph (iv), the demand for loans stemmed from domestic and foreign borrowers and aimed mostly for both productive and consumptive purposes.[17] In general, the loans were secured by property collaterals worth at least double the value of the loans and the interest rate they carried varied depending on the risk of the venture for which the loans were advanced and other considerations.[18] Examples abound. Amemiya (2007, 86–87) for instance describes in detail the terms and the interest rates lenders charged for bottomry loans. They varied on account of the risks of the journey and the season that it took place, since ship losses during winter times were higher than similar journeys during summers. The view that emerges from the evidence is that much like today, there prevailed a whole structure of interest rates, which moved up or down depending on the direction in which the conditions in the credit market moved the equilibrium

---

16 The issue of price controls in classical Athens is a mute one. Migeotte (2009, 143–152) has looked into the nature of the influences of the state on the prices of the aforementioned commodities and in page 149 he concludes that:

> ...It thus seems that, in practice, the fixing of wholesale and retail prices depended primarily on negotiations between the merchants and the magistrates, and on the magistrates' power of persuasion.

17 In the relevant literature, there is a lengthy debate regarding the nature of the loans that were advanced by Athenian bankers. Before the 1980s, the dominant position was that the loans were mostly for consumption. However, when the evidence was revisited by Cohen (1990), it became apparent that the methods by which researchers had selected and assessed the evidence were subjective and biased toward the hypothesis that they wished to confirm. Since then, the balance of opinion has changed and now most economic historians side with the view that the loans were advanced predominantly for productive purposes. In our analysis, we adopt the latter view and extend it to include loans for trading as well as pure speculation. But it should be clear that the consistency of our analysis and the conclusions we derive from it do not depend on the nature of the loans. Even though, we are aware of the implications of this issue, as well as the significant disagreements among economic historians, whether Athenians borrowed for consumptive or productive purposes, the market for loans would determine an equilibrium interest rate and this is sufficient for us in the present research endeavor.

18 It should be clear that the volume of acceptable "bankable" collateral would be a strongly limiting factor restraining credit growth and enhancing stability in the economy. But at the same time, it would retard economic growth by curtailing the expansion of the money supply.

interest rate. In other words, assuming that the credit market determined a basic relatively riskless interest rate, the structure of interest rates guided lenders on how to adjust it in order to reflect the circumstances that applied to the particular borrowers, the intended uses of the loans, the quality of the property offered for security, etc.[19]

Drawing on the above, let us return again to the question we posed earlier regarding the equalization of the equilibrium interest rates in the markets for deposits and loans. Consider an equilibrium interest rate r' in the credit market which is slightly higher than $\bar{r}$. The margin of the former interest rate over the latter would signify that the bankers are able to make a pure profit rate[20] on the deposits they manage to attract. However, in a competitive market with uninhibited circulation of information, this situation cannot last for long. The reason is that the pure profit on the part of bankers will motivate enough depositors to withdraw deposits and instead become themselves direct lenders. As a result, while the curve S^d in Graph (iii) would start moving slowly rightward, thus leading to a downward pressure on the equilibrium rate for deposits, the curve S^{cr} in Graph (iv) would move rightward more violently as bankers lose deposits. Hence, eventually, as the interest rate r' in the loans market declines faster than the interest rate in the market for deposits, the two interest rates would come to rest in the same lower equilibrium interest rate, which allows the bankers to earn only the normal net rate of profit, which by assumption is included in curve D^d of Graph (iii).

6.4 Equilibrium in the money market

Figure 6.2 depicts in graphical terms the fundamental blocks which in our view constituted the monetary module of the Athenian economy in classical times, and particularly in the 4th century BCE. It can be expanded by adding modules so as to integrate it with the production of output, the generation of labor and capital incomes, the tax and expenditure operations of the government, etc. Then the model would reflect more realistically the details of how the real and the monetary sectors of the economy functioned. We shall push the analysis a bit further in this direction later on. But what

19 Presumably a "relatively riskless" interest rate would reflect only the rate of time preference. As such it would have to be positive, and hence the whole structure of the interest rates in the economy would be positive. Now, compare this stylized feature of the Athenian economy to the negative interest rates that have emerged in recent years in contemporary market economics. This is another distinct difference between an economy without a central bank and commodity-based money and an economy with a central bank and fiat money. Since in the latter economy savers are confronted by central bank choices that carry the risks of higher losses on their savings, all who save for other than income earning purposes are forced to accept negative interest rates, just to slow down the rate of their losses.

20 We call this profit rate "pure" to signify that it is over and above a "normal" profit rate required by banks to stay in the business of banking. We have assumed that the latter is included in the curve D^d in Graph (iii).

we wish to do here is to summarize our findings regarding the process of convergence to and the properties of the equilibrium in the money market.

In the confines of the markets in Figure 6.2, money consisted of three components: currency, bullion, and bank credits. On this basis, we have shown that their equilibrium quantities were fully determined and indeed in a manner that households, nonfinancial enterprises and bankers should have been pleased with the results, because they achieved the best realization of their plans. To be sure, these results did not come about easily for them since they had to compete fiercely even for marginal gains. But in this process, they were guided effectively in adjusting their plans by three relative prices. The price of the currency in terms of goods and services $\bar{p}^c$ (see Graph (i)); The implicit price of silver bullion $\bar{p}^c(1-e)$; and the price of credit in the form of the additional consumption in some future date, if one is willing to part with one's present consumption, which is indexed by the equilibrium interest rate for bank loans $\bar{r}$ (see Graph (iv)).

Moreover, aside from the above *first best* results for all participants who persevered to the equilibrium point, the results turned out to be also *first best* for the economy as a whole, because the money market allocated the available quantity of bullion into currency, deposits and bank loans in the most efficient manner. To establish this proposition, assume that in Athens existed at the time a central bank which, in order to stimulate investment and economic growth, imposed an upper limit on the interest rate below its equilibrium level $\bar{r}$. In this administratively set interest rate, the demand for loans would be higher than the supply and the loans market shown in Graph (iv) would split into official and unofficial. If one were able at all to obtain loans in the unofficial market, one would have to pay interest rates even higher than the equilibrium interest rate, which would have prevailed in the absence of the said constraint. To keep the analysis brief, the new allocation of the available bullion would be *second best* for the economy, because it would involve fewer deposits, fewer loans and more hoarding, thus defeating the intended results of the central bank policy.

Could a central bank under any circumstances improve on the results of the money market in a monetary system like the one depicted in Figure 6.2? Definitely not, because the central bank, first, ought to have better information about the actual conditions that prevail in the markets than the market participants themselves, and, second, it ought to be able to simulate the preferences of market participants in advance. But this is an impossible problem to solve, because the central bank cannot know the preferences of market participants before they are revealed by their choices.[21]

---

21 It is likely that some readers aware of advanced economic theory may remind us of Samuelson's (1948) theorem of revealed preferences. We hasten to add that even if the central bank were able to predict precisely the preferences of market participants, it would still need to have an automatic feedback mechanism to continuously adjust its policies to the changing circumstances in the markets, and indeed not alone in the money markets. But the design and implementation of such a mechanism lie in the domain of wishful thinking.

Hidden in the above analysis is the following serious social problem which cannot be ignored. Regarding the market process in Figure 6.2, there is no doubt anymore that the great majority of participants as well as the state come out winners in terms of both freedoms and material well-being. But there are also people who take part in various stages of the process and, for reasons that are not of the present to explain, they are left behind or pushed aside. Athenians were very mindful of the social imperative to control income and wealth inequality between certain socially optimal bounds as the latter were understood by the majority of the citizens who participated in the *Assembly*.[22] Between equality of the ends and equality of the means, they placed in actuality the emphasis on the equality of the means, that is, education, and the enlargement of opportunities for all to thrive through commerce and open markets. Yet, at the same time, the state not only provided a social safety net, sufficiently secure to cover those who failed despite their earnest efforts to succeed, but also limited enough to discourage free-riding, corruption and abuses (see Section 5.1.3 on social welfare). In retrospect, it was an experiment in search of economic efficiency within an environment of social cohesion, which was met with remarkable success.

6.5 Summary

Money in classical Athens consisted of two components: the base money that consisted of silver coins and bullion, some part of which was held by banks in the form of primary deposits, and the loans that the banks advanced to their customers for consumption and production purposes. The quantity of money that circulated in the economy at any given time was determined by economic agents interacting in the money market. If in terms of goods and services the value of the drachma was higher than its silver content plus the cost of seigniorage, bullion holders would sense the opportunity for profit and, by turning enough quantity into coins at the mint, equilibrium would be established in the demand and supply for money. On the contrary, whenever the opposite happened and in terms of goods and services the value of drachma fell below that of its silver content, equilibrium between demand and supply for money might be established by melting enough drachma coins for their silver content. We could not find instances of such events, but that was certainly a possibility. This key result, that is, that the quantity of money was determined endogenously in the economy, emanated from the fundamental institutional arrangement that the mint stood ready at some cost to turn bullion into coins on demand.

Presumably, part of the base money was stashed away in response to the demand for hoarding[23]; a second part, multiplied by the so-called "veloc-

---

22 Admittedly, given the instability of Athenian political life in comparison with the glacial stagnation of, say, Sparta, those social bounds must not have been too stable.

23 It would be utterly farfetched not to assume that well-to-do Athenians did not keep a part of their riches in Attic drachma, either at home or in bank vaults. To the extent that they

ity of circulation" was used to carry out the volume of transactions that took place each year, and still a third part was deposited with the banks to earn extra income in the form of interest. Since coins in hand, coins in hoarding vaults and bullion returned no interest, how households and enterprises allocated their holdings in means of payment among currency, bullion, bank deposits and bank loans, was determined by the price mechanism in the framework of the markets exhibited in Figure 6.2. In particular, with the intermediation of banks, household and enterprises were brought into impersonal contact with households and enterprises possessing portfolios of (currency $= q^c$, bullion $= q^b$, deposits $= q^d$, loans $= q^{cr}$), which, under appropriate market conditions, stood ready to restructure into (currency $= \bar{q}^c$, bullion $= \bar{q}^b$, deposits $= \bar{q}^d$, loans $= \bar{q}^{cr}$), given for example a change in the demand for loans from q^{cr} to $\bar{q}^{cr}$. Depending on the direction of this change, the prevailing interest r would increase (decrease), say to $\bar{r}$, the deposits at the banks would rise (decline) to $\bar{q}^d$, and the latter would respond by expanding (shrinking) credit at the multiple of the inverse of their reserve ratio. These adjustments would bring about equilibrium in the markets for bank loans and deposits. But in the process, the change in bank deposits would force the prices in the markets for currency and bullion to change in the directions $p^c \to \bar{p}^c$ and $p^b \to \bar{p}^b$. Finally, as these price changes would take effect, the desired quantities of currency and bullion would change as follows: $q^c \to \bar{q}^c$ and $q^b \to \bar{q}^b$. In short, all financial markets adjusted optimally to accommodate in this case the change in the demand for loans, but the same would happen given any other change as, for instance, an influx of specie into the economy, a shift in the seigniorage margin at the mint or even changes in psychological factors that might influence the propensity to hoarding and hence the velocity of circulation.

Central to the aforementioned sequence of adjustments from the one equilibrium position to the other was the determination by financial markets of the equilibrium reserve ratio in the banking sector. What percentage of each deposit banks retained in order to safeguard their ability to cover withdrawals at any given time was then as paramount as it is today in the prevailing "fractional-reserve" monetary systems. But in classical Athens, there was no lender of last resort and the banks were obliged to hedge against risks on their own by balancing their urge for profit against the trust and the loyalty of their depositors.[24] Some banks, like the one run by Pasion, managed the inherent risks with success and became famous, whereas others failed and vanished into historical oblivion together with the deposits of their customers.

---

did, they practiced hoarding which implies that the amount of currency involved was eliminated from circulation.

24 There definitely existed a stock of bullion that could be struck quickly and cheaply into coins and lent out at some "penalty rates." The *treasuries of the gods* were also, most likely, not fully invested as manifested by the calls on their funds in cases of fiscal emergency. In risk management, the larger the emergency pool, the more stable the system. Hence, the argument for not having each bank manage its risks alone made good sense. However, we found no evidence of any scheme on the part of the Athenian financial institutions to manage collectively the risks involved in their business.

7 An assessment of comparative performance

Above, we established that the equilibrium quantity of money, the equilibrium interest rate, the equilibrium reserve ratio and the equilibrium relative prices were all determined in the economy. Now, we can add that all these crucial variables were *real* and directly *observable*. They were real in the sense that no authority in the state interfered in any way to alter their informational content for whatever reason, and they were directly observable because between them as instruments of information and the economic agents who made choices on them did not intercede any veil-like money, which forces people to make decisions on the *nominal* or *fiat money* equilibrium values of these variables.

As we shall argue later on, the merits of commodity-money based market systems in terms of democracy and political economy advantages can be hardly overstated. But perhaps the monetary system in classical Athens, as presented in the preceding chapters, fell short by reference to the objectives central banks are instructed to pursue in our times. Hence, before returning to the main issue of necessary reforms in the established regime of central banking, we must first assess the comparative performance of the monetary systems in classical Athens, where as we saw there was no central bank and money was endogenous, and the United States, where the Fed injects base money into the economy and presumably controls overall money supply through the policy instruments at its disposal.

To set the stage for this assessment, recall from the introductory chapter, that the Fed is mandated to pursue four objectives: namely, first, to stabilize the general price level, which has been interpreted to imply a long-term inflation rate in the neighborhood of 2%[1]; second, to minimize unemployment

---

1 Experiments have shown that people generally perceive a 2% pay cut with no change in the inflation rate as unfair, whereas they also perceive a 2% pay raise when inflation runs at 4% as fair. Economists attribute this phenomenon to the psychology of economic agents in fiat money market economies and invoke it by referring to the so-called "money illusion" syndrome in order to rationalize the argument that with prices that are *inflexible* or *sticky* downward, small levels of inflation, say of 1% or 2% per annum, are actually desirable.

by aiming at the so-called natural rate of unemployment, commonly thought to lie around 4%[2]; third, to stimulate economic growth by steering the economy close to its productive potential,[3] but without promoting the formation of asset bubbles that later burst and create financial crises and panics; and fourth, to bring about a moderate long-term interest rate, which on federal government ten-year bonds may be conceived to imply two percentage points over the trend rate of recent inflation.[4] In the longer past, "central banks" used to revise the target values for these objectives in the light of actual developments and the results from credible empirical analyses. However, in more recent decades, they have adopted them as inherent to the institutional and structural setup of market economies. So, we feel comfortable to employ them as standard gauges of the prevailing normal.

Lastly, since the Fed serves to a significant extent as banker of the word, we wish to look into the influences that its policies exercise on world indebtedness and the stability of the international financial system. As technological developments in recent decades have integrated U.S. financial markets with those of the world and shocks can be transferred almost instantaneously among countries, the margins for errors have shrunk to extinction and preventing major worldwide financial crises demands new ideas and bold

---

Drawing on analyses like this, the Fed construes that inflation at the rate of 2% is most consistent over the longer run with its mandate for price stability. In other words, price stability in the United States is defined to attain at this rate of inflation.

2 The adoption in macroeconomics of the presumption that the rate of unemployment in modern market economies is inversely related to the rate of wage inflation dates back to the late 1950s. It is called the Phillips curve, bearing the name of the researcher who was the first to formulate it as a testable hypothesis and identified it empirically using data from the British economy. Drawing on the correlation between these two rates, what is claimed is that, because of frictions in the search process for jobs and other downward wage and price rigidities like the minimum wage and the "money illusion" of economic agents, at every rate of wage inflation there is an inversely related percentage of workers who are caught in the transition from one job to the other. Later on, assuming that wage inflation translates into price inflation at a certain markup, researchers expressed the Phillips curve as an inverse relation between the rates of price inflation and unemployment. Hence, if for a market economy it is found that because of its institutional arrangements the so-called "natural rate of unemployment" is 4% achievable at a rate of price inflation of 2%, the effectiveness of monetary policies that aim at *full employment* and *price stability* should be assessed on how close to these targets they steer the economy.

3 The productive potential of the economy is computed by following approaches like that described in Section 7.3 below. Bitros (2019) has found that the estimates of the potential output are very sensitive to the measurement of the capital input. But, in any case, research analysts in the United States view them as valid gauges of potential economic growth.

4 The interest rate objective that the *1977 Federal Reserve Reform Act* sets for the Fed to pursue may not target the so-called "nominal" or "fiat-money" interest rate. The latter is defined this way because its basis is the U.S. dollar, the value of which in terms of goods and services varies inversely with the rate of general inflation. This detail is important to keep in mind, because shortly we shall differentiate it from the so-called "real" interest rate, which is free of general inflation distortions.

reforms. So, given that Athens did play a similar role with its hard currency in a period of openly interconnected ancient economies, at least either as a member-state of the *Delian League* (478–454 BCE) or from the position of leadership in the *First Athenian Alliance* (454–404 BCE), perhaps, we may gain some insights from its case for a safer way forward in the present precarious circumstances.

7.1 Price stability

Presently, when we refer to prices, we think either about the changes in the *general price level* and talk about the issues of inflation–deflation, or about the changes in the *relative prices* and talk about the flexibility of markets to adjust to endogenous and exogenous shocks. From Loomis (1998, 240–250), but not only, we know that for Athens in classical times, the relevant evidence is extant and that it relates to changes not in the general price level, but in the prices of select goods and services, and indeed to a limited range of them.[5] So, it is impossible to assess the performance of the economy in this regard with certainty. However, this does not preclude arriving at some credible guesses by drawing on the available indications and indirect ways of thinking.

7.1.1 Inflation in part and in general

Recall that the economy of Athens in the classical period, and particularly in the period 480–430 BCE, was exposed to two huge streams of silver flows. The one emanated from the mines in Laurion and the other from the tributes Athens received from its allies in the context of the *First Athenian Alliance*. A similarly huge inflow of precious metals repeated again in the 4th century, springing from the treasures in gold and silver that Alexander the Great captured from the Persians, but not earlier than 330 BCE. From several historical events, we have come to suspect that whenever such large amounts of specie pour into a country, the price level of certain goods and services tends to increase relative to the precious metals. For example, consider the huge inflows of silver into Spain from the Americas, which occurred between the second half of the 16th and the first half of the 17th centuries. Many scholars have associated with them the so-called *Spanish Price Revolution* by suggesting that they resulted on the average in an "inflation" of about 1.3% per annum.[6] But they do not clarify whether they mean

---

5 This is certainly true for wheat and *alphita* (milled barley), which were the two most important grains. We know also that silver depreciated relative to gold.

6 According to Lynch (1991, 184), during the period 1501–1562 AD prices rose on the average at the annual rate of 2.8%, but in the period 1562–1600 AD the rate of inflation retreated to 1.3% per annum.

inflation as changes in the "general price level," to which we shall refer as *general inflation,* or inflation as price changes on the level of a particular basket of "goods and services," to which we shall refer as *partial inflation* or for brevity just *inflation.* Given that there were no data on general inflation at the time, we take it that they mean inflation. So, adopting it until further notice, did the large silver flows into Athens give rise to noteworthy inflation in this limited sense?

7.1.1.1 Evidence regarding inflation

In the period 480–430 BCE, the silver from the Laurion mines and the allied tribute would have increased the supply of money by shifting rightward the surface $\hat{q}^m$ in Graph (ii) of Figure 6.2. Could it have generated persistent inflation? To find out, we shall concentrate first on the silver flows from Laurion. In the absence of hard evidence, Figueira (1998, 493) rates the likelihood of inflation quite high. He suggests that the working hypothesis should be that Athenians experienced "significant" inflation in the 5th century because it is unlikely that the supply of "goods and services" increased in proportion to the increase in the money supply. Instead, we vouch in favor of a low probability of "significant" inflation from this source on the grounds of the following thinking.

Before silver from the Laurion appeared in the markets in the form of currency, bullion and bank deposits, its mining and processing expanded employment and incomes, and hence GDP. By implication, the latter's composition would have changed and with it certainly the relative prices, but the aggregate demand for "goods and services," should have increased pretty much in proportion with their aggregate supply because silver was a tradeable commodity that could be exported freely in the form of currency and bullion. If the prices for foodstuffs and other household and enterprise implements increased in the short run owing to supply of silver-induced excess demand, profit margins would have tended to increase and by stimulating imports in the medium run prices would have returned to an equilibrium. So, with regard to this source, we fail to see how the abundant production of an internationally tradeable commodity like silver would lead to "significant" inflation. But the large allied tributes constitute a different case. Let us see why.

The revenues from this source entered into the coffers of the Athenian state and by authority of the *Assembly,* they were employed to finance all sorts of public expenditures. The following quotation from Loomis (1998, 243) highlights succinctly what transpired:

> The possible c. 50% rise in wages from c. 450 to 432 would be the natural result of enormous tribute revenues pouring into Athens year after year. With the transfer of the treasury of the *Delian League* from Delos to Athens by 453 and the elimination of the Persian military threat by the

Peace of Kallias in 449, more money was available for expenditure in Athens itself, for (the raw materials for) public works, and for the wages of public officeholders, soldiers and sailors, and public construction workers. The increasing amount and circulation of this money, in the context of a (presumably) less rapidly increasing labor supply, would have been the cause of the wage increases in this period.

That is, gradually, year by year, the state raised the wages of public magistrates, soldiers and sailors across the board; it spent lavishly in the construction of luxurious public buildings and city beautifications; it established programs of social welfare, festivals and other cultural activities, etc. As a result, we may contemplate the following implications: In conjunction with the slower rising supply of labor, the increasing amount and circulation of the allied currency inflows raised wages in the public sector and expanded the production of nontradeable goods and services; rising wages in the public sector raised the wages and the cost of materials in the private sector; as the latter entered into a phase of cost-push inflation, Athens lost international competitiveness and the Attic drachma lost value relative to other currencies; the exports of tradeables slowed down; the gap in the balance of trade widened; and eventually, the economy entered a period of inflation. Clearly, this smacks as the first ever case of the so-called *Dutch disease*.[7] But it was not because all indications are that during this period, the production of tradeables increased, and, as most likely, the abundant production of silver kept incomes increasing, the domestic demand for tradeables brisk and the balance of trade at ease, since increased imports of grains could be settled by paying in silver drachmae. Yet there still remained the element of cost-push inflation.

That is why we believe that Figueira's (1998, 493) hunch that in the 5th century BCE, the Athenians experienced "significant" inflation may be right. The culprit though was not the huge quantities of silver from the Laurion mines. Rather, the inflationary price spiral should have started from the way in which the state spent the elevated net revenues from the allied tribute.[8] Still, what was the range of inflation requires some clari-

7 More specifically, in the case of Holland, heavy income transfers from abroad emanating from the sale of gas or oil increased domestic spending. This, in turn, drove up the prices of the nontraded goods and services, for which the price levels are formed in the home market. Finally, as the higher prices of nontradeables translated into wage increases via inflation indexation, collective bargaining and other processes, manufacturing, the competitive product prices of which cannot deviate from world market prices, lost competitiveness and contracted substantially. In the case of Great Britain, which had a flexible exchange rate system, exchange rate appreciation because of the oil revenue inflows had the same effect, that is a major contraction of the manufacturing sector. This explains why the term *Dutch Disease* is sometimes referred to as *de-industrialization*.

8 The view propagated in the literature is that Athens under Pericles was able to finance the increased public expenditures because of the large inflows of currency from the allied

fication. For this purpose, we return to Loomis (1998, 243). From his ex-haustive search in the sources, he conjectures that in the period 450–432 BCE, public sector wages increased by about 50% or roughly about 2% per annum. Quite reasonably, assume that the wages in the private sector increased annually by the same rate and that the value added of labor to the GDP was 80%, implying that the value added from inputs like capital, materials and energy was 20%. Then the Consumer Price Index (CPI) year in and year out would have increased at an average rate of less than 2% per annum, depending on how much the cost of production of all other inputs might have been influenced by the rise in wages. Again, from this analysis, it follows that inflation in the period under consideration could not have been higher than 2% per annum.

During the 30 years following the start of the Peloponnesian War in 431 BCE, we know that the flows of silver from the Laurion mines declined and that in 413 BCE, they came to a stop when Spartans captured the fort of *Deceleia* and 20,000 slaves who worked there escaped. The mines operated on and off until they were shut in 1982 AD. But the silver output left little surplus above operating costs and in the 4th century, the revenues it gener-ated for the state dwindled to a trifle. Similarly, the tributes from the allies and tax revenues from the war savaged economy were insufficient to cover the public expenditures and Athens, after a period of borrowing head over fist from the temples, was obliged to enter into a sharp wage cutting mode across all ranks of public servants. For example, Loomis (1998, 245) finds that in 403/402, that is, shortly after its defeat in 404 BCE, Athens cut the wages of its army and possibly naval personnel by 33.3%.[9]

From that period on to 330 BCE, as we have mentioned in several places earlier, Athens recovered gradually some of its previous strength and glory, particularly under Euboulos and Lycourgos. But never had the financial re-sources to repeat the largesse and the extravagances of the Periclean era. As documented by Loomis (1998, 247), in the 70 years to 330 BCE, the wages in the public sector increased 1% per annum from the low base they hit at the close of the Peloponnesian War. Hence, since wages in the private sector would have adjusted to those set administratively in the public sector,[10] the

---

tribute. To us this seems significantly exaggerated because it fails to account for the large proportion of military expenditures that the allies recaptured by offering services to Attic forces, sharing in Athenian colonization, undertaking expenditures for garrisons and bases in their territories, and, most importantly, from the reliance of Attic forces on merchants for the provisioning and sustenance of their forces. This explains why we have placed the emphasis on the net, not the gross, revenues from the allied tribute.

9 Perhaps Athens would have been forced to adjust wages downward in the public sector much earlier, if the nominal scale of allied tribute had not been raised 2.5–3 times in 425 BCE.

10 However, during the period 400–330 BCE there were no extraordinary inflows of species into Athens and hence prices increased only because of the rise in the wages of public servants by the state.

trend of inflation during this period should have been closer to 1% rather than the benchmark of 2% per annum in the peacetime period of the 5th century.

Lastly, referring to the years after 330 BCE, Westermann (1910, 215–216) hypothesizes that the effects on prices from the Persian treasures that flowed into the Athenian economy, directly through the very generous remuneration by Alexander the Great of the soldiers that fought with him and returned to Athens, and indirectly from the large sums he donated to various Greek cities and communities in Asia Minor, "must have been great." But the meaning of terms changes over lengthy periods of time and what was "great" in 330 BCE Athens might be considered "hyper" or "modest" in the early 20th century that he was writing. So, in order to become more specific by comparison to a more recent historical event, he parallels the possible inflation that might have occurred then with the inflation that California experienced from the discovery of gold mines in 1848. In this case, he informs us, the average prices of all commodities from 98.7 in 1849 rose to 109.1 in 1853, thus giving an inflation of about 2% per annum. Was it "great?" It appears that it was because in the preceding several decades, Athenians had been accustomed to an inflation close to 1%.

7.1.1.2 The case of general inflation

The above relate to the notion of inflation as used by economic historians. Now, let us return to the issue of general inflation. Consider an economy with two goods, say, bread and silver. Denote the unit price of bread in terms of silver as p_b^s, that is, two obols of silver per weight unit of bread, and the unit price of silver in terms of bread as p_s^b, that is, half the weight unit of bread per obol of silver. By implication, we have $p_s^b = 1/p_b^s$. Next, assume that the available quantity of silver doubles, while the available quantity of bread remains constant. Since double the quantity of silver will buy the same quantity of bread, p_b^s will increase to $2p_b^s$, whereas p_s^b will decline to $p_s^b/2$, and hence it will continue to hold that $p_s^b = 1/p_b^s$. This proves that while the increase in the quantity of silver changes the *relative prices*, the general price level remains unchanged and hence general inflation is 0. This transpires because, whatever percentage of value silver loses in terms of bread, the latter gains exactly in terms of silver. Does this proof generalize to an economy based on so-called commodity money with many goods and services? We think it should, provided that the commodity money maintains its integrity and that it is not debased, since then it acquires qualities nearly similar to fiat money.[11] Does this proof apply to Athens in classical times? It

---

11 Sussman, Zeira (2003) have shown that commodity money can lead to general inflation through debasements, which act like devaluations. Otherwise, in the absence of currency debasement, it should hold that in an economy in which the quantity of commodity money M circulates with velocity V, giving a value of transactions MV, if the relative prices of

does because, as we stressed earlier, Athens did not mingle up with money supply and guarded strenuously against adulteration of its currency. Therefore, even though there was inflation in the prices of particular baskets of goods and services, other baskets of goods and services probably deflated and general inflation remained 0 throughout.

To sum up, while during the period 400–330 BCE, the prices mainly of necessities might have inflated at an average annual rate of 1%, in the periods 480–430 BCE and 330–300 BCE, inflation of such basic goods and services was close to 2%. Excluding the years of the Peloponnesian War, the indications are that over 150 years of relative peace in the two centuries under consideration, such inflation ranged narrowly around 1.5%. But quite likely general inflation was 0 because the Attic drachma, except for a short period at the end of the Peloponnesian War, was never debased. Hence, while the general price level in Athens remained stable, in the United States over the period 1960–2015, prices increased at the rate of 3.8% per annum.[12] Thus, with regard to the rate of inflation, the evidence establishes a fundamental advantage of economies with money based on a commodity standard over economies with fiat money, which is issued and systematically devalued by central banks through general inflation, either in the course of trying to achieve high employment or in complacency and acquiescence to the governments of the countries that they serve.[13]

7.1.2 Relative prices and economic flexibility

Now, suppose that we observe an economy with just two goods, coffee and tea. Owing to a prolonged period of drought in the countries producing coffee, assume that its world supply declines. Then, upon news of this event in the media, the price of coffee would climb from p_c to $\bar{p}_c$, pushing downward its purchases from q_c to $\bar{q}_c$. If asked to explain what would transpire in the market for tea, a novice would say that its purchases would increase from q_t to $\bar{q}_t$, thus pushing upward its prices from p_t to $\bar{p}_t$, because the two

---

some goods and services increase by a certain percentage, for the transactions to be exactly executed, the relative prices of the remaining goods and services must decrease by the same percentage, and hence the general level of prices remains unchanged.

12 This rate was computed using the Consumer Price Index (CPI), given as series CPALT-T01USA661S in the database of the Federal Reserve Bank of St' Louis (Link: https://fred.stlouisfed.org). For the changes of inflation in various periods during 1960–2016, see Table 1.1 in the introduction.

13 This claim is consistent with the results which have been reported by Rolnick, Weber (1998, 14) who find that:

...on average, inflation rates are also higher under fiat standards. The average inflation rate for the fiat standard observations is 9.17 percent per year; the average inflation rate for the commodity standard observations is 1.75 percent per year. And, once again, every country in our sample experienced a higher rate of inflation in the period during which it was operating under a fiat standard than in the period during which it was operating under a commodity standard.

goods are substitutes and some consumers would find it to their advantage to switch from the relatively more expensive coffee to the relatively cheaper tea. However, even a highly trained economist would not be able to say how fast and at what prices and quantities the two markets would settle again, because the speed of the convergence to the new equilibrium prices and quantitates depends on the fluidity with which the two markets absorb the shock of the sudden decline in the world supply of coffee. The more *agile* are the relative prices of coffee and tea and the more *adjustable* are the two markets, the quicker the convergence will take place and the least possible will be the divergence among the new and the old equilibrium prices and quantities in the economy. This much we know with certainty and it might not be worth repeating. But it helps bring to the fore an important property, that is, *economic flexibility*, which in essence is synonymous to the *efficiency* with which markets help economies achieve the best use of the resources at their disposal. So, what we intend to do here is to attempt a comparative assessment in this regard between Athens in classical times and the United States in recent decades.

The ease, the safety and the cost at which transactions take place are key determinants of *economic flexibility*. In a market economy, all three have to do with the *quality of institutions,* which depends on the *quality of governance* and the degree of *economic freedom* that prevail. Table 7.1, based on World Bank and Fraser Institute data, presents two sets of indices showing how ancient Athens and the United States compare in these two areas relatively to Hong Kong that stands at the top of the rankings. However, before commenting, some clarifications are in order regarding the scores for Athens in the upper half of the table. We have taken the liberty to fill in the six shells by drawing on the following considerations:

*   *Voice and Accountability*: Athens was a direct democracy. Policy decisions were taken in the *Assembly* where all citizens could attend and vote. In fact, because there was a quorum of 6,000 citizens for the *Assembly* to be in session, those who came first up to this number received 3 obols, so everybody had an incentive to participate. Also, there was complete freedom of expression and association and, according to the boast of Pericles in his *Funeral Oration*, there was even tolerance of one another's behavior.
*   *Political stability and absence of violence*: With the exception of two brief oligarchic episodes in the late phase of the Peloponnesian War, there was neither political instability nor politically motivated violence or terrorism in the contemporary meaning of the terms. But there were political aberrations in the form, first, of *ostracism*, which was pursued through the *Assembly*, and, second, of narrow middle class that Aristotle considered *sine qua non* for political stability.
*   *Government effectiveness*: Athens had no elected political administration. The *Assembly* exercised all state powers under due process. With the exception of certain officials, such as *generals*, *tamiai* and *judges*,

Table 7.1 Quality of governance and economic freedom in Athens in the 4th century BCE, and the United States and Hong Kong in 2014[a]

	Quality of governance[b]					
	Voice and accountability[1]	Political stability and absence of violence[2]	Government effectiveness[3]	Regulatory quality[4]	Rule of law[5]	Control of corruption[6]
Athens[c]	100.00	95.00	100.00	90.00	100.00	100.00
United States	81.77	65.71	89.90	88.94	89.90	89.42
Hong Kong	65.52	90.95	98.08	99.52	94.23	92.31

	Economic freedom[d]				
	Size of government[7]	Legal system and property rights[8]	Sound money[9]	Freedom to trade internationally[10]	Regulation[11]
Athens (8.8)[e]	9.90	6.10	9.60	9.60	8.60
United States (7.81)	6.41	7.10	9.39	7.57	8.58
Hong Kong (9.0)	8.63	8.08	9.38	9.48	9.42

1 Voice and accountability capture perceptions of the extent to which a country's citizens are able to participate in selecting their government, as well as freedom of expression, freedom of association and a free media.

2 Political Stability and Absence of Violence/Terrorism measures perceptions of the likelihood of political instability and/or politically motivated violence, including terrorism. We do give Athens a perfect score because of two oligarchic uprisings that took place during this period.

3 Government's effectiveness captures perceptions of the quality of public services, the quality of the civil service and the degree of its independence from political pressures, the quality of policy formulation and implementation and the credibility of the government's commitment to such policies.

4 Regulatory quality captures perceptions of the ability of the government to formulate and implement sound policies and regulations that permit and promote private sector development.

5 Rule of law captures perceptions of the extent to which agents have confidence in and abide by the rules of society, and in particular, the quality of contract enforcement, property rights, the police and the *Courts* as well as the likelihood of crime and violence.

6 Control of corruption captures perceptions of the extent to which public power is exercised for private gain, including both petty and grand forms of corruption, as well as "capture" of the state by elites and private interests.

7 Size of government captures the degree to which a country relies on personal choice and markets rather than government budgets and political decision-making. Countries with low levels of government spending as a share of the total, a smaller government enterprise sector and lower marginal tax rates earn the highest ratings in this area.

8 This index captures the existence of rule of law, security of property rights, an independent and unbiased judiciary and impartial and effective enforcement of the law.

9 Sound money indexes the growth of money supply, inflation and the freedom of citizens to maintain foreign currency bank accounts.

10 This index measures the presence of a wide variety of restraints that affect international exchange: tariffs, quotas, hidden administrative restraints and controls on exchange rates and the movement of capital.

11 A very important index. It measures the presence of a wide variety of restraints that limit the freedom of exchange in credit, labor and product markets.

(Continued)

a We take 2014 as basis for reference and comparison because one of our sources of information refers to this year.
b The figures in the upper half of the table rank the United States and Hong Kong on the
   basis of the percentiles they occupied in 2014. Their source is: http://info.worldbank.org/
   governance/wgi/index.aspx#reports.
c The figures shown for Athens in this row give the scores that we assign to the six indices on
   the basis of our interpretation of how the definitions reported under one to six above might
   apply in the context of classical Athens.
d The figures for Athens come from Bergh, Lyttkens (2014) and refer to Athens in the 4th
   century BCE. Those for the United States and Hong Kong come from www.fraserinstitute.
   org/economic-freedom.
e The figures within the parenthesis stand for the total score.

who were appointed by ordination and served longer, public administration was run by magistrates elected by lot for one year and under
very strict monitoring and accountability procedures. The draw process
limited corruption and ensured transparency in the selection of public
officials (Hansen 1999, 341–342). The magistrates were assisted by civil
servants, who secured the necessary continuity of the state. We surmise
that because they were elected by lot and for a very short term of service, magistrates did not have the time to carry their political views in
their tasks and that the civil servants were very independent and felt
respectful to citizens. Also, cases of corruption of public magistrates
were few (Christ 2006; Pritchard 2014, 8) because, with two exceptions,
the term of their service was annual (Aristotle, *Athenian Constitution*,
54.2; Hansen 1999, 222–223); in normal circumstances, appointed officials did not have the time to develop corruption links effectively; and
as we explained in Section 3.1.3, the auditing process was very strict.

• *Regulatory quality*: The public administration was responsible for the
  implementation of the laws that the citizens passed in the *Assembly*. Presumably, citizens knew what was best for their state and how the private
  sector might assist in promoting their collective objectives. However,
  as domestic and import–export markets for cereals and certain other
  foodstuffs were less than totally free from government intervention,
  given their relative importance in the economy, most likely they introduced some regulatory rigidities.

• *Rule of Law*: According to Harris (2015), the rule of law contained such
  elements as:

> …peaceful resolution of disputes by fixed rules, obedience to laws
> enacted by the community, equality before the law, accountability of
> all public officials, fairness in trials, speedy resolution of disputes…
> This built the trust necessary for market relations and reduced trans-
> actions costs by reducing what modern economists call "asymmetry
> of information.

In other words, there was regulation by law, not by the magistrates and
certainly not by functionaries of the state. Moreover, officials were

personally responsible for their conduct and subject to very serious punishment for abuses.

- *Control of corruption*: The state could not be captured by political interests because it was governed by the citizens themselves. Certainly, some petty theft and corruption did exist. But politicians were relatively weak to use the state for their private advantage.

We believe that if a regime of direct democracy like that in Athens existed in our times, its *quality of governance* would get top scores, ahead of Hong Kong and certainly well ahead of the United States.[14] This explains our initiative to advocate in Chapter 9 in favor of transforming the soonest possible today's representative democracies into variants of democracy controlled and governed directly by citizens. As for the comparison of the U.S. with Hong Kong, looking across the upper half of the table, observe that the United States has a considerable advantage over Hong Kong in political freedoms (see first column), which is counterbalanced by the greater political instability and the presence of violence (see second column). These differences most likely reflect differences in the approaches that the two countries take to personal freedoms, which are not amenable to value judgments. But that the United States lags behind Hong Kong in all other quality of governance indices suggests that its economy is not as *flexible* as it could be by comparison to the top ranked country, and hence to ancient Athens. This inference is particularly reinforced by the index of "regulatory quality." For reasons that need not occupy us here, but which have been summarized excellently by the former chairman of the Fed Greenspan (2004), deepening state interventions in the United States continue to introduce rigidities into its markets, thus raising the frequency and the severity of financial crises.

Consistent with this conjecture are also the indices that pertain to *economic freedom,* displayed in the lower half of the table. We see that the United States ranks on a par with Hong Kong, but both lag behind Athens in the quality of money. Athens achieves an edge over United States and Hong Kong in this area because of its better experience in the front of inflation proper. But in all other indicators, the United States lags behind ancient Athens and Hong Kong and particularly in the areas of the "Size of the government" and the "Freedom to trade internationally." In the last two to three years, the differences of the indices in these two fields appear to widen against the United States, indicating that recent policies may have a bias toward expanding the role of the U.S. government and introducing additional restraints to international trading.

---

14 To anticipate a possible criticism or counterargument asserting that going back to direct democracy would increase the politicization of communal life, we suggest that Greeks nowadays are very politized individuals anyway, but without the benefits of control over the nature and the processes for pursuing a common good.

On account then of the remarkable economic flexibility that prevailed in Athens, prices would be expected to be fluidly adjustable. Is there hard evidence attesting to this expectation? The following examples are indicative of what we know:

- A *medimnos* of barley cost 2 drachmae in 422 and the same in 329 BCE. A *medimnos* of wheat cost 3 drachmae in 422 and 5 to 6.5 between 414 and the beginning of the 4th century (a period of uncertainty and supply difficulties due to the ranging of the Peloponnesian War). Its price declined to 3 drachmae in 393, increased to 9 during 340–330 BCE, and then it declined again to 5–6 between 330 and 324 BCE.
- Shoes cost 8 drachmae in 388 BCE and about 6 in 330 BCE.
- An auction of slaves in 414 BCE registered prices from 60 to 360 drachmae (360 for a skilled artisan jeweler), while prices during the 4th century fluctuated from 50 to 150 drachmae for unskilled, and 180 to 600 for skilled metal workers, etc.
- Skilled stonemasons working in 409 BCE on the Erechtheion building in the Acropolis were paid 1 drachma, irrespective of whether they were Athenian citizens, *metics* or *slaves*. By the end of the next century (329–308 BCE), wages ranged from 1.5 drachmae for unskilled to 2–2.5 for skilled workmen.

From these and numerous other similar examples, in conjunction with the superior overall economic flexibility in Athens,[15] we surmise that commodity prices and wages were flexible upward as well as downward; wages followed a slow positive trend, which might be indicative of rising incomes and upward pressures from the wages in the public sector that were set administratively; wage differentials between skilled and unskilled labor were substantial, suggesting the existence of shortfalls in skilled craftsmen; and there was absence of pay discrimination on the basis of worker's social status.

7.2 Unemployment

The average annual unemployment rate of all persons 15–64 years old in the United States over the period 1960–2015 was 6.15%.[16] Earlier, we noted that the target rate for unemployment was 4%. Hence, even if *full employment* is defined at this rate of unemployment, Fed's policies throughout the postwar period failed to prevent the overshooting of unemployment by 50%. Did Athens fare better or worst in this front? The evidence is that it fared far far better. Let us look into this claim.

---

15 We believe that this assessment is warranted even in the presence of the negotiated price setting of the prices for the life-sustaining goods we mentioned earlier.
16 This rate was computed from series LRUN64TTUSA156N, reported in the database of the Federal Bank of St' Louis (link: https://fred.stlouisfed.org).

In the preceding section, we assessed the determinants of economic flexibility and found that the scores of Athens regarding both its quality of governance and economic freedom were significantly higher than those in the United States. On this ground, we concluded that markets in Athens were very resilient and that the prices of commodities and wages must have changed smoothly in both directions. In particular, wages could not have been sticky downward, because there existed no dichotomy between "real" and "nominal" prices, and hence households, enterprises and workers were not motivated to alter their behavior in order to preserve the purchasing power of their incomes. General inflation most likely was 0 and hence there was no reason for the existence of "money illusion." Therefore, the prevailing institutional arrangements were such as to permit full employment of all who were willing to work at the going wage rate. In other words, the normal for the Athenian economy was full employment at 0% inflation in the long run, whereas the normal for the Fed has been 4% unemployment at 2% inflation. But is full employment for Athens in line with the available empirical evidence? We think that it is and indeed not only on the basis of the historical data that we presented earlier regarding the structure of the Athenian economy and its economic flexibility but also on account of the following more focused references to the existing sources.

In his contribution to the political economy of Athens in 355/354 BCE, Xenophon (*Ways and Means*) highlights the excellent prospects of its economy by drawing the attention of Athenians to the comparative advantages on which the glory of Athens was founded in the past and the potential that they provided for the future. He touches upon all sources of wealth creation: the key location, the mild climate, the security and the ease of access to the ports, the mining, the industrial strength (see Sections 5.2.2.2 and 5.2.2.3), the knowledge and the institutions of governance as well as commerce, etc. From this treatise, we wish to transfer here just a few exceedingly illuminating passages regarding employment in the sector of mining, which played such an important role in the golden decades before the Peloponnesian War. Xenophon (*Ways and Means*, IV, 3–8) writes:

> Now, we all agree that the mines have been worked for many generations. At any rate, no one even attempts to date the beginning of mining operations. And yet, although digging and the removal of the silver ore have been carried on for so long a time, note how small is the size of the dumps compared with the virgin and silver-laden hills. And it is continually being found that, so far from shrinking, the silver-yielding area extends further and further.
>
> Well, <u>so long as the maximum number of workmen was employed in them, no one ever wanted a job; in fact, there were always more jobs than the labourers could deal with. And even at the present day no owner of slaves employed in the mines reduces the number of his men; on the</u>

contrary, every master obtains as many more as he can (Underlined by the authors). The fact is, I imagine, that when there are few diggers and searchers, the amount of metal recovered is small, and when there are many, the total of ore discovered is multiplied. Hence of all the industries with which I am acquainted this is the only one in which expansion of business excites no jealousy.

Further than this, every farmer can tell just how many yokes of oxen are enough for the farm and how many labourers. To put more on the land than the requisite number is counted loss. In mining undertakings, on the contrary, everyone tells you that he is short of labour. Mining, in fact, is quite different from other industries. An increase in the number of coppersmiths, for example, produces a fall in the price of copper work, and the coppersmiths retire from business. The same thing happens in the iron trade. Again, when corn and wine are abundant, the crops are cheap, and the profit derived from growing them disappears, so that many give up farming and set up as merchants or shopkeepers or moneylenders. But an increase in the amount of the silver ore discovered and of the metal won is accompanied by an increase in the number of persons who take up this industry. Neither is silver like furniture, of which a man never buys more when once he has got enough for his house. No one ever yet possessed so much silver as to want no more; if a man finds himself with a huge amount of it, he takes as much pleasure in burying the surplus as in using it (Underlined by the authors).[17]

In the lines that we have underlined for emphasis, we are told in no uncertain terms that when the mines were operated at maximum capacity, there was not a single worker who wished to work and didn't find a job. Or, even more to the point, we are told that mining enterprises could not secure all the workers they wished to hire and that the excess pressure on the labor market was not transitory because the demand for silver was practically insatiable.

Certainly, the pressure of excess demand for workers that emanated from silver mining and processing industries could be expected to spill over to all labor markets in the economy. But still, given the dearth of data to back it, generalizing to this level by relying on Xenophon's description of the full employment conditions that prevailed in these sectors would be suspect. To

17 Considering the time this paragraph was written and the unsurpassed clarity with which Xenophon describes the law of diminishing returns in agriculture and how the price mechanism guided producers in deciding whether to stay in a market or to exit from it in search of better profit opportunities, to us it seems altogether amazing that so much ink was wasted by authors writing in support of the "primitivist" and later on "substantivist" conceptualizations regarding the structure of the Athenian economy in classical times. The only excuse we can think of is perhaps that Xenophon's *Ways and Means* for some unknown reasons escaped the attention of economic historians.

bridge the gap, we searched for indirect evidence in the variation of the number of *metics* and slaves. For, since it was mostly them who moved the economy, one might reasonably expect that their number would be fluctuating in tandem with the employment opportunities in the economy. The estimates that Amemiya (2007, 36) compiled from the relevant literature are shown in Table 7.2. Looking at the third and fourth rows, we see, respectively, that the number of *metics* increased in the middle of the 4th century BCE and then declined, whereas the number of slaves increased faster than the *metics* during the former decades and then remained stable. Admittedly, these estimates reflect the effects of wars, diseases and the myriad of other social factors that determine the changes in the rates of births and deaths. But if we ignore the possibility that these factors affected differently the two categories of the population, we can draw the following tentative inferences: In the period to the middle of the 4th century BCE, as *metics* flocked into Athens, lured by the enlarged opportunities for applying their skills and trades, particularly under Euboulos expansionary fiscal policies, the number of slaves accelerated. Most likely, this was a period during which the demand for labor outstripped supply and full employment together with rising wages and incomes was the norm. Then in the period to 322 BCE, while the number of *metics* declined, perhaps because after the defeat of Athens in Chaeronea in 338 BCE occupational and entrepreneurial opportunities became bleak, the number of slaves remained flat. This asymmetry might be interpreted to imply that the slaves continued to be in good demand at reduced remuneration though because they did not have the mobility to leave Athens.

To conclude, with completely flexible product prices and wages, in principle, it was unlikely that Athens in classical times experienced systematic spells of unemployment. From time to time, market restructurings because of shifts in consumer demand and other social and natural events might have given rise to small percentages of unemployment. But these were transitory and labor markets returned to full employment over the long haul. No central bank was needed to glimpse through the looking glass of a Phillips curve, and if it had been invented at the time, its intervention would have produced results inferior to those that were achieved by markets themselves. Full employment was another major advantage.

Table 7.2 Estimates of the size and composition of the population in Athens during classical times (thousands)

	431 BCE	*Mid-4th century*	*322 BCE*
Adult male citizens	30–60	21–35	21–30
With families (times 4)	120–240	84–140	84–120
Metics	24–25	20–30	10–25
With families (times 2)	48–50	40–60	20–50
Slaves	30–100	50–150	50–150
Total	198–390	174–350	154–320

7.3 Economic growth

Currently, economic growth accountants think of a country's rate of economic growth within a year by drawing on the production function:

$$Q_t = A_t L_t^{1-\alpha} K_{t-1}^{\alpha}, \quad \alpha, A_t > 0, \tag{2}$$

where the symbols stand for: Q_t = real Gross Domestic Product (GDP) in year t; L_t = billion hours worked in year t; K_{t-1} = real value of the capital stock in year $t-1$; A_t = Total Factor Productivity (TFP) in year t; and the parameter α stands for the income share of capital in the value of output.

Transforming equation (2) into logarithmic form, differentiating totally the resulting expression, and setting $\alpha = 0.3$, on account of the empirical evidence that the payments to owners of capital in industrial market economies have averaged in the postwar period roughly 30%, yields:

$$\%\Delta Q_t = \%\Delta A_t + 0.7 \cdot \% \Delta L_t + 0.3 \cdot \% \Delta K_{t-1} \tag{3}$$

This equation states that the growth rate of GDP equals the growth rate of TFP plus the weighted average of the growth rates of labor and capital. Or, to express it in a way indicating that TFP is computed as a residual, the growth rate of A_t is equal to the growth rate of Q_t not accounted for by the weighted average of the growth rates of L_t and K_{t-1}.

Referring to equation (3), and before turning to our main task, a few remarks are in order. In its generic form, it can be employed to compute the potential output, and hence the potential rate of economic growth, of any country with a market economy and at any period of its history. But while doing so, one must be aware of the significance and the implications of the parameter α. As we said above, setting $\alpha = 0.3$ reflects the postwar experience of income distribution in industrial economies. What this implies is that the trends in the potential GDP that prevailed were shaped also by the institutions, which determined that 30% of GDP went as income to capital and the rest to labor. If the social, fiscal, regulatory and labor arrangements in classical Athens were biased against excessive income inequality and as a result they led, say, to $\alpha = 0.15$, the potential output would have expanded at much lower rates, since the streams of consumption would have been much higher and the streams of investment much lower than otherwise. This clarification is important to keep in mind because it helps understand the crucial role institutions play in the speed by which countries become wealthier than others or why they grow at different rates in different periods in their history.[18]

---

18 We shall explain later on that the value system of the Athenians and their institutions were bent toward encouraging maximum efforts on the part of individuals, but without allowing excessive inequality to undermine social cohesiveness. In business they condone making "moderate profits" and using them in responsible manners for promoting social

In the framework of equation (3), central banks are presumed to influence economic growth through two channels. That is, investment and aggregate demand for output. The analysis on how a central bank may attempt to do so is standard. Since investment is related inversely to the interest rate, by decreasing (increasing) the cost of funds it lends to the banking system, the central bank may stimulate (retard) investment, which in turn boosts (decelerates) the quantity and the quality of the capital stock of the economy, thus raising (reducing) its growth rate. As for the aggregate demand for output, the instrument of the central bank is the quantity of money. In particular, by increasing (decreasing) the quantity of money, the central bank is presumed to increase (decrease) initially the aggregate demand for output, thus driving the intensity of the utilization of the capital stock upward (downward). Then, depending on whether enterprises perceive the change in the aggregate demand as temporary or permanent, they adjust the hours of work, the number of workers employed and/or investment, thus raising the rate of economic growth through L_t and/or K_{t-1}.

Until around 2000, the Fed based its policies on the quantity of money, defined variously as M1, M2 or M3.[19] In the years that followed gradually, it emerged that it had lost control of the quantity of money and it switched to targeting the interest rate. However, as it can be ascertained from Bitros (2015, 2018), an increasing number of researchers in recent years have reported empirical findings showing that the Fed has lost control of the interest rate as well, thus raising serious concerns about the effectiveness of monetary policy. It is not the proper place here to review this literature. But perhaps the readers may appreciate the basis of the strong evidence in this regard by looking at Figure 7.1, which juxtaposes the trend components of the series[20]: GDP = Gross Domestic Product; M1 = Money supply in the form of cash; M2 = Money supply in the form of cash plus near-cash means

---

well-being. Hence, it is no surprise that by all accounts capital formation was low, thereby missing the opportunity to boost Total Factor Productivity (TFP) through the embodiment of technological advances in new means and methods of production.

19 Further to our remarks in the introduction, there are multiple ways to define money supply depending mainly on the ease and the cost of turning the marginal asset included into cash. Money defined as M1 includes coins and paper currency, demand deposits, travelers' checks, and other checkable deposits. M2 consists of M1 plus the so-called near money, which consists of savings deposits, money market securities, money market mutual funds and other time deposits. M3 comprises M2 plus assets that can be converted into cash, but which may have significant restrictions on a timely conversion and/or a lack of guarantee that the investment's stated worth will be retained in the conversion to cash.

20 In the econometrics literature there have been for some time now lingering doubts about the appropriateness of the Hodrick-Prescott filter for estimating the trend component in macroeconomic time series. Even though we have missed the opportunity to apply it in its boosted form that Phillips, Shi (2019) recommend, we are confident that the conclusions reached in the text would not have changed, had we have the benefit of their most remarkable refinement in the estimating technique of the filter. The data come from the database of the Federal Bank of St' Louis and correspond in particular to the series

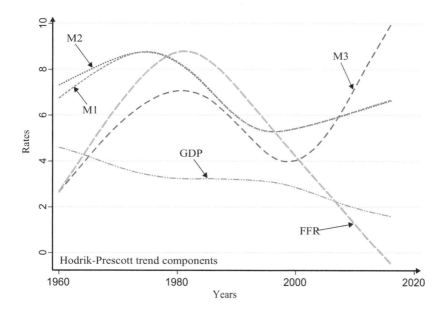

Figure 7.1 Growth rates of real GDP, FFR, M1, M2 and M3 in the United States over the period 1960–2015.

of payment; M3 = Money supply more as store of value rather than a medium of exchange, and the effective FFR = Federal fund Rate in the United States over the period 1960–2015.

Table 7.3 displays how monetary policy instruments moved within three roughly distinct periods in the years 1960–2015. On closer observation, we see that irrespective of the particular stance of monetary policy, GDP trended continuously downward to secular stagnation. The most monetary policy might have accomplished would be to slow down the rate of this trend. But to have done so, the Fed ought to have moved its policy instruments in a consistent way. Looking at the direction of the arrows, has this been the case? We do not think so, because: (a) in the periods 1960–1980 and 1980–2000, the money supply (M1, M2, M3) and the interest rate (FFR) moved in the same direction, which implies that the Fed had lost control of its policy instruments; and (b) during the period 2000–2015, in the span of which we know that it abandoned any effort to target the quantity of money, the Fed just pushed desperately the interest rate toward the zero bound. To be sure, one would find it hard not to concede that the three waves of quantitative easing in the advent of the 2007–2008 crisis did not prevent a

labeled in the text by the symbols GDP = A191RL1Q225SBEA, FFR = FEDFUNDS, M1 = MANMM101USA189S, M2 = MYAGM2USM052N, and M3 = MABMM301USA657S.

Table 7.3 Long-term shifts in the direction of monetary policy instruments and the real GDP in the United States over the period 1960–2015[1]

Periods	GDP	FFR	M1	M2	M3
1960–1980	↓	↑	↑	↑	↑
1980–2000	↓	↓	↓	↓	↓
2000–2015	↓	↓	↑	↑	↑

1 Based on the annual rates of change of the corresponding variables.

serious break downward in the trend rate of GDP. However, the evidence depicted in Figure 7.1 provides solid support to the well-known caveat that the operations of the Fed do not matter in the long run. But a great deal of research has shown that the same is true in the context of the business cycle.[21]

If there is still any doubt, consider the recent seminal book by Gordon (2016). He investigates over two dozen processes that may be responsible for the declining living standards in the United States. Not surprisingly, keywords like monetary policy, money supply, interest rate and the likes are not even mentioned in the subject index. On the contrary, one finds frequent references to such money-related facilitators of economic growth as banking, consumer credit, mortgage finance and installment loans. Apparently, the only channel through which the Fed might be able to affect economic growth is through its supervisory role of financial markets, even though this is not directly mandated by the *1977 Federal Reserve Reform Act*. Yet this channel is way too indirect, the Fed's probable effectiveness is limited to the enhancement in the efficiency of financial markets, and this holds mainly if microprudential policies stimulate the incentives of private agents for strict monitoring of the performance of financial institutions. So, eventually the crux of the matter is how keenly competitive are the financial markets and this brings us to the case of Athens where there was no central bank and banking was unregulated.

The silver currency in classical Athens was issued on a monopoly basis by the state. But not its quantity, since bullion holders could turn it into currency on demand at the mint. This arrangement rendered the currency endogenous to the economy. Moreover, on account of the policies adopted by the *Assembly* and the institutions that were put in place, as attested for example by *Nicophon's Law*, the coins maintained their integrity in silver content, thus becoming the currency of choice in the Eastern Mediterranean

21 Just for two examples, consider the results obtained by Rolnick, Weber (1998), regarding the relationship of GDP to the quantity of money, and Lee, Werner (2018), regarding the relationship of GDP to the interest rate. Using samples of countries including the United States, the former find that if a country uses fiat money, increasing its rate of growth will not increase its rate of output, whereas the latter reject the view that interest rates affect economic growth.

and beyond. With such a currency, every economist today would agree that economic agents could plan their activities without the uncertainty of inflation, which constitutes one of the preconditions for encouraging the undertaking of investment and thereby boosting economic growth through the expansion of employment and physical capital accumulation.

Another precondition to the same effect is the availability of credit. In Section 2.2.1, we mentioned that at its peak, the money and banking industry numbered 30 *eponymous* bankers and many more anonymous, because of the secrecy under which they conducted their business. Also, in Section 5.5.2, we explained that the bankers offered a large number of services, including loans. Recall that in the literature, there is some controversy as to whether the loans were given for consumption or production purposes. But in the light of the evidence presented by Cohen (1992, 33) and Harris (2016), there is no doubt any more that the Athenian bankers in addition to consumer-advanced production loans, thus supporting financially both the demand and the supply of output. Nor is there any doubt that the Athenian bankers created credit and invented ingenious forms of payments based on bank credit (see Cohen 2008, 76–83).[22] In further confirmation of these findings, Cohen (1992, 216–222) reports and comments on a number of bank failures, which occurred presumably because their owners had miscalculated the competitively determined own reserve ratios and they had extended more credit than it was safe for their depositors.

Still two other preconditions are for the state, first, not to crowd out financially the private sector and second, to establish the necessary legal and administrative mechanisms for the protection of property rights and the enforcement of contracts. Regarding the first aspect, we saw earlier that the public budget on both the current and the capital account was financed partly from tax and other revenues of the state, partly by citizens and *metics*, who undertook to finance and maintain various services that fell in the categories of *trierarchy* and *liturgies* and partly from loans that were contracted on interest with the *treasuries of the gods*. Consequently, the public and the private sectors were financially segmented and the effects of changes in taxation affected only indirectly the structure of the interest rates and the availability of credit in the private markets. As for the second aspect, we have documented already that the quality of governance in classical Athens was on a par with that of Hong Kong in our times, implying that it was very friendly to economic growth, as it can be further ascertained from Harris (2016), even though of course heavy interventions by inspectors like the ones described by Figueira (1986, 164) in the case of grain dealers risked

---

22 We find it disappointing that in this age of digital cloud and lightning information dissemination the literature on *free banking* has failed to take notice of the money and banking case in classical Athens. We would have thought that the seminal contributions by Cohen (1992, 2008) and others would have been noticed much much earlier, because they provide evidence many centuries older than the controversial case of Scotland in the 17th century.

destroying the autonomy of markets and might result in undesirable social consequences over the longer run.

With these arrangements in place, one would expect that economic growth would have been quite robust, albeit in premodern terms. Did it materialize in any meaningful way? Having looked at this question, Amemiya (2007, 63) concludes that: "There is no evidence of economic growth in Athens during the fifth and fourth century." But by calling attention to the evidence presented by Morris (2004), which is based on the index of per capita consumption over the period from 800 to 300 BCE, he concurs that economic growth in the period under consideration may have been about 0.14% per annum, and that it compares favorably with the increase of 0.2% per annum in the Netherlands from 1580 to 1820 AC. Moreover, three years later came along a paper by Ober (2010), which provided further evidence and arguments in support of these estimates. As for the future, we are confident that through tireless digging for hard evidence, in conjunction with the adoption of ingenious new computational approaches, results will continue to fill the gap in our knowledge on this issue.[23]

For example, the discussion in the blog Pseudoerasmus (2015) contains already several new hypotheses to revise or even supplement the assumptions of the neoclassical growth model underlying equation (3) and, if anything is certain, more evidence will come by in the coming years to enable us to discriminate among alternative theories of ancient Greek economic growth. But while endeavoring in this direction, one should be aware of the risk that applying modern growth accounting techniques to this ancient economy may be misplaced. To explain the reason, suppose that institutions and culture in classical Athens evolved inherently to promote high and sustainable economic growth rates. Then, certainly, in the absence of substantial rates of growth by U.S. standards in the last 200 years, that market economy was a complete failure. But what if the institutions and the culture had not been oriented toward facilitating fast and sustainable GDP growth? What if they had been ordained to achieve other objectives like promoting a good life, as understood at the time, or social cohesion through means oriented egalitarianism, or even other forms of happiness and *eudaemonia* like participating in the democratic process and shaping the future of their state? Would we

---

23 By the standards of the last 200 years in Western type democracies estimates of economic growth in premodern periods are always low. However, we doubt strongly that economic growth in Athens was as low as estimated by the aforementioned authors, even though they find them sufficiently high to warrant talking about Wealthy Hellas. Quite certainly Total Factor Productivity (TFP) might be low because of insignificant technological advances. But as per equation (3) the rate of economic growth depends also on labor and capital. If Athens added several thousand slaves and *metics* each decade from 480 to 430, as demographic research might support, the economy ought to have grown swiftly even without incremental productivity growth. We are indebted to Figueira for drawing our attention to this possibility and keep his very interesting intuition in our files marked "future research."

then judge their performance on a binary scale of success or failure using economic growth criteria of contemporary vintage? In our view, aside from measures based on GDP, an index including all achievements would place classical Athens at the top of a unique rank of its own.

Certain authors argue that the wealth Athens amassed would not have been possible without the tributes paid by the city-states participating in the *Delian League*. But French (1964, 92–93, 96–97) notes that Athens absorbed tremendous costs in leading this alliance and that when the *funds* of the league were merged around 440 BCE (Blamire 2001, 99), Athens had already attained a high level of wealth (French 1964, 136–137). This claim is again a strong argument in favor of the view that Athens' economic strength during the 5th century (the "empire" period) and the 4th century was mainly not the result of the economic exploitation of its allies, but of its own economic dynamics in creating and distributing wealth to its constituents. Through its political- and market-based institutions, Athens managed to become wealthy, to afford the glorious monuments we so admire today, and to give impetus to the intellectual accomplishments that later became the basis of Western civilization.[24]

In conclusion, the Fed does not have the means to deliver on its economic growth mandate. The remarkable postwar economic growth in the United States was achieved not because of Fed's policies but in spite of them. Even more ominous is that by pursuing these policies, the Fed as banker to the world has contributed significantly to the current problem of unsustainable indebtedness in Western-type democracies, as well as to the increased frequency and severity of financial crises. Perhaps this explains why we hear now all the more frequently acclaimed voices calling for its abolishment and the adoption of some variant of *free banking*.[25]

7.4 The interest rate

In equation (2), the symbol K_{t-1} stands for the undepreciated value of the means of production used in conjunction with labor L_t to produce output Q_t; and the interest rate r^{cr} used in Graph (iv) in Figure 6.2 measures the income that the owner of the means of production earns per unit of K_{t-1} for having committed his funds and /or those that he borrows from the market in the particular line of production. In the literature, the percentage rate of this income is referred to alternatively as return on capital, price of capital, remuneration of

---

24 As already mentioned, Morris (2004) and Ober (2010, 2015) provide evidence to the effect that Athens during classical times achieved relatively low but significant economic growth by the then prevailing standards. Bresson (2007, 2016a), Harris (2016), and others hold the same view.

25 For a compilation of the bibliography on free banking that existed up to the 1980s see Selgin, White (1994). For the literature since then, see White, Vanberg, Kohler (2015).

capital, yield or real rate of interest.[26] In contrast to this notion of the income derived from a productive investment, commonly we think of the interest income one earns by making a deposit in a commercial bank. Ultimately, the interest income earned from a deposit in a bank is not unrelated to the interest income earned from investing the same deposit in the production of goods and services. The reasons can be explained easily by reference to Graphs (iii)–(iv) in Figure 6.2. But they become a little more complicated in monetary systems where the currency is paper, the value of which depends on the trust of the issuing government. Let us see the source of the complications.

Monetary systems on a fiat standard differ from those on a commodity standard in at least one fundamental respect. This is that in the former systems, financial markets drive a wedge between "nominal" prices, that is, in the present case, fiat money denominated interest rates, and the "real" prices, that is, purchasing power or inflation free denominated interest rates. If the symbols r^{cr}, i^{cr} *and* θ denote the long-term rates of the real interest, nominal interest and inflation, respectively, it can be shown that this wedge translates into the following equation:

$$r^{cr} = i^{cr} - \theta \qquad (4)$$

In the United States, where the monetary system is on a fiat standard, the Fed is expected to bring about "moderate long-term interest rates." The *1977 Federal Reserve Reform Act* is not clear whether this mandate is set in terms of the "nominal" or the "real" interest rates. However, given that the government, the households and the enterprises form their plans under the veil of fiat money prices and the monetary authorities define price stability at $\theta = 0.02$, the Act may be construed to imply that the Fed should strive to attain moderate real long-term interest rates, r^{cr}, by steering appropriately its policy rate[27] toward the lowest possible long-term nominal interest rate, i^{cr}. On the contrary, in ancient Athens, where the monetary system was on a commodity standard, the integrity of the currency was maintained throughout and the general price level remained stable, the real and the nominal interest rates coincided, thus rendering the interest rate directly observable. Our first objective in this section is to assess the effectiveness of Fed's interest rate policies and to comment on the results by reference to the interest rates that prevailed in ancient Athens.

Aside from the above, the two monetary systems differ markedly on account of the nature and range of government activities in the financial

---

26 The preceding can be summarized more succinctly by reference to the following quotation from Ricardo (1821, 511):

> The interest of money is not regulated by the rate at which the Bank (Authors: He means the Bank of England) will lend,..., but by the rate of profit which can be made by the employment of capital, and which is totally independent of the quantity or of the value of money.

27 According to Bullard (2016, 6), the Fed sets a short-term interest rate, in particular the Federal Funds Rate (FFR), which in turn influences all other nominal interest rates.

markets, and hence on their influence in the determination of the real long-term equilibrium interest rate. Recall from Section 3.3 that Athens did not run budget deficits and whenever unintended ones arose for whatever reason they were covered by loans from within the public sector. By contrast, the government in the United States has been running consistently budget deficits throughout the postwar period and covers them by floating various types of debt certificates in the financial markets where it stands in competition with households and businesses. As a result, ignoring the problem of its scale, the U.S. government influences the formation of interest rates through three channels, that is, deficit spending, debt servicing and the formal and informal cooperation it extracts from the Fed. Our second objective is to trace the interest rate, political economy and wider democracy ramifications that emanate from these institutional arrangements.

7.4.1 *Real interest rates in the United States and ancient Athens*[28]

Let us go back for a moment to the production function in equation (2). The marginal product of capital is given by the expression:

$$\frac{\partial Q_t}{\partial K_{t-1}} = \alpha A_t \left(\frac{L_t}{K_{t-1}} \right)^{1-\alpha}, \; \alpha, A_t > 0. \tag{5}$$

We observe that it is positive and that it declines as the capital input K_{t-1} increases while the labor input L_t remains fixed. This is the famous law of declining marginal products, and we invoke it here in order to establish the proposition that since capital in the United States is certainly more abundant relative to labor than it was in ancient Athens, the interest rate in the former country can be expected to be lower than in the latter. Moreover, given the decline in the labor-capital ratio in the United States since the 1960s, we would expect the interest rate to have trended significantly downward. How far has this expectation materialized? Have Fed's interest rate policies precipitated developments in this front and, if in the positive, have they been successful? Below, we turn to these questions in the same order.

7.4.1.1 *The interest rate in the United States in the postwar period*

Kravis (1959, 943) has reported that during the period 1949–1957, the average nominal interest rate in the United States was 8.66%. Over the same period, the implicit GDP deflator increased on the average 2.42% per annum, thus leading to an average economy-wide real interest rate 6.24%.

---

28 Henceforth, and unless indicated specifically otherwise, whenever we refer to the "interest rate" we shall mean the "real interest rate."

Approximating the rate of inflation by the implicit GDP deflator,[29] the International Monetary Fund (IMF) estimates that for the period 1961–2015, the real interest rate in the United States averaged 3.88%.[30] As expected from equation (5), the annual return on capital declined on the average by 37.8%. This is our first finding.

Now, looking through the lenses of equation (4) and allowing for an inflation rate of 2%, during the period 1960–2015, the Fed targeted the interest rate by changing the policy rate, that is, the Federal Funds Rate (FFR). So, let us see what happened in the credit markets. Figure 7.2 displays the trend components of three key interest rates in the United States. Their mean values, standard deviations and confidence intervals are exhibited in Table 7.4. Looking from left to right at the rows labeled r^{cr}, *rgov* and *rcorp* observe that the annual average cost of borrowing that the Fed targeted and the cost of borrowing by the government and the corporations varied narrowly around 3.17%, 2.44% and 3.43%, respectively. In conjunction with the above estimate of the overall return on capital, these figures imply that the Fed overestimated the cost of borrowing by the government to the tune of 23.1% [(2.44/3.17)−1] and underestimated the cost of borrowing by corporations and borrowers at large by 8.2 [(3.43/3.17)−1] and 22.4[(3.88/3.17)−1][31] percent, respectively. Therefore, if the Fed aimed, as it ought, at the long-run real economy-wide cost of borrowing, year in year out they missed the target they set quite significantly. This is our second finding.

Table 7.4 Means, standard deviations and confidence intervals of the trend components of the public, private and policy interest rates in the United States over the period 1960–2015[1]

Variables	Definitions	Means	Standard errors	95% confidence intervals
r^{cr}	Fed's policy rate[2]	0.0317	0.00221	0.02214–0.04126
rgov	Government bond yield[3]	0.0244	0.00298	0.01844–0.03037
rcorp	Corporate bond yield[4]	0.0343	0.00298	0.02832–0.04208

1 All data come from the database of the Federal Bank of St. Louis.
2 This interest rate has been computed by subtracting from the effective Federal Funds Rate (FFR) the expected rate of inflation of 2%.
3 The ten-year government bond yield is the series IRLTLT01USQ156N.
4 Moody's corporate bond yield is series Aaa.

29 Computed from the series GDRDEF, which is found in the database of the Federal Reserve Bank of St' Louis, the average annual rate of inflation over the period 1961–2015 was 3.42%
30 International Monetary Fund, World Development Indicators, Series FR.INR.RINR.
31 We assume here that households borrowed at the average real interest rate over the period 1961–2015.

An additional finding worth noting is that consistently the government borrowed at 1% less than the interest rate paid by prime business borrowers. To some extent, this difference certainly reflects the standard tax-related forces that render governments on the average less risky than household and business borrowers in the loan markets. But in the case of the United States, we consider that this margin is actually smaller than it would be warranted because it reflects the perception of lenders that the government via the Fed controls the issuing of dollars and as a result, if bad developments come to worse, it will not default. However, as we emphasized in the introductory chapter, if a worldwide crisis erupts no one can guarantee that the U.S. dollar will remain invincible, at least not under the current U.S. foreign policies.

Finally, let us shift attention to Figure 7.2. We saw earlier that up until 2000, the Fed targeted the money supply and that it did so unsuccessfully because in 1960–1980 (1980–2000), increasing (decreasing) money supply was accompanied by increasing (decreasing) of the Federal Funds Rate. That is, the policy turned out to be internally inconsistent to have real effects, if did have any at all, and as a result the Fed switched to targeting r^{cr} by pushing r^{cr} along its downward trend that had started back in 1980. Observe that with considerable time delay, eventually this policy dragged downward both the government and the corporate bond yields. But even though from 1980 to 2000 the economy grew smoothly enough to call it a period of "great moderation," slowly but steadily many fundamentals worsened, and as argued by Bitros (2015), the international financial crisis that erupted in 2007 was instigated to a large extent by omissions and commissions of not only

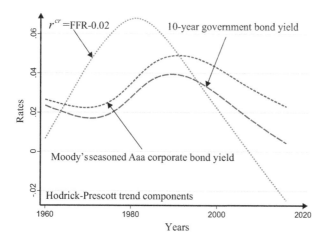

Figure 7.2 Long-term real public and private interest rates in the United States over the period 1960–2015.

the U.S. fiscal but also monetary authorities. In particular, because of the highly accommodative Fed policies, public and private indebtedness has skyrocketed and become unsustainable, saving has declined dramatically, capital formation has slowed down, the capital stock is growing old to the detriment of productivity gains, etc.

7.4.1.2   The interest rate in ancient Athens

From Sections 3.3 and 5.2.2.4, it follows that in ancient Athens, there existed two distinct money markets: The one operated in the public sector and handled the financial exchanges of the state with the *treasuries of the gods*, whereas the other operated in the private sector and catered to the financial needs of households and enterprises. Moreover, the two money markets were interconnected through the channel of the demand and supply for bank deposits (see Graph (iii) in Figure 6.2), since the *treasuries of the gods* deposited their surpluses with the banks in the private sector to earn interest income. In this context, recall from Section 3.3 that the interest rates in the former money market varied in the range from 1.2% to 6%, whereas those in the latter varied for "landed" loans around 12% and for "maritime" loans over 100%. So, the question is how we might explain these big differences.

In the money market, that was internal to the state sector, the level of interest rates was much lower than that in the private sector for at least three reasons. The first is well known and has to do with the difference between individuals and the state regarding the so-called pure time preference. Human beings are under a fundamental dimension of uncertainty. That is, they face a measurable probability of death at any moment, which renders the enjoyment of future rewards from their efforts uncertain. Because of this condition, they become inherently impatient and demand to receive payment of commensurate interest in order to abstain from present consumption and thus release resources for investment or loans, that is, future consumption. Because of their impatience, we say that individuals have a pure time preference in the sense that they prefer present to future consumption. On the contrary, since it is an institution with infinite horizon, the state is free of any impatience, present and future state consumption is of equal value, and hence pure time preference is zero. Therefore, some portion of the large difference between the interest rates in the two money markets emanated from the impatience of individuals because of the inescapable probability of death.

Well known is also the second reason for which the interest rates on loans contracted by the state are generally lower than those paid by private borrowers. This comes down to the difference in the risk of default by borrowers and the loss of capital and interest by lenders. As is the case today, the loans to the Athenian state by the *treasuries of the gods* carried limited risk of default because ultimately their repayment was guaranteed by the authority of the *Assembly* to raise the necessary funds through taxes or other means. There is no doubt that in periods of war and/or in periods when the climate in the *Assembly* was dominated by strife among political factions, the riskiness of state debts increased and vice versa. Nor is it there any doubt that in such periods, the interest rates in this money market would move in unison with those in the private money market, since the managers of the *treasuries of the gods* would have first-hand knowledge of the changing financial conditions in the economy. But such shifts would explain the variability of the interest rates within the indicated ranges, not the difference in the levels, which related to the perceived differences in the risks of default.

The third source of influences that determined the wide difference between public and private interest rates is the difference in the competitive structure of the two money markets. The one in the state sector functioned pretty much like the well-known model of bilateral monopoly.[32] On the one side were the representatives of the *Boule*, and hence ultimately of the *Assembly*, and on the other, the leadership of the *treasuries of the gods*. Owing to its scale and the fact that the state was the main source of the wealth they managed, quite certainly, the former enjoyed strong bargaining power over the latter and thus they were able to bargain for low interest rate relatively to those that prevailed in the private sector. But the bargaining setup should not be interpreted to imply that the heads of the *treasuries of the gods* were devoid of all independence because they bore their own responsibilities for the management of the wealth with which they were entrusted by the state.

Perhaps no other example is more suitable to highlight this point than the issue of ownership over the statue of Athena in the Acropolis, which was covered with clothing and ornaments of gold with an estimated value of 700–1,000 talents. The *treasury of Athena* served three financial functions. It kept the state's short-term cash balances to smooth out the management of the state's budget; it received donations from the state as well as from private donors and certainly up to the beginning of the Peloponnesian War, it stood as guardian of the tributes contributed by the allies for the common cause of the defense against the Persians. On these grounds, it is not surprising that an issue of ownership emerged as to whom the wealth in the statue belonged. For, if it was owned by the *treasury* itself, the ultimate owner was the state and no interest was due for its use in exceptional circumstances. But if the owner was the goddess Athena, the heads of the *treasury* acted on her behalf and were obliged to exact from the state an interest rate that was appropriate for the risks that prevailed at the time of the loans.

---

32 Bilateral monopoly is a market structure which consists of one monopoly on demand side, called monopsonist, that is sole buyer, and a monopoly on the supply side, called monopolist, that is sole seller.

7.4.1.3 Comparative assessment

In the years leading to the 1960, the interest in the United States was a little over 6%. Since then and up to 2015, the interest rate has declined to around 2.7%, with government borrowing at rates varying narrowly around 2.44% and the safest business borrowers at around 3.43%. The decline by almost 50% in the overall interest rate reflects the decline in the return on capital, whereas the difference between the government and the business interest rates reflects the difference in the risk of default between the two categories of borrowers.

Most likely, the significant decline in the overall interest rate in the United States would have been much more sizable, if particularly in dec-ades after 1980, both the government and the public had not resorted to excessive borrowing and accumulation of debt, which by all accounts have become by now unsustainable. Consequently, the Fed, which has accom-modated if not encouraged the development of these ominous trends, at long last must reverse trends toward normalcy by taking the lead in rais-ing the interest rates so as to slow down the massive government deficits, mainly for consumption purposes, stimulate saving and the return to healthy economic growth through investment in physical capital expansion and modernization.

Unlike the government in the United States, the state in ancient Athens ran neither deficits nor accumulated debts and, whenever circumstances compelled it to borrow for periods longer than expected, the funds origi-nated from previous budget surpluses that had been donated to and man-aged by the *treasuries of the gods* for unforeseen contingencies. Borrowing from this facility involved paying interest at rates which varied according to the scarcities and the risks that prevailed in the financial markets. However, we do know that the interest rates charged for such loans were less than 6% and at times as low as 1.2%. Considering that we are talking about state loans 25 centuries ago, these low interest rates compare astonishingly well with those of government loans in the United States during the postwar pe-riod. We dare even surmise that relatively to senators and congressmen, the Athenians in the *Assembly* who decided on the terms of borrowing should have felt more comfortable to paying these interest rates, since they knew that the corresponding interest expenditures would be stashed away as in-come of the *treasuries of the gods* and be available again for borrowing in the future.

The interest rates in the private sector of ancient Athens were two to four times those in the United States in the postwar period. Hence, draw-ing as we should on the established proposition that the interest rates are related inversely to the level of a country's economic development, it is rather surprising that based on this index, the Athenian economy stood relatively to the United States to where many emerging countries stand today.

7.4.2 Public goods and the rate of interest

Earlier, we emphasized in several places that throughout classical times, ancient Athens operated on balanced budgets or at least it balanced whatever unforeseen deficits arose with loans from the *treasuries of the gods*, that is, from within the public sector. This policy was applied with two provisions. First, that they cared to achieve surpluses in previous years so as to accumulate enough reserves to cover unforeseen contingencies; and second, that these reserves did not remain inactive but returned to the economy with the mediation of the *treasuries of the gods* to earn high interest income. Also, we emphasized that balancing the budget did not in any way hinder the construction and operation of large and small government buildings, water system, monuments and a great assortment of other public goods and services. In applying these policies, Athenians acted many centuries ahead of Keynes as if they had been inspired by his advice, spelled out in the quotation that we cited in the introductory chapter. That is, they employed the capital account of the budget to combat short patches of unemployment and avoided the accumulation of deadweight unproductive debt.

All decisions to invest in public goods were taken in the *Assembly*, where the male Athenians thought and behaved as guardians of their state, that is, for the common good. If budget surpluses came short and the state had to borrow from the *treasuries of the gods* to finance these investments, they made sure that they paid the lowest possible interest rate under the circumstances and that the loans were repaid so that the resources might be available again in the future. From the evidence, we know that at times they authorized payment of interest rates between 1.2% and 6% per annum. But in their private lives, they paid interest rates of 12% or even higher. Naturally, there arises the following question: why were Athenians as private individuals willing to pay interest rates so much higher relative to the ones they negotiated and authorized as members of the *Assembly*? Even though speculative, we believe that the following arguments may provide an answer.

As members of the *Assembly,* the Athenian citizens acted on behalf of an entity, that is, the state, with which they associated properties like: *longevity* for many generations to come; *reduced uncertainty*, since the potential cost of unexpected calamities might be spread through taxation over many people; and *allegiance* to unborn generations to whom the current generations felt obliged to contribute as their forefathers had done for them in the past. So, the calculus that they applied to the state's saving and investment affairs differed significantly from the individualistic criteria that they employed in their own private saving and investment decisions. To highlight the difference, recall that under Pericles, Athens built several monuments so luxurious and sturdy that some like the Parthenon continue to defy the relentless savages of man and time by standing in the places where there were erected, whereas the beauty of what is left from others may be appreciated in the new Acropolis Museum of antiquities in Athens.

From the decisions to commit the huge resources that were required for their construction, it follows that the citizens who participated and voted favorably in the *Assembly* must have felt as if the timing and the social value of the services from these public goods mattered for them only to the extent that they enriched the lives of future generations of Athenians. Or, expressing the same feeling more technically, they exercised extreme patience, which implies that they assigned to these investments zero time preference and looked to borrowing, if necessary, the required funds at the lowest possible interest rate, not from the market, but from the *treasuries of the gods*. We shall call the harmony in this behavioral dualism of the Athenian citizens as the *Miracle of Direct Democracy*. For, it must spring from its mechanisms that the structuralist–individualist nature of human beings was molded through *paideia* into the character of Athenians as citizens responsible for their city.

How striking and unique this property is in comparison to the developments in contemporary representative democracies may be appreciated by reference to the two approaches to public investment found in the literature on *cost-benefit analysis*. The first, advocated among others by Baumol (1968) and Harberger (1972), suggests appraising the feasibility or not of a public project on the basis of the so-called *Social Opportunity Cost* (SOC). According to it, a public project is worth undertaking only if the value of social benefits that will result exceeds the loss of removing from the private sector the necessary investment resources. Dominant in this approach is the idea that generally investment resources should be applied to those sectors where they are most efficient on the basis of market valuations. The second approach, advocated by Sen (1961), Feldstein (1964) and others, argues that the proper criterion is the so-called *Social Rate of Time Preference* (STP) or *Social Discount Rate* (SDR). To arrive at this recommendation, for example, Feldstein (1964, 365–366) poses and answers positively the following questions:

> Economists have long believed that individuals irrationally discount future pleasures merely because of their futurity. Should not the government correct this error, the argument continues, by substituting its own interpretation of the "public good" for the opinions of public preference expressed through the market or ballot-box?

Both approaches miss the uniformity of decision-making in the context of the Athenian democracy. But the one suggested in the above quotation is also fundamentally flawed because: (a) it erodes the legitimacy of representative democracy by allowing governments as agents to override the preferences that the citizens as principals reveal through the electoral process; (b) it ignores the reality of politics and politicians as expressed in Franklin's appraisal mentioned right in the beginning of the introductory chapter; and (c) it substitutes authority for voluntarism and by doing so it undermines the trust and the bonds of citizenship among present and future generations.

7.5 The two currencies from an international perspective

Having come out of the big war in the 1940s victorious, having sponsored the generous Marshall plan for the reconstruction of European and other countries and having skillfully drawn on the relative scale and strength of its economy ever since, the United States has managed to turn its currency into the preeminent international means of payments and store of value. Even though in the meantime certain other countries and their currencies have gained ground in international financial transactions, as we saw in the introductory chapter, by all metrics, the position of the dollar remains to a great extent invincible. In particular, according to Despres, Kindleberger, Salant (1966), since the 1960s, the United States has attained and maintains the status of the "banker of the world," whereas gradually in more recent decades, Gourinchas, Rey (2007) document that it has evolved also into the dominant "venture capitalist of the world."

Exactly like the United States in 1945 AD, Athens in 480 BCE had emerged victorious against the Persians in the battle of Salamis and embarked with its allies on political and economic arrangements that were destined to lead to the achievements, collectively known as the *golden age* of Greece. Recall that shortly after that battle, Athens managed in 478 BCE to establish the *Delian League*, also referred to in the literature as the *First Athenian Alliance* and Athenian Empire, which lasted until 404 BCE. At various times, the alliance numbered from 150 to 330 member-states; initially, its headquarters were on the island of Delos and from 454 BCE in Athens; and its main objective was to provide security to its members against renewed threats from the Persians. Considered in this context, but keeping in mind the analogies of time and scale, the consolidation in the use of the Attic drachma among the member-states of the alliance and beyond that Figueira (1998, 469–478) describes by reference to the available evidence and van Alfen (2011) fully ascertains is reminiscent of the process through which the dollar gained dominance in the decades since the war. So, what we should like to attempt in this section is to identify the driving forces in the two cases and assess the significance of their similarities and differences.

7.5.1 The U.S. dollar in the postwar period

To the world dominance of the dollar certainly has contributed a confluence of military, geopolitical and other strategic U.S. advantages. For example, President Trump has demonstrated publicly and for that matter, brazenly how the long-standing security arrangements under the North Atlantic Treaty Organization (NATO) have been used by U.S. administrations to promote exports of various weapons systems, and not only, as well as how military might projected through numerous land and naval bases around the world may be turned into powerful levers for pursuing "America first" objectives and proclamations. But concomitantly with them, various policies that the U.S. federal government and the Fed adopted over the decades have been instrumental in shaping the international economic and financial order in the national interests of the United States.[33] Central to the latter and most relevant to our analysis are the foreign exchange and the international trade policies that the United States adopted, brief summaries of which are presented below.

7.5.1.1 *From fixed exchange rates to freely floating fiat currencies*

More than anything else, the structure of the international monetary system that was agreed in 1944 at Bretton Woods reflected the choices of the United States. The aims of the system were to stabilize exchange rates, prevent competitive devaluations among the signatory countries and promote economic growth. To pursue them, the delegates to the conference set up two institutions, that is, the International Monetary Fund (IMF) and the International Bank for Reconstruction and Development (IBRD) or World Bank as it is known today. The IMF was endowed with contributions by the 29 founding member-states reckoned on their relative positions in the world economy and its mandate was to monitor the system of the exchange rates that was put in place and to take care of the imbalances that might arise in their balance of payments. As for the IBRD, its mandate was to provide assistance for the reconstruction of the war-savaged economies in Europe and elsewhere.

According to the agreement, the United States was expected to peg its currency at 35 dollars an ounce of gold and going forward to issue dollars in quantities appropriate to create and sustain the confidence in the convertibility of the dollar at this rate, whereas the other participating countries would peg their national currencies to the dollar at predetermined

---

33 The fundamental doctrine in the U.S. international relations since the war has changed only in form, not in substance. Until very recently policy makers tried to appear mindful and tactful regarding the implications of the constraints that emanated for their national policy choices from the institutions of the world order they themselves had put in place. But whenever the U.S. national interests called for, they would not stop short of destabilizing the international system to take advantage. At least this is what we understand from Volcker's (1978, 4) clear cut statement that:

> It is tempting to look at the market as an impartial arbiter ... But balancing the requirements of a stable international system against the desirability of retaining freedom of action for national policy, a number of countries, including the U.S., opted for the latter.

However now, in the advent of the bold push toward "America first" priorities, the Aeolus sac has opened and it is every country for itself. That is why we are afraid that the world will start moving on a path similar to the one that brought about the breakdown of the *First Athenian Alliance*, gave impetus to the Peloponnesian War, and eventually led to the downfall of Athens.

fixed rates with an allowable deviation of plus or minus 1%. Clearly, by its very structure, the system rendered the U.S lender of last resort and thus ultimately its sustainability depended on the condition that the United States would not borrow from the world more than the value of its stock in gold. The system entered into full operation in 1958 and performed quite successfully for over a decade. But during this period, the United States ran persistent balance-of-payment deficits that were covered by issuance of dollars and as a result the situation came to a heading in 1971. In particular, since the foreign-held dollars exceeded the value of U.S. stock in gold and it became apparent that the dollar was significantly overvalued, in the summer of that year, the U.S. government canceled the convertibility of the dollar to gold and let its exchange rate float freely in relation to the other currencies.

From the above brief narrative follows that over the years leading to 1971, the United States enjoyed a strong hegemonic currency status. Although it had agreed to follow domestic policies, which would preserve the above-mentioned dollar exchange rate, the United States adopted policies well in line with advantages like the one Eichengreen (2011, 3–4) has called "Extravagant privilege" and pointedly explained in the following quotation:

> …It costs only a few cents for the Bureau of Engraving and Printing to produce a $100 bill, but other countries have to pony up $100 of actual goods and services in order to obtain one. (That difference between what it costs the government to print the note and a foreigner to procure it is known as "seigniorage" after the right of the medieval lord, or seigneur, to coin money and keep for himself some of the precious metal from which it was made.) About $500 billion of U.S. currency circulates outside the United States, for which foreigners have had to provide the United States with $500 billion of actual goods and services.

Had the United States not undermined the quasi-gold standard of the Bretton Woods system, quite likely it would have lasted much longer than it did. But its demise helped bring to the fore a grave issue. This is that an international monetary system based on the dominance not of the United States but of any country is ominous for the financial stability of the world.

To reinforce this view, consider what has happened since 1971 under the present free floating system of fiat exchange currencies. Figure 7.3 displays the trends in the exchange rates of the dollar against the deutsche mark, the euro and the pound over the period 1971–2018. During these years, the $ depreciated 60% against the DM-€ and 37.5% against the £. Just for an example, let us assume that on the average, the dollar depreciated against all other currencies 50% or about 1% per annum. Even approximately, the implications are very serious. Let us see why. According to the World Bank, in the third quarter of 2018, the gross external debt of the United States reached 19.56

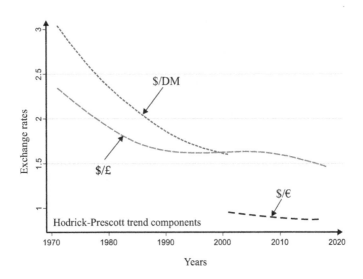

Figure 7.3 Exchange rates of the U.S. dollar ($) against the German deutsche mark (DM), the euro (€) and the British pound (£), 1971–2018.

trillion and of this, 16.38 were in dollars.[34] Assuming that this debt accumulated at a steady rate, its average each year amounted to 8.19 trillion. Hence, at the depreciation rate of 1%, it turns out that the countries holding this debt transferred to the United States goods and services worth 4.08 trillion dollars (= 8.19 × 50 × 0.01). Clearly, a subsidy of this order by the world to the United States is far more striking than Eichengreen's "Exorbitant privilege." So, it is high time that the United States should coordinate with other reserve currency nations to stabilize the exchange rate of the dollar.

This issue is urgent for at least two more key reasons. The first is to forestall the rising probability of an accident with devastating world repercussions. The United States is not as big as it used to be. As it was reasonable and expected, other countries like Germany, China and India have grown more rapidly in the meantime and have taken shares away from the United States in many important metrics. For example, even though it is far richer in per capita income, one may argue that the United States is not the biggest economy in the world anymore, since in Purchasing Power Parity values, the GDP of China is higher, and moreover its central bank holds in reserves a great deal of dollars. Therefore, it is fair to surmise that the dreadful scenario Eichengreen (2011, Ch. 7) describes is not so farfetched or unlikely to be ignored. For, if China and the other reserve countries mentioned above had not cooperated the last time around, the U.S. government and the Fed

---

34 See World Bank at https://databank.worldbank.org/data/embed-int/Table-2-SDDS-new/id/7857d781

would not have been able to control the 2007 housing crisis from spreading quickly across the globe and causing a financial Armageddon.

The second reason springs from the following dilemma: The domestic policies, which for 50 years have boosted United States exports by driving down the value of the dollar, run increasingly the risk of a sudden stop, that is, if some foreign dollar asset holders determine for any reason that they have had enough of losses and decide to sell them, the collapse of the dollar can be catastrophic. Controlling this risk recommends adopting domestic policies that will help halt the further depreciation of the dollar. However, in the process of removing this bias, the policies should not lead to a significant appreciation of the dollar because there looms another risk, which derives from the excessive dollar-based indebtedness of emerging and poor countries. In particular, if the dollar appreciates, it may help boost economic growth in these countries by stimulating their exports, but at the same time, it will raise the burden of servicing their debts and we cannot be certain as to the relative magnitude of these two effects. Therefore, thinking ahead of this risk, it is high time for international policy coordination among the world's main reserve currency countries or some other international arrangements to put the genie of world financial instability back into the bottle.

To summarize, as puzzling as the anomaly of the continued world dominance of the dollar is, the quest for an international monetary system the stability of which will be based more on institutions of world markets and less on the interests of a particular country or region is urgent. And it has become even more so because of the uncertainty created by the highly unsettling approaches to foreign trade that are pursued by the current U.S. administration.

7.5.1.2 Foreign trade policies

Up until very recently, U.S. trade policies in the post war period were based on a long honored doctrine pursued through two approaches. Referring to the doctrine, this is that lowering tariffs and expanding free trade go hand in hand with economic growth, reducing poverty and raising the trust of the world in liberty and free markets. As for the two approaches, the first aimed at introducing a rule-based international free trade system, whereas the second aimed at bilateral Free Trade Agreements (FTA), locally or internationally, but without undermining the general system of regulations. United States efforts following the former approach started soon after the end of the war. Initially, they led to the enactment of the General Agreement on Tariffs and Trade (GATT) in 1947 and culminated in 1995 with the establishment of the World Trade Organization (WTO), the membership of which expanded from 123 founding member-states to 164 as of December 2017.[35]

---

35 Under GATT, and to some degree because of it, the level of tariffs among major trading countries declined significantly. In particular, the average tariff levels from about 22% in 1947 were reduced to 5% in 1999.

On the other hand, beginning with the *Canada–United States Free Trade Agreement* (CUSFTA) in 1988, the United States has signed several FTAs with Canada and Mexico, as well as other countries that are far away such as with the ASEAN Free Trade Area countries in the South-East Asia.[36]

Even if we were able, we find it inappropriate to review here the arguments in favor or against the above two approaches. We believe that they are complementary and that they can help any country accelerate its rates of economic growth and at the same time develop comparative advantages in productive activities with pertinent resources and energies. Free trade under bilateral or multilateral agreements cannot be anything else but beneficial to all countries involved by their own accord. Instead, we should like to highlight the results of U.S. trade policies in terms of the degree of integration of its economy into that of the world. Table 7.5 shows three relevant indices. Column (6) displays foreign trade as a percentage of GDP. We observe that overall trade increased almost by a factor of 3.5, that is, from 8% in 1950 to 27% in 2017. This finding corroborates that the U.S. economy has become more intertwined now than ever before, even though its foreign trade is the lowest among advanced countries with the exception of Japan. Moreover, comparing columns (4) and (5), it turns out that: (a) the trade balance was in favor of the United States before 1971 but reversed thereafter; (b) while exports and imports grew modestly up to 1971, since then they have expanded very rapidly; and (c) given that after 1971, the dollar depreciated significantly against all other reserve currencies, exports did not increase as it might have been expected, quite likely because of losses in competitiveness that emanated from the decline in the long-term total factor productivity.

Unfortunately, the degree of U.S. globalization reflected in the indices of Table 7.5 was accompanied by benefits and costs that were unevenly distributed among social classes and regions. Mainly, human and physical capital holders residing in large urban centers benefited tremendously, whereas lower skilled inhabitants of isolated regions were hurt. Whole industrial sectors were decimated; jobs were transferred abroad; wages barely kept with inflation and in general, both republican and democratic federal and state administrations failed to undertake the balancing act that was required for this process of trade liberalization to continue bearing the fruits of rapid economic growth in advanced, emerging and poor countries. What happened in the United States transpired also in other matured economies, although the effects took different forms. As a result, we have entered into an extremely precarious juncture with a U.S. administration bent on slapping high flat tariffs on imports from both allied and adversarial countries alike,

---

36 On November 30, 2018, Canada, the United States and Mexico signed the new Canada-United States-Mexico Agreement (CUSMA). For more details, see www.international. gc.ca/trade-commerce/trade-agreements-accords-commerciaux/agr-acc/cusma-aceum/ index.aspx?lang=eng

Table 7.5 Globalization indices of the U.S. economy[1]

Years	Exports	Imports	GDP[3]	Exp/GDP	Imp/GDP	(Exp + Imp)/GDP
	(1)	(2)	(3)	(4) = (1):(3)	(5) = (2):(3)	(6) = [(1) + (2)]/(3)
1950[2]	12.36	11.61	299.83	0.041	0.039	0.080
1960[4]	25.94	22.43	542.38	0.048	0.041	0.089
1971	59.68	60.18	1164.85	0.051	0.052	0.103
1995	794.39	890.77	7639.75	0.104	0.117	0.221
2017	2351.97	2903.35	19488.39	0.121	0.149	0.270

1 All level figures are in current billions of dollars.
2 Figures for exports and imports of goods and services for 1950 derive from the series EXPCS and IMPGS found in the database of Federal Reserve Bank of St Louis.
3 The GDP figures come from the same series in the database of Federal Reserve Bank of St Louis.
4 Figures for exports and imports for all other years come from the website: www.census.gov/foreign-trade/guide/sec2.html#bop.

and who knows what else is in the offing besides the threat of ousting its chairman, if the Fed raises interest rates. Thus, as precisely described by Eichengreen (2011, 153–154) in the following quotation and few thought it as likely, where the world stands now is a trigger short of the abyss:

> One trigger could be political conflict between the United States and China. The simmering dispute over trade and exchange rates could break into the open. American politicians, who see China's failure to revalue its currency more quickly as giving it an unfair competitive advantage, resulting in a chronic trade imbalance and U.S. unemployment, could impose an across-the-board tariff on imports from the country. Beijing would not take this lying down. Or the United States and China could come into conflict over policy toward rogue states like North Korea and Iran. Imagine that the United States took military action against one of those regimes, contrary to the wishes of Beijing. Again, China might be tempted to do something significant to register its protest.
>
> One way for China to vent its anger and exert leverage over the United States would by using its financial weapon. Official Chinese agencies hold 13 percent of all U.S. government securities. Dumping them would send the bond market into a tizzy. As soon as they realized that the Chinese government was selling, other investors would pile on. Interest rates in the United States would spike. The dollar would crater. This demonstration of its vulnerability could cause exporters, importers, and investors to abandon the dollar permanently.

Can the leadership of the great U.S. democracy allow the situation to unravel? We should like to postpone assessing the odds until the next chapter.

7.5.2 *The drachma in classical times*

All along in the preceding discussion, we implied that there is an international credit market in which surplus-saving countries offer loans in various currencies to deficit-saving countries to cover the shortfalls that they experience each year in the current and capital accounts of their balance of payments. Implicit in the discussion was also the understanding that countries cannot borrow ad infinitum from this market, because in the short run, they pay increasing borrowing costs in the form of higher interest rates and national currency depreciation, whereas over the long run, the credit market may shut down on them altogether. By contrast, in classical times, Athenian deficits and surpluses from foreign transactions had to be settled with coins, bullion or in kind. This is not to imply that credits among local and international merchants and even among states were unknown. Drawing on the following quotation, Amemiya (2007, 106) argues that making payments for cross-border commerce-generated credits certainly was practiced:

> There was no paper money in classical Athens, but there was an equivalent of bank checks. When Stratokles needed funds available at the distant Black Sea, he did not take his money with him; instead, he carried a bank guarantee of payment issued by Pasion's bank, where Stratokles had a deposit (Isocrates *Trapezicus*, 35–7). "When the merchant Lykon was leaving Athens and wanted to make payment of 1,640 drachmae to a business colleague, he directed that funds on deposit at Pasion's bank be paid at a future time to Kephisiades (Demosthenes, *Against Callippus*, 3)". (Athenians called this kind of cashless settlement *diagraphè*. The verb *diagraphò* means "cross out").

Or, for a few more examples, Aeschines (3.104) refers to a loan of one talent at an interest rate of 12% that Demosthenes had advanced to the people of Oreus, the Athenian politician Androtion made a loan without interest to the people of Arsinoe and the *Temple of Appolo* on Delos made loans both to Delians and to foreigners and neighboring states. But such loans were not widespread or institutionalized, so it is safe to proceed on the conceptualization that there was no international credit market of any significance.

On this stipulation, Athens did not borrow from abroad; it had neither external debt nor payments for debt and interest; and hence its balance of payments consisted only of the current account, an imaginary configuration of which would have looked like that in Table 7.6 below. In Section 5.2.4, we concluded that because of the high imports of grains, the balance of trade in row (1) was perennially in deficit, that is, Imp −Exp > 0 and that the shortfall was covered by other means of payment like those reported in row (2). The composition of the sub-accounts in rows (3)–(5) requires some more careful consideration, but we cannot be here anything more than sketchy. The

Table 7.6 Athenian balance of payments

Debits	Credits
1. Exports (Exp)[1]	1. Imports (Imp)[1]
2. Exports of coins and bullion	2. Imports of coins and bullion
3. Transfers in kind	3. Transfers in kind
4. Transfers in currency and bullion	4. Transfers in currency and bullion
5. Bank deposits from abroad	5. Bank withdrawals from abroad
Balance: 0	

1 Nonfiduciary exports and imports.

states that participated in the *Delian League* in the 5th century paid tribute to Athens, presumably for defraying the costs of common defense. At least initially some contributed by offering fully equipped and manned *triremes*, whereas others paid their dues in acceptable means of payment. The former had no footprint on the Attic economy, whereas contributions in kind would show in row (3) and contributions in currency contributions in row (4) on the Debits side. If any subsidies in kind and currency were advanced by the *hellenotamiai* in Athens to allied states, they would appear in rows (3)–(4) on the Credits side. On the other hand, bank deposits and withdrawals by foreigners like the merchant Lykon in the above quotation would be recorded in row (5). What cannot be disputed is that by one way or another, year in year out, the current account would be balanced. They did not have the diplographic accounting system we have today to assemble and publicize the results of international financial transactions, but the algorithm of balancing dues and claims was reflected in their actions.

Our objective in the sequel is to highlight the arrangements through which the Attic drachma attained its exemplary status in the Eastern Mediterranean and beyond in classical times

7.5.2.1 State commitment to no debasement

For a currency to be accepted globally as a means of payment and store of value, the state that backs it must inspire by its behavior and institutional structure the confidence that it will defend its integrity even under extraordinary national circumstances. In the case of the drachma, this condition was fully satisfied by the fact that the supreme governing body of the state, that is, the *Assembly*, was controlled by the same people who would be hurt by a decision to debase the currency.

How extreme and farfetched such a possibility must have been considered at the time, we had the opportunity to stress earlier when we mentioned the incident with the golden ornaments of the statue of the goddess Athena in the closing years of the Peloponnesian War. In particular, recall from the introduction to Chapter 5 that in 404/403 BCE, Athens reached the end of the road in its fight with Sparta and leaders scraped the bottom of the *treasury* vaults for leftovers. So, the choice came down to either debase the currency or use the gold in the ornaments of the statue. Under those trying circumstances and in the light of the order they had adopted for drawing on the reserves, we surmise that their decision proved revealing of their convictions and wise because, while the ornaments could be recreated later on, debasing the drachma would have destroyed the confidence in the honor of Athens and its governors, that is, the Athenian citizens themselves.

Additionally, Athens was motivated to maintain its commitment for a stable drachma by market and institutional constraints. One example is the circulation of parallel currencies. In view of the competition that prevailed among coins from various foreign mints, Athens must have been dissuaded from adopting policies like imposing high seigniorage charges, which would have discouraged access to its mint and placed the drachma at a competitive disadvantage.[37] There was another constraint in this. Assume that Athens ran sizable fiscal deficits, which in the view of drachma asset holders created the prospect of imminent imposition of taxes. Rationally thinking many of them would try to switch from taxable to nontaxable forms of assets. In the process, they would substitute drachma for non-drachma holdings, which would create a wave away from the drachma and into foreign currency denominated assets. Hence, Athens had to be very prudent with its fiscal policies to prevent such incidences. Still, a third constraint emanated from the legislative efforts to spread the use of the drachma among its allies. If it expected through the *Coinage Decree* in the 5th century and *Nicophon's Law* in the 4th to convince them to shut down their mints and adopt the drachma, Athens ought to honor its commitments with regard to its currency.

7.5.2.2 Safeguarding the integrity of the drachma through democratically controlled institutions

In Chapter 2, we explained in good detail the network of institutions, which were in charge of the currency. In all stages, that is, from the assignment of permits to private contractors to extract the ore from the Laurion mines, to taking the silver to the mint to strike the coins and to making sure that the currency in circulation retained its integrity, the supervising magistrates were elected by lot, appointed for terms of one year, held individually responsible to carry out the specific tasks with efficiency and honestly and remained fully accountable until audited.

---

37 Alternatively, given that no allied or adversary state had access to the silver to compete with the drachma, the Athenians might have understood intuitively that high minting fees were counterproductive.

At the top of the state apparatus in all currency matters was the *Boule* which, as we explained in Section 2.1, acted as the executive branch of the government and reported to the *Assembly.* Therefore, ultimately, all responsibility for setting the objectives of the policies in the domain of the currency, as well as for the effectiveness and transparency of operations with which they were pursued by the authorized public servants, rested with the Athenian citizens. From our reading of the evidence, we surmise that the whole supply and manufacturing chain of the currency had been set up on the principle that "absolutely no one is to be trusted." Citizens were appointed to tasks by selection processes that aimed at minimizing the opportunities for favoritism and corruption, but even so they performed under the ever presence of *bouleutai.* In the front desk of the currency services were the *dokimastai* in the markets of Athens and Piraeus and the People's Court for speedy adjudication of disputes that arose in the process of testing the purity and the origin of coins. The testers were slaves, and hence purposely open to severe punishment in cases of gross errors or abuses, and the law of Nicophon empowered them to impose stiff penalties including the confiscation of the whole lot of tested coins, if found adulterated.

7.5.2.3 Market determined exchange rates

In Chapter 6, we established that the determination of the supply of money was left to the "currency," "silver bullion," "deposits" and "credit" markets as depicted in Figure 6.2. According to this setup, the equilibrium prices of the currency were determined by the interplay of currency demand and supply that emanated, respectively, from the supply and demand for goods and services. For methodological reasons, we conducted the analysis in that configuration of the monetary module as if the Athenian economy was closed to the world, even though we know that it was not. Hence, now we shall relax this assumption so as to incorporate the implications of the activities in Table 7.6 for the exchange rate of the currency.

Let us go back to Graph (i) in Figure 6.2 and assume that the equilibrium price of the drachma increased from $\bar{p}^c$ to $\bar{p}_1^c$. Then each drachma in circulation would buy more goods and services than before, thus stimulating their production at home and raising their imports from abroad. In turn, owing to the increased demand pressure, the prices of goods and services produced locally would rise gradually relative to the purchasing power of the drachma, leaving the general price level unchanged. The standard effect in fiat currency systems of differential inflation on the exchange rate would be absent. Now, given that the current account was always balanced, the question is: how might the increase in the demand for imports affect the exchange rate of the drachma in relation to the exchange rates of the currencies in the states from where the imports would originate? To simplify the analysis for an answer, we assume that all additional imports would be procured from the nearby island of Aegina, which minted its own silver currency called the *Aeginitan stater* or *chelone*, showing a turtle on the obverse.

As both economies were open,[38] soon after the price of the drachma in Athens increased, the price of the chelone would increase as well through arbitrage, and their exchange rate would be maintained. But the appreciation of the chelone in terms of goods and services in Aegina would not lead to deflation, because the rise in demand by the Athenian importers would push the prices of goods and services upward, leaving again the general price level in Aegina unchanged. Therefore, as long as the exchange rates of currencies were based on the fixed quantity of silver that they contained, the prices of goods and services would adjust in all states so that the exchange rates would remain unchanged everywhere.[39]

The last issue has to do with the effects of foreign currency deposits and withdrawals, which would have been reported in row 5. These represented inflows and outflows from a stock of such assets and in any one year, the balance could be positive or negative. So, let us trace the potential implications by focusing on Graph (iii) in Figure 6.2. Their stock would have increased the "money base" of the Athenian economy by shifting the curve S^d to the right, expanding credit by the inverse of the average reserve ratio of the banking system, pushing the interest rate r^{cr} downward and possibly increasing investment and economic growth. No matter whether they had been attracted into Athens for speculative or transactions purposes, the drachma would have appreciated because of the standard differential interest rate effect. Moreover, depending on their size, the drachma might have appreciated further because of secondary effects from the expansion of incomes. But over the long run, the exchange rate would have returned to the international price of the silver contained in the various currencies. As for the flows, these might serve for signaling the course of probable developments in such sensitive areas as political stability and fiscal policy shifts.

38 We use the term "open" to imply that the two economies exchanged goods and services through some markets which functioned competitively. If the authorities in the one or the other economy prohibited the exportation or importation of certain goods, as it was the case with the exports of grains in Athens, such prohibitions did not render the economies less open than the United States that prohibit the exports of certain advanced electronic devices.

39 It is not at all surprising that Finley (1965, 23) arrived at the same conclusion in the following quotation:

> Unless Athens stopped all trade outside the Empire and unless she controlled all sources of raw silver, she could not 'trade away' Athenian money 'at Athenian valuation' in the sense in which that phrasing has been used. After all, the need is not on all one side. Athens had few surpluses, other than silver, and many shortages. Before she could manipulate coin-values to substantial advantage, she would have to exercise a compulsion on the exchange of goods in the Aegean far beyond anything proposed or even dreamed of. How, for example, could she have compelled others to bring in corn and slaves for her to purchase with over-priced drachmae, and at the same time have compelled others to buy Athenian vases, olive oil, or wine with the same coins but at a different coin-value?

7.5.2.4 Foreign trade policies

Import–export trade took place in an area specifically dedicated to such activities called *emporion*. In the port of Piraeus, this area was adjacent to the *agora*. Similarly, with the latter, it was delineated by a stone wall and it bordered on the sea front. All exchanges that took place in this area were carried out under the provisions of specific laws, which were enforced by the magistrates whom we mentioned in Table 5.1 with the title *epimelitai tou emporiou* or "overseers of the port."[40] In contemporary jargon, transactions in the *emporion* belonged roughly to the category of "wholesale trade," whereas those in the *agora* fell in the category of "retail trade" and were monitored by the magistrates called *agoranomoi*. That Athens invested the resources it took to build these vast structures with the ancillary docking, transporting, warehousing and hospitality facilities is clear proof of the importance it assigned to foreign trade for its survival and economic growth.[41]

Closely coordinated with the above were also the policies that Athens adopted in order to keep the sea lanes open to shipping and safe not only for its own trade but also that of its allies. When the *Delian League* was founded in 478 BCE, certainly the primary objective was common defense against the Persian threat. But later, when that threat vanished, the alliance turned into serving other purposes like fighting piracy in the Aegean. In the following quotation, Bresson (2016a, 302–303) gives us a very good glimpse into the services Athens provided in this respect:

> …Throughout its fifth-century empire, Athens policed the Aegean seas. Leaving from Athens or other naval bases on the Aegean, and operating almost everywhere, Athenian ships clearly provided decades of

---

40 For a comprehensive description of the functions that the *epimelitai tou emporiou* performed, the roles of the duty assessors and collectors, the rules that applied in the closing of contracts, the technology of selling and buying on the basis of *deigma* (sample), and many other minute but insightful details of what was going on in the area of *emporion,* see Bresson (2016a, Chapter 12).

41 As for the analysis of the reasons why foreign trade is such an important source of wealth, simple Athenian citizens and leaders were well informed by philosophers and economists. For example, Pseudo-Xenophon (*Constitution of the Athenians* 2.11–13) declared:

> …If some city is rich in ship-timber, where will it distribute it without the consent of the rulers of the sea? Again if some city is rich in iron, copper, or flax, where will it distribute without the consent of the rulers of the sea? However, it is from these very things that I have my ships: timber from one place, iron from another, copper from another, flax from another, wax from another…In addition, they will forbid export to wherever any of our enemies are, on pain of being unable to use the sea. And I, without doing anything, have all this from the land because of the sea; yet no other city has even two of these things: the same city does not have timber and flax, but wherever there is flax in abundance, the land is smooth and timberless. There is not even copper and iron from the same city, not any two or three other things in a single city, but there is one product here and another there.

peace in the Aegean. The tribute paid by the cities, which was in most cases modest, was in a way the price to be paid for security. Most of the tribute must have gone to pay for the fleet of warships... With the fall of Athens in 404 BCE... no longer had the means to police the seas as it had done during the preceding century. If the Athenians launched naval expeditions, it was first and foremost to protect their own maritime routes, and the consequences for other cities were, so to speak, only a collateral outcome.

That is, not too different policies than the ones contemporary superpowers adopt in order to ensure that the high seas remain open and secure for commercial fleets.

In Section 4.2, we presented the policy initiatives through which Athens encouraged its allies in the *first* and *second* alliances to adopt the drachma as their currency or at least apply common coinage standards when minting their own currencies. From the evidence, we concluded that indeed many member-states complied. They stopped minting and, considering also that they were obliged to pay the tribute in the Athenian currency, the drachma gained wide acceptance. In turn, its establishment as the dominant currency of the times reduced transactions costs and boosted trade throughout the region. In this process, Athens did not enjoy, like the United States does, the "Exorbitant privileges" that are associated with the world dominance of the U.S. dollar, but still it reaped considerable benefits. As we explained in Section 5.2.2.2, Athens and especially the port of Piraeus became a center where a merchant could find all sorts of commodities for re-export, with the exception of grains; obtain credit to finance his trading ventures; exchange his funds in one currency into another; deposit his money with the Athenian banks for later use; etc. In short, it was the enhanced value added from these services that helped Athens bridge the deficits in its trade account.

Moreover, at least during the *first* alliance or otherwise called imperial period, by controlling the routes of the sea trade through its naval power, in conjunction with the overarching dominance of its currency in the Eastern Mediterranean, Athens was able to influence the terms of trade agreements in its favor. To corroborate this assessment, the following quotation from Thucydides (*The Peloponnesian War*, 1.120.2) explains how the Corinthians described the consequences for those Peloponnesian states, which would refrain from participating in the war against Athens:

> ...For ourselves, all who have already had dealings with the Athenians require no warning to be on their guard against them. The states more inland and out of the highway of communication should understand that if they omit to support the coast powers, the result will be to injure the transit of their produce for exportation and the reception in exchange of their imports from the sea; and they must not be careless

judges of what is now said, as if it had nothing to do with them, but must expect that the sacrifice of the powers on the coast will one day be followed by the extension of the danger to the interior, and must recognize that their own interests are deeply involved in this discussion.

If they abstained and Athens had its way, Corinthians warned them, they risked losing access to the export markets to place their products, most likely the lesser loss by comparison to the loss of import markets to meet their needs. Hence, either explicitly by granting permits to trade in the expansive *emporion* of Piraeus and providing security in the Aegean trade routes, or implicitly by projecting its military might, Athens maintained and exploited a strong bargaining position both with regard to its allies and its adversaries.

Finally, given that the bulk of the deficit in the trade account emanated from imports of a few products in permanent or semipermanent scarcity, it is worth noting that foreign trade policies were characterized by various degrees of government intervention which aimed at smoothing their supply chains and discouraging profiteering. Top in this list were the grains, mainly wheat and to a lesser degree barley, olive oil, charcoal and timber. Export and re-export of grains were completely forbidden and at times the state would appear even as buyer on the demand side to make sure that their prices did not exceed certain officially determined levels (Bresson 2016a, 420–425). In other less pressing times, the import prices of these goods would be set after persuasive discussions among the *epimelitai tou emporiou* and the importers (Figueira 1986, 164). However, as the importation of these goods depended on many uncontrollable factors and government intervention risked causing greater harm than benefit to citizens, in the light of government intervention, their prices might be in less or more serious disequilibrium in the short run, but over the long haul, they converged to those determined internationally.

7.6 Summary

In this chapter, we assessed the performance of two distinct monetary systems. One based on a paper standard with a central bank mandated by the government to pursue four money-related objectives, and another based on a silver standard without a central bank, in which the government limits itself to the control of the qualities of the commodity currency, that is, form, weight and precious metal content, and the market determines everything else. Namely, the quantity of the currency, the quantity of money, the amount of bank deposits, the average reserve ratio of banks, the interest rate and the price of the currency in terms of goods and services. In particular, drawing on the *1977 Federal Reserve Reform Act*, we compared the performance of the monetary system in the United States in the postwar period with that of Athens in classical times by reference to the rates of inflation, unemployment, economic growth and the long-term interest rate. Additionally, given that in those times the drachma became in the Eastern Mediterranean and beyond as dominant as the U.S. dollar in the world during the postwar period, we assessed the two currencies from an international perspective. So, the task now is to summarize our main findings.

Already from the 1960s, the Fed had acceded to the view that because of market rigidities and "money illusion" on the part of workers, relative prices had become sticky, giving rise to a rather stable relationship between the rate of inflation and unemployment, that is, the well-known Phillips curve. As a result, drawing on numerous estimates of this curve, they interpreted their mandate for stable prices and full employment to imply objectives of 2% general inflation and 4% unemployment. For monetary policy, this has been the normal ever since. Instead, over the period 1960–2015, we calculated that the average rates of inflation and unemployment were, respectively, 3.8% and 6.15% per annum. The Fed failed on both counts because of impotence in the paper standard-based policy instruments, lack of appropriate coordination with fiscal policies or other developments in the state and the economy, which are beyond the domain of their responsibility. By contrast, in classical Athens where relative prices were fully flexible, all indications drawn from theory and the available historical evidence favor a normal of stable prices at 0% general inflation and full employment at 0% unemployment. We believe that this remarkable performance has very much to do with the combination of direct democracy, the limited role of the state in the control of the currency, the silver-based monetary standard and the determination of the quantity of money in the markets for currency, silver bullion, and bank deposits and credit. Even though the merits of the Athenian silver standard over the U.S. paper standard may have become clear by now, we shall return for further analysis in the next chapter.

Helpful in understanding the difference in the performance between these two monetary standards are the differences in the economic flexibility that characterized Athens in classical times and the United States more recently. For, if the quality of governance and economic freedom, which are primary determinants of economic flexibility, differ significantly, their differences might go a long way toward explaining the differences in the rates of inflation and unemployment. The evidence that we were able to put together on this issue is not just revealing but highly illuminating. With regard to the quality of governance, and on account of reasonable guesses, Athens was considerably ahead of the United States and very close to where Hong Kong is presently, whereas, with regard to economic freedom, Athens came ahead even of Hong Kong with the exception of a slight lag in the scores of the indices "Legal system and property rights" and "Regulation." Therefore, with reference to these findings, we surmised that economic flexibility in the United States has declined and hence it is no surprise that relative prices have become so sticky as to lead to higher inflation and unemployment rates.

Unsuccessful have been also the Fed's efforts to stimulate economic growth, irrespective of whether it targeted the growth rate via the demand or the supply channels. To corroborate this assessment, we investigated the relationship between the long-term trend in the standard instruments of monetary policy and the long-term trend in the growth rate of GDP over the period 1960–2015. Not unexpectedly, our findings ascertained the long-held view that monetary policy does not matter. It has no effect whatsoever. Perhaps for a short while, it is able to stall the decline in the growth rate, but nothing more than that and quite likely not without socially undesirable unintended consequences. On the other hand, in the case of Athens, the issue of economic growth has been a mute one. Owing to the lack of statistical data, economic historians have been looking for traces of economic growth at the time in indices like the size of dwellings and the per capita consumption. However, so far their efforts have been met with limited success and the puzzle of how the Athenians managed to build the magnificent monuments we all admire today and maintain their grip of control in the wider region of Eastern Mediterranean for nearly 2 centuries remains unresolved.

Next, we turned to the Fed's mandate regarding the interest rate. Since the target inflation rate is reckoned at 2%, we interpreted the provision in the law to imply that the central bank ought to set the Federal Funds Rate i^{cr} such as to achieve moderate long-term real interest rates. We found that while the Fed set the long-term real average interest rate r^{cr} at 3.14% that which prevailed in the economy was 3.88% or 18% higher. By implication, the Fed failed to bring about the moderate interest rates it aspired to achieve. In all probability, this failure transpired because the Fed erred in gauging accurately the demand for savings mainly by the U.S government to cover its rapidly accumulating fiscal deficits, as well as from abroad where world savers could find higher interest rates elsewhere. As to the collateral damages from this failure, we mentioned above that the average annual rate of inflation during this period was 3.8%, that is, almost 100% higher than the targeted rate.

On the contrary, the state in Athens could not and did not run budget deficits, unexpected shortfalls and surpluses were balanced through the *treasuries of the gods*, and the interest rates the state paid for loans from within the public sector varied in the low range 1.2%–6%. In the private sector, depending on the risks of the loans, the interest rates might even exceed 100%. But according to the available evidence, the normal interest rate was around 12%. When compared to the interest rates in many countries of the Organization of Economic Cooperation and Development (OECD) in the postwar period, these interest rates indicate that Athens must have attained a remarkable level of economic development. Yet, because of the lack of pertinent data, for the time being such indications have to remain in abeyance.

Lastly, we looked into the main drivers for the international dominance of the two currencies. In both cases, we found that: (a) unmatched military power and diligent deployment of its deterrent to keep open and safe the routes of trade in the high seas; (b) building alliances, which encourage cross-border cooperation; and (c) leadership based on stable and credible political and economic institutions, are very important because they lead to the reduction of transactions costs, the lowering of tariff and nontariff barriers and the increase in international trade that benefits all countries involved. Additionally, to the dominance of each currency contributed other reinforcing factors. For example, the drachma received exceptional support from the money-related institutions and policies that we presented in Chapters 2–5 as well as in Section 7.5.2. Certainly, these emerged because of other more fundamental accomplishments like: the establishment of direct democracy, which offered the prospect of continuity; the discovery of the silver mines in Laurion, which enable Athens to maintain its military power and at the same time provide a cohesive economic and social environment; the setup of an efficient public administration based on the election of officials by lot and for short terms of service; the protection of property rights, which became the basis for domestic and international transactions, etc. In short, there was a confluence of clearly identifiable factors that propelled the drachma to dominance in classical times and maintained its wide acceptability well into the Hellenistic period.

On the other hand, the U.S. dollar became dominant in two phases. The first one started with the Bretton Woods' agreement right after the big war and ended with the abolishment of its convertibility into gold in 1971. In this phase, as the United States enjoyed and rightfully so the status of the leader and savior of the free world, the countries that participated accepted to fix the exchange rates of their national currencies to the dollar. This was a period much like that after the battle of Salamis in 480 BCE when the leadership and the power of Athens among its allies were unquestionable. Issues started to arise only when peace was established and attention turned to the national-interest first priorities. The same happened after 1971. The United States started to undermine the cohesiveness of the free world by following domestic policies which in the eyes of its allies created major world imbalances. Financing of increasing fiscal deficits required lose monetary policies; the latter fueled inflation; inflation eroded the value of the dollar; through the depreciation in the value of the dollar, the United States got accustomed to reaping "Extravagant privileges," whereas emerging countries have been deluged with "Exorbitant debts" instigated by the Fed's policies, which pushed the dollar interest rates to the zero bound; and all of this while the reserve currencies of the European Union, China and a few other countries have not been able to gain significant shares and thus loosen the grip of the dollar on the world financial markets.

As we stated in the introductory chapter, we believe that the world is now in an ominous juncture. The dollar-based international monetary system has stopped serving the interests of the community of nations. We do not like what we see because we cannot preclude that the soft war, which goes on in the international financial markets, will not break into a very destructive hot war. The present painstaking study of the unique monetary system in classical Athens offers considerable insights for confronting the challenges facing the world today. Looking forward, in the next chapter, we shall attempt to highlight the possibilities in this regard in the expectation that they may attract the attention of leaderships in the United States and the other reserve countries of the world.

8 Alternatives to common central banking

Let us go back to Section 1.2 and specifically to the underlined part of the quotation from the *1977 Federal Reserve Reform Act*. As we read and explained its meaning in the first paragraph, the leaders in the U.S. Congress who authorized this Act made it crystal clear that they did not seek in any way to undermine the independence of the Fed in pursuing the stated objectives at its own discretion. A year later, they repeated exactly the same wording, albeit with an important qualification, by declaring in Section 108 of the *1978 Full Employment and Balanced Growth Act* that:

> Nothing in this Act shall be interpreted to require that the objectives and plans ... be achieved if the Board of Governors and the Federal Open Market Committee determine that they cannot or should not be achieved because of changing conditions: Provided, that in the subsequent consultations with, and reports to, the aforesaid Committees of the Congress pursuant to this section, the Board of Governors shall include an explanation of the reasons for any revisions to or deviations from such objectives and plans."

Since then and for several decades, the issue of the Fed's discretionary powers remained dormant. It was debated hotly in academic conferences and journals, but until the big financial crisis erupted in 2008, it received scant attention from the U.S. Congress in the context of its constitutional responsibilities.[1] Eventually though, in 2013, that is, the year of the centennial of the establishment of the Fed in 1913, the House Financial Services Committee, acting in the framework of the *Federal Reserve Centennial Oversight Project*, introduced the *Centennial Monetary Commission Act of 2013* and a year later, the *Federal Reserve Accountability and Transparency Act of 2014*.

---

1 Article 1, Section 8 of the U.S. Constitution, gives to the U.S. Congress the power "to coin Money" and to "regulate the Value thereof." Even though the words "coin money" and "regulate" are least precise and have created a lot of controversy, it will prove helpful for later in the present chapter to clarify that at the time of the constitutional convention, it was widely understood that the term "Money" meant metallic money, not fiat money. From this, it follows that what the Founding Fathers of the United States had in mind was a commodity standard (either silver or gold, or both), not the paper standard currently in force.

The thrust of these initiatives was evident. The Centennial Monetary Commission was expected to provide a public forum for experts to evaluate the performance of the Fed and to recommend possible institutional and operational rearrangements so as to strengthen its mission going forward. Presumably, the commission's recommendations would not bind the U. S. Congress to undertake any particular legislative action. However, they would provide Members of Congress with valuable information to determine whether or not such actions were necessary.[2] Quite likely, the *Federal Reserve Accountability and Transparency Act of 2014* was inspired by the deliberations and the proceedings of the Centennial Monetary Commission. Its main feature was to require the Fed to adopt a *monetary rule* in place of its traditional discretionary posture. The Fed would have flexibility to choose among alternative monetary rules. But its flexibility would be restricted to monetary rules belonging to the genre of the so-called Taylor Rule, which bears the name of John Taylor, professor of economics at Stanford University.

Although the House of Representatives of the U.S. Congress passed it, the *Accountability and Transparency Act of 2014* was killed in the U.S. Senate, and the same fate met repeated attempts by the House of Representatives to frame the Fed's discretionary powers. Hence, in view of these experiences and our assessments in the previous chapter, the following question comes to mind. Given that the Fed (a) has failed by significant margins to achieve the objectives that the laws set for it to pursue throughout the postwar period; (b) by all available indications the monetary policies under its leadership are prone to creating financial crises which keep increasing in frequency and severity; (c) manages the world's preeminent currency, which renders its monetary policies particularly precarious for the stability of the international monetary system; and (d) has lost control of the quantity of money and it is strongly doubtful whether it maintains still some control of the interest rate, would efforts in the direction of a rules-based monetary policy suffice?[3] Introducing a constitutional wedge of this form would

---

2 The hearings of the Centennial Monetary Commission covered a wide variety of issues ranging from the assessment of Fed's performance to the gold standard and the securities used in open market operations.

3 In addition to the above evidence-based weaknesses of the common central banking, there are many others "based on principal." Just to recall them, here is a summary in the words of Friedman (1962a, 50–51):

> Any system which gives so much power and so much discretion to a few men that mistakes—excusable or not—can have such far-reaching effects is a bad system. It is a bad system to believers in freedom just because it gives a few men such power without any effective check by the body politic—this is the key political argument against an "independent" central bank. But it is a bad system even to those who set security higher than freedom. Mistakes, excusable or not, cannot be avoided in a system which disperses responsibility yet gives a few men great power, and which thereby makes important policy actions highly dependent on accidents of personality. This is the key technical argument against an "independent" bank. To paraphrase Clemenceau, money is much too serious a matter to be left to the Central Bankers

strengthen the resistance of central bankers to pressures by politicians to influence the economic and electoral cycles via seigniorage so as to enhance their chances of reelection. But their incentives, which give rise to multiple moral hazard problems, would not be affected and this would be a major weakness. Moreover, referring to the provisions of the *Accountability and Transparency Act of 2014*, Dorn (2014) and many likeminded researchers answer in the negative by arguing that:

> By using the Taylor Rule as the baseline, the Act is implicitly constraining the Fed to an interest-rate target. If the Fed deviates from the Taylor Rule, it would have to explain why and would be audited by the General Accountability Office. Nevertheless, the Fed would still have a large amount of discretion, and no one would be held liable for departing from the adopted rule—whatever it is.

Some others, like for example Binder, Spindel (2017), would answer that imposing a monetary rule is superfluous because the Fed is controlled already by U.S. Congress in many direct and indirect ways; and still some others thinking along the arguments presented by Bitros (2015, 82–84) hold the view that in order to enhance the probability for the monetary rule to prove effective, it must be supplemented with institutional reforms which will place whatever margins of discretion are allowed under vigilant democratic control.

Be the state of the literature as it may, if recent results showing that the Fed has lost control even of its sole policy instrument, that is, the Federal Funds Rate, are ascertained by further research, sooner or later it will become impossible to escape abolishing it altogether. In view of this prospect or even before a major international financial crisis erupts, we must think ahead of the available alternatives to common central banking and assess their feasibility from a social perspective. This is exactly the task to which we aspire in this chapter and our plan is to pursue it by drawing also on the leads that we gained from the case of money in classical Athens.

8.1 Central bank as the fourth power of the state[4]

In contemporary representative democracies, personal and civil liberties are protected from the abusive inclinations of those who are elected to govern through the separation of powers. By assigning the exercise of the main functions that spring from the collective power of the people to distinct and

---

4 The original idea of embedding monetary authority in the constitution belongs to Buchanan (2010, 257). In his words:

> ... monetary authority must be formally constitutionalized by amending the Constitution, a process that, in itself, would modify public attitudes.

independent authorities, their capability to engage in illegal and unauthorized practices is inhibited, first, because their domain of authority is reduced and, second, because of the so-called checks and balances among them. An example of efficient separation of powers can be seen in the United States, where governance is entrusted by the people to three entities: judicial, legislative and executive. Although these entities are independent of each other, the constitution ensures that each one may check and balance the other two so that none of them may acquire absolute power. The top judicial authority is the Federal Supreme Court, which corresponds to the *Heliaia* in ancient Athens. The legislative authority is exercised by the U.S. Congress, which is divided into two bodies: The House of Representatives and the Senate. The U.S. Congress performs the legislative functions of the *Assembly* of ancient Athens.[5] Finally, the top executive, the President, governs with the assistance of Secretaries (Ministers) that he selects and are appointed after due diligence about their moral standing and experience by the Senate.

In a monetary regime consistent with the above institutional setup, the independence of the central bank might be conceived on grounds similar to those of the other three branches of government. For example, the judicial branch in the United States is independent from the legislative and the executive branches. But its independence is bounded by checks and balances, which preclude members of the Supreme Court from exercising absolute power—that is, power irreverent to the objectives pursued by the other two branches of government, as expressed and mandated through the laws. Analogously, the executive and the legislative branches are independent but obliged to respect the decisions arrived at by the Supreme Court. Hence, it would constitute a major regime change if by a constitutional amendment the Fed was upgraded into a fourth branch of government, bounded only by the checks and balances that would be spelled out in the amendment. In this framework, the independence of the Fed would be circumscribed by the law and honored as such by the other branches of government. Like the Supreme Court justices, the governors in the Fed would be appointed for life so that all their incentives to capitalize on their knowledge and social prestige

---

Then, in Buchanan (2015, 55) he elaborated further on the same idea by stating that:

> In the American context, a formal amendment to the U.S. Constitution would be required, one that would establish and legitimize an independent body charged with the task of securing the single objective, that of maintaining the value, as defined, of the monetary unit, the dollar.

This section draws heavily on the argument in the same direction presented by Bitros (2015).

5 Between 1630 and 1650, the communities of New Anglia in the United States applied many principles of the Athenian democracy. Moreover, according to de Tocqueville (1840, 39–42), Rhode Island adopted direct democracy without representatives. How strong was the influence of the ideas on liberty and democracy from ancient Greece on the American intellectuals mainly in the 18th century has been analyzed thoroughly by Winterer (2002).

by jumping to private practice would be quashed. The differences among the political parties regarding the orientation of monetary policies would be reflected in the views held by those who are appointed as governors and in the influence they might exercise on the stance of the Fed as a collective entity. Finally, monetary policy would be driven by concerns to serve the long-run interests of society, not the short-run interests of politicians and organized pressure groups.[6]

In the heat of everyday debates about inflation, unemployment, debt sustainability, exchange rate valuation and competiveness, the position of the governors of the Fed would differ significantly from that of Supreme Court justices. Their decisions quite frequently would be dragged into bruising battles among the political parties. Many would read in them biases toward one group or another, and they would be accused of social insensitivity. To reduce the adverse influences of such divisive debates on the credibility of monetary policy, perhaps the proposed upgrading of the Fed may be supplemented with a monetary policy rule that would make policy transparent and enable the Fed to stay firm in the course of bubble-neutral monetary policies. Moreover, in the interest of better coordination and enforcement, it may be advisable to bring micro- and macroprudential policies and agencies under its authority, if further research showed that the moral hazard problems of regulation would be reduced.

To emphasize the advantages of this alternative approach to the common central banking over recent proposals aimed at enhancing the "independence" of the Fed, it suffices to consider two benchmark cases. The first one can be extracted from the report on "Rethinking Central Banking" that 16 world-renowned economists in the *Committee on International Economic Policy and Reform* submitted back in 2011. In page 28, they state:

> Central Bank independence ultimately rests on political consensus—on the convergence of views among leading political interests that society's broader economic goals are best served by this independence.

That is, the solution they propose is to render the Fed "independent" through "political consensus." Does this proposal have any real value? It does not, for at least two fundamental reasons: (a) political parties in representative democracies are beset by moral hazard problems that make political consensus extremely unlikely, and (b) democracy stands on the principle of not granting independence to any person, collective entity or institution—even

---

6 This expectation should be contemplated with a lot of skepticism because, with the exception of a few federal judges who remain within rigorous constructionist bounds, the rest creep gradually to judicial latitude. So, it is doubtful whether governors appointed to the new Fed would not represent the interests of their own guild.

  Perhaps, recalling the Athenian maxims for good governance that "nobody is to be trusted" and that "every official is elected by lot, for short service, and audited ex post for his conduct" may provide some guidelines for institutional innovation.

if it were certain that this would serve society's broader goals. As for the second case, consider the proposal to place the Fed under a fully empowered *Office of Inspector General* (OIG for the Fed), that is, like those in all other federal agencies.[7] Is it reasonable to expect that such an auditing framework may ever pass through both the U.S. Congress? Not really because: (a) all other agencies are constrained by their budgets, and hence they are fundamentally different than the Fed; (b) we have now the precedent mentioned above that the House of Representatives failed repeatedly in more recent years to impose on the Fed even the lesser requirement of a monetary rule; and (c) representative democracy rarely leads to circumstances that the private interests of those elected in the U.S. Congress align with those of the United States, and of course less so with the interest in the stability of the international financial system.[8]

The 2008 crash in the United States showed that while a rules-based monetary policy may be necessary to prevent central banks from contributing to the creation and bursting of assets bubbles, it may not be sufficient. The reason is that under the present institutional circumstances, the relations of central banks to politicians, regulators and organized pressure groups are beset by serious moral hazard problems, which induce them to deviate from the monetary rule when push comes to shove. This problem is generic to all countries organized as representative democracies with more or less free-market economies, but it applies especially in the case of the Fed because the U.S. dollar is the world's leading reserve currency. As recent events made obvious, its fallibilities may bring down the whole international financial system. That is why the question of how to forestall another and perhaps bigger crash in the future is most urgent. Assuming that the Fed can control the quantity of money or the policy interest rate, thinking ahead of events would recommend upgrading the Fed's constitutional status to a fourth power of government, much like the judicial branch, and passing a constitutional amendment that binds the Fed by a fairly malleable monetary rule. By establishing its independence within the framework of checks and balances, appointing its governors for life to stem the moral hazard problems, and following a monetary policy rule, the Fed may be able to stay the course in pursuing a bubble-neutral monetary policy.[9]

---

7 For a brief introduction into the details of this proposal, see Foster (2009).

8 Moreover, even in the unlikely case that it is placed under a fully empowered Office of Inspector General, judging on the basis of the spectacular failures of federal regulators, as revealed recently by the 2019 grounding of Boeing's new 737 MAX plane, due to two crashes and the death of over 300 people, and the numerous stories in the press highlighting how Inspectors General side consistently with the party having the greater power, for all practical purposes the independence of the Fed cannot be guaranteed.

9 Subject to the stated condition, it should be clear that from an institutional standpoint the constitutionalization of the Fed is a better best approach to confronting the issue of the independence of monetary policy than placing it under the supervision of an Inspector General.

However, the ability of the Fed to control its target variables is questionable and, if the existing doubts are confirmed by further research, soon a dilemma will arise as to the appropriate reforms. In view of this outlook, some experts hold that the Fed can reestablish control over its target variables provided the government introduces a wide range of reforms, while other experts argue that the Fed has lost control and there is no going back to money or interest rate targeting. Acting along the first approach would require a far-reaching reform of the existing monetary system like the one presented above for the constitutionalization of money, whereas proceeding along the second approach would require scrapping the Federal Reserve System and replacing it with a market-based monetary regime along the ones presented below.

8.2 Currency and credit based on free banking

The search for institutional arrangements to curb the discretionary power of central banks is as old as central banks themselves. To wit, consider in the following quotation the sharp criticism that Ricardo (1809, 3, 21–22) addressed to the Bank of England for the manner in which it managed the quantity of banknotes early in the 19th century:

> By lessening the value of the property of so many persons, and that in any degree they pleased, it appeared to me that the Bank might involve many thousands in ruin. I wished, therefore, to call the attention of the public to the very dangerous power with which that body was entrusted; but I did not apprehend, any more than your correspondent, the signature of "A Friend to Bank Notes," that the issues of the Bank would involve us in the dangers of national bankruptcy.

He sensed that the bank violated the time-honored objective of price stability and that by doing so, it risked ruining many people and driving Britain to bankruptcy. However, notice that he did not call on experts to devise mechanisms in order to tame the power of the central bank, as the great majority of monetary economists are doing in our times. He appealed to the public—the ultimate source of power in democracies—by stressing that if the Bank of England was left unchecked, it has too much power and may use it with devastating consequences for the citizens and the country. Perhaps the constitutionalization of money in the manner explained above would earn Ricardo's approval. But still this alternative would leave the monopoly of money and as it is well known monopolies are hurtful to citizens, irrespective of whether they are controlled by state or private interests. The alternative of free banking, which we are going to consider in this section, replaces the monopoly of the state over money and monetary policy with competition as in all other commodity and services markets.

After lengthy debates in the 19th century, and in the light of the frequent financial crises and at times rampant inflation, the School of Free Banking was revived in the 1970s with a flurry of publications by Hayek (1978/1990), White (1984/1995), Friedman, Schwarz (1986),[10] Selgin (1988), and many other distinguished researchers.[11] The main thrust of the arguments they put forward is that on the grounds of the available historical evidence, as well as long accepted imperatives of economic analysis, abolishing the monopoly of the state in the supply of money and leaving its provision to private banks under the general institutional setup that applies in all other markets is a superior arrangement for the monetary system in comparison to the one now in place. However, with the exception of this common feature, one finds in this literature multiple models of free banking that differ significantly depending, first, on whether the precedent to which they refer derives from historical free banking episodes in the United States, Britain or other countries,[12] and, second, on where they place the emphasis regarding issues like the nature and functions of money, the convertibility of banknotes into specie, the clearing mechanism of banknotes issued by banks, and the determination of the reserve ratio, if the holding of reserves is imposed exogenously. Hence, it is beyond the scope of the present and certainly it would be superfluous to review here all these models. Instead, we shall concentrate on the *model of Scottish free banking* which in our view offers the nearest feasible and superior alternative to the established monetary system, even though looking forward we consider the likelihood of it ever being adopted far smaller than the constitutionalization of money in the form outlined above.

8.2.1   An adaptation of the White-Selgin (WS) model of Scottish free banking

The model in question was presented by White (1984/1995) in the first edition of his book in 1984. Immediately it attracted a lot of attention and praise, but also some quite sharp criticisms. Over the following several years, he defended his interpretations of the historical evidence in a series of publications and then incorporated his responses in a revised and extended edition of his book in 1995.[13] In the meantime, Selgin (1988) enhanced and formalized further the model, whereas other researchers enriched the literature

---

10 This paper marks a complete turnaround by Milton Friedman from his outright rejection of free banking in Friedman (1960) and his timid reconsiderations in Friedman (1962b).
11 To get a glimpse into the ideas and the protagonists who paved the way and gave impetus to the revival of the School of Free Banking, see Yeager (1962).
12 For nine such episodes, see Dowd (1992).
13 However, he did not respond to certain particularly thorny issues raised by Sechrest (1993/2008, Ch. 5).

on free banking with many more historical episodes from various countries and the theory with new analytical conceptualizations. We take it that when the publication by Selgin, White (1994) appeared in the prestigious *Journal of Economic Literature,* the ideas of free banking had made already considerable inroads into the ways we should think about market-driven monetary arrangements. So, after a few brief introductory references to the structure and performance of Scottish banking in the period of interest, we shall proceed to adapt the model by drawing on Sechrest (1993/2008, 18–43) for our own purposes.[14]

According to White (1984/1995) in the 150 years from 1695 to 1845, the banking system in Scotland evolved from 5 private banks in 1740 to 35 banks in 1826.[15] Of the private banks that were active in 1845, 19 issued banknotes and operated 363 branches, providing coverage of one branch per 6,600 persons as compared to one branch per 16,000 persons in the United States. And as to its structure and performance in page 32 we read that:

> There were many competing banks; most of them were well capitalized by a large number of shareholders; no single bank was disproportionate large or dominant; all but a few of the banks were extensively branched. Each bank issued notes for £1 and above; most banks' notes passed easily throughout the greater part of the country. All banks of issue participated in an effective note-exchange system. All offered a narrow spread between their deposit and discount (loan) rates of interest.

From this assessment, one is tempted to surmise that the banking system functioned at the time as in a *laissez-faire* environment in which entry and exit of banks were completely uninhibited, the banks converted always their banknotes into specie on demand, there were no state interventions that conferred privileges to particular banks, etc. Since White drew attention to the Scottish case, further scrutiny of historical events has revealed certain significant differences of fact and interpretation. For example, in the light of the computations by Sechrest (1993/2008, 83–86) of the frequency of bank failures, the stability of the Scottish banking system may not have been as superior as claimed by White (1884/1995, 39) in comparison to the banking system, which operated in England under the authority of the Bank of England. However, none of these differences has been decisively critical to shake the trust in the view that the Scottish banking system at least after the 1770s and until 1845, operated as nearly competitively as one might ever expect to find in actual life.

---

14 In Chapter 8, Sechrest (1993/2008) provides a comprehensive and to our view definite rebuttal of all known criticisms of free banking. Consequently, we find no reason to extend our presentation beyond these remarks.

15 Free banks started to appear several years after the monopoly charter of the Bank of Scotland expired in 1717. The second private bank by the name Royal Bank of Scotland was founded in 1727.

We turn now to the model and start with certain definitions and conventions. The specie, that is, coins and/or bullion of precious metals, stood as the "cash reserves" or "outside money" of the banking system. Let this money be accounted in dollars and denote its unit price and quantity as (P^s, q^s), capital symbols indicating nominal values. The "inside money" consisted of banknotes and deposits. Banknotes did not bear interest. Deposits carried two prices: one on demand and the other at a future date. In the same way as banknotes, the price of checkable deposits was their purchasing power in terms of commodities, whereas the price of time deposits was the nominal interest rate denoted by R. Banknotes and checkable deposits, of unit price and quantity denoted as (P^n, q^n), made up the quantity of money for transactions purposes. On the other hand, time deposits of unit price and quantity denoted by (R, q^d) served as loans. At each point in time active in the free banking sector were on the demand side households, enterprises and banks that demanded "outside money" and "inside money" in the form of "notes" and "time deposits," and on the supply side, households, enterprises and banks supplying "outside money" and "inside money" in the demanded forms. Based on the quantity of outside money in their vaults q^s, the banking system created liquidity in the amount of $(q^n + q^d)$, implying $q^s = k(q^n + q^d)$, k being the reserve ratio. Finally, in order to link the banking system to the wider economy, we assume that $Y = Py = vq^n$, in which (Y, y) stand for the nominal and the real national product, respectively, p is an index of the general price level and v denotes the velocity of circulation of the quantity of notes used in transactions. The issue at hand now is to highlight the equilibrium allocations and prices $(\bar{q}^s, \bar{q}^n, \bar{q}^d, \bar{P}^s, \bar{R}, \bar{Y}, \bar{P})$ for given values of the parameters (k_0, v_0) so that we can analyze the model's comparative statics properties .

Figure 8.1 displays a graphical representation of the model.[16] Graph (iii) shows the market for outside money q^s, whereas Graph (iv) depicts the apparatus through which the banking industry converts outside money into inside money consisting of q^n notes and q^d time deposits. Notice in the latter graph that the reserve ratio k_0, which we treat initially as a parameter, is given by $q^s / q^n = q^s / q^d$. To keep the analysis simple, we assume that the specie seldom appears in circulation and that the equilibrium quantity $\bar{q}^s$ is acquired or rented by banks at the equilibrium price $\bar{P}^s$. Given the reserve ratio k_0, the banking industry maximizes profits at point A. To this, it is led by the market for time deposits, shown in Graph (v), and the market for

---

16 Observe the difference in Graphs (ii) and (iv) in Figures 6.2 and 8.1. The shaded surface in the former figure is convex to the origin, whereas the one in the latter figure is convex to the $q^n q^d$ plane and upward sloping. It signifies a fundamental difference in the nature of "inside money". In classical Athens, it was partly commodity money, that is, silver coins and primary deposits in silver coins and bullion. On the contrary, in the Scottish model it was money created totally by banks in the form of notes and time deposits. In the words of Selgin (1988, 158):

> Inside money... is after all not a commodity "produced" in the usual sense of the term but a vehicle of credit representing outside money lent to banks at call.

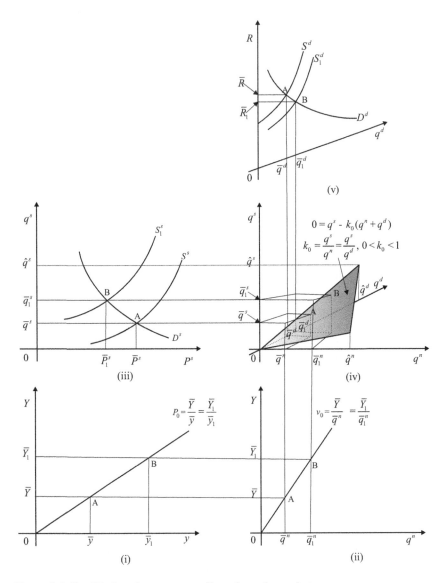

Figure 8.1 Equilibrium in money, credit and goods markets.

goods, shown in Graphs (i)–(ii). The former market determines the equilibrium values of the time deposits and the interest rate $\left(\bar{q}^d, \bar{R}\right)$, assuming that the interest rate offered to depositors by banks is included in the demand curve D^d. On the other hand, as shown in Graph (ii), given the velocity of circulation v_0, the banking industry is led to the equilibrium supply of notes $\bar{q}^n$

to finance the equilibrium nominal national product $\bar{Y}$. Lastly, with the equilibrium nominal national product thus determined and an index of the general level of prices formed in the goods markets, in Graph (i), the model determines the equilibrium level of real national product $\bar{y}$. What we wish to do next is to employ the model to trace the effects on the equilibrium values of certain ad hoc changes in the factors held constant.

The curve S^s in Graph (iii) stands for the supply of outside money. Among others, its position reflects the state of specie hoarding that prevails in the economy. Everything else remaining constant, let the demand for hoarding decline so that the curve shifts leftward to S_1^s. As a result, cash reserves in the banking system will expand to q_1^s while their unit cost will decline to P_1^s; profit maximizing equilibrium in the banking industry will shift to point B; the equilibrium values for notes, time deposits, nominal and real national product will increase to $\bar{q}_1^n$, $\bar{q}_1^d$, $\bar{Y}_1$, and $\bar{y}_1$, respectively; and the equilibrium nominal interest rate will decline to R_1. Similar (opposite) changes to the equilibrium values would come about if the reserve ratio k_0 declines (increases). For then, the banking system would be able with the same amount of cash reserves to increase (reduce) the quantity of inside money. On the contrary, if the velocity of circulation v_0 changes, the only variables that would change in the same direction are those for nominal and real national product. Drawing on these thought experiments, many significant questions like the following come to mind: (a) Could the banks in this free banking system resort to overissuing of inside money and thus driving the economy into a devastating financial crisis? (b) Holding the velocity of circulation constant at v_0, changes in inside money change the nominal and the real national product in the same direction along the ray P_0 (see Graph (i)). If the velocity of circulation increases, say to v_1, how might $\bar{Y}, \bar{y}$ and P_0 be affected? and (c) If a free banking regime was in place in the United States in the postwar period, which would be some indicative but striking differences?

Let us consider the first question by assuming that in their effort to maximize profits, free banks enter into an operating mode that drives $k_0 \to 0$. Gradually, the shaded surface in Graph (iv) would tend to become horizontal at the level of the available specie, thus leading to ever expanding quantities of inside money. From Graph (v), we see that the interest rate R would be pushed downward, and hence the revenues of the banking sector would decelerate. At the same time, the continuous expansion in the inside money would increase the costs for its management by the banking sector. These two trends would be expected to squeeze the profitability of banks and thus discourage the reduction of k_0 beyond its equilibrium point. Rationally behaving free banks would not overissue for still another reason. As k is reduced well past its equilibrium value, banks would have to face the increasing risk of a run on their cash reserves through convertibility. Therefore, while for any particular bank it is a possibility, in a free banking system populated with many moderate-sized banks that operate in an environment of nearly perfect competition and under the watchful interest of their owners and depositors, general overissuing of money convertible into specie is impossible.

With regard to the second question, consider an increase in the velocity of circulation from v_0 to v_1 as per Graph (ii) in Figure 8.2 below. Under flexible prices in the economy, the equilibrium nominal and real national product would rest at the level of full employment $(\bar{Y}_1, \bar{y}_1)$ shown by letter A in Graph (i). Thus, with the shifting of the general price level from P_0 to P_1, the nominal national product inflates from $\bar{Y}_1$ to $\bar{Y}_2$. However, the rise in inflation would be transitory because over the longer run, nominal national product would return back from $\bar{Y}_2$ to $\bar{Y}_1$ through the following sequence of reactions. Since general inflation would not change relative prices, the price of specie will rise by the rate of inflation; cash reserves in the banking system will decline; inside money will shrink from $\bar{q}_1$ to $\bar{\bar{q}}_1$; and finally, the dollar value of national product will decline from $\bar{Y}_2$ to $\bar{Y}_1$, that is, sliding from point B to C in Graph (ii). This analysis corroborates that prices in a free banking system like the one under consideration may be expected to be stable because free banks have an incentive to keep inside money growing at the rate of real national product.[17] In turn, this implies also that nominal and real values of variables like the price of specie P^s and the interest rate R coincide.

The third and last question relates to issues of practical importance. An impressive difference certainly would show in the rates of inflation since, as we reported in Section 7.1.1, over the period 1960–2015 prices in the United

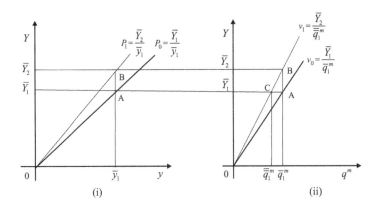

Figure 8.2 Effects of a change in the velocity of circulation.

17 Using a more elaborate model of free banking, Selgin (1988, 102) finds that:

> Free banks maintain constant the supply of inside money multiplied by its income velocity of circulation. They are credit intermediaries only, and cause no true inflation, deflation, or forced savings

States increased at the rate of 3.8% per annum. By contrast, under a free banking regime, dollar prices would have remained stable or even declined in view of the persistent increase in Total Factor Productivity (TFP) from technological advances. Another similarly forceful difference would emanate from the level of government indebtedness. Observe from Figure 1.1 in Section 1.1 that the explosive rates of federal debt took hold after 1972. In that year, we have noted already that the U.S government stopped the convertibility of the dollar. As a result, by cutting off this anchor of the dollar from the price of gold, the government won ample, nearly uncontrollable, leeway to run budget deficits, accumulate debts, cheat citizens out of their savings and in general to condone the deliberate erosion in the value of the dollar. Still another major difference would be that the observable prices in the economy would be real and economic agents would not be misguided by various degrees of "money illusion" and "guessing errors." Last, but not least, dollar interest rates would not have declined to the low levels to which they were artificially reduced by the U.S. government and the Fed, and now the world would not be under the dreadful dilemma of the nonsustainability of international debt, particularly by emerging countries.

These and many other advantages over common central banking should not be interpreted to imply that free banking is foreign to problems. Since banks in general are not infallible, they can be expected to make bad loans, mismanage the banknotes they issue, lose the confidence of depositors and some eventually fail. Also, unanticipated discoveries of new deposits of specie, technological breakthroughs in the purification of precious metals and even shifts in consumer preferences will create disequilibria that may take time to restore. But relatively speaking, from pure theoretical analyses and the experiences from many historical episodes, it does follow that free banking is superior than contemporary central banking because it is not prone to generating inflation, bank failures are isolated events almost never contagious, losses and profits from saving and investing are matched in the same decision maker, thus making everybody more responsible, etc. However, as we indicated earlier, the likelihood of it ever being adopted is as small as that which pertains to representative democracy ever returning from the established practice of deficit spending for purely political reasons to balanced budgets and debt-free governance.

8.3 Attic drachma: private currency with state standards

While research results regarding the model of free banking were gaining space in professional journals and time in conferences, doubts about its empirical underpinnings in the Scottish experience continued to appear unabated. Having looked into these lingering reservations, we are fairly confident that their primary source can be traced in the following quotation from Friedman, Schwartz (1986, 8, 11), which summarizes their assessment of the evidence at the time:

History suggests both that any privately generated unit of account will be linked to a commodity and that government will not long keep aloof....If free private competitive enterprise can produce a viable money without government, it has yet to do so.

To ascertain that this is still the case, consider Timberlake (1998, 181). Even though he is writing over ten years later and the relevant literature has been enriched with many more country episodes of free banking and considerable rebuttals by its leading advocates, he expounds the same assessment by giving prominent emphasis in the above quotation. So, we take it that the dominant dissenting view continues to be that "if free private competitive enterprise can produce viable money without government, it has yet to do so." In this context, that is, the continuing search for a paradigm of "viable money" with the least possible direct involvement by the government,[18] we should like to draw attention to money in classical Athens.

The story we have told so far draws on several strands of literature patiently put together particularly over the last 40–50 years by economic historians, numismatists, sociologists, political scientists, etc. As such, it stands on adequate evidential grounds to claim that the Attic drachma functioned in an institutional environment in which: (a) the state enacted and enforced laws and regulations that aimed at safeguarding the integrity of the currency component of money, leaving the functioning of credit markets to the laws that applied in all markets; (b) in carrying out the operations of public finance, the state acted as the dominant but not the sole provider of currency; (c) the supply of money was determined by competitive forces in financial markets; and (d) all equilibrium level and rate variables like, for example, the prices and quantities of silver in the forms of currency and bullion, the amount of bank credit and the reserve ratio, and the interest rate were determined by supply and demand conditions. The objective in this section is to reaffirm this claim with a brief summary of our main findings.

1   The world status of Attic drachma[19] started to change precipitously after the discovery of the Laurion silver mines in 483 BCE, the victorious Battle of Salamis in 480 BCE and the successful inauguration of the *Delian League* in 478 BCE. For, as it follows from van Alfen (2011), in

---

18 We do not think that by using the terms "without government" these world renowned monetary experts meant the absence of government even from its general institutional and regulatory tasks in the economy.

19 Thomas Figueira has told us that, in and before 500 BCE, monetarized economies were still in their infancy. Even Athenian minting was still at a modest level. The supply of fractional coins to enable retail business or for making change was very limited. Money on the Aeginitan standard was both more common and less standardized or rigorously produced (though Aeginitan coins themselves were of very high quality). Money was used to a large extent for levies and disbursements, transfers of assets and the establishment of household reserves.

order to finance the huge public programs mainly in the fronts of rearmament and state infrastructures and beautifications, Athens embarked on a massive striking of *tetradrachms*, drawing on the voluminous streams of silver from its Laurion revenue, the allied tribute and the tax revenue paid in currency and bullion. With the impetus that the public expenditures from these programs gave to import–export activities, the Attic *tetradrachm* spread rapidly across allied and nonallied states and became the preeminent currency in the Eastern Mediterranean and beyond. The following quotation from Rathbone and von Reden (2014,153) leaves no doubt about its astonishing staying power over the centuries:

> In classical Athens the principal coin was the silver *drachma* which numismatic studies have shown was minted at a target weight of 4.32g.… In 170s BCE the Attic *drachma* was apparently reduced in weight to around 4.20g, and similar reductions happened to some other Greek coinages.

That is, from the 480s BCE to the 170s BCE, the silver content of the drachma was reduced by only 2.78%. It is not surprising therefore that it became the first international reserve currency extending its dominance well into the Hellenistic period.[20]

2　In Chapters 2–5, we explained in great detail the policies and the activities through which Athens pursued the dominance of the drachma locally and internationally. Instrumental in this regard were achievements in the following fronts:

- The shapes, the forms, the stamps, the silver content and in general all the minute technical details that pertained to the currency were decided in the *Assembly* and enforced by the *Boule* with the collaboration of state appointed magistrate and supervisors at the mint.
- Throughout the decades, even in times of despair, like when Athens succumbed in 404 BCE to Sparta, the state showed unrelenting

---

20　By contrast, it is worth noting that in 594 BCE Solon introduced an ingenious devaluation like currency reform, which by most accounts kept social peace by enabling debtors to reduce the burden of their debts up to 27%. In particular, by replacing in circulation the Aeginitan by the Attic drachma, which was worth 27% less, Solon enabled indebted Athenians to get significant relief on their debts and thus preserved social peace. Illuminating in this regard is the following quotation from Plutarch (*Solon*, 15.4):

> Some writers, however, and Androtion is one of them, affirm that the poor were relieved not by a cancelling of debts, but by a reduction of the interest upon them, and showed their satisfaction by giving the name of 'disburdenment' to this act of humanity, and to the augmentation of measures and the purchasing power of money which accompanied it. For he made the mina to consist of a hundred *drachmas*, which before has contained only seventy-three, so that by paying the same amount of money, but money of a lesser value, those who had debts to discharge were greatly benefited, and those who accepted such payments were no losers.

determination to protect the integrity and the international reputation of its currency. For this purpose, it put in place institutions to guard against all those who might attempt to adulterate it for profit. The *modus operandi* in governance was "nobody is to be trusted, not even after passing all due procedures of appointment to public office." Materials used and coins fabricated were checked in the presence of *bouleutai* and *epistatai*; *dokimastai* were located in the markets of Athens and Piraeus to verify the purity and origin of coins; cheating of all sorts was discouraged by stiff punishments; and irreconcilable conflicts that arose among merchants regarding currency matters were resolved quickly in the so-called *People's Courts*.

- At times, Athens adopted one-sided policies to promote the adoption of the drachma among its allies. For example, by demanding payment of their tributes to the alliance in Attic drachmae, and by keeping the minting and seigniorage charge low, most other allied states were led gradually to shut down their mints. However, as attested by *Nicophon's Law* and the presence in Athens and Piraeus of *argyramoiboi*, Athens never restricted the parallel circulation of foreign currencies, although the official policy under the *Kallias Decree* aimed at the wider possible adoption of the Athenian currency in the context of the *First Athenian Alliance*. Witnesses have reported that when foreign merchants brought their goods to the port of Piraeus, they sold them at significant price discounts to customers who paid in drachmae. Such was the trust and the esteem for this currency that it was used as a select medium for storing wealth.

- That Athens managed to stand by the integrity of its currency in peace and in war is closely related to the doctrine of public finance that they had adopted. Public budgets were balanced as a matter of principle and conviction; to cover unexpected shortfalls, they withdrew cash from surplus funds stashed away at the *treasuries of the gods* in previous years; in exceptional circumstances, if cash on demand was not available, they borrowed from these *treasuries* on interest and made sure to repay promptly the state's debts; the *treasuries of the gods* deposited their surplus funds with the banks in the private sector and in turn subsidized the interest rates on the loans they advanced to the state; and last but not least, it is worth noting that since all matters regarding public revenues and expenditures were under the control of the *Assembly*, where the consequences of decisions concerned first and foremost the citizens who decided, direct democracy certainly served their best interests.

3   Main customer of the mint was the state itself. But at the same time, the mint was open for business to all, Athenians and foreigners, who had silver bullion and wished to turn it into drachmae on the payment of some small manufacturing and seigniorage charge. By implication,

this arrangement rendered the supply of the currency endogenous. In particular, if the drachma was dearer than bullion in terms of goods and services, bullion was converted into drachmae and the supply of the currency increased. On the contrary, in extremely rare cases when bullion became dearer than the drachma in terms of goods and services, we would expect coins to be melted for their silver content and the supply of the currency to decline.

4   The state did not mingle up in the functioning of the banking sector. Unlike the Scottish and the other episodes of free banking, in classical Athens circulated only one commodity medium of exchange issued by the mint. But its supply at least at the margin was in private hands; the laws against profiteering, usurious abuses and fraudulent practices applied in banking as in all other markets; there was no lender of last resort; depositors had to be watchful of the bankers to whom they entrusted their savings; bankers were liable with all their property in case of failure and this made them extra careful in their loan decisions; and if conflicts arose between banks and their customers, which could not be resolved quickly by friendly intermediation, the differences were resolved in the regular *Courts*.

5   In classical Athens, there operated not less than 30 *eponymous* banks. We do not know how many of them run concurrently. But even if half or even a third of them functioned at any one time, the banking sector was well populated, considering the period we are talking about and the probable level of per capita income and wealth. The banks offered a wide range of local and international services, extending into investment and tax counseling as well as in the undertaking of business ventures. Most importantly, banks offered loans well above the deposits they received and their own funds. Therefore, as we explained in the graphical representation of the Athenian model of free banking in Section 6.2, the banks operated as in a fractional reserve system in which the equilibrium interest rate on loans is determined simultaneously with the equilibrium reserve ratio and the other key variables in the monetary sector of the economy. In this setting, since bullion could be converted easily into coins on demand at the cost of only a small charge, money consisted of three components, that is, coins of various denominations, bullion and bank deposits. By distinguishing bank deposits into primary and secondary, money might be defined narrowly to include only the former or broadly to include both. In any case, it is known that bank deposits may function as part of the money supply as long as there is confidence in their easy conversion into acceptable means of actual payment.

To summarize, in classical times, Athens pursued the dominance of its commodity currency locally and internationally by putting in place institutional and administrative arrangements as creative and farsighted as all other aspects that glorify the civilization they inherited to future generations. They succeeded because by strokes of collective ingenuity and perhaps chance, they made public choices which were consistent with the private interests of those who decided. In particular, since the maintenance of the integrity of the Attic drachma served the geopolitical interests of Athens and at the same time the interests of citizens who were paid in drachmae and participated in the *Assembly*, public and private interests coincided and this in turn rendered chosen policies effective.[21] With the exception of the currency, in the market of which the state was very influential, all other matters of money were left to financial markets and free banks. We believe that the latter played a much larger role than can be documented by reference to available evidence. Thus, the model of money that emerged is significantly different from the one based on the Scottish experience, so perhaps it has a better chance to escape the criticisms of the Scottish model of free banking.

8.4 On the evolving prospects of electronic money

In order to understand the nature of *electronic money*, suppose you place an order in a well-known internet megastore for a certain commodity and that you pay with your credit card in U.S. dollars. Even though all processes from placing the order to the dispatching of the commodity to your address are carried out electronically using digital technologies, the money used in the settlement of the bill is not electronic money. It is fiat currency and/or credit in fiat currency that you have in the bank which issued your credit card. Instead, electronic money consists of *electronic currency* and/or *electronic credit* held in nonphysical digital form. For the time being there are no platforms through which one can obtain electronic credit. We know that several commercial and even central banks are experimenting and do plan to introduce such platforms. But until electronic credit becomes widely and easily available, transactions will be limited to electronic currencies, which are distinguished into *virtual* and *cryptocurrencies*. Their fundamental difference being that virtual currencies have no value beyond the narrow *virtual communities* in which they are used.[22] Hence, since it is only the cryptocurrencies (henceforth cryptos) that have real world value, for now it is they that draw attention.

---

21 In the next chapter, we shall argue that the coincidence of public and private interests is a unique advantage of the *direct* over the *representative* democracy because, in contrast to the latter, the former is not subject to Arrow's (1963) famous theorem, which establishes the impossibility of representation of preferences in groups.

22 In April 2019, J. P. Morgan, a huge U.S. bank, entered into the market of electronic payments with its own digital coin. Details about this venture are available at: www.jpmorgan.com/global/news/digital-coin-payments. This particular coin is not a cryptocurrency. It is a virtual currency in the service of J.P. Morgan's virtual community.

The market for cryptos opened in 2009 with the entry of Bitcoin (BTC). The objective of its inventor was to create a digital currency for carrying out and settling transactions from peer-to-peer over the internet under conditions of security and private secrecy. For this purpose, and in order to keep a detailed and secure record of the transactions among the peers, the inventor adopted the advanced cryptographic ledger technology called *blockchain*, whereas in order to provide a mechanism for the supply of coins, the inventor created a mine-like mathematical algorithm through which the peers could mine coins by incurring increasing costs, that is, exactly as it would happen in a silver mine that necessitates going deeper and deeper for less and less rich ore until the vein is exhausted. Within a few years bitcoin gained considerable popularity and as it happens in such cases it created a lot of excitement over its perceived potential. But soon also started to surface technical and economic bottlenecks that blurred its prospects as a likely alternative to commodity and fiat currencies.[23] An indicative sample of these bottlenecks would certainly include the following:

1   Bitcoin is a block of ultra-safe data registered in the computer ledgers of the peers that participate in the network. When a transaction takes place among two or more peers, all ledgers are updated. This requires in turn that all computers be available to the network and as a result the consumption of electric power increases very fast with the expansion of the network, thus limiting its upward scalability. The same drawback besets also the process of mining. Before a bitcoin can be spent, it has to be mined. Initially the discovery process was profitable. But after a large percentage of its potential supply was mined, the consumption of electricity increased exponentially, thus rendering the mining process subject to diminishing returns and its upward scalability prohibitive.[24]

2   In the last few years, the constraint of scalability has been confronted in at least two ways. First, via the entrance into the market of several hundred, if not thousands, of new cryptos, and second via improvements in the energy efficiency of the adopted digital technologies, which allow expanding of the ceiling of the potential supply further and further. For example, in the case of Ethereum, most calculations indicate that the total supply of Ether will reach but not exceed significantly the 100 million

---

23 Even though below we relate the bottlenecks to Bitcoin, to a smaller or larger extent they hold for every known cryptocurrency. So, our references should not be interpreted to imply that they are exclusive to the Bitcoin.

24 It should be noted that in the case of the bitcoin, the total number of coins that will ever be in supply is capped at 21 million. Since 2009, the amount of coins already mined is about 17 million. The last whole bitcoin is expected to be mined around 2040, whereas the mining process will come to an end in roughly 100 years. At that time, the cost of mining will have gone through the roof, the yield will have declined to a minute fraction of a coin, and its price will be determined solely by supply and demand conditions.

mark. Even though the constraint of scalability is relaxed by leaps and bounds still the problem remains.

3   Above we said that in the event of a transaction the ledgers of all peers in the network are updated. By implication, as the number of peer increases, registration and verification of transactions places an upper limit to the number that can be executed per second. In turn these processes create congestion in the network and lengthen the waiting periods for the execution of any one transaction, and particularly for those that carry no fee and are given least priority in the queue. On the contrary, credit card transactions can be executed quickly because the issuing institutions may expand the capacity of supporting networks through further investment. To alleviate somewhat the long delays in the transactions, more recently issuers of cryptos have resorted to attaching a facility which takes the form of a hard fork from the original currency. In the case of the bitcoin, for example, this facility is referred to as Bitcoin Cash (BTH). This has expedited the processes of registration and verification significantly. But the underlying problem of network congestion is ever present.

4   Bitcoin's price experiences more frequent and much wider changes compared to the prices of the currencies in advanced economies. For example, in 2010 the Bitcoin was worth 25 cents to a U.S. dollar ($). In November 2017 its price climbed to $11,000; shortly afterward it dropped to $9,000, and in more recent months it has varied around $3,500. This excessive volatility renders bitcoin unsuitable for holding wealth over extended periods. At least for the time being, one cannot invest one's savings and retain peace of mind because the value of the investment might skyrocket as well decline to zero. Risk loving investors though may take their chances and when successful with bitcoin they can always turn their profits into more stable currencies.

In view of the above, experts are ambivalent about the future of digital currencies. On the one extreme, there are all those who do not see much potential in them, despite the interest shown by central banks, and not only. The gist of their thinking is best expressed in the following quotation from Rogoff (2018):

> Many crypto-evangelists insist that bitcoin is *digital gold*, in part because the long term supply is algorithmically capped at 21 million. But this is nutty. For one thing, unlike gold-which has always had other purposes and today is employed widely in new technologies from iPhones to spacecraft-bitcoin has no alternative use. And even if bitcoiners manage to find a way to lower the *phenomenal energy cost* of verifying transactions, the very nature of decentralized ledger systems makes them vastly less efficient than systems with a trusted party like a central bank. Take away near-anonymity and no one will want to use it; keep it and advance-economy governments will not tolerate it.

On the other extreme, there are many evangelists of cryptos who insist that bitcoin is indeed digital gold. But their argument is more subtle and certainly not based on the cap of the potential supply. Instead they argue that once possessed by somebody, bitcoin like gold or silver cannot be in any way another person's liability. There is no trust involved. If one holds bullion, the only way one loses ownership is by selling it or by losing it to thieves. Bitcoin has the same exact property. Once in one's wallet, it cannot be cloned and stays firmly in one's possession. The only way bitcoin leaves one's grasp is either through sale, theft, or losing in some way one's wallet. Drawing on this specie like advantage of cryptos these evangelists go as far as to declare that[25]:

> A more energy efficient and secure form of Bitcoin will possibly emerge as a World Currency, like the Globo. An easily programmable blockchain ledger, like Etherium, will possibly emerge as a replacement for Stocks and Bonds, and other contracts that are securities. The Bitcoin equivalent in Etherium, Ether, can possible also emerge as a World Currency.

Finally, there are those who look into the future through the lenses of the trends which have propelled over the millennia the dominance of a single currency in any one national jurisdiction. Their views fall in between the above mentioned extremes by allowing an open window to technological breakthroughs that may render cryptos viable nongovernment established currency. At least this is our interpretation of the following quotation from Eichengreen (2019, 13):

> ...the broad tendency, it is fair to say, has been in the direction of one currency for each political jurisdiction and common economic space, where in practice those political and economic spheres coincide. The question is whether digital currencies will now reverse this trend, given the apparent ease with which they can be created. At the moment such digital units are proliferating. But the information sensitivity of those units, as evident in the fact that they trade at varying prices against one another and the established numeraire, suggests that they fail to provide the core functions of money. So-called stable coins are intended to bridge this gap by providing a reliable store of value, means of payment and unit of account, but whether they can be scaled up at reasonable cost (when fully collateralized) or maintain their stability (when not) is doubtful.

Considering what governments in the United States have done to the value of the U.S. dollar in the postwar period, as well as the dangers looming ahead should a major financial crisis erupt, our view in this book has been all along that overhauling central banking is long overdue. To this end, we

---

25 See Akwei (2018).

view the case of cryptos as a paramount process of pressure for change, because the monopoly of governments on money has become contestable and the more central banking reform is delayed, the more likely it is that technological change will overcome the issues of scalability and price stability of digital currencies.

Inherent in the established model of central banking is centralization. Not exactly like the central planning apparatus in the old Soviet empire, but the same in spirit and consequences. Central bankers pretend that they know where the economy stands at every moment and that they have the means to stir it in the direction of achieving certain socially desirable objectives. In essence though they know very little about what is going on in the economy and there are grave doubts whether they have any control on their policy instruments. That is why central banking is buckling under its own weight. On the contrary, when it was introduced in 2009, bitcoin represented a true revolutionary departure from this model because for the first time in history it highlighted the possibility of establishing a totally decentralized system of payments, that is, one regulated neither by the government nor by any private entity. Although it has no intrinsic value, bitcoin stands conceptually on a par with so many ingenious mathematical and computational constructs used in today's miraculous technological applications. Digital currencies in general are much close to being equivalent to digital gold and in our view it is only time until technological breakthroughs confront the issues of scalability and stability. The only true risk we see is that when success finally comes in these fronts, the government with its arm in the Fed will step in and take control ostensibly to protect citizens from tax evasion and other illicit activities that may be associated with the anonymity of the cryptos. Yet, expectedly, a workable middle ground will be found in which the Fed will offer a digital currency for the state to interact with the private sector, but without its potentially dreadful implications for civil liberties,[26] leaving the markets for cryptos to function as every other market under the law.

---

26 If in doubt of the seriousness of these implications, consider the following. Since the United States is in reality a *virtual community*, it should be obvious that the Fed may turn the dollar into a *virtual currency* transferred via permissioned ledgers or pseudo-blockchains. In this event the dollar would not be a cryptocurrency. It would continue to serve exactly as in the traditional financial system. At the same time, though it would be completely centralized and *eponymous* in the sense that it would facilitate real-time tracking of customer transactions, all those with bad credit record might be excluded, tax authorities might have access to records, etc. But such powers at the Fed would endow the government and the regulators with sophisticated forensics tools, and hence with unprecedented insights into the spending habits and social behaviors of citizens. If this prospect is dreadful for citizen sovereignty in democracies, only digital technology in the service of personal liberty may dissuade it.

8.5 Clues for money from classical Athens

In the last 100 years, through peace and war, the United States has established itself as the preeminent empire in the world. Along with its political, military and cultural might has come the dominance of the U.S. dollar. Therefore, what happens to its value and what policies the U.S. fiscal and monetary authorities conduct are issues of worldwide importance. Relatively speaking, Athens in classical times found itself in a similar position. Even after its defeat by Sparta and the end of its so-called "empire" period in 404 BCE, the Attic drachma continued to dominate in domestic and international transactions throughout the Eastern Mediterranean and beyond, and gave to Athens a comparative advantage that contributed significantly to its renaissance in the 4th century. Focusing on the parallels of these two cases, our objective has been to exploit the rich evidence that has accumulated in recent decades regarding money and banking in Athens during those times to draw any lessons that may be useful in the present challenging context in the United States and the world.

8.5.1 *Central bank with nonconvertible paper currency*

The combination of representative democracy with the issuing by a state-controlled central bank of nonconvertible fiat currency on a monopoly basis since the 1970s has proved deleterious more or less everywhere with few exceptions. In the United States, aside from allowing the piling up of unsustainable public debts and failing consistently and significantly to deliver on its mandates regarding inflation, unemployment, economic growth and the long-term interest rate, the Fed is now at a crossroad. For, not only it has lost control of the quantity of money, but also institutional and structural developments may have rendered policy initiatives based on the nominal interest rate ineffective, if not dangerous. Consequently, following the golden rule of balanced budgets established by Athens 25 centuries ago, the soonest possible and in any case before the stability of the international monetary system is threatened by the next major crisis, intoxicated democracy in the United States should be relieved from its addiction to deficit spending and debt.

To this effect, it is high time that the Fed is empowered to withstand the apparent bias of the political system toward overissuing of nonconvertible dollars. In doing so, an effective reform may be to turn the Fed into a fourth branch of state power, along with the executive, legislative and judicial, since with its newfound independence within the United States system of checks and balances, it might stem the exorbitant postwar government profligacy. Moreover, encouraged by this bold upgrading reform, the Fed may find it reinforcing to look into the possibility of adopting some version of electronic currency or even return to convertibility.

However, proceeding in this direction would be warranted only if it is certain that the Fed can exercise effective control over the Federal Funds

Rate. On this issue, the bulk of the available empirical evidence is negative. But the econometric analyses employ data that pertain to the present institutional setup in which the Fed is subject to direct and indirect interventions from the U.S. Congress and the Office of the President. Therefore, since we cannot know what the case under the proposed reform will be, reconstituting the Fed should be viewed as a provisional regime conditioned on the proof that monetary policy does remain viable. Otherwise, if this is not the case or if overriding political circumstances and/or a cataclysmic financial crisis render it imperative to abolish the Fed altogether, the choice will come down to adopting a decentralized monetary system. In that event, free banking will emerge as a realistic alternative and the question will be which model is the most appropriate. The presentation below is devoted to this issue.

8.5.2 Free banking with commodity-based currencies: the Athenian vs. the Scottish model

From Figures 6.2 and 8.1, but also from our explanations regarding their structure, it follows that the Athenian model of free banking, henceforth called Model A, differs markedly from the one that has been associated with the Scottish experience, henceforth called Model S. A first difference springs from the nature and the number of currencies in circulation. In Model A, there is only one commodity currency, whereas in Model S circulate as many currencies as the number of notes-issuing banks. Compared on this basis, the advantages of the former model over the latter are that: (a) it does not require a costly central mechanism to clear transactions executed in different paper currencies; (b) because of the intrinsic value of the commodity currency, it is less prone to *counterparty* and *liquidity* risks that are associated with the banknotes; and (c) by being uniform, the commodity currency enhances the efficiency of exchanges by reducing transactions costs, since the prices of goods and services need not be stated in different paper currencies.

Another fundamental difference has to do with the role of the state. In Model A, the state has monopoly over seigniorage. Depending on who governs, this may be an advantage or disadvantage. If government is exercised by a king or a dictator, history suggests that the commodity currency will be debased in emergency situations to raise state revenues. Under such circumstances, state monopoly over seigniorage is certainly a disadvantage. But in classical Athens, in addition to the evidence that the Attic drachma circulated in parallel with foreign currencies, thus rendering state monopoly contestable, the government was in the hands of many citizens who had an immediate interest to maintain its integrity. Now, consider the case of Model S. Will the government abstain from mingling up with the integrity of outside money? Drawing on the following quotation from Friedman, Schwartz (1986, 43), we do not think so:

Historically, a single unit of account linked to a single dominant outside money has tended to emerge, initially via a market process of transactors settling on a particular commodity, followed almost invariably by government's exercising control over one or more aspects of the issuance of outside money-typically with the ostensible purpose of standardizing the coinage and certifying its quality (purity, fineness, etc.).

Finally, a third significant difference lies in the distinction between "outside" and "inside" money. In Model A, all money is "inside" because the commodity currency, that is, coins and bullion, circulates simultaneously with the credit money generated by banks. On the contrary, in Model S, there are two categories of money. That is, commodity currency, that is, coins and bullion, which stands for "outside money" and circulates rarely if ever, and banknotes together with checkable and time deposits, which constitute "inside money" redeemable on demand into "outside money." Providing for these two types of money may be an advantage of Model S, because it prevents the wide circulation of precious metals, and hence it economizes on their use. But on the other hand, it exacerbates counterparty and liquidity risks that diminish by far the significance of this advantage.

Therefore, Model A is far superior than Model S because it is more in line with the historical precedent of a uniform currency; even under representative democracy, it provides for a constructive role on the part of the state while limiting its ability to act on the worst inclinations of politicians; and all money is "inside," which implies that inherently the financial system is characterized by reduced counterparty and liquidity risks.

8.5.3 *Free banking with digital currencies*

Looking forward, it is still quite early to tell how the introduction of bitcoin and the numerous other cryptos will integrate into the monetary systems in advanced democracies. Central banks are churning out one discussion paper after another and the same keen interest is shown by big domestic and international U.S. banks. But suppose that circumstances lead to the abolishment of the Fed. In that event, what is the likely structure of free banking that we might expect to emerge? In our view, it is safe to expect a banking industry closer to Model A rather than to a completely decentralized one based on full anonymity of citizen-miners, henceforth to be referred to as Model C. Let us explain why.

Anonymity is synonymous with the protection of civil liberties. But like fire, wind and the other powers of nature, if left unbounded, civil liberties can be very destructive to society. By guaranteeing complete anonymity, cryptos provide citizens with unlimited opportunities to resort safely to illicit actions. Therefore, the state as ultimate guarantor of the law cannot become complicit to violating the law by dealing in transactions carried out in cryptos. In the absence then of a central bank to offer an official digital currency, the state has to establish a mechanism, say a *Digital Mint*, to supply it at the discretion of *eponymous citizen-miners*. Given that all transactions with the state will be carried out in this particular digital currency, it goes without saying that quite likely it will gain a dominant position among all digital currencies in circulation. In other words, it will perform like the Attic drachma in model A, with the only difference that it will be in the form of *digital silver*.

However, on the other hand, governments in present-day democracies are not free of grave fallibilities. Particularly in view of the budget deficits, the huge debt overhang, the depreciation of the U.S. dollar in the postwar period, and so many other crude government forays into private lives, a great many principal-citizens in the United States and across the world have lost much of their trust in their agent-politicians and have turned into indifferent private individuals. What this implies is that at times governments in representative democracies can be harmful and, if technological breakthroughs enable them to keep safe, citizens will chose anonymity as the ultimate line of defense for their civil liberties. For this reason, we concur with the position expressed in the following quotation from Berentsen , Schär (2018, 104):

> History and current political reality show that, on the one hand, governments can be bad actors and, on the other hand, some citizens can be bad actors. The former justifies an anonymous currency to protect citizens from bad governments, while the later calls for transparency of all payments. The reality is in between, and for that reason we welcome anonymous cryptocurrencies but also disagree with the view that the government should provide one.

Therefore, the free banking industry likely to emerge would consist of two sectors. One populated by *eponymous* citizen-miners associated with the government operated *Digital Mint*, and another populated by *anonymous citizen-miners* associated with various cryptos. That is, pretty distant from Model C and quite close to Model A, albeit using digital not commodity silver that was the case in classical Athens.

8.6 Concluding assessments

Recently, we were informed by world news outlets that the economic advisor to the current U.S President asked the Fed to lower immediately the Federal Funds Rate by half a point.[27] We always knew that the central bank in the United States was never independent. We glimpsed in the data. So, what we learned from Binder, Spindel (2017) was simply a confirmation. But never before have we witnessed such an open and for that matter brazen intervention of the U.S. government into the institutional standing of the Fed. That

---

27 http://trumploveswinning.com/oan-newsroom/fed-should-cut-rates-by-half-a-point-kudlow-tells-axios/.

is why now, more than any time before, we are convinced, first, that the prevailing trends in the management of the U.S dollar signal significantly elevated risks for the stability of international financial markets, and, second, that overhauling central banking in the United States is long overdue.

The main issues in this regard are threefold. The first is how to enhance the independence of the Fed in the expectation that it might stem the exorbitant profligacy of U.S. governments in the postwar period. Since the United States cannot continue running budget deficits and piling up deadweight debts to the detriment of future generations, economic growth and the stability of the international financial system, this long established ominous trend must be broken. And one likely path to returning to fiscal sanity a la classical Athens is by upgrading Fed's institutional status into a fourth branch of state powers, along with the executive, the legislative and the judicial. The second issue has to do with the accumulating evidence that monetary policy is ineffective and according to a sizable group of experts, potentially harmful. If this proves to be the case after enacting the proposed reform, central banking will have run its course and the Fed should be replaced by some form of free banking. The third and indeed preponderant issue is that in view of the grave moral hazard problems that beset representative democracy, the prospects for gradual peaceful adoption of these far-reaching institutional changes are slim. But they might become inescapable in the event of a financial crash of monumental proportions and/or an upheaval in the U.S. political system.

In that dismal social juncture, drawing on the experiences of Athens during classical times, we believe that the Athenian model of free banking, properly adjusted to allow for the developments in the front of digital currencies, is most appropriate because:

- In line with the historical precedent, it provides for the state to determine the standards of a Uniform Official Currency (UOC) in which it is prepared to conduct its business with the private sector and all entities in foreign jurisdictions.
- The UOC is tied to gold, silver, any other suitable commodity or even to a basket of such commodities. In case the UOC is digital, it remains *eponymous* and convertible to the individual or collective commodity to which it is tied for accounting purposes. Moreover, at their own discretion, banks and other currency issuing institutions may use UOC as "outside money."
- Responsible for issuing the UOC is an official mint. But the state does not mingle up with its quantity in circulation. The latter is determined endogenously, that is, strictly by the demand addressed to the mint from *eponymous* individuals, banks and other financial and nonfinancial institutions.
- Banks, other financial institutions, and in general all wishing and able to enter into the money markets may issue their own paper and/or

digital *eponymous* and anonymous currencies, as well as advance credit and hold assets in such currencies.
- Equilibrium reserve ratios and counterparty and liquidity risks are all determined in the money markets by the interplay of interests between currency issuers and currency holders.

In a system of money and banking with the above key attributes, will the U.S. government be able to continue running consistently budget deficits, amassing public debt, exploiting "exorbitant benefits" from abroad by deliberately eroding the value of the dollar, projecting an example of representative democracy to be avoided, etc.? Drawing on our findings in Chapter 7 from the comparative assessment of the performance in Athens during classical times and the United States in the postwar period, we are confident that in this system, the United States will have an opportunity to rediscover the virtues of sound money and leadership in the world.

8.7 Appendix: on the inversion of Gresham's law in classical Athens

If one visits the Wikipedia for information about Gresham's Law, one will learn that in a monetary system in which there is parallel circulation of several currencies based on some commodity like gold, silver and bronze, this law states that "bad money drives out good money." Also, one is told that in the lineage of its inventors, the first to allude to it was Aristophanes in the following passage from his comedy *Frogs*[28]:

> Many times it seems to us the city has done the same thing with the best and the brightest of its citizens as with the old coinage and the new gold currency. For these, not counterfeit at all, but the finest it seems of all coins, and the only ones of the proper stamp, of resounding metal amongst Greeks and foreigners everywhere, we never use, but the inferior bronze ones instead, minted just yesterday or the day before with the basest stamp. So too the citizens whom we know to be noble and virtuous, and righteous and true men of quality and trained in the palaestra and dancing and music, these we despise, but the brazen foreigners and redheads worthless sons of worthless fathers, these we use for everything, these latest parvenus, whom the city before this wouldn't have lightly used even for random scapegoats.

However, what Aristophanes is saying in this quotation, and certainly implies Gresham's law, contradicts the evidence we cited in Section 8.3 to the effect that the silver content of Attic drachma remained practically stable

---

28 See Aristophanes (*Frogs*, 718).

for 300 years and that it dominated domestic and international exchanges during those centuries. Hence, our objective in this Appendix is to explain: first, why this contradiction is more apparent than real, and, second, why most likely in classical Athens the law applied inversely, namely, that "good money drove out bad money."

8.7.1 Aristophanes' circumstantial evidence

According to most sources, Aristophanes wrote this comedy sometime close to the year 405 BCE, that is, toward the end of the Peloponnesian War in 404 BCE. In this text, we mentioned that during the few years leading to their defeat, Athenians decided to melt the golden clothing of the statue of the goddess Athena to make both ends meet. They were in terrible financial straits, circumstances forced them to move out of the ordinary, and in this case, they issued silver-plated coins with cores made of bronze. Therefore, what Aristophanes must have observed and commented on was the well-known behavioral aberrations of people under siege, when everybody fights for survival and good money and quality goods disappear from open markets and are channeled at exorbitant prices only through "black markets." However, while these circumstances led the sharp-eyed Aristophanes to highlight the first instance of Gresham's law, these hard times were transitory because, as we mentioned in the text, within a few years after 404 BCE, Athenians returned to their previous best practices by minting drachmae in the pristine Attic standard while at the same time they withdrew the plated ones from circulation.

8.7.2 In classical Athens good money drove out bad money

In the text, we cited ample evidence attesting to the effect that during the first half of the 5th century, and certainly after 376 BCE when *Nicophon's Law* applied, the monetary system of Athens was based on free banking. In particular, private banks operated freely; owners of silver bullion could convert it into coins at the mint on demand; and the issuing of coins of small value from bronze was exclusively in private hands.[29]

During these periods, the mints of several allied city-states continued to issue their own commodity currencies and, as the latter circulated in all states in parallel, competition among them was keen because, as we have argued by drawing on the dominant interpretation found in the literature, *Nicophon's Law* did not outlaw explicitly the parallel circulation of good foreign coins.

---

29 No paper bank notes circulated because paper had not yet been invented in the Mediterranean. But apart from this difference, it maintained strong similarities with the monetary systems in the Scottish and the other country episodes of free banking that we mentioned in the text. For, private paper bank notes in these cases were covered by gold and silver reserves; they were redeemable on demand; and hence, the anchor of these monetary systems, as in classical Athens, was the quantity of gold and silver in the reserves.

The crucial point in this context is that Gresham's law operates only if the state forces market participants to accept undervalued currency as the only legal tender. Under free banking and currency competition, as was the case in Athens, Gresham's law operated inversely.[30] This, we maintain, is a very important result of currency competition, and in the first hand not surprising advantage of free banking. Let us explain where it springs from.

First, under currency competition, no market participant had an incentive or obligation to accept undervalued or bad currency. Thus, since only good currencies were accepted, bad ones were driven out of circulation.

Second, since the quantity of currency was determined partly by the demand to convert bullion into coins, the mint's integrity guaranteed that no private person could ever introduce debased coins into circulation.

Third, exacting seigniorage, small in percentage in Athens but overall not negligible as a source of revenue because of the large amounts of bullion converted into coins, was possible only if the currency was good. This again was a strong incentive to keep the Athenian currency "pure" in terms of stable silver content.

Fourth, the quality of the currency was linked to the trade predominance of Athens and Piraeus as the main Mediterranean *entrepôt*. Athenians understood that in order to attract trade, they had to have a good and internationally accepted currency. Linked to this consideration was the need of Athens for huge grain imports. Obviously, traders would not bring grain into Athens, if they were to be paid in debased currency.

Fifth, Athenian coins were one of the main export items of Athens, covering in today's terminology its trade deficit. Again, this would not have been possible with a debased currency.

Sixth, there were strong institutional provisions for the circulation of good currencies. We mentioned in the text that under *Nicophon's Law* counterfeit, Attic coins were confiscated and put out of circulation. At the same time, the existence of the testers provided, if needed, symmetric information to

30 In cases of currency competition, as in Athens, where individuals had a choice among various currencies, if Athens had declared drachma as the sole legal tender for the payment of taxes, *liturgies*, expenditures, etc., the following situation would have emerged, if Athens had decided, hypothetically, to debase its own currency. An Athenian citizen could pay all his obligations to the state with the debased bad Athenian currency and keep the good foreign parallel currencies for free market transactions, since market participants would not accept the debased currency at par, but if at all, at a discount. Thus, the good currencies would gradually force the bad one out of market transactions. Moreover, citizens providing services to the state would realize that the debased currency with which they were paid traded in the markets at a discount. Thus, since they had the decision-making power in the *Assembly*, they would vote against the debasement, reestablishing the real value of the currency, as did happen after the end of the Peloponnesian War with the withdrawal of the debased silver-plated currency. Again, the interplay of market forces and incentives with direct democracy would work as an inverse Gresham's law, that is, good currency driving out the bad.

parties involved in the exchanges because they revealed the quantity of pure silver contained in the tested coins. *Nicophon's Law* actually functioned as a deterrent against Gresham's law and a strong force for its inversion: bad currencies were legally driven out of circulation.

Last, but not least, it was the political and strategic setup: As we emphasize in the text, under direct democracy, the citizens decided also on all monetary issues. Since the majority of citizens were paid for services offered to the state in Athenian coins, they had a strong incentive to keep the currency good. Hence, at the same time, they were the decision-making body (in contrast, say, to medieval monarchs) and they provided for this.

As to the strategic context, during times of war, alongside the citizen *hoplites*, rowers, sailors and cavalrymen, it was necessary to employ specialized mercenaries, such as Cretan archers, javelin men and slingers (mainly Aetolians and Thracians). But, in order to attract them, in an international competitive market, they had to be offered pay in good currency, or else they would seek service with the foes of Athens, if they were paying in higher value currency. The attraction of mercenaries was another aspect of currency competition at work.[31]

So, on account of the above forces that pushed for the maintenance of the integrity of the Athenian currency, as far as we know, we had in Athens a unique case in which Gresham's law was inverted because bad copies of the coins minted in Athens were considered counterfeits and confiscated, whereas good foreign coins and copies of the Athenian coins were not forbidden by the law explicitly from circulation.

31 At the beginning of the 14th century, the then Byzantine emperor, Andronicos II Paleologos, took into his service the Catalan joint stock mercenary company to combat the Turks. Although the Catalans fulfilled their part of the contract, driving back the Turks to the depth of Asia Minor, the emperor realized that he did not have sufficient gold coins to pay them as per contract. He tried to pay them with debased coins, which the Catalans of course understood. The end result was that the company turned against their former employers, devastated and plundered Thrace, before retiring to establish in 1311 a Spanish Duchy in today's Athens and Boeotia. The ancient Athenians never experienced such a situation. Another case of nonpayment of mercenaries occurred after the end of the first Punic War, when Carthage was unable to pay her mercenaries, who revolted leading to protracted war in North Africa.

9 Why back and how to direct democracy

In ancient Athens, the distances citizens had to travel in order to participate in the *Assembly* were not small. The distance from Piraeus to Athens
is approximately 8 kilometers and for a person to reach *Pnyx*, where the
Assembly convened, would have taken the better part of the previous day.
Yet, despite these adverse circumstances, surviving texts confirm that Athenians did not spare personal sacrifices in order to exercise their rights in the
governing of their state. They felt foremost citizens and secondarily private
persons and considered it a great honor to take part in their state's affairs,
even if it meant traveling great distances. But they were relatively limited in
number, they spoke the same language and they shared the same traditions
and customs, so their capability to assemble, to communicate and to govern
themselves in all public affairs was relatively easy.

The process of democracy in the *Assembly* was conducted under strict
procedural arrangements. However, in as much as deliberations and
decision-making were orderly, the thousands of male Athenians who participated accepted and behaved in line with the following principles, proudly
declared by Pericles in his *Funeral Oration* (Thucydides, *History of the Peloponnesian War*, 2.34):

- The government was not in the hands of few, but of many (i.e., *the
  majority principle*).
- In legal affairs, all citizens were equal for the settlement of their private
  disputes (*the principle of equality before the law*).
- Public honors and offices were conferred not because citizens belonged
  to a particular class or race, but because of personal merit (*the principle
  of meritocracy*).
- There prevailed freedom from suspicion of one another in every pursuit
  in one's life (*the principle of personal liberty*).
- Every citizen had an independent "voice" to all state matters (*the principle of isegoria*).
- In relation to the freedom of speech, it was the "duty" of any citizen to
  speak freely the truth for the common good, even at his personal risk (*the
  principle of parrhesia*). This principle conveyed high moral standards and
  required conscious and active citizens who stood in favor of the common
  good. *Parrhesia* could also be seen as the Athenian antidote to *demagogy*.

- All state departments and services were subject to auditing by citizens (*the principle of transparency*).
- Citizens were educated to praise democracy, spill their blood to defend it and have a strong spirit of solidarity (*the principle of solidarity*).
- Violations of the law and particularly those that influenced the general spirit of society were severely punished after due process (*the principle of justice*).
- The state cared for the children of those killed in wars as well as for the less well to do (*the principle of compassion*).
- In the supposedly Solonian tradition, whatever was not forbidden explicitly by the laws, it was considered legal behavior.

Moreover, to control manifestations of extreme individualism, exchanges were conducted in a context of values and institutions providing for: (a) utmost respect for private property; (b) freedom to use property rights in order to promote one's material welfare; (c) social use of wealth; (d) complementary state activities emphasizing the implementation of law and order, the undertaking of projects of public infrastructure, the regulation of food markets in response to prevailing supply shortages, as well as safeguarding the integrity of the currency; and (e) enforcement of tax laws through democratically controlled procedures.

The towering statesmen who drafted the U.S *Declaration of independence* and the *Constitution* in the last quarter of the 18th century were well aware of the above principles. They embraced the classical Athenian political and intellectual culture and sought to establish a nation close to the prototype of ancient Athens.[1] But they did so with one key difference. In particular, they constituted the United States as a *Republic* based on the *principle of representation*, rather than as an Athenian Democracy based on the *principle of self-government*. To emphasize its importance and at the same time remain consistent with the terms we used in earlier chapters, henceforth we shall refer to the republican form of government as representative democracy and to the Athenian as direct democracy.

The idea to set up the United States form of government as representative democracy was proposed by Madison (1787) in his famous essay better known as "On factions." In this, he argued that:

1   Self-government is a bad institutional setup for decision-making in the public interest because it accentuates divisiveness and promotes factionalism. In his own words:

> The instability, injustice, and confusion introduced into the public councils, have, in truth, been the mortal diseases under which popular governments have everywhere perished.

---

1 For an assessment of the influence that ancient statesmen and philosophers exercised on the thinking and the decisions of the founding fathers of the American Democracy, see Richard (2009) and Lehmann (2015).

2   Delegation of decision-making to "proper guardians" is more likely to serve the long term interests of the country, since:

> …by passing public views through the medium of a chosen body of citizens, whose wisdom may best discern the true interest of their country, and whose patriotism and love of justice will be least likely to sacrifice it to temporary or partial considerations. Under such a regulation, it may well happen that the public voice, pronounced by the representatives of the people, will be more consonant to the public good than if pronounced by the people themselves, convened for the purpose.

3   The vast landed area of the country, in conjunction with the then available modes of transportation, rendered frequent assembling of people in a given place extremely difficult, if not impossible. Moreover, these natural difficulties were further reinforced by the lack of homogeneity among the U.S. citizens in terms of their country of origin, language, culture, values, etc.

With regard to them, it is worth noting that a little over a decade earlier Smith (1776/1977) had published his Magnus Opus on the wealth of nations and that his assessments about the performance of representative democracy in England were damning. Madison, who certainly was aware of them, chose to insist on (1)–(2), although it was clear that: (a) the size of the United States and the heterogeneity of its population validated (3) and rendered governance by delegation imperative, and (b) "self-government" in ancient Athens was hardly ochlocratic. However, in retrospect, he proved right even on the basis of (2) since, from the 150 years to the crisis of 1929, by most historical accounts representative democracy in the United States performed close to the expectations of its founders, perhaps because there was substantive commitment to subsidiarity wherein elements of more direct rule existed locally. So, the question that arises is: would a similar assessment be warranted for more recent decades?

Having argued in the preceding chapters to the effect that U.S. fiscal and monetary authorities failed to manage the state budget and the money prudently, we could answer in the negative and conclude with a brief explicatory epilogue. But then we would risk leaving in abeyance the ultimate causes of this failure. For if, for example, governance in the United States has suffered significant losses of democratic legitimacy, as it seems to be the case, this mismanagement and the undesirable social consequences associated with it would be secondary effects. Hence, for a more comprehensive answer, our plan in this last chapter provides for four tasks. These are, first, to highlight certain core weaknesses of contemporary democracy, which have been always there in a more or less dormant state, but became pronounced in the United States after the war and particularly after the 1970s; second, to identify the roots from where some of these weaknesses emanate and explain why they are extremely difficult, if not impossible, to confront; third, to identify the advantages of direct democracy as practiced in Athens during classical times and to highlight the piecemeal approaches, which have been proposed in order to ameliorate the drawbacks of representative democracy; and fourth, to make a case for returning to direct democracy by drawing on its undisputed advantages in view of the improved prospects from the unprecedented developments in the digital and communication technologies.

9.1 Core weaknesses of contemporary democracy

Smith (1776/1977) was aloof about the state's potential to indulge in wasteful and illiberal activities. For this reason, he supported limiting the state's domain to a bare minimum. But he did not expound upon why and how the institutional arrangements he observed allowed British governments to behave as reprehensibly as he expressed. More explicit on this was Mill (1861, 136, 156–156, 160) who, almost 100 years later, noted that the most important problems of representative democracy emanated from the opportunities it offers for: (a) incompetent individuals to be elected to positions of power; (b) state powers to fall into the hands of groups of individuals having private agendas alien to the interests of the general public; and (c) various groups with common professional and/or commercial interests acting in unison to extract from governments by various means decisions in their favor and against the public interest. Madison considered the "recall" procedure an adequate safeguard for getting rid of incompetent and corrupt officials. But the weaknesses under (b)–(c) remained wide open and it is through them that democracy in the United States has been eroding in recent decades on account of deleterious processes like the following.[2]

9.1.1 The self-interest of politicians[3]

Since Downs (1957) presented his economic analysis of democracy, it has been widely accepted that the decisions and actions of politicians are driven largely by their private interests. Citizens have limited ability to accumulate wealth compared with politicians, many of whom become obsessed with the so-called syndrome of leadership.[4] Once autonomous from the control of citizens, politicians may expand their power through public spending, and more generally, through the expansion of the state's activities into the economy.

---

2 For an extensive coverage of the issues discussed in this and the next section, see Bitros, Karayiannis (2013, 25–99).

3 Recall also the quotation from Franklin (2005, 87) in the introduction to Chapter 1.

4 An interpretation of this syndrome is given by Froelich, Oppenheimer, Young (1971). According to them, its source is the pursuit by some people to become leaders in society, because of the "leadership surplus" they may enjoy, which is not necessarily material (i.e., income), but may be psychological, such as the fulfillment of ambition and vanity.

The question is: how the self-interest of politicians was controlled prior to 1929, namely during the long period of classical democracy when the state was small? One explanation may be that the values and the living conditions that prevailed in the United States obliged politicians to remain more committed to pursuing the public interest. Another may be that after the Second World War, reelection campaigns became expensive and this made politicians prone to using the power of the state to help themselves by giving in to the demands of various private interests. Finally, a third explanation is that with the shifting of government policies toward *statism*, various small groups of citizens became aware of the opportunities to organize and, by using their money and political clout, extracted various benefits from the state at the expense of the tax-paying citizens. Thus, rent-seeking, about which we shall say more shortly, took roots and flourished as a significant dysplasia of contemporary democracy.

9.1.2 Bureaucracy

Weber (1947) has argued that the objectives of civil servants are to maintain their position and to serve their country. Today, the prevailing view is that civil servants seek to maximize their incomes, job security, working comforts, the desire to act arbitrarily so as to show self-value importance and even the ability to decide in line with their own political affiliations.[5] The extent to which civil servants attain these objectives depends on three factors: the amassing of bargaining power; the ease with which they can use it to extract benefits from the state; and, lastly, the extent of autonomy they enjoy, which allows them to become a "state within the state."[6] In addition to promoting rent-seeking and corruption, bureaucracy increases transaction costs and weakens economic growth.[7]

---

5 Niskanen (1975) and others have confirmed this behavior in the USA. Therefore, we can reasonably assume that the situation will be worst in countries with less transparent and more authoritarian democratic regimes.

6 The great dangers that emanate from this process for democracy have been stressed by many philosophers and economists. For an example, consider the following warning by Popper (1945, II, 181):

> ...It is undoubtedly the greatest risk of interventionism - particularly of every direct intervention-that leads to an increase in state power and bureaucracy. Most supporters of interventionism do not care about it or close their eyes, which increases the risk.

7 Bureaucracy hampers economic growth not only because it stifles innovative activity but also because, as argued by Williamson (2000), it prevents the correction of various imperfections of the free market economy. In this respect, it has been corroborated theoretically and empirically (see, for example, Ardagna, Lusardi, 2009) that the more government regulations in starting, operating and closing enterprises, the less economic growth. Another derivative of many state regulations is that they render the profession of lawyers most attractive. But from Murphy, Shleifer, Vishny (1991), we know that economies with many lawyers instead of engineers have low economic growth potential because, while lawyers increase transaction costs, engineers increase the efficiency and innovative activity of businesses.

The concentration of bargaining power takes place by expanding the number of civil servants and by allowing or even encouraging the formation of powerful labor unions in the state sector. Given that greater bureaucracy offers more opportunities for new hires, promotions and salary increases, it is not surprising that in a period when unionism in the private sector has been declining in the public sector has been expanding. Hayek (1960, 120–121) predicted that as the share of civil servants in total employment would expand, their clout in the political market would increase, thus enabling them to claim economic policy concessions. He was right. Moreover, let us not forget that the various policies are designed and implemented by government technocrats, thus enhancing their ability to bias legislation to their favor. Finally, it should be noted that the tenured or quasi-tenured regime of employment of civil servants reduces their performance unless, as Tullock, Seldon, Brady (2002, 11–12, 58–59) have found, their performance is monitored closely.

9.1.3 Uncoordinated administrative polycentrism

Large multinational companies like Nestle, Siemens, Toyota and Coca-Cola have manufacturing facilities in many countries and at the close of each day, despite the time differences among various geographical regions, they are able to know the results of their operations as well as the main problems they face in each country. How do they achieve this remarkable coordination? They achieve it through decentralized management systems, in which their managers in each country may decide freely within certain general limits set by the center and expressed in terms of market shares, profitability and other indicators of measurable performance for which they are held accountable. But why even in the United States, the mightiest representative democracy of all, the government is unable to govern effectively? This is a difficult question and answering it would require us to write a separate book, even if we could. So, we will limit ourselves to the following remarks.

Basically, governments are unable to govern effectively because, among other shortcomings, they lack the prerequisites that have been worked out by contemporary management science. In particular, the objectives they set to achieve are at best broad and uncertain. Their information lags constantly behind the current state of the economy or of the problems they are called to face. The ministers in the various ministries, including their advisors, rarely know the operation of the civil service departments they undertake to work with, thus leaving much leeway to the technocrats and bureaucrats to undermine the enacted policies for their own purposes. Since the objectives pursued are often obscure and immeasurable, growing conflicts among ministers allow them to pull the efforts of the governments in various directions, etc.

However, none of the above organizational weaknesses undermines so decisively the effectiveness of governments than the lack of automatic mechanisms to coordinate the information, which is necessary to confront a problem of general national interest and which is diffused across many ministries and state agencies and organizations. We know from experience how all these administrative units safeguard their importance by sitting tightly on the information they collect regarding the tasks to which they have been assigned, so we consider it safe to surmise that the difficulty of elected governments to control the centers of power within the public sector is a fundamental weakness of representative democracy.

9.1.4 Rent-seeking

Rent-seeking may be pursued by all sorts of citizen groups. The objective of those who do so is by using various means to convince governments to grant them services at less or no cost. This does not imply that the citizens who benefit give nothing in return. What they give is received by politicians and the political parties, rather than the state. As such, providers and recipients benefit at the expense of the general public, which often bears the cost of the illicit privileges exchanged in the process of rent-seeking. A typical example is the imposition of, say, tariffs to protect certain businesses or whole sectors of the economy from foreign competition. In particular, instead of investing to improve the productivity, and hence the competitiveness, of their businesses, entrepreneurs often manage, through lobbying and other pressure means, to induce governments to impose duties on competitive goods imported from abroad. As a rule, the results are that: (a) the domestic prices of the protected goods are maintained at higher levels than their prices abroad, thus harming the consumers and (b) the protected businesses do not develop the necessary competitive advantages and to a large extent they have losses and eventually close down. So, the question is why rent-seeking was limited before 1929 but flourished afterward, contributing significantly to the expansion of the state in the U.S.

According to Olson (1965), rent-seeking activities are most successful when pursued either by small and tightly organized groups of citizens, whose size allows them to pass unnoticed by the general public, or by groups with clearly defined objectives and recipients of the benefits (e.g., workers in a particular business or sector of economic activity). Less successful are large groups, which give rise to a noticeable "free rider's problem," and groups that aim at a wide diffusion of the expected benefits (e.g., all workers). In light of this analysis and the technological changes in the transportation and communication industries that occurred after 1929, organized lobbying of the government and politicians for rent-seeking purposes was embraced by small local and regional groups. With little extra cost, insignificant population groups could elicit important benefits from the government at the expense of the general public, causing the phenomenon to flare up.

Rent-seekers gain unilateral transfers of unearned resources from politicians by exercising implicitly or explicitly the electoral power and financial support of their membership. No direct bribes or other forms of corruption are involved. In contrast to such cases, there are others in which politicians and government agencies offer favors to specific private interests as if they are in their service. These have become quite widespread and deserve separate consideration.

9.1.5 Regulatory and state capture

Suppose that state agency A is established to regulate the activities of industry A in the public interest. We say that it is captured when its activities fall under the influence of groups or individuals within the industry A. Is regulatory capture illegal? It may be but not necessarily. Is it corrupt? It may be but again not necessarily. It is corrupt only when the regulators and/or the politicians who pass the regulation serve the interests of the industry A because of a bribe, some other incentive or threat. Such cases need to be distinguished from those in which there is a process of interest representation in the design of legislation. For example, when local politicians are asked by voters in their electoral region to mediate in the design of some legislation which concerns their neighborhood, they are not involved in state capture. Nor are state capture practices of business intermediation by trade associations and other legitimated bodies of representation, bargaining and compromise in the design of policies. These forms of intermediation are not corrupt because they do not involve the payment of incentives. In short, *regulatory capture* concerns the loss of independence on the part of the regulatory body to the industry over which it has regulatory authority, whereas *state capture* refers to the actions of individuals, groups or firms to influence the formation of laws, regulations and other governmental policies to their own advantage by offering illicit and nontransparent benefits to public officials.

In the literature, we find many examples of evidence-based regulatory and state capture in the United States Below we present briefly two, chosen for their relevance to the issues we have discussed in this book. They refer to the roles of banking industry regulation in the 2008 crisis and the tax policies in reference to the rise of inequality in income and wealth, respectively.

9.1.5.1 Banking industry regulation and banks too-big-to-fail

The *Glass-Steagall Act of 1933* separated the business activities of commercial banks from those of investment banks. In particular, the Act prohibited commercial banks participating in the fractional reserve system from using their depositors' money to pursue risky investments. They could advance adequately secured loans to households, enterprises and the state, but not invest in stocks and bonds of private issuers. Only investment banks could deal in such financial instruments.

Through the decades, as the economy grew and money supply expanded, commercial banks grew larger and larger. Eventually they became excessively big and powerful and, as it was to be expected, they managed to undercut the restraints set by the Act. In particular, starting in the 1970s large banks claimed that the provisions of the Act were rendering them less competitive against foreign securities firms. Soon loopholes started to open and gradually commercial banks expanded their investing activities into high risk securities reserved only for investment banks. The culmination of this textbook case in regulatory capture led to the 2008 crisis and may be best corroborated by the following excerpt from Williams (2018):

> After the 2008 financial crisis led to a massive government bailout of U.S. banks, lawmakers expanded their regulatory oversight. Dodd-Frank was instituted in 2009 to address the systemic risk of large banks. Since then, this 22,000-page regulation has crushed small banks in compliance costs, incentivizing merges and exacerbating "too big to fail". Ironically, the laws and regulations aimed at reducing the influence of big banks made them more powerful. Big banks are bigger than ever, and community banks are quickly disappearing........
>
> In banking, the people with the specialized knowledge required to navigate and regulate financial markets are often bank compliance officers and current regulators. This means the people most qualified to regulate banks for the government are often former or current bank employees. Similarly, former government regulators are ideal candidates to become regulatory compliance officers in the private sector. This manifests in a revolving door of experts moving between the public and private sectors, which creates the perception – if not the evidence – of corruption.

In periods before 1929, too-big-too-fail banks would have been broken down by regulators to reduce the risk posed to the U.S. economy by the failure of any such bank. Today, regulators are satisfied to play it "fiddler in the roof" in full knowledge that the only sustainable policy consistent with the prevention of another horrible financial crisis is the breaking down of the big banks. Moreover, the readers should not conclude that regulatory capture holds only in the United States Even though the 2008 crisis did not start from the European Union (EU), the meticulous narrative presented by Lauk (2014) leaves no doubt whatsoever that regulatory capture holds equally widely in the EU banking sector.

9.1.5.2 Concentration of capital ownership and inequality

Bitros and Karayiannis (2008, 2010) have argued that while ancient Athenians discouraged *sterile inequality* that results from inherited wealth and leads to conspicuous consumption, at the same time they believed that there is a positive correlation between economic progress and *creative inequality* that stems from entrepreneurial activities. So, to some degree, they condoned it. Ancient Greek texts show that the prevailing beliefs on this issue were in line with the curve E'E shown in Figure 9.1. Up to point A, inequality was tolerated because it stimulated the wealth producing incentives of people, and hence the rise of tax revenues for Athens. However, from that point on, they discouraged it because it was considered counterproductive and a major threat to democracy by creating divisiveness and instability.

The existence of segments E'A and AE has been confirmed by researchers working with data from various Western type democracies. Either too little or too much inequality is bad for economic growth and democracy. Among others, Piketty (2014) has argued that the United States in recent decades has entered into a phase of too much inequality. In his view, as the ownership of capital has become increasingly concentrated in less and less people, the share of capital in GDP has nowhere to go but up, and hence, the culprit of rising inequality is none other than a systematic bias in the core foundations of the market system. Acemoglu, Robinson (2015) remarked that this proposition lacks empirical validity because, first, it derives from an analytical framework that abstracts from the rebalancing powers of the political and economic institutions, and second, it is in conflict with past economic history. However, the results of the 2016 U.S. elections confirmed that inequality and relative poverty have increased to dangerous levels and that this happened mainly because the "political and economic institutions" remained passive throughout this period. We believe that what this proves is that powerful economic and financial centers have captured the taxing and other rebalancing institutions and policies in the United States, even though factors such as the spread of substance abuse, legal and illegal competition

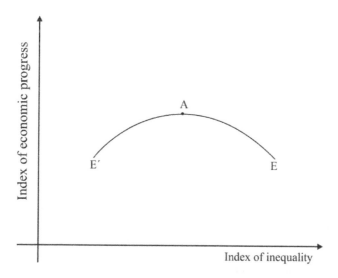

Figure 9.1 Presumed relation of economic progress and inequality.

from immigrants, educational declines below the upper middle class and the creation of urban and rural underclasses, have contributed also to the polarization of the body politic toward this populist electoral outcome.

9.2 Sources of inherent weaknesses in contemporary democracy

Some of the aforementioned weaknesses may become eventually reversible. For example, sometime in the future, conceptual and technological breakthroughs in management, information and communication sciences may render it feasible to administer decentralized decision-making in the public interest as efficiently and transparently as in the large multinational companies. But some others will perpetuate because they spring from innate drawbacks in the way contemporary democracy has been set up. In other words, it is structurally defective. Let us explain.

9.2.1 Impossibility of representation in groups

Schumpeter (1942, Chapters 12, 13) established that under certain quite demanding conditions, representation in Western style democracies could be feasible and effective. But as he was writing almost a decade before Arrow (1951) and three decades before Akerlof (1970), he derived them from an analytical framework, which ignored the implications of the so-called Arrow's impossibility theorem and Akerlof's asymmetry of information in the context of politics. So, the key question for representative democracy continues to be: through elections, can citizens delegate their choices over policies in a consistent way and hold politicians accountable for their implementation? Drawing on these two more recent pioneering studies and the numerous applications to which they have led, in this and the next few sections we shall show why, even if it were feasible in principle, in reality representative democracy would fail.

Suppose a candidate for the U.S. Congress from a district in New York wishes through his campaign to get a precise idea about the ordering of the priorities of his prospective voters. In his speeches, he presents a large assortment of policies supported by his party and shortly before the elections he asks from those present in a town hall meeting to order for him from the most to the least urgent a number of policies suitable for the district. Can he expect to come out from their responses enlightened? In other words, will he be able to obtain an ordering that if elected, he can take to Washington and state to his colleagues in the party that this is the order of priorities that represents the preferences of his constituents, irrespective of whether they voted for him or not? The answer is most surprising. Arrow's theorem ascertains that from the responses of his constituents, there is no way whatsoever to construct a "collective ordering" such that every one of those who took part in the process would be able to recognize as his own,[8] provided of course that the constituents we are talking about satisfy certain reasonable criteria concerning their autonomy and the rationality of their preferences over the policies in question.

Being unable to obtain a "collective ordering" out of the stated preferences of his constituents, if elected, by necessity the Congressman will vote according to his own perception of this ordering, hoping that he may guess correctly.[9] If he does, most likely he will get reelected. If not, he stands a good chance to become a one-term Congressman. But this uncertainty is unlikely to leave his congressional behavior unaffected. For, having started eager to serve his district, and thereby his homeland, he will view his presence in the U.S. Congress as a one-off opportunity for self-promotion. And when that happens, the problems for democracy will start because in his voting calculus, his short-term personal and party's interests will take precedent over the longer term ones of his constituents and his country.

9.2.2 Asymmetry of information

The vast majority of people lack the knowledge and skills to understand complicated public issues and take decisions in the common interest. Also, ignoring the responsibilities that spring from citizenship, many people detest participating in the solution of problems that arise from everyday living. So, they are glad to entrust these tasks to "proper guardians," or more commonly "politicians," who are presumed to have the necessary capabilities. The process of selection among all those who offer to undertake these assignments usually takes the form of elections every so many years over local and national levels, and thus the elected officials–politicians become *agents* of the citizens as *principals*. Thus, beyond the thorny issue of representation, contemporary democracy is beset by a second fundamental problem known

---

8 Frequently, it is suggested that the relative frequencies of items mentioned in opinion surveys may be considered a good proxy of the "collective ordering" of the preferences of the people who participate. However, even if the sample of the respondents is representative of the wider population in statistical terms, the said frequencies are not a proper index of the ordering sought because, after the results of an opinion survey are announced, many of those who take part disagree that the frequencies coincide with their ordering.

9 Since guessing on the missing "collective ordering" generalizes to the whole political system, it should be clear that the lack of representativeness poses a major problem. Munger (2012, 341) has articulated it as central by suggesting the need for:

> Democratic coherence: How can collective-choice institutions be designed to limit the possibility that voting outcomes will be perceived as either arbitrary or imposed? Given the Condorcet-Arrow problem, this problem bears on both the moral legitimacy of democratic choices and the practical stability of democratic governments.

We believe that no institutional remedy is possible short of switching to direct democracy. But we shall return to elaborate further on this later on.

in the literature as the *principal-agent problem* or *dilemma*. Let us see how it arises in the context of our previous example.

Upon entering into the U.S. Congress, the Congressman will be appointed to committees tasked with various subjects. Naturally, in carrying out his duties, he will gain a lot of information available only to a very narrow circle of people and hence potentially of considerable monetary value. Will he be tempted to use it for his own advantage? The paramount odds are that he will succumb not only because of the uncertainty about his reelection but also because of self-excuses like others in his position would do the same, electoral campaigns are costly and so on. As a result, given that informational asymmetry confers exploitable advantages to the political system as a whole, one must ask: can citizens do something about it, and if so, how may they deter politicians from deceiving them?[10] The answers found in the literature follow two general approaches. The first maintains that the mandate citizens give to politicians should be specified in strict terms. In other words, what this approach recommends is that the government should be assigned a specific range of policies or projects, without any discretion to deviate from certain explicitly defined limits (*strict agency*). The second approach suggests that the mandate should be completely open (*free agency*).[11] That is, once elected politicians should be free to decide according to their own perception of correctness, without even taking into account the preferences of their voters. History and experience show that only the latter approach has been adopted. Hence, it is not surprising that as a rule in contemporary democracies elected officials deceive citizens and introduce measures to strengthen their authority, quash accountability and insulate themselves from the control of the public.

The problems that emanate from asymmetric information become even more insurmountable when we turn to the implementation of the enacted policies. For then, the ultimate principals, that is, the citizens who pay the bills, are passive, the immediate principals are the elected-politicians who act autonomously and quite likely for their own interest, and agents are the unelected employees in the narrow and the wider public sector. Since they are the latter who produce and control the data on any one subject and as a rule provide the continuity of service in the public administration, while their political supervisors come and go, the asymmetries of information they enjoy may enable them individually and collectively through their labor unions to act as "a state within a state" (recall the analysis in Section 9.1.2 above). To be sure, the installation of digital monitoring systems in recent

---

10 One of the most striking cases of deceptive practices by politicians, for citizens everywhere in contemporary democracies to remember, is the challenge George W. Bush, Sr., addressed to the American voters in 1988. In order to persuade them that he would not increase taxes, he proclaimed: "Read my lips: No more taxes." Not only did he impose taxes, but they were also quite high.
11 This distinction was already made in the 18th century by Burke (1774).

decades may have stemmed widespread attempts by employees in the public sector to take advantage of hidden knowledge and hidden actions. But on the other hand, the continuing enlargement of the state may enhance the opportunities for such aberrant behaviors, and hence on balance the situation may be worsening.[12]

9.2.3 The deleterious role of political parties

As their views had been shaped by the study of the Athenian democracy and their experiences under the British rule, most of the founders of the U.S. democracy were distrustful of political parties. Madison in particular appears in his essay *On factions* to believe that they would not emerge. Yet he and the other founding fathers were proven wrong because already in the 1790s, two parties were established and started to compete fiercely. As a result, even though the *Constitution* does not make any mention to them, from very early political parties became a *de facto* institutional complement of representative democracy in the United States.[13]

The general assessment by experts is that in the 19th century, the political parties contributed significantly in the establishment and operating maturity of the principles and institutions that the founders provided for in the U.S. constitutional order. They managed to create governing majorities by focusing electoral campaigns on the issues rather than on the personal traits of the politicians that were involved. After elections, party leaderships were flexible to bargain and compromise as in a process of search for the policies that would serve best the long-term interests of the country. By raising the reputation of the legislative branch, they were able to check the accumulation of excessive power by the executive since, on the one hand, they articulated the voices of the citizens, whereas on the other, they reinforced the separation of powers, and in general, they acted as a mechanism that mediated among the state powers and assisted them to run relatively efficiently.

---

12 Political scientists have long been trying to devise mechanisms in order to mitigate the undesirable consequences from a social point of view of the *principal-agent problem* both in policy design and policy implementation. In our view, the results so far are not encouraging because controlling of the practice of opportunism by politicians and bureaucrats carries exorbitant costs on the part of citizens. For an assessment of this literature, see for example Lane (2013).

13 Madison did not take long to realize that the great dispersion of power that he had embedded in the *Constitution* would render the formation of governing majorities extremely difficult. That is why, according to Postell (2018), he started to view the usefulness of political parties in the following context:

> Within a few years of writing No. 10, Madison had shifted his focus from the fear of majority tyranny to the difficulty of organizing the majority in the first place. Without a majority capable of acting collectively, he now believed, the government would fly out of its proper orbit, no longer following the people but rather following its own interest. What was needed, he argued, was a mechanism for mobilizing popular will and exerting its influence over the government.

However, in the 20th century and particularly after World War II, the political parties lost their orientation. Already in the first quarter of the last century, when Weber (1921/1946, 94) was writing by drawing on his visits to the United States, it did not escape from his sharp observational lenses that "The management of politics through parties simply means management through interest groups." But the capture of the political parties by special interests was still in its infancy at the time and Weber thought that only large, organized parties could oppose bureaucracy as a tendency toward a caste of mandarins, removed from the common people by expert training, examination certificates and tenure of office. Had he lived into the 1980s, most likely he would have concurred with Barber (2003, xxxiii) who in the 1984 edition of his book penned down the following assessment[14]:

> Political scientists continue to hope that the crisis in participation is a function of party realignment of the kind that occurs in twenty or thirty-year cycles in most democratic societies. But there is evidence that the party system is breaking down or breaking up, and that representative party democracy may be being replaced by dangerous new variants of neodemocracy-the politics of special interests, the politics of neopopulist fascism, the politics of image (via television and advertising), or the politics of mass society.

And the decline has continued ever since. To highlight where the situation stood 20 year later, here is how Barber (2003, ix–x) saw it in the 20th edition of his book in 2003:

> The democratic deficit that was becoming apparent in the 1970s has become far more widespread, both within the United States and beyond its shores. The number of nominal democracies has continued to increase-which nation does not today affect to call itself a democratic regime?-but the number of nations in which democracy is seriously practiced remains restricted and cannot even be said with conviction to always include the United States.

As for more recently, poll after poll reveals that more Americans today identify as independents than with either of the two major political parties. Citizens do not miss the opportunity to emphasize their distance from either Republicans or Democrats.

In short, experience and evidence demonstrate that political parties behave as large enterprises, acting to maximize the interests primarily of their organized members, secondarily of their sponsors and lastly of their

---

14 At the same time though, it is not farfetched to presume that the analyses of "interest-based political representation" may have intensified "interest-based politics" by activating even marginal professional and social groups to seek particular favors from political parties in exchange for electoral support.

supporters in the electoral body. As foreshadowed by Franklin (2005, 87), rarely maximizing the interest of the country. These assessments are based on at least the following considerations. First, and foremost, is the pretext of the need for governmental stability. Regarding this claim, as Gehl, Porter (2017) established, the political market has been transformed into a tightly controlled oligopoly with no real competition and two large parties alternating in power. This structure, which is supported by multifaceted legal and other constraints, renders the entry of new parties exceptionally difficult and allows the political system to become autonomous, and hence indifferent to the preferences and interests of citizens. Second, as the political system becomes autonomous, the relationship of representation deteriorates and voters become alienated from politics,[15] stop caring about the common interest and even worse they may try to maximize their own private interests by attaching to the clientelist system of the political parties. Third, voter alienation erodes solidarity and social cohesion.[16] During periods of such deficit, political parties introduce costly and inefficient programs, mainly in the context of the "welfare state," in which the beneficiaries feel more allegiant toward the initiators of these programs rather than to the citizens who pay the costs through their taxes. Fourth, by attaching to the political parties, the citizens become addicted to the restrictions of their rights and liberties and become tolerant to the enlargement of the state at the expense of the private economy.

We find no better way to conclude this section than to describe the insoluble problem that political parties pose for representative democracy with the following quotation from Lyon (1996):

> Parties and businesses, however, have a strong vested interest in restricting competition. In the case of business, government regulations limit the ability of corporations to choke off competition. But parties control the only body-the government-that can regulate them.

---

15 An index of the alienation of citizens in the representative democracies is the percentage of those who abstain from the elections. As Barber (2003, xxxiii) notes:

> Mean voter turnout in America since World War II hovers around 50 percent for presidential elections-lower than every other non-compulsory democracy in the West. In a country where voting is the primary expression of citizenship, the refusal to vote signals the bankruptcy of democracy.

16 In certain democracies where the parties often alternate in government, either through implicit or explicit agreements, changes are introduced for the purpose of perpetuating their hold on power. In the United Kingdom, for example, a government can hold majority in the parliament, despite receiving only one-third of the votes of the electorate, enabling it to vote for laws opposed by the vast majority of the population. Governments that are elected by nonproportional electoral systems, inspire doubt about their representativeness, thereby undermining the quality of democracy. In turn, the lack of representativeness induces citizens to perceive government decisions as illegitimate, and to resort to behaviors that aim to annul the results intended by the laws.

9.2.4 Deficit spending

In the previous chapters, we stressed that as a rule, Athenians strived to balance the public budget, if not within each year, at least through balancing short period deficits with short period surpluses.[17] By behaving as they did in their own households, whenever they were called to decide on borrowing for the state from the temples and the *treasuries of the gods,* where they themselves had deposited surpluses from previous years, they would borrow by paying interest. We know that borrowing from these institutions of last resort created always a big commotion in the *Assembly,* which had to decide on the terms of the loans and the particulars for their repayment. But at the end, they were able to compromise because it was ingrained in their values that passing debts to unborn generations of Athenians was unjust.

In the long decades leading to the 1929 crisis, representative democracies managed public budgets in an Athenian like fashion. Debts created during periods of wars would be settled in the following years through budget surpluses. The same spirit against systematic deficit spending was echoed also by Keynes (1936, 220, 378–380; 1942, 277–278; 1944, 366–367) in the 1930s and 1940s. But under the leadership of the so-called Keynesians, his warnings were set aside and the Aeolus sac of deficit spending opened for good and in all democracies across the world. Thus, governments in the United States started to run budget deficits to achieve initially "full employment" and later on various other socially appealing objectives to justify in the eyes of citizens the self-promoting agendas of politicians and bureaucrats through deep expansion of the state into the private sector. By the time Hayek (1960, 304–305) took notice of the serious mutations in the problems that were afflicting the economy and Buchanan, Wagner (1977) held Keynes responsible for what was happening, the addiction of the body politic to deficit spending and the accumulation of public debt had become irreversible. To confirm this assessment, it suffices to note the following. In 2016, that is, the last year of his presidency, Barack Obama, whom the successor U.S. president considers as super progressive, meaning leftist, proposed the so-called Constitutional Balanced Budget Amendment. However, a series of leading economists, including four distinguished Nobel laureates, opposed it by arguing, among others, that[18]:

17 Recall from Sections 3.1.1 and 3.1.3 that there were strict procedures in place so that revenues matched expenditures by reallocating funds from surplus to deficit activities, as well as making sure that expenditures were effected in line with the provisions and guidelines laid down by the responsible authorities. The *logistai* and *euthinoi,* who headed these tasks, acted as the modern-day controllers and auditors, and, if they found discrepancies, they filed lawsuits against those who were in charge. As mentioned earlier, the auditing procedures that the Athenian state applied were known as *logodosia* and *eisangelia.*

18 See   www.epi.org/publication/economist-statement-constitutional-balanced-budget-amendment

A balanced budget amendment would mandate perverse actions in the face of recessions. In economic downturns, tax revenues fall and some outlays, such as unemployment benefits, rise. These built-in stabilizers increase the deficit but limit declines in after-tax income and purchasing power. To keep the budget balanced every year would aggravate recessions.

As far as we know, even full-hearted supporters of balanced budgets have never proposed balancing the budget every year. What they have proposed is balancing the budget over a full business cycle. That is, realizing surpluses in the upturn, when the economy risks overheating, and spending these surpluses in the downturn mostly in infrastructural investments in order to stimulate aggregate demand and prevent the economy from going into deep recession. Such a policy would prevent the accumulation of public debt, which by skyrocketing in recent decades places the stability of the U.S. economy and the international financial order at the risk of another major crisis. Therefore, we fail to understand the reasoning of these renowned economists, who opposed the proposal as anything more than a defense of the status quo, long favored by intellectual supporters of the big state.

Even worse than the above, there are economists of world status who claim that debt does not matter because Americans owe it to themselves. For an example, take the *New York Times* columnist, Paul Krugman, another Nobel laureate, who looks down on economists expressing concern about uncontrollable deficits and out-of-hand federal and private debt. However, the multifaceted distortions to the economy, summarized concisely by Edwards (2015), are real and would not go away because he pushes them under the rag. Simply he is wrong and this explains why the large majority of economists are exceedingly concerned with the economic and particularly the political implications of debt for democracy in the United States and in the world.

9.3 The superior advantages of direct democracy

Recall from earlier chapters that Athens practiced direct democracy and that the same is true with many other Greek city-states (e.g., Robinson 2011) and Federations (Mackil 2013).[19] The supreme governing body was the *Assembly*. After hearing the expert initiators on an issue, the participating citizens decided by voting case by case, as for example, for the economy, through the adoption of *Nicophon's Law*, or defense through the adoption of *Themistocles Naval Decree*. In the executive branch, with the exemption of a few posts that were filled by voting from lists of knowledgeable and

---

19 For example, when in 191 BCE, the Achaean Federation managed to unify all of Peloponnese under its authority, it comprised more than 103 democratically governed city-states.

experience-distinguished candidates, all positions were filled by lot for short terms of service and all officials were strictly accountable. Every citizen could come forward and defend or reject the "common good," as he perceived it, in full freedom but also with conduct worthy of an Athenian. This is the context on which Pericles reflected when in his *Funeral Oration* (Thucydides, *History of the Peloponnesian War, 2.*37) declared that:

> While we are thus unconstrained in our private business, a spirit of reverence pervades our public acts; we are prevented from doing wrong by respect for the authorities and for the laws, having a particular regard to those which are ordained for the protection of the injured as well as those unwritten laws which bring upon the transgressor of them the reprobation of the general sentiment, ...

On these grounds, we surmise that direct democracy emerged and flourished in Athens because it allowed its citizens to shape the political framework within which they could pursue freely but orderly their economic activities, and to live their lives as they wished, without undue interference from the state.

The model of the Athenian direct democracy remains unique to the present-day. It has not been adopted anywhere over the centuries, so we lack the advantage of knowledge through experimentation. As a result, what evidence we find in the literature comes from applications of direct democracy processes for the resolution of specific issues of general interest to the people of a country or a local community. For example, in more recent decades, numerous studies, among which Feld and Matsusaka (2003), Matsusaka (2005a, 2005b, 2010) Blume, Miller, Voigt (2009), Feld, Fischer, Kirchgässner (2010) and Blume, Voigt (2012), using data from isolated incidences of direct democracy in the United States, Switzerland and the rest of the world, have assessed its advantages in comparison to those of representative democracy and have shown the superiority of the former over the latter in various key economic issues. We consider these research endeavors very valuable because by having demonstrated the practical benefits from the introduction of piecemeal direct democracy processes in various countries, they have brought the great prospects of this model of governance to the forefront of public attention across the world. But our objective here is not to review these literatures. Rather, what we plan to do is to highlight the superior advantages of the Athenian model of democracy over the one that dominates in the United States and the other advanced representative democracies.

9.3.1 No representation, no political parties, no voter alienation

Unlike the model of representative democracy, in which governments are formed by the political parties that win in the elections, the Athenian model is free of political parties. The citizens govern themselves in a political and organizational framework of self-government. In turn, this fundamental difference implies that while the former model is beset by the problems of representation that we reviewed in the preceding section, the latter model offers a far more effective mechanism, first, for arriving at the ordering of citizen preferences over policies, second, implementing them promptly and efficiently, third, keeping the citizens engaged in the governance of the state and fourth, ameliorating significantly the problem of asymmetric information. Relegating the latter for the next section, here we shall concentrate on former three advantages.

The source of the first advantage of the Athenian model is that because of the intermediation of the political parties, representative democracy does not permit citizens the possibility of unbundling, that is, to vote for the policy option, say on education, proposed by the A party, on health by the B party, on defense by the C party, etc. As a result, the ordering of citizen preferences is not revealed, at least not precisely. On the contrary, in the Athenian model, the decisions are taken by voting on a case-by-case basis and the true order of citizen priorities is arrived at by applying the majority rule among those that vote. This setup, we believe, delivers the true essence of democracy.

The second advantage is the selection and appointment of most officials by lot, for short service, holding them personally responsible for carrying out their duties legally and ethically, and absolving them from all *euthine* only after audit. In the previous chapters, we had the opportunity to comment on the contribution some of these institutional arrangements made to the exemplary quality of governance in classical Athens. For example, since they operated under the understanding that absolutely no one was to be trusted because of the frivolity of human nature, we suggested that in order to limit the corrupting influence that authority exerts on the character of those holding office, with few exceptions, they kept the term of service to one year.[20] Here then, we should like to expand a bit on the merits of selection by lot or sortition. The candidates for state office were proposed by the citizens who were registered with the ten tribes. The criteria for selection at that level were known in advance and very demanding. The information on the proposed candidates was passed and checked independently at the state level before the names of those admitted were placed in the urn. Finally, those appointed

---

20 In representative democracies, elected officials are appointed usually for four years. On the contrary, the leaderships of public corporations, among which one identifies giant multinational corporations, are elected for one year. Even though by comparison to classical Athens, where officials were also appointed for one year, it would be extremely lenient to admit, let us assume that this striking difference might have been justified in the past because the social cost of running elections every year would be absurd. But what about now that technology has rendered digital elections as easy as buying our everyday groceries over the internet? Our answer for now is that appointment for four years is not justified anymore, but we shall return later on to document it.

were selected through random drawing. By implication, the system assured that: (a) all competent and interested citizens had an equal chance of holding public office; (b) factionalism was minimized, since there was no point making promises to win over key supporters; and (c) clientelism in the form of distributing state benefits to particular groups of voters so as to get reelected was absent. All these merits made for a vastly better functioning democracy in comparison to today's highly biased electoral processes.

The third advantage, that is, efficiency, derives from the superior institutional flexibility of the Athenian model. To highlight it, consider the case of the British exit from the EU, that is, Brexit. It seems that many British citizens had second thoughts about leaving the EU and the popular sentiment in favor of holding a second referendum gained momentum. But institutionally, this presents considerable problems both at the political and the legislative levels. It is a difficult issue for the prime minister, the ministers, members of the parliament of all parties, etc. Under the Athenian model, the solution would be simple, straightforward and could be implemented fast. An initiator would just have to propose a new vote in the *Assembly* and if the outcome was different from the previous one, the new decision would be implemented.

A famous example in this regard is the one reported by Thucydides (*History of the Peloponnesian War*, 3.36–49). In 427 BCE, the *Assembly* decided to punish the rebellious citizens of Mytilene (a member of the Athenian League) by putting to death all adult males upon their surrender after a long siege. An Athenian ship sailed bringing the order of execution to the Athenian general of the island. The next day, the Athenians had second thoughts on the harshness of the punishment and the *Assembly* took a decision to annul the previous one and to execute only the leaders of the revolt. A second ship was sent, countermanding the previous order, with its Athenians commanders promising the rowers extra pay as an incentive if they arrived in time to save the Mytileneans. The second ship did overcome the first and the Mytileneans were saved. Presumably, if Athens followed Brexit procedures, the decision would have not changed at all, or not in time to save the citizens of the island and the *Assembly* would have committed a terrible mistake.[21]

Lastly, of singular significance is the third advantage. We mentioned earlier that in contemporary democracies, citizens have been disappointed by the behavior of governments and political parties and that they have distanced themselves from public affairs. They have become indifferent to

---

21 The evidence is that Athenian democracy in the 4th century became less radical in the sense that after 403 BCE, they introduced two new institutions, that is, "*graphe paranomon*" and "*nomotherai*," which acted as further checks and balances mechanisms regarding the decisions of the *Assembly*. Readers interested in the role of these institutions may start with Lyttkens, Tridimas, Lindgren (2018), regarding the former, and Harris (2013), regarding the latter.

what is happening at the state level and they show it by abstaining from elections, denigrating politicians and opening their hearts and minds to currents of ideas and populist political parties that seek to abolish democracy altogether. The looming threat and the quest for an alternative model of democracy is succinctly described in the following quotation from Barber (2003, xiv):

> When the public yields its basic governing functions to representatives, it has begun a process of alienation that in the end taints the very idea of public goods and common ground. This alienation in turn trivializes democracy, transforming what should be ongoing deliberative participation in governance into a cynical preoccupation with media-hyped elections.... In a word, then, privatization, alienation, and the abuse of civic deliberation are actually easier in a representative democracy than in a strong participatory democracy- which is one more argument in strong democracy's favor.

In the sequel, we shall argue and hope to show convincingly that the strong democracy Barber is after may very well be a close adaptation of the Athenian model.

9.3.2 Procedural counterbalancing of informational asymmetries

The citizens who participated in the Athenian *Assembly* came from all walks of life. They were not presumed by any means to have expert knowledge on any of the multifaceted functions of their state. The only thing they were presumed to have was common sense and motivation to serve the "common good." To carry out their duties, they listened to expert initiators of the various policy initiatives and depending on their understanding, they stood ready to speak freely their mind in favor or against the proposed policies and at the end to vote accordingly. In fact, according to Kyriazis, Economou (2015), the Athenian citizens were trained to listen and being guided by experts.

For example, let us go back to *Nicophon's Law* to which we referred in Section 4.3.2. Nicophon was a monetary expert in the service of the *Assembly*. So, to win support for his proposals, we can assume that he strived to explain what the objectives of his draft law were and how they might be achieved. Speaking in the presence of at least 6,000 people, the great majority of whom knew little or no monetary economics, he had to communicate his ideas in simple but not simplistic terms. In the process, every citizen present shared the same information, which formed a basis for his vote. Therefore, the asymmetry of information between Nicophon and the prospective voters in his audience was reduced and the decision was carried out with a better understanding of the pros and cons by those who voted and would be called to share the consequences of the law, if adopted.

To appreciate the wisdom of the above procedural approach, consider the following quotation from Tirole (2017, 12):

> ...the problem of limited (or "asymmetric") information is everywhere at the heart of our institutional structures and our policy choices and at the heart of the economics of the common good....Based on this asymmetry, populism can exploit the ignorance and prejudice of voters" (*ibid.*, 28)....the market for goods and services is a mechanism to exchange and diffuse information, thus facilitating choice. If the public had a better understanding of economic mechanisms, this would be a public good.
>
> (*ibid.*, 31)

Taking the latter analogy into politics, we may argue that the *Assembly* functioned as a market for the exchange and competition of "ideas." Every initiator brought forward and tried to "sell" his own proposal, for which he had to offer specific and convincing information (arguments) that would make it superior to that of other initiators on the same issue. In turn, this exchange of arguments among all present, counterbalanced informational asymmetries and established a common ground which facilitated "informed" choices. Helpful in this regard was also the fact that those who participated in the *Assembly* spoke the same language, shared the same code of ethics and adopted the same practices in politics. Furthermore, a citizen who wished to speak or to propose (known as, *ho boulomenos*) or even to accuse somebody openly in the *Assembly* was free to do so, but he knew that whatever he said could be potentially used against him, if his proposal hurt eventually the state's interests. Hence, as we have argued already, every citizen who participated in the *Assembly* behaved responsibly by adhering to the principle of *parrhesia*. Ancient philosophers were fully aware of the importance of these attributes for the orderly governance of the state's affairs and concurred with Aristotle who stressed that the supreme value of a state (*politeia*) is *homonoia*, meaning order, unity and steadfastness of minds in the pursue of a common purpose.

Today the question would be: may we, or even better, should we trust simple citizens to decide on complex issues? Hidden in this question is the mistrust regarding the abilities of the average citizen to take part in such deliberations and assume responsibility in the adoption of such decisions. Drawing on the Athenian experience, we think that this is wrong on multiple grounds. First, yes, average citizens may err. But "proper guardians" and "experts" do err as well and perhaps even more often and more seriously, if they lack "morals" and may escape from absorbing the consequences of their errors. Second, in direct democracy, individual rights, responsibilities and consequences fall on the same person. So, for citizens, this setup is a process of "learning by doing" through potentially costly errors.

Third, as we argued above, there is no such thing as "voter alienation." Instead, what develops is a sense of "belonging." We know this from Manville, Ober (2003), who characterize Athens as a "Company of citizens" because it expanded and enhanced the meaning of "belonging" to a community—making membership available, real, practical and emotionally satisfying. On pages 82–83, they explain why the Athenian political model of direct participation of citizens into politics succeeded. They write:

> Cleisthenes and his colleagues transformed the existing status of "being an Athenian." They gave it deeper meaning, with language and passionate rhetoric celebrating the values of freedom and equality. They also made citizenship more reliable by formalizing the procedure of membership enrollment and certification…Now it was not some elite ruler but your fellow citizens as a community who guaranteed for you your status of citizenship. You became a citizen through a vote by the citizens, and no one but your fellow-citizens could ever take citizenship away from you. The formalization of that status created a new and stronger sense of individual security. That in turn allowed for the growth of the deep mutual trust on which a true company of citizens must be built.

Lastly, fourth, the many thousands of citizens who participated in the *Assembly* had a greater probability to reach decisions that matched the preferences of the average Athenian than if their number was a miniscule percentage of the total population. That this is the case we know now from the theorem of large numbers, which guarantees that the results obtained from a large number of voters should be close to the average, and that the results will converge closer to the average as the number of voters increases.[22]

Thus, by corresponding best to the interests of the average citizen, the decisions on the "common good" by the *Assembly* drew wide acceptance and support, which in turn contributed to the efficiency and success of their implementation.

9.3.3 Election, accountability and personal responsibility of all officials

In Section 5.1.1.1, we described in brief detail the structure of the public administration in classical Athens. With the exception of a small force of civil servants, who were appointed to maintain the records and provide the necessary continuity in the provision of public services, and a small number

---

22 We cannot digress here to cover these issues. But interested readers may find it convenient to look at www.kaispiekermann.net/blog-native/epistemic-theory-of-democracy and https://global.oup.com/academic/product/an-epistemic-theory-of-democracy-978019 8823452?cc=gb&lang=en&#.

of officials such as the *strategoi (generals)*,[23] who were elected by vote from lists of candidates distinguished for their knowledge and experience, all other officials were elected by lot, for short terms of office, and remained accountable until after they were relieved by the auditors. Athenians, but ancient Greeks in general, believed that election to all state posts is one of the cornerstones of democracy and they would not understand today's proliferation of nonelected officials heading the ever expanding plethora of regulatory bodies and independent quasi-state authorities. For an Athenian, as honorable as it was to serve in a public post, the same held true when one assumed the mantle of the defender of the public interest. This is a crucial difference with today's democracies.

Any citizen could step forward in order to defend the public interest, as he understood it, and many did in small and big ways characterized by a mentality of *parrhesia*. Let us stress this missing link in our times by reference to a famous example, that is, the controversy *On the Crown*. In 340 BCE, Demosthenes, acting as initiator, persuaded the *Assembly* to undertake defensive measures to thwart Macedonian expansionism under King Philip II. He convinced Athenians to prepare for war and to entrust him with the building of an alliance of Southern Greek city-states against Macedon, which he brought about successfully. The Athenians offered him an honorary crown for his services. But in 338 BCE, the allies were beaten by the Macedonians at *Chaeronea*, with the Athenians losing 1,000 men. Years after that battle, Aeschines, Demosthenes political rival, accused him of leading the *Assembly* astray and harming the common interest. We see that a previous favorable vote in the *Assembly* did not exonerate the initiator of his responsibility, if ex post his proposals proved disastrous for the state. Aeschines did not have to prove any personal harm or damage he sustained as a result of Demosthenes' proposal. A defender of the public interest or common good could accuse an initiator in front of the *Assembly*, the *Popular Courts* or both. In the particular case, Demosthenes, through his oration *On the Crown* (one of the all-time masterpieces of rhetoric dating to 330 BCE), won. If he had lost, he would have faced grave consequences, fines, exile or even death. Thus, initiators had to be cautious, responsible and above all, courageous when proposing. It was as if an "Invisible Hand of Courage" guided their proposals on grave issues.

In most of today's democracies, single or groups of citizens cannot come forward as defenders of the common interest against measures taken by

---

23 The institution of ten Athenian *generals* was considered very important because it was connected to the survival of the state itself. It required skillful, knowledgeable and highly experienced leaders to hold the post, and obviously this could not be safeguarded by lot. For this reason Athenians selected them by ordination. Again, as we argued in Section 3.1.1, the same applied for the *tamias tes koines prosodou*, the *chief tamias*, whose duties were more or less similar to those of a modern Finance Minister, and other posts.

government or other public authorities that they consider harmful to common interest.[24] In order to gain recourse in front of a court of justice, citizens have to prove not only that a law or measure is for example unconstitutional but also that the particular measure harms them personally. This is another crucial difference as to how the public interest was understood then and now. Defense of the public interest has been degraded to personal interest.

To summarize, all public officials were fully accountable, being audited at the end of their term of office, and they were open to prosecution by any citizen in front of the *Courts*. This made them as well as the initiators very cautious in their service to the state and served as barrier to populism, contrary to what happens now in many countries. Through hearing the expert initiators and participating in the *Assembly*, Athenians gained knowledge and mostly made correct decisions. In the *Assembly*, the "wisdom of the majority" prevailed, to paraphrase the well-known Condorcet Jury Theorem.[25]

9.3.4 Resiliency through multiple checks and balances

The Athenian democracy reemerged after only one year of authoritarian rule in two cases at the end of the Peloponnesian War (411 and 403 BCE) and again, at the beginning of the 3rd century, after an interregnum of absolutist/oligarchic rule, which was imposed by the Macedonians in 322 BCE upon defeating Athens in the *Lamian* war and lasted until 307 BCE. Until Athens was destroyed by the Romans in 88 BCE, its democracy endured for about four centuries in total, thus being the longest lasting in history. In comparison, the longest lasting presidential democracy of the United States is 243 or 236 years (depending on whether one calculates from the beginning, 1776, or the end, 1783 of the American Revolution), whereas the oldest representative democracy in Europe, that is, that of England (and after 1707 the UK), dates 330 years, but partial suffrage of the urban male working class in England and Wales was introduced for the first time with the presentation of the *People Act of 1867*, known also as the *Reform Act of 1867*.[26]

---

24 From Figueira, we have learned that in the United States, fraud can in fact be attacked by private citizens through *Qui tam* suits, whereas corruption through the path offered by the *Racketeer Influenced and Corrupt Organizations (RICO) Act*.

25 This assessment should not be interpreted to imply that the *Assembly* was immuned from highly damaging decisions. For example, the Sicily campaign in 415 BCE, which ravaged the Athenians finances and undermined deeply the military capability of the state, and the conviction and death of the Athenian *generals* after the battle of Arginusae in 406 BCE, in which Athens was victorious and where the *generals* fell prey to a series of conspirators, were two such decisions. Our assessment should be interpreted to hold on the average.

26 Under such a perspective, democracy in the UK, related to political suffrage of male citizens, has a history of 152 years. Other nations followed later such as New Zealand where adult suffrage was first established in 1893.

We mentioned already above one of the main factors for this remarkable resilience of the Athenian democracy. It was the strong sense of belonging that Athens gave to its citizens. Paraphrasing the dictum of king Louis XIV,[27] Athenians felt and behaved as if declaring with pride and justification "The state is us." When the bonds of citizenship become this strong, citizens are willing to fight and even spill their blood for democracy, as Athenians did on many occasions, for example fighting and expelling the 30 tyrants in 403 BCE. A second main factor was the trust Athenians had in the institutions that solidified their sovereignty over the governance of their state. And by this, we mean the multiple layers of checks and balances through which Athenians made sure that governors and governed would abide by the deecisions taken in the *Assembly*.

Baron de Montesquieu (1748/1989) is considered the first to have pioneered the notion of the separation of powers in the modern world, thus leading to a constitutional system of checks and balances able to constrain the overarching power of political leaders. Athenians and other Greeks practiced a system of checks and balances at least 22 centuries before Montesquieu. The first instance was in the *Assembly* itself, where checks and balances applied at two levels, one informal and another formal. The informal emanated from the legislative procedures in the *Assembly*. For all issues, contrasting proposals were put forward by initiators to be debated, as for example by the opposing pairs Themistocles-Aristides, Kimon-Pericles and Demosthenes-Aeschines. In the case of Themistocles Naval Law, the two proposals were: Use the Laurion money to finance the building of a fleet (vote for the common good defense, Themistocles) or distribute the money equally among citizens (vote for private consumption, Aristides or his supporters). Since there were always two or more proposals, citizens had to hear them all and compare the one against the other until all but a convincing one were checked out.[28]

The formal check was accountability and the potential threat that an initiator might be sued if his proposal proved eventually to be harmful for the common good. It was formal because the complaining citizen(s) had to turn against an initiator (or any official) in front of the *Assembly* or the *Courts*. modern democracies have of course a system of checks in parliamentary debates. But they are attenuated for three reasons: first, because governments are aligned usually with the political parties that hold the majority in the parliament, and hence they can pass the proposed laws irrespective of the outcome of the debate; second, because the party-controlled parliamentary majority rarely if ever breaks ranks with the government; and third,

---

27 Louis XIV dictum was: *L' etat c'est moi.* (The state is me).
28 In addition to the checks and balances aimed at guiding the application of political power toward the common good, there was also one more demanding imperative. This was that political leaders had to be guided by virtue. In ancient constitutional theory, the marrying of both requirements as attributes of the preferred *politeia* started with Aristotle's *Politics*.

because, as we suggested in the previous section, citizens can hold public officials accountable only if they have suffered some personal injury, which may be traced to their decisions.

Lastly, there was a third level of institutional checks and balances, the most well-known being the *graphe paranomon*, which was introduced sometime between the end of the 5th and the beginning of the 4th century, possibly in 404 BCE. According to this, new proposals by initiators in the *Assembly* had to be examined in order to determine if they were compatible with existing law (Schwartzberg 2004, 319). In modern terms, this was an examination of the constitutionality of the proposals and it was carried out by two new boards: the *nomothetai* (meaning those who are establishing new laws) and the *thesmomothetai* (meaning those who are establishing state institutions).[29] The *nomothetai* had to certify that a draft law did not conflict in any way with other existing laws (Harris 2013, 244–245). If this was the case, the proposed laws were rejected. The members of this board were drawn from the annual group of judges serving in the *Courts*. It was actually a two-tier board where the first board (elected by the *Boule* of the 500 men) had also the right to propose new laws, while the second (elected from the Athenian municipalities—*demes*) voted on whether to ratify each law and add it to the archives of existing laws. Characteristically, Harris (2013, 244) argues that:

> In the fifth century, the constitution of the Athenians placed that power in the hands of the *Assembly*, in the fourth century, in the hands of the *Assembly* and the *nomothetai*.

On the other hand, the *thesmothetai* was a board of six *archons*, whose duties were to preside over *Courts* and review the laws annually, to determine whether there were inconsistencies, duplications or invalid laws in force and, if so, to inform the *nomothetai* to rectify this situation. As a result of these reforms, the dominant view of experts is that democracy in the 4th century became less radical as the political system grew less volatile and democracy more mature than in the 5th century.

Aside from the preceding, Athenians applied also for the first time in history the principles of Montesquieu on the separation of state powers. In contemporary terms, among many other functions, the *Assembly* was the

---

29 During the preclassical era after Solon, Athens's main official court was *Areiopagos*, manned only by members of the elite as judges, who had previously been *archons*. The *archons* were eventually nine. Earlier, their office was said to have had a ten-year term. But later, their term became annual. During classical times, of the nine *archons*, six dealt with judicial matters, and for this reason, they were called *thesmothetai* (thesmoi equaling laws), whereas, as we mentioned in Section 2.1, one was in charge of defense, and the other two were tasked with responsibilities like supervising the disposition of confiscated and sacred properties.

state's Legislature. As we stressed above, it provided the forum for the discussion and enactment of Laws and Decrees. The *prytany* segment of the *Boule* was in charge of running the day to day affairs, and thus in today's terms, it served as the Executive. Contrary to today's practices according to which draft laws are submitted to parliaments for authorization by governments, the *Assembly* and the *Boule* in ancient Athens were independent on two essential grounds. First, initiatives for new legislation emerged mainly from within the *Assembly*,[30] and second, while answerable to the *Assembly*, the members of the *Boule* were elected directly by lot, not appointed or chosen by the head of government (President or Prime Minister), as is the case in today's representative democracies.

Also, independent from the other two powers was the *Judicial.* With the possible exception of *nautodikai,* the members of the *Popular Courts* were elected by lot, and court rulings were definitive in the sense that no other public authority could change them. This again is an important difference with the institutional setup in some modern democracies. In the United States, for example, Presidents can circumvent the judiciary, either by refusing to abide by court rulings or by using the presidential pardon, and even more so by changing the numerical composition of the *Courts*, adding or eliminating members, presumably as it suits to the President and his administration (Levitsky, Ziblatt 2018, 128).[31]

Moreover, the composition of the *Popular Courts* remained constant over the centuries, that is, 6,000 jurors elected by lot for each year, sitting in chambers of 201, 501, etc. members, according to the importance of the cases they judged. Given that ordinary citizens sat in the *Courts*, their verdicts, especially on political trials (like the Demosthenes-Aeschines case) reflected the public opinion, since the jurors were a microcosm of the totality of the Athenian citizen body. This arrangement had both advantages and disadvantages. The advantage was that decisions reflected public opinion. The disadvantage was that as jurors were burdened with the judging of the

---

30 Proposals for new laws might be submitted by any citizen (*ho boulomenos*) either in the *Assembly* or through the *Council.* If the proposal was submitted through the latter, the *Council* retained the right to modify the proposal before submitting it to the *Assembly* or even rejecting it altogether.

31 The members of the Supreme Court are nine, and their number has remained unchanged for the last century. But its composition changed during the 19th century. Roosevelt tried to "pack the court," increasing its numbers in the 1930s. However, his attempt was vitiated by the Senate and the House, although he had a majority, democratic senators and members of the House voted against, in a good demonstration of the effective working of checks and balances (*ibid.*, 118–199, 132–133). U.S. presidents have the right even to pardon themselves! An example of circumvention of the Supreme Court's rulings was by Lincoln when he refused to abide by the Court's ruling, which rejected his suspension of the writ of habeas corpus during the civil war (*ibid.*, 128). In ancient Athens, neither the *Assembly* nor the *Boule* could circumvent or annul the rulings of the *Courts*.

laws as well as the facts of the case in front of them, *Popular Courts* reflected the prejudices and intolerance of the mass, the most famous case being the condemnation to death of the philosopher Socrates (which the Athenians regretted soon after, going so far as to erect his statue as a gesture of amends to his memory).

9.4 The long march back to citizen sovereignty

Great civilizations and strong nations rarely decline abruptly. Before they fade away precede many decades, if not centuries, of growing internal discords which weaken the solidarity among citizens and undermine their willingness to defend the order that worked for them in the previous glorious periods. The same malaise appears to have taken hold in the great U.S. republic in the postwar period. After almost 2 centuries during which favorable political and economic developments overshadowed the precarious drawbacks of representative democracy, for several decades now it has become clear to an increasing number of political scientists, economists, sociologists, ethicists, legal experts, etc., that the established order is crumbling under the weight of citizen disenfranchising trends that seem irreversible.

In this light and the looming risks for the democratic way of life, critics of the established order, depending on their diagnoses of the elementary forces that drive the aforementioned trends, recommend reforms along various paths for returning to "substantive democracy" by which we mean a political and economic order where citizen sovereignty in local and national affairs dominates over political parties and elected politicians. Our objective in this section is to present a widely known model of reforms that may lead eventually to substantive democracy, and juxtapose to it the Athenian model of direct democracy in classical times, the advantages of which we explained in the previous section.

9.4.1 Gradualist pathways to substantive democracy

Any attempt to challenge the status quo in today's representative democracies anywhere in the world is bound to meet with strong resistance from the entrenched political and economic interests on which they stand. Hence, the choice of reforms and the mode of their introduction for best results are dividing lines among the various models that aim at paving the way toward substantive democracy. One that has attracted much attention in the relevant literature is the model of "strong or participatory democracy," which has been proposed by Barber (2003, Ch. 10).

The author's motivations derive from the following assessment of the disintegrating allegiance among citizens and its implications for everyday community life (Barber 2003, 220):

In representative democracies such as the United States, citizens define themselves as legal persons and as autonomous parties to a sovereign compact. Their civic identities tie them not to one another but to the government, first as sovereign contracting parties, second as subjects or beneficiaries. The citizen is a citizen exclusively by virtue of his relationship to the government, of which he is both author and subject. His relations with his fellow citizens are entirely private and have nothing of the civic about them. This privatization helps to explain the fearsome civic anomie that has bereaved the Western democracies of almost all civility and has made representative democracy so hostile to the idea of communitarian ties among citizens.

At the time, that is in 2003, the author witnessed a deep estrangement among U.S. citizens, which forebode anything else than more trouble, if it were not reversed the soonest possible. Yet since then, the situation has worsened and this explains why his proposals have remained as current as ever. So, let us turn to the model.

Its objectives are twofold: first, to raise the degree of citizen engagement in local affairs over the medium run, and second, to improve the prospects for dominance of citizen sovereignty over the political parties and the politicians in the long run. To achieve them, the model provides for a process and a program of specific reforms. The proposed process and the rationale for adopting it are explained in the following quotation (Barber 2003, 308):

> ...the prudent democrat reforms by adding participatory ingredients to the constitutional formula, not by removing representative ingredients. The objective is to reorient liberal democracy toward civic engagement and political community, not to raze it-destroying its virtues along with its defects. To call for the abolition of parties is to call for utopia. To call for a constitutional convention is to invite disaster. The American system (like entrenched democratic constitutions everywhere) survives by evolving and evolves by accreting new institutional layers that conform to the contours of a historically tested practice even as they alter the system's dimensions and center of gravity.

In other words, for example, even though the constitution makes no mention of political parties, the idea is not to challenge their presence and activities, but to start building parallel to them layers of appropriately designed institutions and/or civic arrangements that aim at the above stated objectives. The author is fully aware of the risks involved, since by tinkering with the institutions of representative democracy, the social frictions may get out of hand. However, he remains hopeful that grass roots democratic reformers will have the wisdom to embed into the reform process sufficient restraints to avoid all out confrontation with the status quo and most likely defeat.

With this proviso in mind, and the concerns that one may express regarding their efficacy and implications based on the U.S. experience, he proposes the following list of new institutions and civic arrangements (see Barber 2003, 307):

1 A *national system of neighborhood assemblies* from 1 to 5,000 citizens; these would initially have only deliberative functions but would eventually have local legislative competence as well;[32]
2 A *national civic communications cooperative* to regulate and oversee the civic use of new telecommunications technology and to supervise debate and discussion of referendum issues;
3 A *civic videotex service* and a *civic education postal act* to equalize access to information and promote the full civic education of all citizens;
4 Experiments in decriminalization and informal lay justice by an engaged local citizenry;
5 A *national initiative and referendum process* permitting popular initiatives and referenda on congressional legislation, with a multichoice;
6 *Experimental electronic balloting*, initially for educational and polling purposes only, under the supervision of the *civic communications cooperative*;
7 Selective local elections to local office by *lottery*, with pay incentives;
8 Experiments with an *internal voucher system*[33] for selected schools, public housing projects and transportation systems;
9 A program of *universal citizen service*, including a military service option for all citizens;
10 Public sponsorship of *local volunteer programs* in "common work" and "common action";
11 Public support of experiments in *workplace democracy*, with public institutions as models for economic alternatives;
12 A new architecture of civic and public space.

These reforms, if applied, are expected to insert into representative democracy a graft of "strong democracy" in the form of a newly awakened communitarian spirit, which over time through growing citizen participation may evolve into "substantive democracy."

Other models, less ambitious than the above, aspire to the same objectives but by focusing on the mobilization of citizen interest in common affairs through the mechanism of referenda. This approach has a long history and

---

32 For each item in the list, the author provides brief details about its implementation. However, the issue of whether the reforms should be introduced in some sequence or simultaneously is left mute.
33 As "internal voucher system" is defined as one that offers a choice among public but not private schools.

the literature is rich in country studies, range of subjects and organizational techniques, and results. However, we are unable to gauge their net effect on the outstanding issue of return to substantive democracy. For, while on the one hand by asking citizens to decide on various local and national issues some form of democracy does apply, on the other, conducting select referenda may very well deflect the attention of citizens from the lacunae of representative democracy, thus allowing a bad democratic order to get worst. But aside from this problem, we have a general objection to all models that are based on the presumption that the future of substantive democracy depends on the success or failure of the efforts to reinvigorate the spirit of togetherness and the interest of citizens to engage in local and national affairs.

The thread of our objection springs from the quotation we cited earlier from Pericles's *Funeral Oration* (see page 242). Athenians minded freely their own business. In their private lives, they were totally unconstrained. But they had something that tied them with the other Athenians and they had to be watchful of their public actions. This was their ownership of the state. In other words, they had two properties to attend to: one private and the other common, which included the laws. And they knew that the mismanagement of the one property would damage the other. That is why, allowing for the possibility that their public actions might hurt their common property, they acted in line with the written and unwritten laws of their community. By implication, the only reform, which is necessary in present-day democracies, is for the ownership of the state to pass from the control of the fake owners, that is, politicians, bureaucrats, big corporations, lobbyists and rentiers, and return to the true owners, that is, the citizens. This goal lies at the core of the Athenian model of direct democracy to which we turn next.

9.4.2 Radical return to direct democracy

Suppose that the founding fathers of the United States were alive today and that they were called to decide anew the form of democracy they thought appropriate to embed in the U.S. Constitution. Would they have decided to establish a representative or a direct democracy? We believe that including Madison who was much opposed to popular settings for decision-making in the public interest, they would have opted in favor of direct democracy, not because they were unaware of its limitations under the Athenian model, but because technological developments in electronic communications have brought its superior advantages well within reach.[34] To corroborate this

---

34 The Athenian model of direct democracy has been subjected to several criticisms. They vary from the rather moderate view that "while Athens is described as a democracy, votes were held by only a minority of the male population, who held authority over the remainder—women and slaves" to the assertion that "there was no real democracy in Classical Athens": and many objections in between drawing on the weaknesses in the way in which it operated. We are running out of space and we cannot summarize here the

claim, consider the following example of how shareholders control nowadays the management of major multinational corporations, whose shares are distributed worldwide and traded in most international exchanges.

Once a year, at a specific place, day and time, the management of a large multinational corporation must appear in front of its shareholders and, on account of their accomplishments on behalf of the corporation, ask for their vote of confidence. Well in advance of the meeting, the management dispatches to all shareholders, irrespective of the number of shares they own, full documentation together with the agenda of the meeting, including the proposals of the management regarding the appointment of new directors, revisions in the articles of incorporation, changes of external auditors, etc. The whole package of documents that goes to an *eponymous* fund in New York or Tokyo, which may hold several thousand or million shares, will go also via e-mail to an Eskimo who resides in the North pole, inviting them all to either take part in the meetings in person or authorize an independent representative to vote their shares according to their instructions. The technology involved is now standard and, given the capabilities of teleconferencing, it is more than certain that soon shareholder meetings will become all electronic.

So, in view of this real-life experience, the key question that arises is: If multinational corporations with shares spread around the globe can be controlled electronically by shareholders as successfully as so many examples ascertain, why setting up an Electronic Pnyx, which would be equivalent to the *Ecclesia of Demos*, at each level of government would not serve best the interest of any country? Having assessed most of the key objections that might be raised, Bitros and Karayiannis (2013, 179–185) conclude that the sole impediment in returning to a regime of self-government is that the representative democracy in the United States and everywhere has been captured by organized minorities based on conglomerations of political and economic power, and that under normal circumstances the prospects for self-government via Digital Direct Democracy (DDD) will remain in abeyance until a major crisis erupts that will render the radical overhauling of the established order inescapable.[35]

---

arguments and counterarguments found in the literature. For this reason, we close by suggesting that, if the Athenian model of direct democracy is stripped of its historical delimitations, in the present technologically advanced communications environment it offers a feasible and desirable framework for governance from the people for the people.

35 Many concerned with the current unsettling trends in democracies find superficial the idea that an electronic system may substitute for the face to face contact that the participants enjoyed in the *Ecclesia of Demos*, and thereby extend the potential for active participation to millions of people. For them there is a problem of scale that electronic systems cannot overcome. On the contrary, Cartledge (2011) argues that:

If we are all democrats today, we are not -and it is importantly because we are not - Athenian-style democrats. Yet, with the advent of new technology, it would actually be

Is this prospect relatively near or far into the future? Drawing on what we have learned from the present research journey, we believe that if the trends that dominate the political and economic developments chiefly in the United States are not checked soon, the demise of representative democracy as we know it will come sooner than later. But whether this dreadful experience will translate into popular demand for a return to direct democracy will depend on the readiness of citizens to assume the responsibilities that will come with this revolutionary change.

9.5 Summary and concluding remarks

Even though Smith (1776/1977) was very critical of the way representative democracy functions in Britain, the founders of the United States as a republic did not have much choice to adopt the ancient Athenian model of self-government they so much admired. The United States stretched over vast areas of land; the population was the least homogeneous in values, languages, religions, nationalities, etc.; and, not the least, the state of transportation and communication technologies was hardly conducive. So, the adoption in the U.S Constitution of representative democracy with an ingenious framework of checks and balance to avoid the tyranny of a concerted majority, but without rendering the country ungovernable, proved a signature accomplishment of their superb statesmanship.

Through appropriate adaptations to challenges that emerged from time to time, the system of governance the founders set up in the late 18th century allowed the United States in the 19th century to grow fast and assume the leadership in the world in the 20th century. During this period, the functioning of representative democracy was always problematic at both the federal and the state levels owing to its inherent defects discussed in Section 9.2. This explains why it had to be patched frequently to remain workable. But repairing it was possible for as long as the state sector remained limited and it could not be used by organized minorities as instrument to turn the system of public governance to their favor. Citizen sovereignty continued to dominate over political parties and politicians and substantive democracy with all its advantages for personal freedoms, property rights, rule of law, etc., reigned supreme.

Then, the deep economic crisis erupted in 1929 and the situation turned rapidly to the worse. Under the advice of so-called Keynesian economists, but not of Keynes himself, political parties and elected politicians discovered the *deus ex machina* for saving representative democracy in the form of

---

possible to reinvent today a form of indirect but participatory tele-democracy. The real question now is not can we, but should we... go back to the Greeks?

Unlike them, we suggest that the future of democracy lies in the reclaiming by citizens of their sovereignty through digitally aided direct participation in the decision-making at all state levels.

deficit spending and public debt accumulation. By the end of the 1930s, the state sector was growing so fast that Hayek (1944) found it urgent to send a stern warning. Democracy and civil liberties, he noted, are not lost all at once. They are lost little by little and inconspicuously. As citizens become accustomed to the usurpation of their rights by an ever-expanding state and those hidden behind it, the process will lead to a form of slavery from which there will be no return. If his fears at the time were thought excessive or untimely, the developments since then have proved him right. For, in the meantime the state in the United States and generally in all contemporary democracies has grown gigantic, property rights have been encroached significantly, and, as we explained in Section 9.1, citizens have turned from sovereign masters of the state to either beggars for its favors or instrument for extracting various exorbitant benefits to the loss of the general innocent taxpayer. This is a topsy-turvy situation, which has nothing in the offing but crises of increasingly frequency until the next big one.

In view of these appalling developments and the imminent prospects of a potential disaster for the democratic way of life, concerned researchers have been looking intensely for some time now into the elementary forces that drive the underlying trends and suggest possible ways to reverse them. In Section 9.4, we presented a widely known model of reforms, which is presumed by its supporters to hold strong hopes to raise the engagement of citizens in local and national affairs and pave the way toward substantive democracy. We believe that the status quo cannot be fooled into allowing this model of so-called strong or participatory democracy to take roots and flourish in parallel with the established model of representative democracy. Nor is there any hope of making significant progress in the same direction through referenda regarding select local and national issues.

If the road to disaster for the democratic way of life is to be bypassed, gradualist approaches toward substantive democracy are a prescription for self-deceit. To avoid it, there are only two strategies with any hope of success. The one is to mobilize citizens in support of returning right away to direct democracy, and employing the elections to impose it, and the other is to wait until the next major crisis renders representative democracy obsolete, hoping that citizens will be ready at that time for the big switch. Given that the technologies for organizing and conducting *Ecclesia of Demos* or *Electronic Pnyx* at all levels of public governance are now available and routinely practiced by multinational corporations and some states like Estonia, it would seem to us that the time is ripe for grass roots movements to replace the present established order of "nominal democracy" with one based on Digital Direct Democracy.[36]

---

36 If the reader believes that we are alone in the support of this outlook, reading of the analysis in Lyttkens, Tridimas, Lindgren (2018) may dissuade the reader's doubts about its feasibility in the context of the recent technological developments.

References

Ancient Greek authors

Aeschines, (1919), *Speeches: Against Ctesiphon*, Engl. Trnsl. C. D. Adams, Cambridge, MA: Harvard University Press, Perseus Digital Library.

Aeschines, (1919), *Speeches: Against Timarchos* I, Engl. Trnsl. C. D. Adams, Cambridge, MA: Harvard University Press, Perseus Digital Library.

Aeschylus, (1926), *Persians*, Engl. Trnsl. H. W. Smyth, Cambridge, MA: Harvard University Press, Perseus Digital Library.

Andocides, (1968), *Speeches: On the Mysteries*, Engl. Trnsl. K. J. Maidment, Cambridge, MA: Harvard University Press; London: William Heinemann, Ltd., Perseus Digital Library.

Aristophanes, (1907), *Acharnians*, in F. W. Hall and W. M. Geldart (Eds.), *Comoediae*. vol. 2, Oxford: Clarendon Press, Oxford, Perseus Digital Library.

Aristophanes, (1938), *Ecclesiazusae*, Engl. Trnsl. E. O'Neill, Jr., New York: Random House, Perseus Digital Library.

Aristophanes, (1938), *Knights*, Engl. Trnsl. E. O'Neill, Jr., New York: Random House, Perseus Digital Library.

Aristophanes, (1938), *Peace. The Complete Greek Drama*, vol. 2. Engl. Trnsl. E. O'Neill, Jr., New York: Random House.

Aristophanes, (1938), *Plutus*, Engl. Trnsl. E. O'Neill, Jr., New York: Random House, Perseus Digital Library.

Aristophanes, (1938), *Wasps*, Engl. Trnsl. E. O'Neill, Jr., New York: Random House, Perseus Digital Library.

Aristophanes, (1994), *Frogs*, Engl. Trnsl. M. Dillon, New York: Routledge, Perseus Digital Library.

Aristophanes, (2014), *Lysistrata*, Engl. Trnsl. J. Lindsay, New York: Perseus Digital Library.

Aristotle, (1920), *The Works of Aristotle* (*Oeconomica, Atheniensium Respublica*), Engl. Trnsl. E. S. Forster. Oxford: Clarendon Press.

Aristotle, (1934), *Nicomachean Ethics*, vol. 19, Engl. Trnsl. H. Rackham, Cambridge, MA: Harvard University Press; London: William Heinemann Ltd., Perseus Digital Library.

Aristotle, (1944), *Politics*, vol. 21, Engl. Trnsl. H. Rackham, Cambridge, MA: Harvard University Press; London: William Heinemann Ltd., Perseus Digital Library.

Aristotle, (1952), *Athenian Constitution*, vol. 20, Engl. Trnsl. H. Rackham, Cambridge, MA: Harvard University Press; London: William Heinemann Ltd., Perseus Digital Library.

Demosthenes, (1926), *Speeches:* XIV, *On the Navy*, Engl. Trnsl. C. A. Vince, J. H. Vince, Cambridge, MA: Harvard University Press; London, William Heinemann Ltd., Perseus Digital Library.

Demosthenes, (1939), *Speeches:* XVIII, *On the Crown*, Engl. Trnsl. A. T. Murray, Cambridge, MA: Harvard University Press; London: William Heinemann Ltd., Perseus Digital Library.

Demosthenes, (1939), *Speeches:* XX, *Against Leptines*, Engl. Trnsl. A. T. Murray, Cambridge, MA: Harvard University Press; London: William Heinemann Ltd., Perseus Digital Library.

Demosthenes, (1939), *Speeches:* XXI, *Against Midias*, Engl. Trnsl. A. T. Murray, Cambridge, MA: Harvard University Press; London: William Heinemann Ltd., Perseus Digital Library.

Demosthenes, (1939), *Speeches:* XXIII, *Against Aristocrates*, Engl. Trnsl. A. T. Murray, Cambridge, MA: Harvard University Press; London: William Heinemann Ltd., Perseus Digital Library.

Demosthenes, (1939), *Speeches:* XXIV, *Against Timocrates*, Engl. Trnsl. A. T. Murray, Cambridge, MA: Harvard University Press; London: William Heinemann Ltd., Perseus Digital Library.

Demosthenes, (1939), *Speeches:* XXVII, *Against Aphobus* 1, Engl. Trnsl. A. T. Murray, Cambridge, MA: Harvard University Press; London: William Heinemann Ltd., Perseus Digital Library.

Demosthenes, (1939), *Speeches:* XXXII, *Against Zenothemes*, Engl. Trnsl. A. T. Murray, Harvard University Press; London: William Heinemann Ltd., Perseus Digital Library.

Demosthenes, (1939), *Speeches:* XXXIV, *Against Phormio*, Engl. Trnsl. A. T. Murray, Cambridge, MA: Harvard University Press; London: William Heinemann Ltd., Perseus Digital Library.

Demosthenes, (1939), *Speeches:* XXXV, *Against Lacritus*, Engl. Trnsl. A. T. Murray, Cambridge, MA: Harvard University Press; London: William Heinemann Ltd., Perseus Digital Library.

Demosthenes, (1939), *Speeches:* XXXVI, *For Phormio*, Engl. Trnsl. A. T. Murray, Cambridge, MA: Harvard University Press; London: William Heinemann Ltd., Perseus Digital Library.

Demosthenes, (1939), *Speeches:* XXXXIII, *Against Macaratus*, Engl. Trnsl. A. T. Murray, Cambridge, MA: Harvard University Press; London: William Heinemann Ltd., Perseus Digital Library.

Demosthenes, (1939), *Speeches:* XXXXIV, *Against Leochares*, Engl. Trnsl. A. T. Murray, Cambridge, MA: Harvard University Press; London: William Heinemann Ltd., Perseus Digital Library.

Demosthenes, (1939), *Speeches:* LII, *Against Callippus*, Engl. Trnsl. A. T. Murray, Cambridge, MA: Harvard University Press; London: William Heinemann Ltd., Perseus Digital Library.

Demosthenes, (1939), *Speeches:* LVI, *Against Dionysodorus*, Engl. Trnsl. A. T. Murray, Cambridge, MA: Harvard University Press; London: William Heinemann Ltd., Perseus Digital Library.

Demosthenes, (1949), *Speeches:* LIX, *Against Neaera*, Engl. Trnsl. N. W. DeWitt, N. J. DeWitt, Cambridge, MA: Harvard University Press; London, William Heinemann Ltd., Perseus Digital Library.

Diogenes Laertius, (1925), *Lives of Eminent Philosophers. Diogenes Laertius*, Engl. Trnsl. R. D. Hicks, Cambridge, MA: Harvard University Press.

Herodotus, (1920), *The Histories*, Engl. Trnsl. A. D. Godley, Cambridge, MA: Harvard University Press, Perseus Digital Library.

Hesiod, (1914), *Works and Days*, Engl. Trnsl. H G. Evelyn-White, Cambridge, MA: Harvard University Press; London: William Heinemann Ltd., Perseus Digital Library.

Isocrates, (1980), *Speeches: Against Callimachus*, 18, Engl. Trnsl. G. Norlin, Cambridge, MA: Harvard University Press; London: William Heinemann, Ltd., Perseus Digital Library.

Isocrates, (1980), *Speeches: Areopagiticus*, 7, Trnsl. George Norlin, Cambridge, MA: Harvard University Press; London, William Heinemann Ltd., Perseus Digital Library.

Isocrates, (1980), *Speeches: Demonicus*, 1, Trnsl. George Norlin, Cambridge, MA: Harvard University Press; London, William Heinemann Ltd., Perseus Digital Library.

Isocrates, (1980), *Speeches: Panegyricus*, 4, Engl. Trnsl. G. Norlin, Cambridge, MA: Harvard University Press; London: William Heinemann, Ltd., Perseus Digital Library.

Isocrates, (1980), *Speeches: Trapeziticus*, 17, Trnsl. George Norlin, Cambridge, MA: Harvard University Press; London, William Heinemann Ltd., Perseus Digital Library.

Lycurgus, (1962), *Against Leocrates*, I, Engl. Trnsl. J. O. Burtt, Cambridge, MA, Harvard University Press; London, William Heinemann Ltd., Perseus Digital Library.

Lysias, (1930), *Speeches*, VI: *Against Andocides*, Engl. Trnsl. W. R. M. Lamb, Cambridge, MA: Harvard University Press; London: William Heinemann Ltd., Perseus Digital Library.

Lysias, (1930), *Speeches*, XII: *Against Eratosthenes*, Engl. Trnsl. W. R. M. Lamb, Cambridge, MA: Harvard University Press; London: William Heinemann Ltd., Perseus Digital Library.

Lysias, (1930), *Speeches*, XXII: *Against the Corn Dealers*, Engl. Trnsl. W. R. M. Lamb, Cambridge, MA: Harvard University Press; London: William Heinemann Ltd., Perseus Digital Library.

Lysias, (1930), *Speeches*, XVII: *On the Property of Eraton*, Engl. Trnsl. W. R. M. Lamb, Cambridge, MA: Harvard University Press; London: William Heinemann Ltd., Perseus Digital Library.

Pausanias, (1918), *Description of Greece, Attica,* Engl. Trnsl. W. H. S. Jones, H. A. Ormerod, in 4 Vol. Cambridge, MA: Harvard University Press; London, William Heinemann Ltd., Perseus Digital Library.

Plato, (1925), *Gorgias*, Engl. Trnsl. W. R. M. Lamb, Cambridge, MA: Harvard University Press; London: William Heinemann Ltd, Perseus Digital Library.

Plato, (1925), *Menexemus*, Engl. Trnsl. W. R. M. Lamb, Cambridge, MA: Harvard University Press; London: William Heinemann Ltd., Perseus Digital Library.

Plato, (1967), *Protagoras*, Engl. Trnsl. W. R. M. Lamb, Cambridge, MA, Harvard University Press; London, William Heinemann Ltd., Perseus Digital Library.

Plato, (1967, 1968), *Laws,* Engl. Trnsl. R. G. Bury, Cambridge, MA: Harvard University Press; London: William Heinemann Ltd., Perseus Digital Library.

Plutarch, (1914), *Solon*, Engl. Trnsl. B. Perrin, Cambridge, MA: Harvard University Press; London: William Heinemann Ltd., Perseus Digital Library.

Plutarch, (1916), *Plutarch's Lives. Pericles.* Engl. Transl. by. Bernadotte Perrin, Cambridge, MA: Harvard University Press; London. William Heinemann Ltd., Perseus Digital Library.

Pseudo-Xenophon, (1984), *Constitution of the Athenians*, Engl. Trnsl. E. C. Marchant, Cambridge, MA: Harvard University Press; London: William Heinemann, Ltd.

Thucydides, (1881), *History of the Peloponnesian War*, Engl. Trnsl. B. Jowett, Oxford: Clarendon Press, Perseus Digital Library.

Thucydides, (1928), *The Peloponnesian War*, Engl. Trnsl. C. F. Smith, Cambridge, MA: Loeb Classical Library, Harvard University Press, Perseus Digital Library.

Xenophon, (1914), *Cyropaedia*, Engl. Trnsl. W. Miller, Cambridge, MA; Harvard University Press; London: William Heinemann, Ltd., Perseus Digital Library.

Xenophon, (1918, 1921), *Hellenika*, Engl. Trnsl. C. L. Brownson, Cambridge, MA: Harvard University Press; London: William Heinemann, Ltd., Perseus Digital Library.

Xenophon, (1923), *Memorabilia*, Cambridge, MA: Harvard University Press; London: William Heinemann, Ltd., Perseus Digital Library.

Xenophon, (1925a), *Minor Works: Ways and Means*, Cambridge, MA: Harvard University Press; London: William Heinemann, Ltd., Perseus Digital Library.

Xenophon, (1925b), *Minor Works: Constitution of the Lacedaemonians*, Engl. Trnsl. E. C. Marchant, G. Bowersock, Cambridge, MA: Harvard University Press; London: William Heinemann, Ltd., Perseus Digital Library.

Xenophon, (2014), *Oeconomicus*, Engl. Trnsl. H. G. Dakyns, University of Adelaide, https://ebooks.adelaide.edu.au/x/xenophon/x5oe/.

More recent literature

Acemoglu, D., Robinson, A., (2015), "The rise and fall of general laws of capitalism," *Journal of Economic Perspectives*, 29, 3–28.

Acton, P. H., (2014), *Poiesis: Manufacturing in Classical Athens*, Oxford: Oxford University Press.

Ager, S., (1997), *Interstate Relations in the Greek World 337–90 BC*, Berkeley, Los Angeles and London: University of California Press.

Akerlof, G., (1970), "The market for lemons: Quality, uncertainty, and market mechanism," *Quarterly Journal of Economics*, 84, 488–500.

Akwei, J., (2018), "The future of cryptocurrency," https://johnakweil.wordpress.com/2018/01/.

Amemiya, T. (2007), *Economy and Economics of Ancient Greece*, New York and Abingdon: Routledge.

Andreades, A., (1928/1933), *A History of Greek Public Finance*, transl. C. N. Brown, Cambridge, MA: Harvard University Press.

Aperghis, G. G., (1998), "A reassessment of the Laurion mining lease records," *BCIS*, 42, 1–20.

Arafat, K., Morgan, C., (1989), "Pots and potters in Athens and Corinth: A review," *Oxford Journal of Archeology*, 8, 311–346.

Ardagna, S., Lusardi, A., (2009), "Where does regulation hurt? Evidence from new business across countries," NBER Working Paper No 14747.

Arrow, K. J., (1951/1963), *Social Choice and Individual Values*, New York: Wiley & Sons, 2nd edition.

Ault, B. A. (2007), "Oikos and Oikonomia: Greek houses, households and the domestic economy," *British School at Athens Studies*, 15, 259–265.

Austin, M. M., Vidal-Naquet, P. (1977), *Economic and Social History of Ancient Greece, An Introduction*, Berkeley: University of California Press.

Azoulay, V., (2016), *Xenophon and the Graces of Power of Graces: A Greek Guide to Political Manipulation*, Engl. Trnsl. A. Krieger, Swansea: The Classical Press of Wales.

Baloglou, C. P., (2012), "The tradition of economic thought in the Mediterranean world from the ancient Classical times through the Hellenistic times until the Byzantine times and the Arab Islamic world," in J. G. Backhaus (Ed.), *Handbook of History of Economic Thought. Insights of the Founders of Modern Economics*, New York, Heidelberg and London: Springer, 7–92.

Barber, B. R., (2003), *Strong Democracy: Participatory Politics for a New Age*, New York: MacMillan Press.

Baumol, W. J., (1968), "On the social rate of discount," *American Economic Review*, 58, 788–802.

Beaumont, L., (2012), *Childhood in Ancient Athens: Iconography and Social History*, Abingdon and New York: Routledge.

Berentsen, A., Schär, F., (2018), "The case for central bank electronic money and the non-case for central bank cryptocurrencies," *Reserve Bank of St. Louis Review*, 100, 97–106.

Bergh, A., Lyttkens, C. H., (2014), "Measuring institutional quality in ancient Athens," *Journal of Institutional Economics*, 10, 279–310.

Binder, S., Spindel, M., (2017), *The Myth of Independence: How Congress Governs the Federal Reserve*, Princeton, NJ: Princeton University Press.

Bissa, E. M. A., (2009), *Governmental Intervention in Foreign Trade in Archaic and Classical Greece*, Leiden and Boston, MA: K. Brill NV.

Bitros, G. C., (2015), "Thinking ahead of the next big crash," *Cato Journal*, 35, 6693.

Bitros, G. C., (2018), "Monetary policy, market structure and the income shares in the U.S.," *Open Economies Review*, 29, 383–413.

Bitros, G. C., (2020), "Demand adjusted capital input and potential output in the context of U.S. economic growth," *Journal of Economic Asymmetries*, 21 https://doi.org/10.1016/j.jeca.2019.e00140.

Bitros, G. C., Karayiannis, A., (2006), "The liberating power of entrepreneurship in ancient Athens," in Y. Cassis, I. Pepelasis-Minoglou (Eds.), *Country Studies in Entrepreneurship: A Historical Perspective*, London: Palgrave, 11–12.

Bitros, G. C., Karayiannis, A., (2008), "Values and institutions as determinants of entrepreneurship in ancient Athens," *Journal of Institutional Economics*, 4, 205–230.

Bitros, G. C., Karayiannis, A., (2010), "Morality, institutions and the wealth of nations: Some lessons from ancient Greece," *European Journal of Political Economy*, 26, 68–81.

Bitros, G. C., Karayiannis, A., (2011), "Character, knowledge and skills in ancient Greek paideia: Some lessons for today's policy makers," *Journal of Economic Asymmetries*, 8, 195–221.

Bitros, G. C., Karayiannis, A., (2012), "The city-state of ancient as a prototype for an entrepreneurial and managerial society," in G. P. Prastacos, F. Wang, K. E. Soderquist (Eds.), *Leadership & Management in a Changing World: Lessons from Ancient East and West Philosophy*, Heidelberg: Springer-Verlag, 289–304.

Bitros, G. C., Karayiannis, A., (2013), *Creative Crisis in Democracy and Economy*, Heidelberg: Springer.

Blamire, A., (2001), "Athenian finance, 454-404 B.C.," *Hesperia: The Journal of the American School of Classical Studies at Athens*, 70, 99–126.

Blinder, A., (2019), "The economy under Trump is very good. But don't be fooled," *Time*, September 2–September 9, 27.

Blume, L., Voigt, S., (2012), "Institutional details matter – more economic effects of direct democracy," *Economics of Governance*, 13, 287–310.

Blume, L. J., Muller, J., Voigt, S., (2009), "The economic effects of direct democrat – a first global assessment," *Public Choice*, 140, 431–461.

Bradeen, D. W., (1971), "The Kallias decrees again," *Greek Roman and Byzantine Studies*, 12, 469–483.

Bresson, A., (2007), *L'économie de la Grèce des cites. Les structures et la production*, vol. 1, Paris: Armand-Colin.

Bresson, A., (2016a), *The Making of the Ancient Greek Economy: Institutions, Markets, and Growth in the City-States*, Engl. Trnsl. S. Rendall, Princeton, NJ: Princeton University Press.

Bresson, A., (2016b), "Aristotle and foreign trade," Engl. Trnsl. E. M. Harris, in Harris, E. M., Lewis, D. M., Woolmer, M. (Eds.), *The Ancient Greek Economy: Markets, Households and City States*, New York: Cambridge University Press, 41–65.

Brown, G., (2018), "The world is sleepwalking into a financial crisis," *The Guardian*, International edition, September 12.

Bubalis, W., (2010), "The sacred triremes and their *Tamiai* at Athens," *Historia*, 59, 385–411.

Buchanan, J. M., (2010), "The constitutionalization of money," *Cato Journal*, 30, 251–258.

Buchanan, J. M., (2015), "The value of money as a constitutionalized parameter," in L. H. White, V. J. Vanberg, E. A. Köhler (Eds.), *Renewing the Search for a Monetary Constitution: Reforming Government's Role in the Monetary System*, Washington, DC: The Cato Institute.

Buchanan, J. M., Wagner, R. E., (1977), "Democracy in deficit: The political legacy of Lord Keynes," in *The Collected Works of James M. Buchanan*, vol. 8, 51–57. Indianapolis: Liberty Fund.

Buckley, T., (1996), *Aspects of Greek History: A Source-Based Approach*, London and New York: Routledge.

Budin, S. L., (2004), *The Ancient Greeks: New Perspectives*, Santa Barbara, CA: ABC-CLIO.

Bullard, J., (2016), "Safe real interest rates and Fed policy," Federal Reserve Bank of St. Louis, 1–38, www.stlouisFed.org/~/media/files/pdfs/bullard/remarks/bullard_commerce_bank_nov_10_2016.pdf.

Burke, E., (1774), "Speech to the electors of Bristol," http://peter-moore.co.uk/blog/edmund-burke-speech-to-the-electors-of-bristol-1774

Burke, E. M., (2010), "Finances and the operation of the Athenian democracy in Lycurgan era," *American Journal of Philology*, 131, 393–423.

Bury, J. B., (1900), *A History of Greece*, New York: Palgrave.

Camp, J. M., (2003), "The Athenian agora: A short guide to the excavations, Athens," The American School of Classical Studies at Athens, Picture Book No. 16.

Carawan, E. M., (1987), "Eisangelia and euthine: The trials of Miltiades, Themistocles, and Cimon," *Greek, Roman and Byzantine Studies*, 28, 167–208.

Cartledge, P., (2011), "Critics and critiques of Athenian democracy," www.bbc. co.uk/history/ancient/greeks/greekcritics_01.shtml.

Cartledge, P., Cohen, E. E., Foxhall, L., (2002), *Money, Labour and Land*. London and New York: Routledge.

Caspari, M. O. B., (1917), "A survey of Greek federal coinage," *The Journal of Hellenic Studies*, 37, 168–183.

Christ, R. M., (2006). *The Bad Citizen in Classical Athens*, Cambridge: Cambridge University Press.

Christesen, P., (2003), "Economic rationalism in fourth-century BCE Athens," *Greece & Rome*, 50, 31–56.

Christopoulou-Aletra, H., Togia, A., Varlam, C., (2009). "History of medicine," *Archives of Hellenic Medicine*, 27, 259–263.

Coase, R., (1937), "The nature of the Firm," *Economica*, 4, 386–405.

Cohen, E. E., (1973), *Athenian Maritime Courts*. Princeton, NJ: Princeton University Press.

Cohen, E. E., (1990), "Commercial lending by Athenian banks: Cliometric fallacies and forensic methodology," *Classical Philosophy*, 85, 177–190.

Cohen, E. E., (1992), *Athenian Economy and Society: A Banking Perspective*, Princeton, NJ: Princeton University Press.

Cohen, E. E., (2008), "Elasticity of the money supply at Athens," in W. H. Harris (Ed.), *The Monetary Systems of the Greeks and Romans*, Oxford: Oxford University Press, 66–83.

Conophagos, C. E., (1980), *Le Laurium antique et la technique Grecque de la production de l'argent*. Athens. Ekdotike Hellados.

Costouros, G. J., (1978), "Auditing in the Athenian state of the golden age (500–300 B.C.," *The Accounting Historians Journal*, 5, 41–50.

Coy, P., (2018), "The tyranny of the U.S. dollar: The incumbent international currency has been American for decades. Is it time for regime change?" Bloomberg Business Week, October 3, www.bloomberg.com/news/articles/ 2018-10-03/ the-tyranny-of-the-u-s-dollar.

Davies, J. K., (1967), "Demosthenes on liturgies: A note," *The Journal of Hellenic Studies*, 87, 33–40.

Davies, J. K., (1971), *Athenian Propertied Families, 600–300 B.C.*, Oxford: Oxford University Press.

Davies, J. K., (1981), *Wealth and the Power of Wealth in Classical Athens*, New York: Arno Press.

Davies, J. K., (1994), "Accounts and accountability in classical Athens," in R. Osborne, S. Hornblower (Eds.), *Ritual, Finance, Politics: Athenian Democratic Accounts Presented to David Lewis*, New York: Oxford University Press, Inc., 201–212.

Davies, J. K., (2001), "Temples credit and the circulation of money," in A. Meadows, K. Shipton (Eds.), *Money and Its Uses in the Ancient Greek World*, Oxford: Oxford University Press, 117–128.

De Grauwe, P., (2008), "Stock prices and monetary policy," Centre for European Policy Studies, Working Document No. 304.

de Jasay, A., (2007), "Social justice examined: With a little help from Adam Smith," in J. C. Pardo, P. Schwartz, (Eds.), *Public Choice and the Challenges of Democracy*, Cheltenham: Edward Elgar, 35–44.

De Ste. Croix, G. E. M., (1981), *The Class Struggle in the Ancient Greek World from the Archaic Age to the Arab Conquests*. Ithaca, NY: Cornell University Press.

de Tocqueville, A., (1840), *Democracy in America*, 1, New York: Vintage Books, 1954.

Despres, E., Kindleberger, C., Salant. W., (1966), "The dollar and world liquidity: A minority view," *The Economist*, 218(5), 526–529.

Develin, R. (2003), *Athenian Officials 684–321 BC*. Cambridge: Cambridge University Press.

Dobson, J., (1963), *Ancient Education and Its Meaning to Us*, New York: Cooper Square Publishers Inc.

Dorn, J., (2014), "The fed needs truly radical reform, not a timid Taylor rule fix," *Forbes*, July 31, www.forbes.com/sites/jamesdorn/2014/07/31/the-Fed-needs-truly-radical-reform-not-a-timid-taylor-rule-fix/#4e34336a7545.

Dowd, K., (1992), (Ed.), *The Experience of Free Banking*, London: Routledge.

Downs, A., (1957), *An Economic Theory of Democracy*, New York: Harper & Row.

Economou E. M. L., Kyriazis, N. C., (2016a), "The emergence and the development of the Achaean federation. Lessons and institutional proposals for modern societies," *Evolutionary and Institutional Economics Review*, 13, 93–112.

Economou E. M. L., Kyriazis, N. C., (2016b), "Choosing peace against war strategy. A history from the ancient Athenian democracy," *Peace Economics, Peace Science and Public Policy*, 22(2), 191–212.

Economou, E. M. L., Kyriazis, N. C., (2017), "The emergence and the evolution of property rights in ancient Greece," *Journal of Institutional Economics*, 13, 53–77.

Economou E. M. L., Kyriazis, N. C., (2019a), *Democracy and Economy: An Inseparable Relationship since Ancient Times to Today*, Newcastle upon Tyne: Cambridge Scholars Publishing.

Economou, E. M. L., Kyriazis, N. C., (2019b), "The emergence of property rights in Hellenistic Greece and the Ptolemaic Kingdom of Egypt," *Journal of Institutional Economics*, 1–17. doi:10.1017/S1744137419000055.

Economou, E. M. L., Kyriazis, N. C., Metaxas T., (2015), "The institutional and economic foundations of regional proto-Federations," *Economics of Governance*, 16, 251–271.

Edwards, C., (2015), "The problems with Federal government debt," www.downsizinggovernment.org/Federal-debt.

Eichengreen, B., (2011), *Exorbitant Privilege: The Rise and Fall of the Dollar*, Oxford: Oxford University Press.

Eichengreen, B., (2019), "From commodity to fiat and now to crypto: What does history tell us?" National Bureau of Economic Research, Discussion Paper 25426, 1–16.

Ellithorpe, C. J., (2013), "Athenian mercantilism: A new approach to the coinage decree & the law of Nicophon," University of North Carolina at Chapel Hill, Department of History, Unpublished mimeo.

Engen, D. T., (2004), "The economy of ancient Greece," in R. Whaples (Ed.), EH.Net Encyclopedia, http://eh.net/encyclopedia/theeconomyofancientgreece/.

Engen, D. T., (2005), "Ancient greenbacks, Athenian owls, the law of Nicophon, and the Greek economy," *Historia*, 54, 359–381.

Engen, D. T., (2010), *Honor and Profit: Athenian Trade Policy and the Economy and Society of Greece*, Ann Arbor: Michigan University Press.

Fama, E. F., (2013), "Does the control interest rates?" *The Review of Asset Pricing Studies*, 3, 180–199.

Fawcett, P., (2016), ""When I squeeze you with Eisphorai": Taxes and tax policy in classical Athens," *Hesperia: The Journal of the American School of Classical Studies at Athens*, 85, 153–199.

Feld, L. P., Matsusaka, J. G., (2003), "Budget referendums and government spending: evidence from Swiss cantons," *Journal of Public Economics*, 87, 2703–2724.

Feld, L. P., Fischer, J. A. V., Kirchgässner, G., (2010), "The effect of direct democracy on income redistribution: Evidence for Switzerland," *Economic Inquiry*, 48, 817–840.

Feldstein, M. S., (1964), "The social time preference discount rate in cost benefit analysis," *The Economic Journal*, 74, 360–379.

Figueira, T. J., (1981/1986/1998), *Aegina, Society and Politics*, New York: Arno Press.

Figueira, T. J., (1986), ""Sitopolai" and "Sitophylakes" in Lysias' "Against the Graindealers": Governmental intervention in the Athenian economy," *Phoenix*, 40, 149–171.

Figueira, T. J., (1998), *The Power of Money: Coinage and Politics in the Athenian Empire*. Philadelphia: University of Pennsylvania Press.

Figueira T. J., (2011), "The Athenian naukraroi and Archaic naval warfare," *Cadmo*, 21, 183–210.

Figueira, T. J., (2012), "Economic thought and economic fact in the works of Xenophon," in F. Hobden, C. Tuplin (Eds.), *Xenophon: Ethical Principles and Historical Enquiry*, Leiden, Boston, MA: Brill, 665–688.

Finley, M. I., (1965), "Classical Greece," Deuxieme Conflrence intemationale d'-histoire economique: Aix-en Provence, 1962, Paris, 11–35.

Finley, M. I., (1973), *The Ancient Economy*, Berkeley: University of California Press.

Finley, M. I., (1981), *Economy and Society in Ancient Greece*, London: Chatto and Windus.

Fisher, N., (1998), "Gymnasia and the democratic values of leisure," in P. Cartledge, P. Millett, S. von Reden (Eds.), *Kosmos: Essays in Order, Conflict and Community in Classical Athens*, Cambridge: Cambridge University Press, 84–104.

Foster, J. D., (2009), "Transparency and accountability at the federal reserve," The Heritage Foundation, www.heritage.org/markets-and-finance/report/transparency-and-accountability-the-Federal-reserve.

Franklin, B., (2005), *The Autobiography of Benjamin Franklin*, ed. P. Conn, Philadelphia: University of Pennsylvania Press.

French, A., (1964), *The Growth of the Athenian Economy*. New York: Barnes & Noble.

Friedman, M., (1960), *A Program for Monetary Stability*, New York: Fordham University Press.

Friedman, M., (1962a), *Capitalism and Freedom*. Chicago, IL: University of Chicago Press.

Friedman, M., (1962b), "Should there be an independent monetary authority?" in L. B. Yeager (Ed.), *In Search of a Monetary Constitution*, Boston, MA: Harvard University Press.

Friedman, M., Schwartz, A. J., (1986), "Has government any role in money?" *Journal of Monetary Economics*, 17, 37–62.

Froelich, N., Oppenheimer, A., Young, J., (1971), *Political Leadership and Collective Goods*, Princeton, NJ: Princeton University Press.

Fröhlich, P., (2013), "Governmental checks and balances," in H. Beck (Ed.), *A Companion to Ancient Greek Government*, Malden, MA: Willey-Blackwell, 252–266.

Gabrielsen, V., (1994), *Financing the Athenian Fleet*, Baltimore, MD: Johns Hopkins University Press.

Gabrielsen, V., (2013), "Finance and taxes," in H. Beck (Ed.), *A Companion to Ancient Greek Government*, Malden, MA: Willey-Blackwell, 332–348.

Garlan, Y., (1988), *Slavery in Ancient Greece*, Ithaca, NY: Cornell University Press.

Garrison, R. W., (2009), "Interest-rate targeting during the great moderation: A reappraisal," *Cato Journal*, 29, 187–200.

Gehl, K. M., Porter, M. E. (2017), "Why competition in the politics industry is failing America: A strategy for reinvigorating our democracy," *Harvard Business School*, www.commonwealthclub.org/events/2019-03-29/katherine-gehl-and-michael-porter-why-competition-politics-industry-failing.

Giovannini, A., (1974), "Athenian currency in the late fifth and early fourth century B.C.," *Hesperia*, 43, 157–188.

Golden, M., (2003), "Childhood in ancient Greece," in J. Neils, J. H. Oakley (Eds.), *Coming of Age in Ancient Greece: Images of Childhood from the Classical Past*, New Haven, CT and London: Yale University Press, 13–31.

Goldsmith, R. W., (1987), *Premodern Financial Systems*, Cambridge: Cambridge University Press.

Gordon, R. J., (2016), *Beyond the Rainbow: The Rise and Fall of Growth in the American Standard of Living*. Princeton, NJ: Princeton University Press.

Gourinchas, P-O., Rey, H., (2007), "From world banker to world venture capitalist: U.S. external adjustment and the exorbitant privilege," in R. H. Clarida (Ed.), *Current Account Imbalances: Sustainability and Adjustment*, Chicago, IL: University of Chicago Press.

Graham, J. W., (1974), "Houses of classical Athens," *Phoenix*, 28, 45–54.

Greenspan, A., (2004), *Economic Flexibility,* Remarks before the HM Treasury Enterprise Conference, London, www.Federalreserve.gov/boarddocs/speeches/2004/20040126/.

Habicht, C., (1999), *Athens from Alexander to Anthony*, Cambridge, MA: Harvard University Press.

Hallof, K., (1990), "Der Verkauf konfiszierten Der Verkauf konfiszierten Vermögens von der Poleten in Athen," *Klio*, 72, 402–426.

Halkos, G., Kyriazis, N. D., (2010), "The Athenian economy in the age of Demosthenes," *European Journal of Law and Economics*, 29, 255–277.

Hammond, N. G. L., (1959), *The History of Greece to 322 B.C.*, Oxford: Oxford University Press.

Hansen, M. H., (1999), *The Athenian Democracy in the Age of Demosthenes*, London: Bristol Classical Press.

Hansen, M. H., (2006), *Polis: An Introduction to the Ancient Greek City-State*, Oxford: Oxford University Press.

Harberger, A., (1972), *Project Evaluation: Collected Papers*, Chicago, IL: The University of Chicago Press.

Harris, E. M., (2002), "Workshop, marketplace and household," in P. Cartledge, E. E., Cohen, L. Foxhall (Eds.), *Money, Labour and Land*, London and New York: Routledge, 67–99.

Harris, E. M., (2013), *The Rule of Law in Action in Democratic Athens*, Oxford: Oxford University Press.

Harris, E. M., (2015), "Regulating for success," www.greece-is.com/regulating-for-success-2/.

Harris, E. M., (2016), "The legal foundations of economic growth in ancient Greece: The role of property records," in E. M. Harris, D. M. Lewis, M. Woolmer (Eds.),

The Ancient Greek Economy: Markets, Households and City States, New York: Cambridge University Press, 116–147.

Hayek, F. A., (1944/2001), *The Road to Serfdom*, London: Routledge.

Hayek, F. A., (1960), *The Constitution of Liberty*, Chicago IL: University of Chicago Press.

Hayek, F. A., (1976/1990), *Denationalization of Money*, London: Institute of Economic Affairs, 3rd edition extended.

Homer, S., Sylla, R., (2005), *A History of Interest Rates*, Hoboken, NJ: John Wiley & Sons, 4th edition.

Imai, H., (2002), "Hong Kong's high inflation under the U.S dollar peg: The Balassa-Samuelson effect or the Dutch disease?" Stanford Center of International Development, Working Paper No. 126.

Ingham, G., (2004), *The Nature of Money*, Cambridge: Polity Press Ltd.

International Monetary Fund, (2018a), *A Decade after the Global Financial Crisis: Are We Safer*, www.elibrary.imf.org.

International Monetary Fund, (2018b), *World Economic Outlook: Challenges to Steady Growth*, https://www.elibrary.imf.org/view/IMF081/25350-9781484376799/25350-9781484376799/25350-9781484376799.xml?redirect=true.

Isager, S., Hansen, M., (1975), *Aspects of Athenian Society in the Fourth Century BC*, Odense: Odense University Press.

Johnston, J., (1934), "Solon's reform of weights and measures," *The Journal of Hellenic Studies*, 54, 180–184.

Johnstone, S., (2011), *A History of Trust in Ancient Greece*, Chicago, IL: The University of Chicago Press.

Kagan, D., Viggiano, G. F., (2013), *Men of Bronze: Hoplite Warfare in Ancient Greece*. Princeton, NJ: Princeton University Press.

Kallet-Marx, L., (1989), "The Kallias decree, Thucydides, and the outbreak of the Peloponnesian War," *The Classical Quarterly*, 39, 94–113.

Karni, M., (2019), "The growing challenges for monetary policy in the current international monetary and financial system," www.bankofengland.co.uk/-/media/boe/files/speech/2019/the-growing-challenges-for-monetary-policy-speech-by-mark-carney.pdf?la=en&hash=01A18270247C456901D4043F59D4B79F09B6BFBC

Kelen, A., (2001), *The Gratis Economy: Privately Provided Public Goods*, Budapest: Central European University Press.

Keynes, J. M., (1936), *The General Theory of Employment, Interest and Money*, London: Macmillan & Co, 1949.

Keynes, J. M., (1942) "Budgetary policy," in *Activities 1940–1946 Shaping the Post-war Employment and Commodities*, D. Moggridge (Ed.), *The Collected Writings of John Maynard Keynes*, XXVII, London: Macmillan, 1989, 277–278.

Keynes, J. M., (1944), "Post–war employment: Note by Lord Keynes on the report of the Steering committee," in *Activities 1940–1946 Shaping the Post-war Employment and Commodities*, D. Moggridge (Ed.), *The Collected Writings of John Maynard Keynes*, XXVII, London: Macmillan, 1989, 364–372.

Kleiner, F. S., (1975), *Greek and Roman Coins in the Roman Agora*. Princeton, NJ: The American of Classical Studies at Athens.

Kraay, C. M., (1976), *Archaic and Classical Greek coins*. London: Methuen.

Kravis, I. B., (1959), "Relative Income Shares in Fact and Theory," *The American Economic Review*, 49, 917–949.

Kroll, J. H., (2011), "The reminting of Athenian silver coinage 353 B.C.," *Hesperia*, 80, 229–259.

Kyriazis, N. C., (2009), "Financing the Athenian state: Public choice in the age of Demosthenes," *European Journal of Law and Economics*, 27(2), 109–127.

Kyriazis, N. C., Economou, E. M. L., (2015), "Macroculture, sports and democracy in classical Greece," *European Journal of Law and Economics*, 40, 431–455.

Kyriazis, N. C., Zouboulakis, M. S. (2004), "Democracy, sea-power and institutional change: Am economic analysis of the Athenian naval law," *European Journal of Law and Economics*, 17, 117–132.

Lane, J. E., (2013), "The principal-agent approach to politics: Policy implementation and public policy-making," *Open Journal of Political Science*, 3, 85–89.

Lanni, A., (2008), *Law and Justice in the Courts of Classical Athens*, Cambridge and New York: Cambridge University Press.

Lanni, A., (2016), *Law and Order in Ancient Athens*, Cambridge: Cambridge University Press.

Lauk, T. C., (2014), *The Triple Crisis of Western Capitalism: Democracy, Banking, and Currency*, London: Palgrave Macmillan.

Lavelle, B. M., (1993), "The Peisistratids and the mines of Thrace," *Greek Roman and Byzantine Studies*, 33, 5–23.

Lee, K. S., Werner, R. A., (2018), "Reconsidering monetary policy: An empirical examination of the relationship between interest rates and nominal GDP growth in the U.S., U.K., Germany and Japan," *Ecological Economics*, 146, 26–34.

Lehmann, G. A., (2015), "Greek federalism, the rediscovery of Polybius, and the framing of the American constitution," in H. Beck, P. Funke (eds.), *Federalism in Greek Antiquity*, Cambridge: Cambridge University Press, 512–523.

Levitsky, S., Zibblat, D., (2018), *Why Democracies Die*, Cambridge, MA: Harvard University Press.

Lianos, T. P., (2014), "Xenophon's theory of money," *History of Economic Ideas*, 22, 41–53.

Loomis, W. T., (1998), *Wages, Welfare Costs and Inflation in Classical Athens*, Ann Arbor: Michigan University Press.

Lynch, J., (1991), *Spain 1516–1598: From Nation State to World Empire*, Oxford: Basil Blackwell Publishers.

Lyon, V., (1996), "Parties and democracy: A critical view," in A. B. Tanguay, A. G. Gagnon (Eds.), *Canadian Parties in Transition,* Nelson Canada, 530–550, https://democraticreform.net/articles/.

Lyttkens, C. H., (1994), "A predatory democracy: An essay on taxation in classical Athens," *Explorations in Economic History*, 31, 62–90.

Lyttkens, C. H., (1997), "A rational-actor perspective on the origin of liturgies in ancient Greece," *Journal of Institutional and Theoretical Economics*, 153, 462–484.

Lyttkens, C. H., (2013), *Economic Analysis of Institutional Change in Ancient Greece. Politics, Taxation and Rational Behavior*, Abingdon: Routledge.

Lyttkens, C. H., Gerding, H., (2015), "Understanding the politics of Perikles around 450 BC: The benefits of an economic perspective," University of Lund, Department of Economics, Discussion Paper 2015, 13.

Lyttkens, C. H., Tridimas, G., Lindgren, A., (2018), "Making direct democracy work: A rational-actor perspective on the graphe paranomon in ancient Athens," *Constitutional Political Economy*, 29, 389–412.

Mackil, E., (2013), *Creating a Common Polity: Religion, Economy, and Politics in the Making of the Greek Koinon.* Berkeley and Los Angeles: University of California Press.

Mackil, E., van Alfen, P. G., (2006), "Cooperative coinage", in P. G. van Alfen (Ed.), *Agoranomia: Studies in Money and Exchange Presented to John H. Kroll*, New York: The American Numismatic Society, 201–246.

Madison, J., (1787), "The utility of the union as a safeguard against domestic faction and insurrection (continued)," *The Federalist No. 10*, www.constituion.org/.

Maloney, R. P., (1971), "Usury in Greek, Roman and Rabbinic thought," *Traditio*, 27, 79–109.

Manville, B., Ober, J., (2003), *A Company of Citizens*, Boston, MA: Harvard Business School Press.

Marcaccini, C., (2015), "The treasurers of Athena in the late 5th century B.C.: When did they take office?" *Hesperia: The Journal of the American School of Classical Studies at Athens*, 84(3), 515–532.

Martin, F. E., Mukhopadhyay, M., van Homebeek, C., (2017), "The global role of the US dollar and its consequences," Bank of England, *Quarterly Bulletin*, Q4, 1–11.

Matsusaka, G. J., (2005a), "Direct democracy works," *Journal of Economic Perspectives*, 19, 185–206.

Matsusaka, G. J., (2005b), "The eclipse of Legislatures: Direct democracy in the 21st century," *Public Choice*, 124, 157–177.

Matsusaka, G. J., (2010), "A case study on direct democracy: Have voter initiatives paralyzed the California budget?" *The Council of State Governments, Ballot Propositions*, www.iandrinstitute.org/7-Matsusaka.pdf.

McAuley, A., (2013), "Officials and office-holding", in H. Beck (Ed.), *A Companion to Ancient Greek Government*, Malden, MA: Willey-Blackwell, 174–190.

Migeotte, L., (2009), *The Economy of Greek Cities: From the Archaic Period to the Early Roman Empire*, Engl. Trnsl. J. Lloyd, Los Angeles: University of California Press.

Mill, J. S., (1861), *Considerations on Representative Government*, New York: The Floating Press, 2009.

Mill, J. S., (1923), *Principles of Political Economy*, New York: Longmans, Green and Co.

Mohan, R., (2009), "Global financial crisis – causes, impact, policy responses and lessons," *BIS Review*, 1, 1–24.

Montesquieu, (1748/1989), *Spirit of the Laws*, A. M. Cohler, B. C. Miller, H. S. Stone (Eds.), Cambridge: Cambridge University Press.

Morris, I., (2004), "Economic growth in ancient Greece," *Journal of Institutional and Theoretical Economics*, 160, 709–742.

Morris, I., (2009), "The greater Athenian state," in I. Morris, W. Scheidel (Eds.), *The Dynamics of Ancient Empires: State Power from Assyria to Byzantium*, Oxford: Oxford University Press, 99–177.

Morris, I., Scheidel, W., (2009), *The Dynamics of Ancient Empires: State Power from Assyria to Byzantium*, Oxford: Oxford University Press.

Morrison, J. S., Coates, J. F., (1986), *The Athenian Trireme*, Cambridge: Cambridge University Press.

Munger, M. C., (2012), "Self-interest and public interest: The motivations of political actors," *Critical Review*, 23, 339–357.

Murphy, K. M., Shleifer, A., Vishny, R. W., (1991), "The allocation of talent: Implications for growth," *Quarterly Journal of Economics*, 106(2), 503–530.

Niskanen, W. A., (1975), "Bureaucrats and politicians," *Journal of Law and Economics*, 18, 617–643.

Ober, J., (1985), *Fortress Attica. Defense of the Athenian Land Frontier, 404–322 B.C.*, Leiden: E. J. Brill.

Ober, J., (2008), *Democracy and Knowledge. Innovation and Learning in Classical Athens*, Princeton, NJ: Princeton University Press.

Ober, J., (2010), "Wealthy Hellas," *Transactions of American Philological Association*, 140, 241–286. Reprinted in the *Journal of Economic Asymmetries*, 2011, 8, 1–38.

Ober, J., (2015), *The Rise and the Fall of Classical Greece*, Princeton, NJ: Princeton University Press.

Ober, J., (2017), "Inequality in late-classical democratic Athens. Evidence and models," in G. C. Bitros, N. C. Kyriazis (Eds.), *Democracy and Open Economy World Order*. Heidelberg: Springer-Verlag, 125–146.

Olson, M., (1965), *The Logic of Collective Action: Public Goods and the Theory of Groups*, Cambridge, MA: Harvard University Press.

Osiander, A., (2007), *Before the State: Systemic Political Change in the West from the Greeks to the French Revolution*, New York: Oxford University Press.

Papazarkadas, N., (2011), *Sacred and Public Land in Ancient Athens*, New York: Oxford University Press, Inc.

Pownall, F., (2013), "Public administration," in H. Beck (Ed.), *A Companion to Ancient Greek Government*, Malden, MA: Willey-Blackwell, 287–301.

Phelps, E., ([2010]2011), "Three short essays: Past, present, future," in O. Chittenden (Ed.), *The Future of Money*, London: Virgin Books, 173–180.

Phillips, P. C. B., Shi, Z., (2019), "Boosting the Hodrick-Prescott filter," Paper www2.aueb.gr/conferences/Crete2019/.

Piketty, T., (2014), *Capital in the Twenty-First Century*, Engl. Trnsl., A. Goldhammer, Cambridge, MA: The Belknap Press of Harvard University Press.

Popper, K., (1945), *The Open Society and Its Enemies*, I, II, London: George Routledge & Sons, Ltd.

Postell, J., (2018), "The rise and fall of political parties in America," The Heritage Foundation, www.heritage.org/political-process/report/the-rise-and-fall-political-parties-america.

Pritchard, D. M., (2003), "Athletics education and participation in classical Athens," in D. J. Philips, D. M. Pritchard (Eds.), *Sport and Festival in the Ancient Greek World* Swansea: Classical Press of Wales.

Pritchard, D. M., (2012), "Costing festivals and war: Spending priorities of the Athenian democracy," *Historia*, 61(1), 18–65.

Pritchard, D. M., (2014), "The public payment of magistrates in fourth-century Athens," *Greek, Roman, and Byzantine Studies*, 54, 1–16.

Prichard, D. M., (2015), *Public Spending and Democracy in Classical Athens*, Austin: University of Texas Press.

Pseudoerasmus, (2015), *Economic Growth in Ancient Greece*, https://pseudoerasmus.com/2015/04/02/ancient-greece-econ-growth/.

Rathbone, D., von Reden, S., (2014), "Mediterranean grain prices in classical antiquity," in R. J. Van der Spek, J. L. van Zanden, B. van Leeuwen (Eds.), *A History of Market Performance: From Ancient Babylonia to the Modern World*, London and New York: Routledge.

Reibig, A. (2001), The Bücher-Meyer controversy: The nature of the ancient economy in modern ideology, PhD thesis, University of Glasgow.

Rhodes, P. J., (1980), "Athenian democracy after 403 B.C.," *The Classical Journal*, 75, 305–323.

Rhodes, P. J., (1985), *The Athenian Empire*, Oxford: Oxford University Press.

Rhodes, P. J., (2005), A *History of Classical Greek World: 478–323 BC*, Oxford: Blackwell Publishing.

Rhodes, P. J., (2013), "The organization of Athenian public finance," *Greece & Rome*, 60, 203–231.

Rhodes, P. J., Lewis, D., (1997), *The Decrees of the Greek States*, Oxford: Clarendon Press.

Rhodes, P. J., Osborne, R. S., (2003), *Greek Historical Inscriptions, 404–323 BC*, Oxford: Oxford University Press.

Ricardo, D., (1821/1951), *On the Principles of Political Economy and Taxation*, in P. Sraffa (Ed.), with the collaboration of M. H. Dobb, *The Works and Correspondence of David Ricardo* vol. 1, Cambridge: Cambridge University Press.

Ricardo, D., (1809/1951), "The price of gold: three contributions to the Morning Chronicle," in P. Sraffa (Ed.), with the collaboration of M. H. Dobb, *The Works and Correspondence of David Ricardo*, vol. 3. Cambridge: Cambridge University Press, 15–46.

Richard, C. J., (2009), *Greeks and Romans Bearing Gifts. How the Ancients Inspired the Founding Fathers*, Lanham, MD: Rowman and Littlefield Publishers, Inc.

Rizakis, A., (2015), "The Achaian league," in H. Beck, P. Funke (Eds.), *Federalism in Greek Antiquity*, Cambridge: Cambridge University Press, 117–131.

Robinson, E. W., (2011), *Democracy Beyond Athens: Popular Government in the Greek Classical Age*. Cambridge: Cambridge University Press.

Rogoff, K., (2018), "Cryptocurrencies are like lottery tickets that might pay off in future," Theguardian.com, www.theguardian.com/business/2018/dec/10/cryptocurrencies-bitcoin-kenneth-rogoff.

Rolnick, A. J., Weber, W. E., (1997), "Money, inflation, and output under fiat and commodity standards," *Federal Reserve Bank of Minneapolis Quarterly Review*, 22, 11–17.

Samons, L. J. (1993), "Athenian finance and the treasury of Athena," *Historia: Zeitschrift für Alte Geschichte, Bd.*, 42(2), 129–138.

Samons, L. J., (2000), *Empire of the Owl: Athenian Imperial Finance*. (Historia Einzelschriften) Stuttgart: Franz Steiner Verlag.

Samuelson, P. H., (1948), "Consumer theory in terms of revealed preference," *Economica*, 15, 243–253.

Samuelson, P. H., (1973), *Economics: An Introductory Analysis*, New York: The McGraw-Hill Companies, 9th edition.

Schaps, D. M., (1979), *Economic Rights of Women*, Edinburg: Edinburg University Press.

Schaps, D. M., (1996), "Builders, contractors, and power: Financing and administering building projects in ancient Greece," in R. Katzoff, Y. Petroff, and D. Schaps (Eds.), *Classical Studies in Honor of David Sohlberg*, Ramat Gan: Bar-Ilan University Press, 77–89.

Schaps, D. M., (2004), *The Invention of Coinage and the Monetization of Ancient Greece*, Ann Arbor: The University of Michigan Press.

Schumpeter, J. A., (1942), *Capitalism, Socialism and Democracy*, London: Routledge, 2003.

Schwartzberg, M., (2004), "Athenian democracy and legal change," *American Political Science Review*, 98, 311–325.

Sechrest, L. J., (1993/2008), *Free Banking: Theory, History and a Laissez-Faire Model*, Westport, CT; Quorum Books, with new preface to the 2nd printing.

Selgin, G. A., (1988), *The Theory of Free Banking: Money Supply under Competitive Note Issue*, Totowa, NJ: Rowman & Littlefield.

Selgin, G. A., White, L. H., (1994), "How would the invisible hand handle money?" *Journal of Economic Literature*, 32, 1718–1749.

Seltman, C. T. (1924). *Athens, Its History and Coinage before the Persian Invasion*. Cambridge: Cambridge University Press.

Sen, A., (1961), "On optimizing the rate of saving," *The Economic Journal*, 71,479–496.

Shipton, K., (1997), *The Private Banks in Fourth-Century B.C.*, Athens: A Reappraisal, *The Classical Quarterly*, 47, 396–422.

Shiratsuka, S., (2011), "A macroprudential perspective in central banking," Bank of Japan, Institute for Monetary and Economic Discussion Paper No. 2011-E-3.

Smith, A., (1776/1977), *An Inquiry into the Nature and Causes of the Wealth of Nations*, Chicago, IL: Chicago University Press.

Smith, V. C., (1936/1990), *The Rationale of Central Banking and the Free Banking Alternative,* Foreword by Leland Yeager, Indianapolis: Liberty Fund Inc, http://oll.libertyfund.org/.

Spantidaki, S., (2016), *Textile Production in Classical Athens*, Oxford: Oxbow Books.

Stevenson, G. H., (1924), "The financial administration of Pericles," *The Journal of Hellenic Studies*, 44(1), 1–9.

Sussman, N., Zeira, J., (2003), "Commodity money inflation: Theory and evidence from France in 1350–1436," *Journal of Monetary Economics*, 50, 1769–1793.

Taylor, J. B., (1993), "Discretion versus policy rules in practice," *Carnegie-Rochester Conference Series on Public Policy*, 39, 195–214.

Teo, W. L., (2009), "Can exchange rate rules be better than interest rate rules?" *Japan and the World Economy*, 21, 301–311.

Thompson, M., (1939), "A hoard of Greek Federal silver, Hesperia," *The Journal of the American School of Classical Studies at Athens*, 8(2), 116–154.

Thompson, M., Mørkholm, O., Kraay, C. M., (1973), *An Inventory of Greek Coin Hoards*. New York: Numismatic Commission by the American Numismatic Society.

Thorley, J., (1996), *Athenian Democracy*, New York: Routledge.

Timberlake, R. H., (1998), "Gold standard policy and limited government," in K. Dowd, R. H. Timberlake (Eds.), *Money and the Nation State: The Financial Revolution, Government and the World Monetary System*, New Brunswick, NJ: Transaction Publishers, 167–191.

Tirole, J., (2017), *Economics for the Common Good*, Princeton, NJ: Princeton University Press.

Tridimas, G., (2012), "Constitutional choice in ancient Athens: The rationality of selection to office by lot," *Constitutional Political Economy*, 23, 1–21.

Tridimas, G., (2013), "Homo Oeconomicus in ancient Athens: Silver bonanza and the choice to build a navy," *Homo Oeconomicus*, 30(4), 435–458.

Tridimas, G., (2017), "Constitutional choice in ancient Athens: The evolution of the frequency of decision making," *Constitutional Political Economy*, 28, 209–230.

Tullock, G., Seldon, A., Brady, G., (2002), *Government Failure: A Primer in Public Choice*, Washington, DC: Cato Institute.

Van Alfen, P. G. (2011), "Hatching owls: Athenian public finance and the regulation of coin production," in F. de Callatay (Ed.), *Quantifying Monetary Supplies in Greco-Roman Times*, Bari: Edipuglia, 127–149.

Van Wees, H., (2013), *Ships and Silver and Taxes and Tribute. A Fiscal History of Archaic Athens*, London and New York: I. B. Tauris.

Volcker, P. A., (1978), "The political economy of the dollar," Federal Reserve Bank of New York, *Quarterly Review*, 3(4), 1–12.

von Reden, S., (2010), *Money in Classical Antiquity*. Cambridge: Cambridge University Press.

Walbank, F., (1983), "Leases of sacred properties in Attica, Part IV," *Hesperia*, 52, 207–231.

Weber, M., (1921/1946), "Politics as a vocation," in Engl. Trnsl. H. H. Gerth, C. W. Mills, *From Max Weber: Essays in Sociology*, New York: Oxford University Press, 1946, 77–128.

Weber, M., (1947), *The Theory of Social and Economic Organization*, London: Collier Macmillan Publishers.

Welser, C. S., (2011), *Demos and Dioikesis: Public Finance and Democratic Ideology in Fourth-Century B.C. Athens*, https://repository.library.brown.edu/storage/bdr:11246/PDF/

Westermann, W. L., (1910), "Notes upon the ephodia of Greek ambassadors," https://ia601701.us.archive.org/0/items/jstor-262193/262193.pdf.

White, L., (1984/1995), *Free Banking in Britain*, London: Institute of Economic Affairs, reissued 2nd edition.

White, L. H., Vanberg, V. J., Köhler, E. A., (2015), *Renewing the Search for a Monetary Constitution: Reforming Government's Role in the Monetary System*, Washington, DC: The Cato Institute.

Williams, R., (2018), "Regulatory capture in American banking," Center for the sturdy of public choice and private enterprise, www.ndsu.edu/centers/pcpe/news/detail/32605/.

Williamson, O., (2000), "Economic institutions and development: A view from the bottom," in M. Olson, S. Kahkönen (Eds.), *A Not-So-Dismal Science: A Broader View of Economics and Society*, Oxford: Oxford university Press, 92–118.

Winterer, C., (2002), *The Culture of Classicism: Ancient Greece and Rome in American Intellectual Life, 1780–1910*, Baltimore, MD: The Johns Hopkins University Press.

Winters, J. A., (2011), *Oligarchy*, Cambridge: Cambridge University Press.

Woolmer, M., (2016), "Forging links between regions: Trade policy in classical Athens," in E. M. Harris, D. M. Lewis, M. Woolmer (Eds.), *The Ancient Greek Economy: Markets, Households and City States*, New York: Cambridge University Press, 66–89.

Yeager, L. B., (1962), (Ed.), *In Search of a Monetary Constitution*, Cambridge, MA: Harvard University Press.

Contemporary literature in Greek

Andreades, M. A., (1992), *History of the Greek Public Economy I. From the Homeric to the Greek-Macedonian Years*, Athens: Papazisis.

Baloglou, C. P., (1995), *The Economic Thinking of the Ancient Greeks*, Thessaloniki: Historical and Folklore Society of Chalkidiki.

Baloglou, C. P., (2006), *Economy and Technology in Ancient Greece*, Athens, GA: Academy of Athens.

Doukas, P. G., (2007), *Economic Theories, Principles of Management and Ancient Greek Thought*, Athens: Livanis.

Economou, E. M. L., (2018), *Economy, warfare and institutions: The Athenian Democracy from the archaic to the classical period* (750–323 BCE), Athens: Enalios.

Economou, E. M. L., Kyriazis, N. C., (2018), *Economy, warfare, institutions and strategy. The Achaean federation* (389–146 BCE), Athens: Plethora.

Karayiannis, A. D., Baloglou, C. P., (2008), *Entrepreneurship in the Ancient Greek Economy*, Athens, GA: Academy of Athens.

Karayiannis, A. G., (2007), *Ancient Greek Pioneering in Economics*, Athens: Papazisis.

Kyriakopoulos, I., Skiadioti, X. M., (2015), *Money, Banks and Loans in Ancient Greece*, Athena: Batsioulas.

Kyriazis, N. C., (2012a), *Why Ancient Greece? The Birth and Development of Democracy*, Athens: Psychogios Publications.

Kyriazis, N. C., (2012b), "The glue of democracy: War, institutions and economy in classical Greece," in G. N. Economou (Ed.), *Studies on Cornylios Castoriades. The Birth of Democracy and the Modern Crisis*, Athens: Eurasia, 43–57.

Kyriazis, N. C., (2014), *Democracy and War. Histories from Ancient Greece*, Athens: Eurasia.

Kyriazis, N. C., Economou, E. M. L. (2015). *Democracy and Economy. An Analytical History of Democracy since Its Birth until Today*, Athens: Enalios.

Kyrtatas, D., Ragkos, S. I., (2010), *Greek Antiquity. War, Politics, Culture*, Thessaloniki: Triantafyllides Foundation.

Lianos, T. (2012). *The Political Economy of Aristotle*, Athens: MIET.

Lianos, T., Bitros, G. C., (2015), *Economic Phenomena in Antiquity*, Athens: Gutenberg.

Reginos, D. T., (1983), *Ancient and Byzantine Economic History*, Athens: Papazisis.

Sakellariou, M. B., (1989), *The Polis-State Definition and Origin*, Research Centre for Greek and Roman Antiquity, National Hellenic Research Foundation, https://helios-eie.ekt.gr/EIE/bitstream/10442/8419/1/A01.004.0.pdf.

Sakellariou, M. B., (1999), *The Athenian Democracy*, Heraklion: Crete University Press.

Tsakonas, A. D, (2012), *Economic Policy in Ancient Greece, Rome and Byzantium. Precious Lessons for the Current Crisis*, Athens: Ibiskos.

Glossary of Greek terms

Agoge A process for the upbringing of young Athenians and maintaining their *ethos* through life (see also *paideia*).

Agora The main marketplace in Athens where commercial transactions took place.

Agoranomoi A body of ten magistrates who supervised the smooth functioning of the market; the prices to be fair based on the forces of demand and supply; the quality of the products to meet accepted specifications and the currencies to be pure and unadulterated.

Agronomoi Magistrates responsible to supervise the drainage and allocation of rain water.

Altruism Selfless willingness to do things for the well-being of others, even at one's personal sacrifice.

Anasaximon A mine that could be re-equipped in order to be exploited further.

Antidosis A law pertaining to an exchange of property between two parties. A man who was assigned with a *liturgy* such as *trierarchy*, could potentially avoid it by nominating a richer man who was (supposedly) more qualified than himself to perform it. In cases of disagreement between the two parties, the solution was provided by *Courts*.

Aparchai The tributes paid by the allies of the *Delian League* to the city-state of Athens.

Apeleutheroi Those slaves who managed to gain their freedom, such as the case of the wealthy banker and industrialist Passion.

Aphane Not visible property that facilitates its owner to avoid taxation.

Apodektai A group of magistrates served for a year, whose duties were to collect public revenues from the various specified sources and deposit them in the *treasuries of the gods*.

Archons The highest ranking officials in many city-states during the archaic period. An aristocratic body that lost many of its responsibilities during the classical period in Athens (see further, the nine *archons*).

Areios Pagos (also known as *Areopagos*)   In preclassical times, the *Areios Pagos* was a court and its members enjoyed lifelong tenure. It was also a *council* of elders of the city. Its membership was restricted to those who had held high public office. In 462 BC, Ephialtes introduced reforms which, with the exception of murder cases, stripped *Areios Pagos* of all other functions in favor of *Heliaia*.

Argyramoibos (in plural, *argyramoiboi*, known also as *kollybistai*)   Professional money changers who were located in marketplaces and in the port of Piraeus.

Argyrocopeion   Athenian mint. It minted the silver currency issued by the state.

Asclepieia   Large medical centers surrounded by a rich assortment of facilities, like temples, baths, stadiums, gymnasiums, libraries, and theaters.

Astynomia (Police)   A group of 300 publicly owned Scythian slaves (the so called "rod bearers") who were employed under the orders of *astynomoi* to guard public meetings; to keep order in large crowd gatherings and to assist in dealing with criminals, handling prisoners and making arrests.

Astynomoi   A group of ten policemen in the service of the city. Their main responsibility was to watch over the cleanliness public facilities and keep the order in the city.

Athlothetai   A group of ten magistrates elected on four-year terms who were responsible to prepare sport events, the most important among them being the *Great Panathenaia*, the famous athletic games which incorporated religious festivals, ceremonies including prize-giving, athletic competitions, and cultural events.

Atimos   An official condemned for embezzlement, bribery or other corrupt offenses. Those who committed such actions were charged for *atimia* (dishonesty) and, if found guilty, faced severe punishments including deprivation of their civil rights. In a face-to-face society such as Athens, an *atimos* was considered a social outcast.

Board of Poletai   A board managed by ten annually elected financial magistrates, one from each of the ten Athenian tribes. They were responsible for auctioning mining leases to individuals or consortia of individuals; selling the confiscated houses and land of those who were convicted in the *Courts*; renting public lands, including temple estates; and auctioning the rights to collect certain taxes. It reported directly to the *Assembly* and their decisions were subject to various controls.

Boule (also known as the *Boule of 500*, or the *Council of the 500*)   The executive branch of government. One among its others tasks was to prepare the agenda of the deliberations and the *probouleumata* (preliminary decrees) to be discussed and decided upon by the *Assembly*.

Bouleutai   Members of the *Boule*.

Chalkos   A coin of tiny denomination of the Athenian drachma made from copper. It was used for small value retail transactions.

Choregoi The wealthy Athenians who financed the variety of *liturgies* and covered the costs involved known as *choregia.*

Coinage Decree A decree through which Athens attempted to introduce the drachma as the common currency among the more than 300 allied city-states within the *Delian League.*

Decadrachm Ten drachmae.

Decree of Kallias A decree, probably authorized by the *Assembly* sometime between 434 and 433 BC, which introduced certain reforms to render the management of public finances more efficient.

Deigma Sample (here referring to coins).

Demes Municipalities. The Athenian state had 139 *demes.*

Diagraphè Crossing out a debt or other obligation.

Didrachm Two drachmae.

Dikai emporikai Commercial court cases adjudicated by qualified and experienced judges.

Dikasts Judges who heard cases either in the *Popular Courts* (*Heiliaia*) or in the *Areios Pagos.* The *Courts* were called *dikasteria.*

Dokimasia A procedure of demanding scrutiny applied on strict criteria by a special board, appointed by the *Council* or by the *Popular Courts,* with the mandate to assess how a citizen elected to become a *Councilman* might carry out his duties, if appointed.

Dokimastai Two public slaves, one located in the *agora* of the city of Athens and the other in the port of Piraeus. They were tasked with the responsibility to test the coins that were brought to them by merchants and certify that they had been struck by the Athenian mint, or that the quantity of their silver content was the same as that of an Athenian Drachma. Only then the coins could circulate freely in the Athenian economy.

Drachma (in plural, drachmae or drachmas) The currency that the Athenian state issued for undertaking all kinds of economic/commercial transactions. The drachma became a universal coin in the Eastern Mediterranean.

Ecclesia of Demos (also known as *Demos* or *Assembly*) A key political institution in Athens and the other democratic city-states and federations. It exercised all legislative and select ultimate-degree judicial and auditing powers; its membership comprised all adult male citizens; and it was in session when more than 6,000 citizens were present; After 415 BCE its legislative powers were shared with the institution of *nomothetai.*

Ecclesiastica A reimbursement of three obols (half a drachma) provided to each of the first 6,000 Athenian citizens when attending *Assembly* meetings.

Eisangelia A procedure through which in every major meeting of the *Assembly,* called *Ecclesia Kyria,* any citizen had the opportunity to accuse an office holder for not fulfilling correctly his duties, or abusing his position, or acting against the public interest. The accused could defend himself either right in front of the *Assembly* or, depending on the type of the accusation, in front of the *Courts.*

Eisphora (plural *eisphorai*)   A tax reckoned on the assessed value of one's property. At the beginning, Athenians introduced it as an extraordinary measure to apply only in times of extreme need, such as a war. However, during the 4th century, Athenians by vote rendered the *eisphora* permanent and imposed it on the wealthier citizens and *metics*.

Emporion   Wholesale trade.

Enechirodanistai   Lenders who took property as security, that is, acting in the same capacity as modern pawnbrokers.

Enktesis   The right to hold property (of land and houses) in any member city-state within the territory of a federal state.

Ephebeia   A two-year, state-funded and organized program, which focused on the military training of a young Athenian 19–20 years of age, known as *epheboi* (in singular, *ephebos*).

Epigamia   The right of transferring property in the form of women's dowries within the territory of a federal state.

Epimelitai tou Emporiou   A group of ten magistrates who supervised the warehouses of goods, and particularly those of cereals so as to prevent merchants from exporting more than one-third of the cereals they imported.

Epimelites epi ton hudaton   Also known as *epimelites epi ton krinon*. A state functionary responsible to supervise the proper functioning and cleanliness of public fountains.

Epimelitai ton mistirion   They were four magistrates responsible for the proper functioning of the temple of Eleusis.

Epistatai   Officials who supervised the construction of public works. Their number varied from two to five, depending on the scale of the project. They were nominated by the *Council* from lists of citizens maintained in the archives of the state and the municipalities. When large sums had to be spent on the construction or maintenance of public infrastructures, the approval of the *Assembly* was necessary.

Epistates (of the *Prytaneis*)   A post belonging to the institution of *prytaneia*. For one 24-hour period, one member of the 50 *prytaneis* was selected by lot to serve as the foreman (*Epistates*, "caretaker"). He administered the state seal and the keys to the state *treasuries* and archives.

Eponymous archon   The first in hierarchy of the nine *archons*, carried out specific projects and responsibilities. The *eponymous archon* was also considered the "first" citizen of Athens.

Ergasimon   A workable mine leased for three years; after this period, the mine was reclassified again into an *anasaximon*.

Eudaimonia   A state good life and happiness-bliss.

Euthene   A legal procedure through which a ten-member board called *euthinoi* assessed whether a public magistrate had acted according to the laws, if he had carried out his tasks in line with what was considered at the times as good administration, etc. No appointed official, not even the *strategoi*, were spared from undergoing evaluation on how they had performed their duties.

Fund for the military (*Stratiotikon*) It managed the defense budget. In case its revenues fell short of the budgeted expenses because of unforeseen developments, the *Assembly* could decide that the military fund could cover its deficit by reallocation of funds from other sources of funds.

Fund of epimelitai ton neorion It looked after the operation of the naval bases for mooring the warships and possibly merchant ships.

Fund of odopoioi It was responsible for the city's roads network.

Fund of theorikon (*Theoric fund*) It collected and dispensed the money earmarked in the budget for giving two obols to needy citizens to attend theatrical plays that were offered by the state as a public good. This service was known as *theorica*.

Fund of toichopoioi It covered the expenses for the construction and maintenance of the city's walls.

Fund of trieropoioi It financed the building of *trireme* warships.

Glauke Another name of the Athenian drachma coins. It is the Greek name of *owl*, bird of wisdom, which was depicted in observe side of these coins.

Grammateus A post introduced in federal states such as the Achaean *Sympoliteia* (Federation), literally meaning the "secretary" who had responsibilities similar to modern heads of state archives, and further responsibilities that are not yet known.

Grammatistai Teachers who taught courses related to reading, writing and mathematics.

Graphe paranomon It means "suit against (bills) contrary to the laws." The suit could be brought against laws or decrees that had already been passed, or earlier when they were merely proposals. Once someone announced under oath that he intended to bring such a suit, the legislation or decree in question was suspended until the matter was resolved. The thinking was that, new laws should not existing laws.

Guardians of neorion Guards responsible for the security of the shipbuilding installations (*neosoikoi*) and the shipbuilding materials kept in them.

Gynaikonomoi Public officials whose duty was the supervision of women's behavior and public appearance in order to protect the morality and the values of society.

Heliaia (known also as *Popular Courts* or *People's Courts*) The main court of Athens during the classical period. It comprised of as high as 6,000 members, chosen annually by lot among all the male citizens over 30 years old, unless they were in debt to the *treasury* of Athens or disfranchised, namely deprived of their civil rights through the humiliating punishment of *atimia,* literally meaning, dishonesty.

Hellenotamiai A group of ten public treasurers, appointed by the Athenians (one from each tribe, possibly selected by election) to handle the contributions from the allied states. They were the chief financial officers of the *Delian League.*

Hemidrachm Half a drachma.

Hieron episkeuastai A group of magistrates responsible for the repairing of temples and sacred buildings.

Hieropoioi   Civil servants responsible for preparing religious ceremonies.

Hipparchos   Cavalry's highest commander.

Hippeis   Horsemen.

Ho boulomenos   He, who wishes to speak or to propose in the Athenian *Assembly*.

Homonoia   Order and unity of minds in the pursue of a common purpose.

Hoplite (in plural, *hoplites*)   A medium income citizen who could bear arms by personally financing his armament. By participating in the so called *phalanx* (heavy infantry) formation, *hoplites* provided a potent fighting force whenever they were called upon to defend their homeland.

Isopoliteia   The provision for equal political rights between different city-states, usually both being members of a federal state.

Kainotomia   New-cutting of land in search of fresh veins of ore rich in silver.

Kitharistai   Guitarists who who taught children how to play the seven-string lyre and sing the works of lyric poets.

Kollybos (in plural, *kollyboi*)   A tiny coin denomination of the Athenian drachma made from copper. One *chalkos* was equal to two *kollyboi*.

Koprologoi   A group of magistrates in charge of the collection of garbage and all kinds of animal feces found in the streets.

Law of Nicophon   Probably introduced in 375/374 BCE, it provided for procedures and measures to prevent the circulation of counterfeit coins in the economy. The important task of testing for the authenticity of coins that were imported by foreign merchants was assigned to the so-called *dokimastai*.

Liturgy (in plural, *liturgies*)   A special type of taxation imposed on wealthy citizen, who undertook to finance the provision of a public service, such as the costly maintenance of a *trireme* warship for a year.

Logistai   A group of ten magistrates whose tasks entailed checking on whether public expenditures were effected in line with the provisions and the guidelines laid down by the responsible authorities.

Logodosia   The procedure of auditing of the Athenian public magistrates (see more details in the institutions of *logistai*, *synegoroi* and *euthenoi*).

Medimnos   A unit of measurement mainly of agricultural products.

Merismos   A system in the center of the public administration which collected funds from various budgeted sources and allocated them to the accounts of the *Assembly*, the *Council* and the other state entities. Then, from these accounts the latter covered the expenditures provided for in their budgets under their own responsibility and reporting requirements.

Metics   Citizens of other city-states who resided and exercised their professions in Athens.

Metoikion   A personal tax on *metics*, both men and women.

Metronomoi   A body of ten magistrates whose responsibility was to check and make sure that the weights and measures used by sellers of goods in the markets were right. Their post was very important because they prevented profiteering.

Metroon A building dedicated the *mother of the gods* where the archives of the state's laws were kept.

Misthos Meaning compensation ("wage") paid to several office-holders like the jurors, the judges, and the *archons* for their services to the state.

Mother of the Gods An important sanctuary which acted also as *treasury* and *public fund*, just like the rest of the sanctuaries within the city. It collected and managed a large volume of currency.

Nauarchos Admiral.

Naucleros (in plural, *naucleroi*) Captain of a merchant ship.

Nautodikai Experienced judges who adjudicated *dikai emporikai*, that is, cases that arose in the maritime sector.

Neosoikoi Well-equipped docks with cover, enabling the construction and maintenance of the *trireme* warships.

Nicophon's Law See above, *Law of Nicophon*.

Nine archons A body dating back to the preclassical aristocratic period with the primary task of overseeing the implementation of laws, conducting court cases, and performing various other duties of religious and military interest. Their responsibilities were gradually reduced during the classical period.

Nomismatocopeion The Athenian mint which issued bronze coins for low value transactions. But bronze coins were issued mainly by private consortia.

Nomothetai Meaning those who were establishing new laws. The *nomothetai* were drawn from the annual group of judges serving in the *Courts*. They constituted a two-tier board in which those in first tier (elected by the *Council*) had also the right to propose new laws, while those in the second tier (elected from the Athenian municipalities-*demes*) voted on to whether to ratify each law and add it to the existing laws.

Obol A subdivision of drachma; one drachma was equal to six obols.

Odopoioi A group of five magistrates responsible for the maintenance of the city's road network.

Oikos The ancient Greek word for household.

Orphanophylax An institution in charge of caring for the children of the soldiers killed in wars and in general of the orphans.

Paideia Upbringing and educating children. Aside from education in the language, mathematics, music, gymnastics, etc., *paideia* comprised a whole range of arrangements that aimed at shaping the moral character of youth from early childhood to adolescence. In other words, *paideia* included not only training them in technical skills but also all efforts to influence their character and moral standing so as to become more active and responsible citizens and less self-centered individuals.

Paidotribai Teachers responsible for the bodily development of the boys.

Palaistra An athletic installation where the *athletes* exercised in various kinds of sports.

Pankration A mixed martial art throughout ancient Greece, which had been developed in Sparta.

Pantopoleion (in plural, *pantopoleia*) Grocery store.

Parrhesia A principle that conveyed high moral standing. It characterized any citizen who stepped forward in the *Assembly*, the *Courts*, etc. to defend the public interest, as he understood it. *Parrhesia* required conscious and active citizens who stood in favor of the common good even at their own personal risk.

Peltastai Lightly armed infantry with a small shield known as *pelta* throwing javelins.

Pentakosiomedimnoi The highest property class of citizens in Athens, comprising all those whose land yielded at least 500 *medimnoi* of corn or the equivalent in other produce.

Pentekoste Collection of a harbor duty on the value of imports and exports. It equaled "the fiftieth part" of the merchandise's value or 2%. The collection was farmed out for a year to the so called *pentekostologoi* who had offered in the auctioning process the highest bid.

Peripoloi Military patrols by conscript soldiers who were performing their military service.

Phalanx The most well-known and practiced military formation in ancient Greece from the archaic to hellenistic times. It was composed entirely of heavy infantry armed with spears, pikes, *sarissas* (very long spears) or similar pole weapons.

Philopatry Love to the motherland.

Phylai A system for administrative division of the Athenians into ten "tribes." Members of the same *phyle* were known as *symphyletai*, literally meaning, fellow tribesmen. In 508, Cleisthenes reformed this system, into three zones: urban (*asty*), coastal (*paralia*) and inland (*mesogeia*). Each zone was split into ten sections called *trittyes* (thirdings), to each of which were assigned between one and ten of the 139 *demes.*

Probouleumata (in singular, *probouleuma*) "Preliminary decrees" prepared by the *Council*, to be then presented, approved and voted by the *Assembly.*

Prytaneia (also known as *prytany*) The executive branch of the *Council*. Each *prytaneia* consisted of 50 *Council* members from each of the ten Athenian tribes. Each tribe which held the post of *prytaneia* in a rounding basis actually ruled the city with full executive rights.

Prytaneion (also known as Tholos) A luxurius and expensive government building where the *prytaneis* exercised their duties and dined with other high ranking officials and foreign dignitaries.

Psephismata Decisions taken in the *Assembly* which assumed the form of *decrees* and remained in force until revised or replaced by another decision. They covered all state affairs and functions.

Sitophylakes A body of ten magistrates who were responsible to guard the wheat warehouses. Five of them were located in Athens and five in the twin city of Piraeus.

Sitopolai Wheat sellers.

Strategoi (in singular, *strategos*) Literally meaning generals and standing for the highest military officials of Athens. Cleisthenes instituted a board of ten *strategoi* who were elected annually, one from each tribe (*phyle*). They had various duties such as the *strategos epi tas symmorias*, that is, responsible for the equipment of the warships and for supervising the *trierarchy*, the most expensive *liturgy* related to the maintenance of a warship for a year.

Syggrapheis A panel of experts with the task of submitting, in collaboration with the members of the *Council*, special proposals to be discussed in the citizen's *Assembly*.

Synegoroi A group of ten public prosecutors, being themselves public magistrates who were assisting the ten *logistai* on their auditing duties.

Symmories (in singular, *symmoria*) Distinct taxation groups of wealthy Athenians that were introduced in 377 BCE. In 358/357 BCE the system of *symmories* was expanded to include the financing *trierarchy*, which was the most expensive of all *liturgies*.

Sympoliteia (in plural, *Sympoliteiai*) The association of city-states in a federal structure.

Syssitia common meals provided as a part of the Athenian welfare state. This institution was also introduced in other states, a well-known case being Sparta.

Talent The largest denomination of drachma. A talent was equal to 6,000 drachmae.

Tamiai (in singular *tamias*) Treasurers in the *treasuries of the gods* and other money managing state authorities. They collected funds, paid bills overlooked the operations of their institutions and reported to higher authorities for reasons of accountability and transparency. They were relieved of all responsibility only after their comprehensive reports regarding the way they had handled their duties had been checked by the responsible public auditors and were found in conformity with the laws and the accepted principles of good administrative conduct.

Tamias ton koinon prosodon;* also known as *epimeletes tes koines prosodou*, or *tamias epi tes dioikiseos He was responsible for the overall supervision of the system for collecting and dispensing public revenues and reporting to the *Assembly*.

Tetradrachm Four drachmae.

Thesmomothetai A board of six *archons* whose duties were to review the laws annually, to determine whether there were inconsistencies, duplications, or invalid laws in force and, if so, to inform the *nomothetai* to rectify the situation.

Thetes The social group with the lowest income in Athens according to the reforms of Solon. *Thetes* were mostly farmers. Themistocles provided them with the opportunity to upgrade their social status since under him and later on they became rowers for the navy.

Toichopoioi   A group of ten magistrates who were in charge of building and maintaining the walls of the city.

Trapezai (in singular, *trapeza*)   Private enterprises which were providing banking services in the Classical and the Hellenistic periods.

Treasury of Athena   It managed the treasures of Parthenon. It functioned as banker to the state during peacetimes and as a lender of last resort in periods of war. It was run by a group of *tamiai*. Their appointment was annual and during their term in office they were under the supervision of the *Council*.

Treasuries of the (other) gods   These *treasuries* functioned in the same way as the *treasury of Athena*.

Trieropoioi   A group of ten magistrates who oversaw the construction and maintenance of *trireme* warships.

Trireme   The main type of warship of the Athenian navy. Each ship comprised 200 personnel; 170 of them belonged to the low-income social group of *thetes*, who served as rowers.

Ypostrategos   Major general.

Zeugitai   The third property class in Athens. Citizens in this group owned land yielding between 200 and 300 *medimnoi* of corn or the equivalent in other produce and could serve in in the *phalanx* as *hoplites*.

Index

For Product Safety Concerns and Information please contact our EU
representative GPSR@taylorandfrancis.com Taylor & Francis Verlag GmbH,
Kaufingerstraße 24, 80331 München, Germany

Printed and bound by CPI Group (UK) Ltd, Croydon, CR0 4YY
01/05/2025
01858432-0005